MORE PRAISE FOR DR. LAWRENCE H. DILLER'S
RUNNING ON RITALIN

"*Running on Ritalin* describes in vivid detail the performance pressures on America's children, their parents, and teachers that result too often in a prescription for Ritalin—and nothing else. This important book should be read by teachers, principals, counselors, and everyone else interested in the well-being of our children." —Ramon C. Cortines, Executive Director, Pew Network for Standards-Based Reform at Stanford University; Interim Director, Annenburg Institute for School Reform at Brown University

"A very important book . . . Dr. Diller has correctly described the 'chaos' of the current ADHD diagnosis; the disturbing trend of blaming children's social, behavioral, and academic performance problems entirely on an unproven brain deficit; and the consequent enormous and generally inappropriate reliance on Ritalin as the remedy. This is the most thorough and reliable book available to help parents and professionals understand and cope with their crisis." —William B. Carey, M.D., Director of Behavioral Pediatrics, Children's Hospital of Philadelphia; author of *Understanding Your Child's Temperament*

"Parents whose kids take the stimulant Ritalin for Attention Deficit Hyperactivity Disorder usually find themselves wondering about the value of using Ritalin. Anyone with doubts should read this thoughtful book by child psychiatrist Dr. Lawrence H. Diller. He is not anti-Ritalin; he prescribes it for some children. But [he] raises many important issues about why Ritalin use has increased in the United States and whether it is the appropriate response to a child's difficulties."
—*Los Angeles Times*

Running on Ritalin

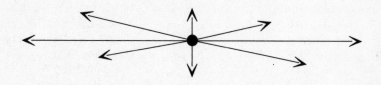

*A Physician Reflects on Children, Society,
and Performance in a Pill*

LAWRENCE H. DILLER, M.D.

BANTAM BOOKS

NEW YORK TORONTO LONDON SYDNEY AUCKLAND

RUNNING ON RITALIN
A Bantam Book

PUBLISHING HISTORY
Bantam hardcover edition published September 1998
Bantam trade paperback edition / May 1999

All rights reserved.
Copyright © 1998 by Lawrence H. Diller.
Cover design copyright © 1998 by Tom Tafuri.
Cover design based on a drawing by Martin Diller, age ten and a half.

Library of Congress Cataloging-in-Publication
Data is on file with the publisher.

ISBN 0-553-37906-2

Published simultaneously in the United States and Canada

Bantam Books are published by Bantam Books, a division of Random House, Inc.
Its trademark, consisting of the words "Bantam Books" and the portrayal of a
rooster, is Registered in U.S. Patent and Trademark Office and in other countries.
Marca Registrada. Bantam Books, 1540 Broadway, New York, New York 10036.

PRINTED IN THE UNITED STATES OF AMERICA
RRH   10   9   8   7   6   5   4   3   2

Dedicated
to
Helen Gofman, M.D., Bayard Allmond, M.D.,
and Alan Leveton, M.D.
and to
My Parents

Contents

Chapter 13

PERFORMANCE IN A PILL:
What Ritalin Says About Us

ACKNOWLEDGMENTS

My wife, who is a writer, told me that writing a book is like running a marathon. I am a sprinter by nature, so I was helped by many people who offered me support, suggestions, and advice over the time it took to write this book.

My patients have been extraordinarily generous. Not only have they given me much of the material for this book by my encounters with them but their support and excitement for this endeavor have astonished me.

I thank supporters of my efforts for their suggestions, advice, or assistance: John Jacobs, Lane Tanner, Tom Boyce, Paul Dworkin, Jon Weil, Sabina Morganti, Mary-Jane Nunes, Sue Parry, Jill Woolfson, Kathy Pavloff, Peggi Levin, and Sarah Pearce.

Robert Coles, Sir Michael Rutter, Robert Reid, John S. Werry, and Paul Genova were generous in giving me their time, ideas, and encouragement. At the Drug Enforcement Administration, initially Frank Sapienza and then, on a continuing basis, Gretchen Feussner were regularly available and ready to provide data and support.

More is published in the professional and lay literature on ADD and Ritalin than for any other combination of childhood psychiatric condition and its treatment. Literally each week brings up another group of articles or books to be reviewed. Furthermore, given the broad scope of this book, I was in dread of both large and small errors persisting in the text. Therefore, I was very fortunate to have the experience and interest of Stephen Hinshaw of the University of California, Berkeley, and Glen Elliott of the University of California, San Francisco, who reviewed the book for technical accuracy. I am extremely grateful for their time and comments.

Helen Reyes, librarian of John Muir Medical Center in Walnut Creek kept her eye out for the interesting article I might miss early in my research. I paid nearly weekly visits to the still spectacular University of California Library Systems—in particular, the Medical Library at the San Francisco campus and the Education/Psychology Library on the Berkeley campus.

Fred Gardner, the editor of *Synapse*, the medical student newspaper of University of California, San Francisco, was the first to tell me there was a book to be written on Ritalin. He also provided early editorial assistance and was crucial in the development of the proposal for this book.

Diana Landau of Walking Street Press in San Francisco, who is my friend and ex-neighbor, took over editing the manuscript. The modestly self-described "Cut and Paste Queen of the Bay Area" provided so much more—wonderful transitions and metaphors as well as "egoless" editing toward the completion of the manuscript. If I could, I would award her an honorary medical degree in "ADDology."

The wisdom and insights of my editor at Bantam, Toni Burbank, guided my efforts toward a sensitive, balanced, and readable book. Her ability to recognize lacunae in the text was uncanny. Robin Michaelson was superbly reliable with logistical support.

I wish to recognize my sons, Martin and Louie, who learned there are more important reasons for appearing on television than for money and are proud of their father's efforts to help children and their families. Martin's concept and initial rendition of the book's cover astonished my wife and me and reminded us that children do indeed listen to adult dinner conversation. My aunt, Sandra Brand, is also a writer. Her interest and support in this endeavor brought us much closer. Lynda Bostrom, my mother-in-law, was given on short notice the task of reviewing the final manuscript. She responded with speed, aplomb, and sensitivity. In the process, my appreciation and respect for this very talented woman grew even deeper.

My wife, Denise, has put up with me for twenty-six years. Her opinions are most dear to me, and her compliments, most precious. I thank her for her support and advice on writing and coping.

Lastly my agent, Beth Vesel of Sanford Greenburger Associates, deserves special credit. It was her vision and her belief that there needed to be a book on children and competition which led her to me. Her representation gave me the opportunity to write a much better book because of the support and assistance I received.

To reach Dr. Diller on the internet:
www.docdiller.com

Running on Ritalin

Chapter 1

←——————→

RITALIN ASCENDANT:
A DOCTOR'S DILEMMA

Something is awry, all right, but something not entirely medical in nature.
—Robert Coles, M.D., *The Mind's Fate*

It's midday at an elementary school in a comfortable American suburb. The lunch bell has just rung, and kids are noisily pouring out of classrooms to enjoy a brief recess in the schoolyard before mealtime.

Inside, next door to the principal's office, the school secretary is arranging bottles of medication on a tray. Scotch-taped to the tray are little photos of fourteen children, labeled with their names and keyed to the bottles. Though by now she pretty much knows who gets what, at the beginning of the school year this system helped make sure she didn't make mistakes—that each of the children taking Ritalin at school received the right pill and dose.

At least a dozen more youngsters among the 350 attending this school took the same medication at home before school but aren't required to take a midday dose. At a nearby school of similar size, the kids getting Ritalin are organized in ten-minute shifts because their number exceeds thirty. And this weekday ritual is carried out—with variations in the number of kids and the personnel responsible for handing out the pills—at schools across the United States.

Attention deficit disorder, or ADD—the condition for which the medication Ritalin is most commonly prescribed—was formerly called hyperactivity, as reflected in its alternative acronym: ADHD (attention deficit/hyperactivity disorder). Its diagnosis is based on problems with attention,

1

focus, impulsivity, or overactivity at school or at home. Since 1990 the number of children and adults diagnosed with ADD has risen from about 900,000 to almost 5 million as we near the end of the decade. This figure—derived from the amount of medication prescribed for ADD—suggests a problem of epidemic proportions.

The sharp rise in ADD diagnosis is directly tied to another startling statistic—a 700 percent increase in the amount of Ritalin produced in the United States during the same time period.[1] An increase of this magnitude in the use of a single medication is unprecedented for a drug that is treated as a controlled substance. Ritalin belongs to the class of drugs known as stimulants, and it is closely related to amphetamine. Although Ritalin has been around for a long time, some people are still surprised to learn that it is essentially a form of speed. Others do know this but believe that the drug has a paradoxical "calming" effect on children, an effect different from the one it produces in adults.

Sorting out myth from fact about Ritalin isn't easy, but the remarkable rise in its use makes it imperative that we try. Perhaps even more important is to explain why the demand for it—and the pressure on parents and physicians to provide it—has become so intense. The phenomena of Ritalin use and soaring ADD diagnoses are related more than statistically. They are deeply intertwined, so that to examine one issue is to examine both, as I will do throughout this book.

The statistics about ADD and Ritalin are embodied as real families and their children in my practice of behavioral pediatrics. At my office in a suburb twenty-five miles east of San Francisco, I evaluate and treat a wide variety of developmental, learning, and behavior problems of children and adolescents. I see children, teenagers, and their families, some of whom bring children as young as two years old for treatment of suspected ADD. Increasingly, adults are among my patients—most of them parents of children diagnosed with ADD who believe they themselves share its symptoms, or people who have heard that I do assessments for ADD.

The families are mostly white, middle- and upper-middle-class. In nearly all cases, at least one parent has a job; in most families, both parents are working. The children are experiencing problems at home, at school, or in multiple settings. Some don't respond to requests; some have unusual or exaggerated fears; some lag behind in school. Some young patients display frequent temper tantrums, language delay, or autism. But more and more often these days, the reason kids are in my office is that their parents, teachers, or primary-care doctors think they might "have" ADD. And more and more, those parents and caretakers are expecting me to supply Ritalin.

"Doctor, do you test for ADD?"

My first phone conversation with Sheila Gordon, the mother of six-year-old Steven, began with this question.* It is a question I first heard only a few years ago, but today hardly a day goes by without a concerned parent raising it. Her voice uneven with distress, Sheila went on to tell me that Steven, her only child, was struggling in the first grade and that the teacher advised having him tested for ADD. She wanted to find out if her son had attention deficit disorder. And she wanted to find out if he needed Ritalin to control it.

Confronted with a familiar dilemma, I shifted uneasily in my chair. How could I tell Sheila over the telephone that, to my knowledge, there *was* no real test for ADD? Perhaps she would think I wasn't well informed about the condition—after all, the teacher had told her to get Steven tested. I wanted to tell her that an ADD diagnosis is complicated, and that the condition now described as ADD can have many causes and many symptoms. In order to help Steven, I would have to evaluate his basic personality, his emotions, his learning abilities, and the demands and responses of his family and school. There was no simple, definitive biological or psychological marker or test I could call on. But I suspected this was not the answer she was looking for.

When someone speaks of "having" ADD (as in having asthma or diabetes), they are implying the condition is biologically based, and that the behavior is neurological in origin. Sheila seemed to accept that Steven's problems might be caused by his brain chemistry. This is a belief widely held today about children with ADD-related symptoms, but one with which I am not entirely comfortable. I believe that brain chemistry expresses itself as personality, that this is inherent and exerts a powerful influence on behavior, but that environment—especially for children—also plays a critical role. I wanted to convey to Sheila that I was uneasy with her perception of ADD—but how to say it without making *her* uneasy? It

---

* The names of all patients mentioned in this book have been changed unless otherwise specifically stated. Nearly all of the personal stories are from my medical practice. I have also changed some of the other details such as their occupations or the number of children in the family to further protect my patients' privacy while attempting to maintain the essence of their problem or situation.

would be better to wait until I met the whole family, including Steven himself, to explain the complex realities of ADD and how they might apply to this child. For the moment, I asked Sheila for more detail about the problems Steven was having in school. He was doing well academically, she said, but the teacher had called home several times to report that he was having trouble "staying on task" when he worked alone, and staying with the group during class activities. He would habitually play with pencils or wander off to the window, for example, when a story was being read. On the playground, he wasn't "keeping his hands to himself," doing an excessive amount of grabbing and some hitting. The teacher had "seen other children like Steven" and suggested he get a medical evaluation. Specifically, she suspected ADD.

Sheila paused briefly and then added: "I know that one kid in Steve's class is taking Ritalin. His parents say it's made a big difference." Again she hesitated, then spoke in a rush: "I *hate* the idea of putting Steve on a drug, but I'm really worried about him not getting along with the other kids. Do you think it might help him? Would it change his personality?"

I understood Sheila's anxiety about her son. I had heard the same note of distress over the phone from many parents, and I've seen the pain and havoc that a seriously unhappy, acting-out child can cause in families. I told her I could evaluate Steven—a process that would take several meetings with him and both parents—and provide an opinion on what was going on and what to do about it. Medication might be part of the eventual treatment, I said—but I would never recommend it as an option before seeing the child.

Sheila seemed relieved, and we set up a first appointment for her and her husband. I'd see Steven later.

It wasn't exactly what I expected when I elected pediatrics, this preponderance of cases clustering around a single diagnosis. Like most aspiring physicians, I had not chosen a specialty at the time I entered medical school in 1972, at Columbia University's College of Physicians and Surgeons. My early impression of med school was that most specialists treated patients more as organ systems than as people. The pediatricians seemed different—perhaps working with children humanized these doctors. So I chose to do pediatrics, with the original intention of being a general pediatrician.

Though I began with a keen interest in human relationships and psychology, my academic experience with psychiatry left me cold and confused. Freudian psychoanalytic theory was still firmly in place, and it was taught with near-religious overtones; the Oedipus complex was presented as fact. At one point I was threatened with a failing grade for strongly urging the nighttime use of a conditioning machine to counter a ten-year-old boy's bed-wetting. The psychiatric instructor insisted that the child's problem was the result of having seen his parents performing the sex act. I wasn't sure if she meant this literally or metaphorically, but I thought the child was being denied a potentially useful intervention.

I didn't discover my professional calling until I came west to do a pediatric internship and residency at the University of California, San Francisco (UCSF). There, in the course of a routine week of training, I was introduced to the pioneering Child Study Unit—and to an entirely new way of approaching children and their families. Since the 1940s the unit has employed a multidisciplinary team to evaluate and treat children with developmental and behavioral problems; on call were pediatricians, a neurologist, a psychiatrist, psychologists, and developmental specialists such as special-education teachers and speech pathologists. In sharp contrast to the Child Psychiatry Department just across the street, the unit's approach wasn't top-heavy with psychoanalytic theory. Rather, it was guided by the nature of a child's personality, and by his or her developmental strengths and weaknesses. And they emphasized the importance of the family as a system, making a practice of seeing children *with* their families. At the time this approach was revolutionary, but to me, treating a child in the context of his parents and siblings made much more sense than seeing him alone.

I valued this experience initially because I thought it would make me a better pediatrician. (Besides the shots and runny noses, parents bring children to the doctor because they're having trouble at school or not listening at home.) But in fact, the encounter changed the course of my career. After completing my residency, I spent three years at the Child Study Unit as a behavioral pediatrics fellow. (At the time, only three such programs existed in the United States; now there are more than fifty.) By 1982, after further training in family therapy at the Mental Research Institute of Palo Alto, California, I could claim the unusual distinction of being a medical doctor, a pediatrician specializing in child development and behavior, and a family therapist as well.[2]

I vividly recall the first time I witnessed the change that some children exhibit when they start taking Ritalin. One of our patients at the Child

Study Unit was a little boy who had never been able to play with a toy for more than a minute without throwing it aside and racing off. After Ritalin, he sat and played quietly for twenty minutes, while his parents and I marveled at the transformation.

Since then I have evaluated hundreds of children and adolescents for the diagnosis of ADD and treatment with Ritalin. Each individual and family has had a unique background, circumstances, and problems—but patterns have emerged. The most obvious pattern has been a distinct shift in the number and kinds of patients referred for an ADD evaluation. Over the first fifteen years of my practice, perhaps two dozen kids each year emerged from my office with an ADD diagnosis. Most of them fit the typical profile long associated with the condition: boys from six to twelve years old, extremely hyperactive and impulsive, functioning poorly (if at all) in a normal school situation. Many of these kids were quite out of control, and intervention with medication (usually Ritalin) was often needed to give other treatments a chance to work.

The parents of these earlier patients were beleaguered and confused: They didn't know what was going on with their kids, were typically accused of bad parenting, and only rarely were aware of the condition called ADD. They may have heard about Ritalin's ability to "calm down" overactive children, but most were fearful of giving stimulant medication to their own son or daughter—I practically had to go on bended knee to get their consent. Some parents were relieved to learn that the problem might spring partly from the child's inherent personality (rather than from their own failure as parents). Others—especially some fathers—didn't buy the concept of ADD at all. Rather than admitting that something might be "mentally" wrong with their child, they preferred to think he just needed more discipline (typically, they thought the child's mother was too "soft" with him).

As of the early 1990s, however, my experience with families and ADD was clearly changing. The sheer volume of my cases went up dramatically, from two dozen a year to more than a hundred at present. I was evaluating more and more children under the age of five for the condition, as well as more children, teenagers, and adults with no signs of hyperactivity—people whose main problem was an inability to pay attention and get their work done. Many of this newer group of patients I judged to be less severely affected by ADD symptoms, and some I thought were doing fairly well. Far more often than in the past, a first-time visit would be prefaced by a phone call like Sheila Gordon's, indicating that someone (usually a parent or teacher) already suspected that ADD was responsible for a child's troubles. Indeed, as ADD became a familiar term, families almost seemed to welcome the diagnosis: Here at least was a clear answer to the behavior puzzles that plagued them.

And though some parents remained uncomfortable with giving medication for behavior problems, in general I encountered far less resistance to Ritalin. I found myself prescribing a lot more of the drug. The difference was simple to measure: California (like many states) requires a distinctive prescription form for Ritalin and other potentially addictive drugs. (In my practice they're used only for Ritalin.) Before 1990 I needed perhaps one pad of a hundred forms every nine months; by 1997 I realized it was one every three months.

What was going on with ADD and Ritalin, and why? I don't remember exactly when I started to feel deeply concerned about the trend I was witnessing and my own part in it. Perhaps it was the fourth or fifth time I saw a young patient who was struggling a bit in school but otherwise seemed to be functioning well enough—a child whom I didn't see as a clear candidate for medication, and yet who had been prescribed Ritalin even before I met him. Or perhaps it was when I realized that only medical solutions were being proposed to behavior problems that I saw as having many possible sources: in overscheduled families or in crowded classrooms, for example. But once I realized what was happening, the questions couldn't be tuned out. Were other doctors worrying about this? Was it unique to our area? Was anyone in the professional literature raising these issues? Was the rise in ADD cases and Ritalin demand a benign phenomenon, or was it time to start looking critically at the matter? These are among the questions that ultimately led to the writing of this book.

Let me introduce some people from this later generation of patients whose situations raise questions for me about ADD and Ritalin:

• Johnny Hester had just turned four when his parents brought him in. His headstrong behavior at home and in preschool had been driving his parents crazy and stressing his teacher, who suggested he might have ADD. Certainly the boy I saw in my office was very intense and determined, but he didn't race around constantly, and he played with toys almost normally. (He did raise a fuss when his parents asked him to put the toys away.) What I saw made me consider him only mildly impulsive and slightly distractible. And even without exploring his situation at school, I felt that family problems were contributing to his behavior. His parents, who had just reconciled after a separation, disciplined him inconsistently. They too were intense, both with full-time, high-pressure jobs. Having read about ADD, they insisted that I prescribe Ritalin on a trial basis.

• Jenny Carter was a ten-year-old who worked too slowly and had trouble completing her assignments at school. Her parents complained that she didn't finish her chores at home, either. Sent to her room to clean up her toys, she'd be found dawdling or playing one of the games she was supposed to be putting away. Both parents worked and wanted her to help take responsibility for her two younger sisters. Jenny would stoically accept her punishments for incomplete work and missed chores, but she sounded sad about her situation when we met.

Jenny struck me as a bright, lovely child who was kind and thoughtful, had many friends, and wanted to please her parents and teacher. It just seemed as if her internal clock was set too slow for the rapid pace and the demands made on young people in late-twentieth-century America. She might have thrived, I imagined, had she been born earlier this century or before compulsory education was adopted. Now she was being evaluated as a candidate for Ritalin.

• Gavin Donaldson was fifteen when I met him. Both his parents were Ph.D.'s, and they were concerned about Gavin; he wasn't getting the top grades they felt he could achieve if he overcame his "concentration problem." They worried about his college options, given his current grade-point average, which hovered just below B plus. Some of his teachers thought he was distractible, others that he was insufficiently motivated.

Gavin himself felt he was doing okay. He didn't mind getting a few B's and C's. He acknowledged that he was easily distracted from schoolwork; he could get A's if he cared more and tried harder, he told me, but he had other interests, such as music and his friends. He was sensitive to his parents' expectations and wanted to please them, but he wasn't enthusiastic about the idea of taking a medication that would affect his brain and personality. I suspected he felt that taking Ritalin would signal that he was inadequate as a person.

I thought the drug could probably improve his performance, focus him more on his schoolwork, perhaps even raise his motivation. His pleasure in doing better and winning his parents' approval might outweigh any loss of self-image caused by taking medication. On the other hand, his performance wasn't bad without it, and I believed his grades would improve once he found something that genuinely engaged him academically.

• Karen McCormack, age thirty-three, single, and a highly talented architect, found me through some friends whose child I had treated. She was happy to learn that I evaluated patients for ADD, for she'd read a book on adult ADD and was convinced that she had it. Karen's sense of design was brilliant, but she struggled to read through reports and felt frustrated by her lack of advancement in the engineering firm where she worked. I thought she might also be depressed—she seemed very hard on herself. Karen was surprised when I didn't offer her medication right away, and resisted my idea that she go for psychological testing for her reading problem and career issues. In her view, I was simply being a roadblock to her getting Ritalin, which, she had learned via the media and the Internet, was the definitive treatment for her problem. She soon went in search of a more cooperative doctor.

How do we explain the kinds of problem behavior now associated with ADD, which causes so much anxiety and disruption in people's lives—a child in constant motion, striking out at his schoolmates, drifting off in class? Or an adult who can't seem to get a reasonable amount of work done or carry on a normal conversation without constantly interrupting or changing the subject? The ancient Greeks, with their ideas about "bodily humors" determining personality, weren't so far off from current models that propose organic origins for every emotional trait. Three hundred years ago, a popular theory about the cause of such disruptive behaviors would have been demonic possession (albeit by a minor devil, compared to one that caused, say, the symptoms of full-blown schizophrenia). Religious explanations might also have claimed that an individual or family was being punished for some wrongdoing: "the sins of the father visited upon the child." Moral turpitude as an inborn trait was once taken very seriously (some still believe in it today, if privately). According to more "advanced" nineteenth-century thinking, criminality and moral deficiency ran in families or could be attributed to certain races and nationalities.

Shortly thereafter, Freudian neuroses became the dominant model in accounting for behavioral aberrations, and through much of this century,

Freudian ideas led most people to accept that "bad parenting" was the prime cause of difficult children. Around midcentury a new explanation emerged: Some psychologists began to see these problems as arising from a lack of "fit"—with a school, a job, a career, a particular set of parents, even an entire society. Many children and adults seem simply to have been born into the wrong family, or into the wrong century or culture.

Lately, American society—in particular, American psychiatry—has moved strongly toward accepting yet another explanation for problems of behavior, motivation, and performance: that they are caused by some dysfunction of the brain. The roots of this movement go deep, and this book will trace them. The message that follows from this model has been unequivocal and powerful: If a problem is neurologically based, it should be treated with a drug.

In many cases, medication is surely called for. In many others, I have doubts. Offering Ritalin can help people who don't fit well into the here and now, I've assured myself. Inarguably, it can help certain kids adapt to an ever more challenging school environment. But I've wondered: Is there still a place for childhood in the anxious, downsizing America of the late 1990s? What if Tom Sawyer or Huckleberry Finn were to walk into my office tomorrow? Tom's indifference to schooling and Huck's "oppositional" behavior would surely have been cause for concern. Would I prescribe Ritalin for them, too?

The surge in Ritalin use tells us volumes about how we explain—and deal with—the problems many children and adults are having in coping with their world today. And the controversy over its use reflects the divide between two competing theories about behavior and performance problems. In one camp are those who believe such problems are chiefly attributable to a child's inherent brain chemistry. According to this view, medication is the best (sometimes the only) treatment. The other side posits that problem behaviors are the result of how children have been and are being treated. According to this view, children develop problems because they are subject to inappropriate or misguided expectations and responses. In other words, there is nothing inherently wrong with the child; what is needed are improvements in parenting, teaching, or the social environment.

The two positions represent the age-old "nature versus nurture" argument, and wherever it concerns children, this argument is played out intensely—because we love them dearly and because they do not yet control their own choices. We, their parents, teachers, doctors, and other advocates, must make the decisions that shape their future.

The "nature" camp has lately gained enhanced scientific status; no longer do we simply talk about the vague concept of "personality" but about parts of the brain that are said to control specific behaviors, and about psychotropic drugs that act upon those sites. These days the "nurture" part of the equation often is simply ignored in the quest to set nature right through chemical intervention.

I'd been troubled for some time by this trend, and when Peter Kramer's *Listening to Prozac* appeared in 1993, I experienced a flash of recognition and appreciation.[3] Kramer, a psychiatrist, was exploring questions similar to the ones I'd been wrestling with—in his case, regarding the antidepressant Prozac. Although Prozac was a new drug and Ritalin had been available for thirty years, both were now being demanded by patients, and prescribed by doctors, in previously unheard-of quantities. In addition, both these psychotropic medications had been demonized in the media with reports (greatly varying in accuracy) of their negative effects: Prozac linked with suicide and homicide, Ritalin accused of stunting children's growth, serving as a tool for mind control, or leading straight to drug abuse.

Kramer's analysis of the Prozac phenomenon helped crystallize issues of diagnosis and treatment that I'd been debating internally: the ambiguities of real-life clinical diagnosis as opposed to fixed psychiatric categories; the risks and benefits involved in prescribing psychotropic drugs in less-than-severe cases; and the ethics of medicating for personality enhancement— what Kramer called "cosmetic psychopharmacology." Both Prozac and Ritalin are being used by millions of people whose emotional or behavioral problems do not signify mental illness or major dysfunction by psychiatric standards, but for whom the drugs provide a little help to let them, the "walking wounded," ease through life more comfortably. What does this mean for all of us?

Despite the author's own hesitations and caveats, it is clear that Kramer's book and the enormous publicity it generated helped foster the now-widespread belief that most emotional disorders are neurochemical in origin and best treated with medication. *Listening to Prozac* made words like *neurotransmitter* and *serotonin* part of the national vocabulary. The "message in the pill," to use Kramer's phrase, is that we are on the verge of a brave new world where friendly chemicals can make most things right. This is

one factor—an important one, I think—in the rise of Ritalin use in tandem
with the ADD diagnosis.

The belief that ADD is a neurological disease—the nature stance—prevails
today among medical researchers and university teaching faculty. Its dom-
inance is reflected in the leading journals of psychiatry, such as the *American Journal of Psychiatry* and the *Journal of the Academy of Child and
Adolescent Psychiatry*. Its eloquent proponents include Joseph Biederman,
chief of the Harvard Medical School Child Psychopharmacology Clinic,
and Edward Hallowell and John Ratey, authors of the best-selling *Driven
to Distraction* and its sequel, *Answers to Distraction*.[4] Russell Barkley, of the
University of Massachusetts Medical School, emphasizes that Ritalin is the
definitive treatment for ADD and may need to be taken throughout the patient's lifetime. All of these experts acknowledge the influence of the child's
world on his or her behavior, but often this strikes me as an afterthought
or lip service. Outside the community of specialists, an audience that includes general physicians, the media, and patients has focused overwhelmingly on the researchers' clarion call: ADD is a neurological disease.

This explanation of ADD is also widely accepted within the leading self-
help group for ADD: Children and Adults with Attention Deficit Disorder,
or CHADD. In less than ten years, this organization has grown to encompass thirty-five thousand families and several hundred chapters around the
country. The group's interests in promoting a neurological cause for ADD
are understandable. For many years, parents were blamed by psychiatry for
their children's problems, but with the new emphasis on biological causation, *no one is to blame*. Welcome relief from guilt, as well as the possibility
of classifying ADD as a medical disorder to win insurance coverage and
disability rights, drives CHADD to embrace a biological basis for ADD.

Along with many researchers, CHADD leaders feel that the 700 percent increase in Ritalin use since 1991 is simply a reflection of treatment
catching up with the identification of a disease. According to Dr. Biederman, 10 percent of America's children have ADD—which would mean
that current treatment rates should double.[5] "Child psychiatry," he asserts,
"is just catching up with adult psychiatry in its use of psychotropic medication."[6]

Is America ready to have 10 percent of its children taking Ritalin? Because boys are disproportionately represented in the total population of
kids diagnosed with ADD, *this would mean giving the drug to one in six boys*

between the ages of five and twelve.[7] This prospect seems not to faze some researchers. In their view, if a medication "works" on a certain condition, then we ought to use it.

There's no question that Ritalin can in most cases bring about short-term improvements in behavior. I and many others, however, find that enthusiasm about the drug's efficacy has obscured a larger, murkier picture. The prospect of Ritalin being given to so many children raises many questions. Among them: How safe is the drug for children and for adults, and what are its possible side effects? Does it help patients overcome their ADD symptoms over the long term? Is there a chance that Ritalin, by addressing symptoms, may mask some of the true causes of behavior problems? And what does the greatly expanded use of such a drug say about the institutions traditionally charged with the "nurture" of children: our homes and families, our schools, our health care system?

Not so long ago, my questions about ADD and Ritalin were confined within the walls of my office, or to conversations with my wife and a few colleagues. But over the last few years the debates I once had with myself have emerged in schools, in self-help group meetings, at medical conferences, in the ivory towers of scientific research, and, inevitably, in the media.

• At a seminar for public school teachers on kids with learning problems, a behavioral expert declares: "It's up to teachers to find the key to motivating the underperforming child." Fed up with feeling scapegoated by society for its failures with children, some of the teachers respond with heartfelt booing.

• "I have thirty-two kids in my class," laments a second-grade teacher. "We used to have a teaching aide, so one of us could spend extra time with the 'difficult' kids. But when there are this many, all I can do is try to get the really tough ones into a special-education class—or get them checked for ADD."

• At an Elks hall in a northern California suburb, a local CHADD meeting takes place. A doctor who claims to diagnose ADD and other behavior disorders with brain scans is the featured speaker. "Withholding medication from these children," he charges, "is a form of neglect."

• At a conference sponsored by the federal Drug Enforcement Administration, narcotics officers talk about how easy it is for kids to buy Ritalin from friends on school premises. Upon learning that doctors sometimes prescribe Ritalin to children after just a fifteen-minute evaluation, one officer remarks: "I wouldn't accept dope from an informer I'd only talked to for fifteen minutes!"

• A Boston University official who tried to cut mandated benefits for students with ADD admits under oath that he referred to some students with ADD as "phonies" and "slackers"; the students win their class-action suit to maintain benefits. But in the same month, a West Virginia judge rules against three medical students seeking extra time to take their exams based on their ADD diagnoses.

• Four young teenagers in San Jose, California, are arrested for the "imprisonment and torture" of a schoolmate. Three agree to sentences; the fourth, and alleged ringleader, is found to have an "apparent abnormality" on a brain scan. His attorneys contend that he is a "victim" of ADD, which caused his violent behavior, and he is remanded to the state for further testing.

• In 1993 the National Collegiate Athletic Association (NCAA) rules that it will not disqualify athletes whose urine tests reveal Ritalin if they have a doctor's letter stating that they are being treated for ADD. The U.S. Olympic Committee, however, continues to forbid Ritalin, as well as other stimulant medications.

In the fall of 1994 I went public with my observations and concerns about ADD and Ritalin in an article sent to some pediatrics journals. When I shared my first drafts with colleagues at UCSF's Child Study Unit (now called the Division of Behavioral and Developmental Pediatrics), many agreed with my perception that something unusual was going on with ADD and Ritalin. They warned me, however, of potential hostility from mainstream psychiatric academia, the pharmaceutical industry, and the ADD self-help organizations—all of which have an interest in promoting ADD as a neurological disease.

Sure enough, the piece was too "hot" for the usual professional journals, as more than one editor told me. But I had also submitted it to the nation's leading bioethics journal, *The Hastings Center Report*, whose editors pounced on this as precisely the kind of issue it was their mission to explore.[8] When my article appeared in mid-1996, among its readers was Gina Kolata, a science reporter for the *New York Times*, who quickly contacted me—it had prompted her to plan a story on the ethics of the Ritalin boom, and could she quote me at length?[9] This was not merely gratifying but a unique opportunity to take the discussion to a national level. The passionate and concerned response to her article—from all sides of the debate—encouraged me to plan this book.

Throughout the long process of research and writing, I have been impressed by how deeply the discussion of ADD and Ritalin use has penetrated American society. A picture emerged of concentric circles of concern that have formed around the issue, representing many points of view. At ground zero, so to speak, are the parents of children diagnosed with the disorder, who struggle every day of their lives with its impact and with decisions about treatment. For them, the questions are very personal and pragmatic: Does Ritalin work? Can it help my child learn how to cope with his personality and get along better with other kids? Could it help with school grades, athletic performance, family relationships? Will it have the apparently miraculous effect on my child that it did on my neighbor's? How safe is it, and what side effects should I be concerned about? Are there any effective non-drug alternatives?

Teenagers and adults also struggle to meet the demands of their lives, and some, on learning about the symptoms of ADD, feel that these symptoms perfectly match their own problems. Receiving an ADD diagnosis may be almost welcome, allowing them to put a name to a vague but deeply troubling malaise. But in order to make informed decisions for themselves, they need to ask: Is there really such a thing as adult ADD? Could my parents and doctors have missed it when I was a child, and only now might I discover it? Is Ritalin safe for adults—could I become dependent or addicted? Will I need to take it my whole life? If I am diagnosed with ADD, what are my rights at school or in the workplace to special help?

Also close to the front lines are teachers and school administrators. They want answers to questions such as: Can I take the time to manage this child without Ritalin, and is that fair to the rest of the class? Will Ritalin help a child who can't seem to get along with his peers? Can it remedy a learning problem? How does an ADD diagnosis qualify a child for special educational services?

Next come the primary-care doctors, mental health workers, and behavioral pediatricians like myself. We tend to see a wide range of cases from the world of ADD, with symptoms ranging from mild to severe. This gives us, I think, a perspective different from that of our colleagues engaged in academic research. But all of us in the medical community must ask similar questions about Ritalin and ADD: What do the studies really tell us about how it works, and how well? When is its use justified—only when there are major signs of ADD-related behavior problems, or anytime we think it may help a child or adult improve his or her performance? Should Ritalin be used alone or in conjunction with other treatments? How can we spot the adolescent or adult who is at risk of abusing Ritalin?

Policy makers, law enforcement officials, and the courts are concerned with Ritalin as a potential drug of abuse. Has there been a rise in the abuse of Ritalin along with its sanctioned use for ADD? Should we maintain current restrictions on its use, including special prescriptions regulated by the government? Or since most patients won't abuse Ritalin, should the restrictions be relaxed? Policymakers must ask other questions, too: How should disability be legally defined for ADD? What are the consequences for our educational system and workplaces of numerous people receiving special allowances because of such a disability? What are the cost/benefit choices of dealing with ADD as a society?

Another powerful group with a huge investment in ADD and Ritalin is the pharmaceutical industry, which has profited enormously from the jump in Ritalin use and would surely benefit from a less restrictive policy on its use. The DEA estimates that pharmaceutical companies earn approximately $450 million a year with stimulants (nearly all legal use of stimulants in the United States is for ADD treatment.)[10] What if the number of American children affected by the disorder really is 10 percent? How would it affect revenues if all those children were receiving medication? How many families will turn instead to the growing number of special diets, food supplements, homeopathic preparations, exercise regimens, and hands-on treatments promising to ameliorate or eliminate ADD-related behaviors?

And, finally, there is nearly everyone else—all the citizens of our hardworking, stress-fueled society. Can low doses of stimulants help anyone—children or adults, ADD diagnosis or not—concentrate better on boring tasks? If it does work this way, why shouldn't anyone try Ritalin? Can it help a person improve his or her performance when some career-related circumstance has raised the bar dramatically?

The ADD-Ritalin issue reveals something about the kind of society we are at the turn of the millennium—for no country besides America is experiencing such a rise in Ritalin use. It throws a spotlight on some of our most sensitive issues: what kind of parents we are, what kind of schools we have, what kind of health care is available to us. It brings into question our cultural standards for behavior, performance, and punishment; it reaches into the workplace, the courts, and the halls of Congress. It highlights the most basic psychological conundrum of nature versus nurture, and it raises fundamental philosophical questions about the nature of free will and responsibility.

Is there a message in this pill? If so, what is the Ritalin boom telling us? Ritalin seems to have become the drug for our day. As competition on every level intensifies, our preoccupations as a culture increasingly center on performance. And our children, whether we realize it or not, have been serving as a proving ground for the premise of medicating to enhance performance. Are we likely to see a time in the not-so-distant future when a large part of America will be running on Ritalin?

Chapter 2

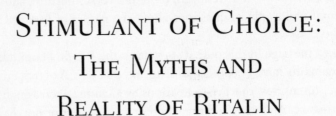

STIMULANT OF CHOICE:
THE MYTHS AND
REALITY OF RITALIN

The totality of the evidence . . . may justify considering stimulant medication as a first-line treatment for many (though not all) cases of ADHD.
> —Russell Barkley, Ph.D., *Psychiatric Times*, 1996

Speed kills.
> —Street gospel, San Francisco, early 1970s

I didn't want to hear the word *Ritalin*, and I especially didn't want to hear it from my husband's first wife." A mother named Alice is describing a turning point in her family's struggle to cope with their son, Joe.[1] Affectionately nicknamed "Rocket Boy" as a toddler, Joe had been "expelled" from preschool and was by this time several months into kindergarten and showing no signs of slowing down. To the contrary, being forced to spend hours in close proximity with his schoolmates seemed to obliterate whatever shreds of self-control he could muster around his parents. On a daily basis, Joe would literally flip out, hurling his body into a group of children, thrashing and screaming. The calls home from his kindergarten teacher, a kind and resourceful woman, came every night.

He'd been an intense challenge since infancy, Alice says, sleeping little, crying lots. As a toddler, he'd sabotaged countless shopping trips with his frequent and unpredictable tantrums. Alice recalls a sympathetic fellow shopper commiserating about the terrible twos: "Little did she know that this was the eighth episode that day!" Over the next few years Joe became kid non grata at other children's homes and birthday parties. Kindergarten caused his behavior to spike even more severely, and a bad cycle set in: In extremis, he would revert to baby talk, whereupon other kids would tease him by imitating it, which prompted him to flip out again.

Alice and her husband, Mark—caring, conscientious, well-educated parents with an "easy" younger daughter—tried all the standard techniques for coping with difficult children: time-outs, positive-reinforcement charts, frequent strategy conferences with the teacher. Joe seemed beyond reach. And his parents suffered the multiple agonies that come with such a struggle: seeing their child miserable and feeling helpless to help him; "losing it" when they got angry at him and then feeling guilty for that; blaming his misery on their own inadequacies as parents (and feeling sure that outsiders were doing the same); anxious about the effects on their younger child.

Finally someone—it happened to be Mark's ex, who worked in the health field—suggested that Joe fit the profile for ADD and that Ritalin might help him. Alice reacted defensively: Joe wasn't that bad, and besides, the idea of giving her child a psychoactive drug every day was repellent. Mark agreed, and they temporized for several more months as Joe continued to deteriorate in school and fell asleep in tears every night, curled in fetal position on the floor of his room. The scale was tipped when he came home with his kindergarten photo, showing his lost, haunted face amid a swarm of giggling five-year-olds.

When they took him to a pediatrician for an ADD evaluation, he was off the chart in most categories on the questionnaires they were asked to fill out. The doctor said some encouraging things about Joe's character and gifts, then sent them home with a mountain of ADD literature—and a bottle of small yellow Ritalin pills.

"My hand shook as I put the pill down next to Joe's cereal bowl that morning," recalls Alice. She didn't tell her son exactly what the pill was for, only that it would help him feel better. She and her husband didn't notice anything dramatically different in Joe's behavior for the first couple of days—but the calls from school stopped coming. Gradually his social life improved; other parents occasionally commented on how he had matured. He didn't turn into a different person, says Alice; he was still difficult and argumentative and hypersensitive. The difference seemed to be that he didn't lose himself in stressful situations. With the help of the drug and continued intensive behavioral work by the family, he could control his swirling energy.

Alice had heard a certain amount about Ritalin before it took its place at the family breakfast table. She knew it was a stimulant that was said "paradoxically" to have a calming effect on children. She had heard that it could suppress a child's appetite, stunt his growth, and interfere with his sleep. She was aware that the Church of Scientology had strongly and publicly opposed its use—which, if anything, led her to think maybe it wasn't so terrible after all. But she did wonder if the drug might alter Joe's personality permanently; she already missed his ebulliant, mischievous side a little. And she was truly worried that it might be addictive—or at least that it might predispose Joe to later problems with drugs.

All in all, Alice's knowledge of Ritalin was about on a par with that of most media-consuming Americans: she knew just enough to be confused and concerned about the drug. Once it was shown to be of significant help to Joe, however, she made it her business to learn more.

In doing so, she had to sort through a great deal of information, misinformation, and myth. Ritalin has been in use in the United States for half a century and has become the most widely used and accepted drug of its type—yet it remains in many ways misunderstood and controversial. Misunderstood because it is both a therapeutic tool and a drug of abuse, and because we don't know exactly why it produces the effects it does. Controversial because its use has been mainly in treating children, whose brains and personalities are still being formed and who do not themselves make the decision about taking the drug. Controversial, too, because there are more and more of these children as time goes by.

RITALIN AND ITS RELATIVES

The family of drugs to which Ritalin belongs—the stimulants—has been both a blessing and a blight on humankind. The stimulants, which include such drugs as caffeine, cocaine, and amphetamine, are so named because of their generalized effects on the body's organ systems, particularly on the heart, blood vessels, and brain. Stimulants increase blood pressure; they make the individual less sleepy. Stimulants such as coca leaves and tobacco have been used for centuries by indigenous peoples for their energizing, pain killing, or medicinal properties. Many of us can't start the day without our hit of caffeine.

Cocaine, the active ingredient in coca, was extracted in the late nineteenth century. It is an effective anesthetic and is still medically used as a local anesthetic for the eye. But until the 1920s it was medically prescribed for its stimulating effects as well, for everything from depression to rheumatism. Amphetamine was first synthesized at about the same time as cocaine and because its mood-elevating effects simply made people "feel better," physicians once prescribed it for a variety of conditions including schizophrenia, heart block, infantile cerebral palsy, seasickness, and persistent hiccups, despite little evidence of its specific benefits.[2] This family of drugs currently includes Dexedrine, Adderall, and Dextrostat.

Methamphetamine—also known as speed, or "crank"—was once prescribed for narcolepsy (involuntary severe sleepiness). It is rarely used medically today, though it is still listed in the *Physician's Desk Reference* under its trade name, Desoxyn. A few doctors prescribe Desoxyn for ADD, but it is much more expensive than other medications available and carries the taint of a street drug.

As for Ritalin, this is actually the trade (or manufacturer's) name for the generic chemical methylphenidate, a derivative of amphetamine.* Methylphenidate was synthesized in Europe in 1944 in an (unsuccessful) attempt to create a stimulant that would not induce addiction or tolerance.[3] It is very closely related to amphetamine; their chemical structures are quite similar, along with the way they are metabolized and their clinical effects.[4] This close connection is the chief reason Ritalin use raises concern among parents and others. Also classed as stimulants but chemically different from methylphenidate are nicotine (found in tobacco products) and pemoline (another medication used for ADD, known by the trade name Cylert).

Introduced into this country in 1955, methylphenidate was first approved for use by the Food and Drug Administration (FDA) for the treatment of drug-induced lethargy, mild depression, and narcolepsy. It acquired its familiar trade name, Ritalin, in the early 1960s, when it was marketed by the pharmaceutical company Ciba-Geigy as a drug to improve the

---

*Throughout this book, I will refer to methylphenidate as Ritalin. However, all references to Ritalin can be understood to apply as well to the generic form of the drug, produced in this country by another manufacturer, MD Pharmaceuticals. Most of what is said of Ritalin also applies to Dexedrine, Adderall, and Dextrostat. While there may be some differences among individuals' responses to these medications, overall their effects are extremely similar. Similarly, in discussing Ritalin's history, I'll continue to refer to its manufacturer as Ciba-Geigy, though that corporation merged in late 1996 with Sandoz, another pharmaceutical giant, to create Novartis, the world's third-largest drug company. I will speak of Novartis when discussing the present and future of Ritalin.

memory of geriatric patients—and for the treatment of various behavioral problems in children.

THE POSITIVES AND NEGATIVES OF AMPHETAMINES

The stimulants—amphetamines in particular—have been alternately embraced and condemned almost since their introduction in modern medicine, in a kind of ongoing love/hate affair. Their "feel-good" properties prompted rather indiscriminate early use without any scientific understanding to back it up.

From 1930 on, however, the amphetamines were extensively studied, and thirty years of research into their effects was summarized in a now-classic 1962 paper by Bernard Weiss and Victor Laties, "The Enhancement of Human Performance by Caffeine and the Amphetamines."[5]

Weiss and Laties's findings seem to portray a wonder drug. They found the amphetamines (including methamphetamine) vastly superior to caffeine at improving human performance in a variety of mental and physical activities. Amphetamine use led to improved vigilance and accuracy in performing tasks, especially repetitive and boring ones. It also improved the subjects' attitude about performing such tasks.

The drug increased physical endurance for both work and sports—not just in endurance events such as swimming or running, but also in one-time events like the shot put. While the improvements in speed were relatively small—on the order of 3 or 4 percent—they occurred across the board, on an entire swim team, for example. And, the authors noted, while 3 percent may seem small, it translates into cutting 7.2 seconds off a runner's time in a four-minute mile—the difference between fame and oblivion. Before Weiss and Laties's paper, it was generally believed that amphetamine worked only on fatigued subjects. In fact, the studies demonstrated that it could produce improvements as good, if not better, in rested individuals.[6]

Another study reviewed by Weiss and Laties made use of a test originally devised to select candidates for aviation training. The subjects were asked to monitor four aircraft-type dials and to keep each dial's pointer at a certain position by manipulating various controls. They were tested at varying lengths of time, and different groups of subjects were given different drugs (plus a placebo control) to determine their effects. Naturally, as the time periods got longer, the subjects would become less vigilant and let the dial pointers drift more. But administering amphetamine counteracted these results of boredom or fatigue in dramatic fashion; the subjects performed much better.

Weiss and Laties also explored the pleasure factor: the euphoric effects of amphetamines. In one study they reviewed, heroin, morphine, amphetamine, or placebo was injected into normal volunteers who didn't know which substance they were receiving. Among these drugs, the subjects overwhelmingly defined the amphetamine experience as the most pleasant. In another study, equal numbers of volunteers from the military were given amphetamine alone or as a platoon-sized group. The latter reported higher degrees and rates of euphoria, demonstrating how group participation enhances the drug experience—a phenomenon familiar to users and abusers.

Most of the studies analyzed by Weiss and Laties were of short duration, and the only negative effects reported from amphetamine use were insomnia and decreased appetite. They did not explore the long-range development of addiction (physiological change that produces craving) or tolerance (the increasing need for higher dosages) that often takes place with continued amphetamine use.[7] Nonetheless, the abuse potential of stimulants had been known since the end of the last century, though consistently downplayed or ignored by the professional community. The appeal of these drugs was the same then as it is now: feelings of euphoria; a sense of power, alertness, excitement, or heightened clarity; an ability to deny the need for rest. Sigmund Freud, the father of psychoanalysis, was among the more famous personalities who regularly used cocaine, and its control over even the most powerful mind was dramatized by Sir Arthur Conan Doyle, who portrayed his fictional Sherlock Holmes as an addict.

The similarly addictive potential of amphetamine had been determined by the start of this century. In any number of animal and human studies conducted from the 1930s on, subjects given the opportunity to self-administer the drug would choose to repeat the amphetamine experience. Laboratory rats will self-administer intravenous amphetamine (and Ritalin) literally to death, repeatedly choosing the drug over food, and thereby starving. Over time, the desired dose would increase, indicating a buildup of tolerance to the drug's effects. Outside the laboratory, a similar pattern of abuse could be observed, and by the late 1960s, the darker side of stimulant use had emerged as a national public health issue.

Stimulants and Child Behavior: The First Link

Among the benefits of stimulants, none has been more important in modern times than their positive effect on children with serious behavior problems.[8] This phenomenon was discovered quite accidentally by a physician named Charles Bradley, who first published his findings in 1937.[9] At the Emma Pendleton Bradley Home in Providence, Rhode Island, a residential diagnosis and treatment center, Bradley worked with children under twelve who were of normal intelligence but demonstrated neurological and behavioral disorders. The discovery was made when Bradley—by all accounts a meticulous and observant man—administered Benzedrine (a mixture of two types of amphetamine) to children who had undergone a spinal tap, in the hope of alleviating the headaches common after this procedure.[10] While this hope was not realized, the treatment had another remarkable effect on many of the children, decreasing their activity level while increasing their compliance and academic performance "in a spectacular fashion," according to Bradley.

"It appears paradoxical," Bradley wrote, "that a drug known to be a stimulant should produce subdued behavior."[11] Bradley went on to theorize that perhaps stimulating certain parts of the brain might lead to inhibition of activity. These observations gave rise to the notion—erroneous but still widespread among parents and doctors—that Ritalin and other low-dose amphetamines produce a calming effect in children that is distinct from its stimulating effect on adults. What Bradley mistook for calm was in reality the children's intensified focus. In retrospect, we know this is essentially the same effect such drugs have on adults, though it may manifest in different ways.

Bradley continued to publish anecdotal accounts of children's behavior on stimulants. His 1937 report involved just 30 children, but in 1950 he reported on a much larger study of 275 children in which both Benzedrine and Dexedrine were used.[12] In this group, 60 to 70 percent of the children were deemed much improved. Despite Bradley's extensive work, however, his accounts of stimulants producing amazing improvements in children's behavior remained unknown to most physicians, circulating mainly by word of mouth. For example, at Babies Hospital of the College of Physicians and Surgeons at Columbia University (my med school alma mater), only one child psychiatrist regularly employed amphetamine with children through the 1940s and 1950s, and it was little used elsewhere.[13] This use of stimulants caught on in a big way only after publication in the early 1960s of substantive clinical trials demonstrating the efficacy of Ritalin and its near-clone, Dexedrine. In 1961 the FDA lent its seal of approval to Ritalin, amending the official list of indications to include treatment for various behavior problems of children.[14]

THE EMERGENCE OF RITALIN

Why Ritalin? Given the close similarity in clinical responses to Ritalin and amphetamine, the chief reason for Ritalin's much greater acceptance among doctors and government regulators for use with children was simply that it was *not* amphetamine. Amphetamine already connoted the potential for danger and abuse. Other factors may have influenced Ritalin's growing popularity.[15] Its quick action and lack of major side effects made it an ideal drug to study in children. Therefore it was studied often—and the more studies there are, the more legitimacy accrues to a drug. Ritalin research fueled many grants and academic careers in the 1960s. And unlike amphetamine, Ritalin was under Ciba-Geigy's patent. This particular formulation could not be copied by other manufacturers, and therefore the company spent money to advertise and promote it to the medical profession—and to fund more studies that supported its use.

Moreover, there is no denying Ritalin's rapid positive effect in many cases; Alice's son, Joe, is a quite typical example of the turnarounds it can produce. For children who have problems with attention, impulsivity, overactivity, and task completion, Ritalin has been shown over and over to help, at least in the short term (that is, weeks and months).[16] Their activity decreases, they become more methodical and less impulsive, they make fewer mistakes, their grades improve, they become more compliant to parents and teachers, their relationships with family and friends get better.[17] Their concentration and attitude may improve enough to mitigate the effects of a learning problem or disability. It is estimated that between 60 and 90 percent of children with attention, behavioral, or school performance problems improve at least somewhat when taking Ritalin.

As yet there exists no complete understanding of exactly how Ritalin works in the brain to modify ADD-type behavior.[18] (See Chapter 5 for a summary of what we do know, or currently surmise.) Its effects on the body are well known, however. Here it's important to distinguish between the normally low doses prescribed for ADD treatment in children and adults and the much higher doses consumed by abusers.

In normal low-dose usage, Ritalin generally produces a quick response and remains in the bloodstream only a few hours. There is no negative reaction to stopping the drug, and dosages can be fairly easily adjusted to achieve the optimum response with the minimum amount of Ritalin. These attributes have made it an attractive drug for use with children, encouraging doctors and parents to think that it's at least worth trying. And in truth, from a pediatrician's point of view, there is little downside to a trial of Ritalin, if the circumstances seem to warrant it. Parents may feel differently, of course.

Ritalin does have confirmed side effects that are significant enough to concern most parents. It's usually one of the first topics raised when I suggest a trial of Ritalin. Alice and her son, Joe, were not my patients, but in discussing their experience with me she emphasized her worry on this score. Alice had heard, for example, that Ritalin might cause Joe to stop eating, lose weight, and even fail to grow properly. While it's true that all stimulants suppress appetite while they are working, as the effects of Ritalin wear off, a normal level of hunger returns. Alice was also worried about Joe's sleeping patterns. Taking Ritalin in the evening or at night will cause insomnia for most people. However, both this problem and loss of appetite are fairly easily controlled by careful timing and amount of the dosage, due to Ritalin's short life in the bloodstream. (Chapter 11 provides more detail about these issues.)

Some early studies raised concern that Ritalin might impede long-term growth, or cause stunting, in children taking it, but later studies have not consistently shown these results.[19] Long-term growth is not currently considered to be an issue. Other effects have been suggested over the years but not proven consistently. For example, a possible connection was proposed between Ritalin use and the development of involuntary movements called tics, associated especially with Tourette's syndrome. Follow-up research failed to confirm a strong connection, however.[20]

Apart from its physical side effects, there has been some concern that Ritalin may have more subtle impacts on cognitive and intellectual processes. Both parents and researchers have noticed that children taking Ritalin sometimes answer questions in ways that seem overly compliant or narrow, suggesting that the drug might restrict creative thinking. One study in the 1980s did show that hyperactive children taking Ritalin offered less varied answers to open-ended questions.[21] But other studies that examined creativity in slightly different ways found no differences between children on or off Ritalin.[22]

THE CONTROLS ON RITALIN TIGHTEN

By the mid-1960s Ritalin had become the primary drug used for the treatment of behavior and performance problems in children. Attempts to estimate the number of children taking Ritalin were limited by the lack of national surveys, so researchers had to rely on an accumulation of local reporting. (The drug's proprietary nature meant that pharmaceutical company data remained unavailable to epidemiologists.) Nevertheless, a best guess was offered in 1970 of 150,000 children taking Ritalin.[23]

But even while acceptance of Ritalin therapy was growing in the medical community, a countertrend was building, soon to be reflected by a change in Ritalin's official status. Recreational drug use and abuse were on the rise through the 1960s; by the end of the decade millions of people were abusing amphetamines.[24] News came also of an epidemic of Ritalin abuse taking place in Sweden.[25] These events prompted the Drug Enforcement Administration (DEA) in 1971 to tighten controls on the stimulants, designating both Ritalin and amphetamine (Dexedrine and others) as Schedule II drugs—a category that indicates significant risk of abuse.[26] (Most of the opiates, including morphine and Demerol, are Schedule II medications. Schedule I, the most dangerous category, is reserved for heroin, LSD, and other drugs that can be used only experimentally.)

This designation had several important consequences. Manufacturers must win approval from the DEA of an annual production quota for each Schedule II drug. These requests are reviewed by the DEA and other government agencies, and the DEA generally approves those based on legitimate need—the amount that pharmacists are selling to patients, supported by physicians' prescriptions. The DEA thus has precise records dating back to the early 1970s on the annual production of Ritalin.

While drug schedules are federally regulated, it's up to individual states to monitor the use of controlled drugs. Currently fifteen states, including New York and California, require physicians to use either a three-part form, known as a triplicate, or prescriptions that are bar-coded for electronic scanning.[27] The states thus can track the prescription patterns of doctors, patients, and pharmacists, and thereby theoretically prevent abuse of the drug. Electronic monitoring, in which the scanned information from each doctor's bar code goes directly into the state's computer, greatly speeds and simplifies this record keeping, and more and more states are moving to this method.

But the requirement of special prescriptions, whatever the form, is perceived as burdensome by some doctors and by many patients (or their parents) who must deal with it. It means, for example, that prescriptions must be written in the doctor's office rather than phoned in to a pharmacy. Some also feel that an unfair stigma automatically attaches to any such controlled drug. As ADD diagnosis rates and Ritalin use coevolved into the 1990s, both manufacturers' quotas and the special prescription requirement became sources of controversy.

ENCOUNTERING RITALIN: A PERSONAL HISTORY

I entered private pediatric practice about a decade after the first big surge in Ritalin use and its designation as a Schedule II drug. I was certainly aware of stimulants and their self-prescribed uses much earlier; like most people who attended college in the late 1960s and early 1970s, I knew people who took Dexedrine or Benzedrine to stay awake and cram for exams or papers. One of my friends became a typical casualty of stimulant-induced delusion: Having stayed up all night to study with the aid of "bennies," he started to crash just before a big test and quickly took a few more. He felt he'd aced the test, but when his paper came back marked with an F, the blue exam book showed two pages jammed with tiny, illegible handwriting. Only then did he realize how depleted and confused he had been.

Professionally, I was introduced to Ritalin, its benefits and possible drawbacks, in 1978, while doing a behavioral pediatrics fellowship at the University of California's Child Study Unit. Within this team of medical, therapeutic, and educational specialists, there was a spectrum of opinion about the value of psychotropic medication for children with behavior or performance problems, but even the most skeptical or concerned professionals among them agreed that Ritalin could be useful in some situations.

About three months into my fellowship at the Child Study Unit, I had a chance to see Ritalin's effects at close range. Part of the training for students like me was to join an ongoing case with an experienced doctor or therapist, and I was sharing some families with the director, veteran pediatrician Helen Gofman, M.D. One day she called me into her office and said, "Larry, I want you to take over the Hanas family. I'll still supervise your work, but I think you can do it and right now I'm busy with other cases. I want you to start by learning to play with Brian."

Play with Brian! All of seven years old, wiry and quick, Brian was one of the toughest kids being treated at the unit—a malevolent dynamo. His last name was pronounced *heinous*, and it seemed no accident. I remember how his eyes darted around when, I imagined, he was planning his next caper. He often hit and kicked his parents, Carlos and Charlene, during family sessions and dominated his larger (but more passive) older brother, Albert. I instinctively didn't like Brian, and in retrospect I realize that may have been why Helen put me on his case—so I could learn to manage or overcome my negative reactions to such "difficult" children. At the time, I dreaded it and saw it as a major hurdle in my young professional life.

It wasn't as bad as I'd feared. During our first play session, Brian challenged me by demanding a big red Tinkertoy piece that I'd started to play with. The first few times he did so, I gave it to him. Later, when I'd started building a tank with it, I refused his command of "Give it to me!" then ignored him and went on building. I wanted to model typical seven-year-old peer behavior so that he could practice coping.

As I watched out of the corner of my eye, Brian at first pushed the other pieces away—though taking care not to push them at me, I noted. Then he abruptly stomped off and began fiddling with another box of toys. I went on with my work, and when I finished my tank (it had two cool turrets on the top), I rolled it back and forth on the table, admiring it out loud. Brian came over to inspect my creation, and I asked, "Do you want to try it out?" He grabbed the tank and rolled it on the floor, making whirring, cranking sounds. "You want to build some houses we can blow up?" I ventured. Brian liked that idea, and we spent the rest of the session working cooperatively. He even helped me clean up, which he rarely did when his parents were around.

After a couple more play sessions also went off with minimal struggle, I was pretty surprised and secretly pleased with myself. Brian wasn't so bad after all, or maybe I just had the right touch with him. Helen and I also occasionally met with the parents, or with the whole family.

One afternoon when I planned to see Brian alone, I went out to greet him and his father, but Brian leaped up and ran past me into the playroom. I looked quizzically at Carlos, who just shrugged. When I got to the playroom, Brian already had three boxes of toys down and their covers off. He lifted one box, dumped the toys noisily on the floor, spent a minute or two playing with them, then got up and dumped the next bin. "Brian, if you want to play with any more toys, first we have to put one of these bins away." He responded with a terse "Yup," but quickly started to build a tall structure, which he promptly destroyed. As he moved toward the third bin I stopped him and insisted he clean up some of the toys. Mechanically but with little efficiency, he scooped up pieces and threw them haphazardly in (or toward) the bin.

To my questions about whether anything different had happened that day in school or at home, he responded in monosyllables, and kept on moving from one toy to the next. He couldn't stay with one for more than three or four minutes. Once he ignored my verbal warning, and I had to physically restrain him from trying to pull down a box that was too high. Finally I gave him a time-out—a few minutes on a chair to settle down (I too needed rest)—but wound up physically having to keep him on the chair. After forty-five minutes I was drained bodily and emotionally, while Brian seemed even more wired. As he dashed out of the room and down the stairwell, I hurried out to meet his father, who seemed unperturbed. "Carlos, there was something really different today," I began. "Oh, yeah," he said. "I'm sorry—I meant to tell you. We forgot to give Brian his afternoon pill. Was he pretty hyper?"

So much for my magic touch. Of course, I'd known that Brian took Ritalin, but at that point in my career I didn't realize what a difference it could make. Not that Brian was easy when he took the drug; he just seemed impossible off it. This was also my first intimation of something I would learn from much experience: that kids often behave better with a doctor, therapist, or teacher than they do with their parents. I instantly felt more sympathy for his parents, who tried hard but were handicapped by their own personalities and by problems in their marriage.

The Hanases continued to use the Child Study Unit for several more years. Brian never did get the consistency he needed from his parents, and by the time he was thirteen, his oppositional behavior was almost a reflex. Around that time, we stopped seeing the family—Brian at least had avoided trouble with the law up to then. He would be almost thirty now. I learned a lot from working with him and hope he's doing all right.

THE SEEDS OF CONTROVERSY

Parents have a natural reluctance to put their children on psychotropic medication. In the early 1970s such misgivings were reinforced by confusing, contradictory, or sensationalized media coverage of Ritalin. An early attack on Ritalin use was published by the *Washington Post* in an article headlined "Omaha Pupils Given 'Behavior Drugs.' "[28] While it inaccurately said that 5 to 10 percent of children in the Omaha public schools were taking Ritalin (it turned out to be 5 to 10 percent of special-education children), the article raised a hue and cry.[29] That same year, congressional hearings were held to clarify the prevalence and propriety of Ritalin use in children. No formal action resulted from the hearings.

The cultural climate in the early 1970s also helped raise the temperature around the issue of Ritalin use. The antiauthoritarian spirit of the sixties encouraged the spread of "nonrepressive" theories of child development and education, such as those practiced at Montessori schools or at Summerhill, the British boarding school embodying the theories of psychiatrist A. S. Neill.[30] Unconventional ideas about psychiatry, as popularized by R. D. Laing and the Ken Kesey novel *One Flew over the Cuckoo's Nest*, demanded that we reconsider the meaning of sanity in an "insane" world. Reaction against an industrialized, technologized, "plastic" society spawned a back-to-nature movement that embraced organic foods, natural healing, and rejection of pharmaceuticals. These trends helped make people wary of any form of "mind control" promulgated by institutionalized medicine and drug companies—and the media played on such sentiments.

This first negative cycle of publicity on Ritalin culminated in 1975 with the publication of a book titled *The Myth of the Hyperactive Child, and Other Means of Child Control*, by authors Peter Schrag and Diane Divoky: a veritable jeremiad against the use of psychotropic medications, especially Ritalin, in children.[31] The book was widely criticized for inaccuracies, and there was speculation, never substantiated, that the authors were members of the Church of Scientology. The church does have a history of opposition to the use of psychotropic drugs in general and Ritalin in particular, going back to the publication in 1950 of Scientology founder L. Ron Hubbard's book *Dianetics*. Mainstream American psychiatry was harshly critical of the psychotherapeutic techniques Hubbard espoused, and in retaliation the church has waged a decades-long media campaign attacking the psychiatric establishment and its advocacy of psychotropic medications. Legal suits and allegations of harassment against individual physicians have been associated with the church, whose members do not necessarily identify themselves.[32] One result of this is that anyone who raises questions about Ritalin, whether legitimately or hysterically, stands in danger of being linked with Scientology.[33]

ADD and Ritalin: Moving in Sync

At the same time as Americans were reacting with suspicion to Ritalin, other forces in medicine and society were poised to trigger an upsurge in its use and acceptability. A cluster of behavior problems that once had seemed to affect relatively few children was about to change its shape and its name, assuming a higher profile in psychiatry and in the culture at large. And from that point into the foreseeable future, the syndrome called ADD would be inextricably linked with the stimulant Ritalin.

Since the dawn of the century, children had been identified with personality-driven symptoms similar to those we now categorize as ADD. Various names were used to describe this related group of behavior problems, including MBD (minimal brain dysfunction) and "hyperkinetic reaction." Whatever name the condition went by, its indispensable symptom was always excessive motor activity, and this could be identified in a relatively small number of children. But in the 1970s researchers, in a crucial shift, redefined the central problem as one of poor attention and distractibility. The next time psychiatry's official guidelines were revised, in 1980, they would include a newly named disease: attention deficit disorder, described in a way that would ultimately encompass thousands, indeed millions of children with no symptoms of hyperactivity at all.

At that time, the relationship between ADD and Ritalin seemed clearcut. Ever since Charles Bradley's discoveries focused attention on the role of stimulants in controlling abnormal child behavior, it had been believed that stimulants worked uniquely on hyperactive children. In other words, it was assumed that Ritalin (and related drugs) worked to correct the problem *only if the problem existed.* This meant that the drug could serve as a kind of litmus test for ADD. A positive response meant that a child "had" ADD. However, in 1978 an important study showed otherwise.[34] Child psychiatrist Judith Rapoport, working at the National Institute of Mental Health (NIMH) in Bethesda, Maryland, reported that *stimulants had essentially the same effects on normal children as on children with attention or behavior problems.*

Working with a group of children—all boys—recruited from the families of her colleagues and staff, Rapoport gave Dexedrine to both hyperactive children and children without any specific behavior or neurological problem. She found that both groups responded similarly, without statistical difference, in lessening their physical activity and improving their attention and performance on a math test. Rapoport later extended her observations to include normal men, who also improved their performances on Dexedrine.[35] The only differences were between the boys (hyperactive and normal) versus the men: While the adults regularly reported euphoric effects from the drug, the children would note only feeling tired or "different" after taking it.

In a sense, Rapoport was merely demonstrating anew the effects of the stimulants as known since the 1930s. Yet her work was pivotal among researchers because it was recent and met current academic standards. And since it disproved the diagnostic role of Ritalin, it showed the need for psychiatry to develop different criteria for identifying ADD—an effort around which there is much disagreement, as we'll see. Yet despite Rapoport's studies, the idea that Ritalin would work to improve performance and decrease activity only in hyperactive children—and could therefore be used as a diagnostic tool for ADD—persists to this day.

By the start of the 1980s, in any event, much of the negative publicity surrounding Ritalin had dissipated, and its use was on the rise. In 1980 it was estimated that between 270,000 and 541,000 elementary school children were receiving Ritalin.[36] (This apparent wide spread is the best estimate achieved through difficult means: extrapolating national figures from local surveys.) In 1987 a national estimate of 750,000 was made.[37] More accurate than these estimates are records kept by the DEA on the annual production quotas of Ritalin.[38] These show a steady annual output of approximately 1,700 kilograms through the 1980s, with slight annual increases or decreases.

Beginning in 1991, however, the production of Ritalin rose sharply, and production has grown significantly every year since. The amount of Ritalin produced in 1993 was 5,110 kilograms, and for 1996 the quota was 11,775 kilos. Although Ritalin continues to be used in treating narcolepsy, and more recently for resistant depression and the mental and neurological deterioration associated with AIDS, virtually all of this increase can be attributed to its use for ADD.[39]

This trend in production was paralleled by accumulating publicity around ADD. Around the start of the decade, newspaper and magazine articles began alerting parents about this hidden disorder that might be affecting their children or themselves. Television talk shows dramatically highlighted the effects of ADD and its "cure," Ritalin. By the summer of 1994 ADD and Ritalin had made the cover of *Time* magazine.[40] They were also the subject of a new book climbing the best-seller lists: *Driven to Distraction: Recognizing and Coping with Attention Deficit Disorder from Childhood Through Adulthood*, coauthored by Edward Hallowell and John Ratey, highlighted the possibility that many adults unwittingly suffered from ADD and had since childhood.[41] Hallowell is a child psychiatrist in private practice, and Ratey is an adult psychiatrist on the Harvard faculty; both are self-acknowledged "adults with ADD" and were using Ritalin.

The burgeoning community of families with ADD children and adults diagnosed with ADD soon began to organize. In 1987, a group of parents of children with ADD formed the organization known as CHADD. At first the acronym stood for Children with Attention Deficit Disorders. By 1993 CHADD had grown to thirty-five thousand members and six hundred chapters nationally, and had changed its name to Children and Adults with Attention Deficit Disorder.[42] Another national organization, the Attention Deficit Disorder Association (ADDA), also formed in the late 1980s but has remained small and primarily focused on education and lobbying efforts. CHADD, on the other hand, has been active in offering support for families, providing information about the condition and available services, and acting as an advocate for families on both local and national levels.

By the fall of 1993 newspapers and television were reporting an apparent national shortage of Ritalin, which had become unavailable in certain communities.[43] It was alleged that, through a bureaucratic oversight, Ciba-Geigy's request for an increase in the Ritalin quota sat on a desk at the DEA for several months. The DEA denied this, contending that the fear of a shortage had been created by letters circulated by the manufacturer itself.[44] Real or not, the shortage became the basis for a later attempt by CHADD and other interested parties to decontrol Ritalin.

Since then, production quotas for the drug have continued to soar. For 1997 the DEA authorized 13,824 kilograms, *an increase of more than 700 percent since 1990.*[45] The amount used annually is quite close to the amount produced because quota requests reflect actual sales by pharmacists. While some claim that the actual increases in Ritalin use remain in line with more moderate increases of the 1980s,[46] the complete available data do not support this.[47] State bureaus set up to monitor triplicate prescriptions have been unable to do their job, overwhelmed by the volume of Ritalin prescriptions. Such a dramatic increase—unprecedented for a Schedule II controlled substance[48]—has raised alarm within the DEA and other international organizations such as the UN's International Narcotics Control Board, based in Vienna.[49]

THE DEMOGRAPHICS OF RITALIN

Who is taking all this Ritalin? Researchers at the University of California, Irvine, Child Development Center, under director Jim Swanson, have tracked ADD diagnosis rates and Ritalin use since 1990.[50] In that year they found 900,000 people diagnosed with ADD nationwide. By 1993 the number had grown to 2 million. Of those with the diagnosis, 90 percent were prescribed medication and 71 percent of those received Ritalin specifically (the latter percentage strikes me and many of my colleagues as low). According to this study, then, about 1.3 million people were taking Ritalin in 1993. Extrapolating from projected 1997 production levels, we can estimate that about 3.5 million persons used Ritalin in 1997. Another 1.4 million used other medications, most likely Dexedrine.[51]

Research supports the general observation that males are much more likely to be diagnosed with ADD and to take Ritalin and related medications than females, in all age groups. In Swanson's study, males outnumbered females by a ratio of between four and five to one.[52] Based on 1994 data and U.S. census estimates of the population of children ages five to seventeen, 5.8 percent of boys and 1.5 percent of girls had been labeled as ADD by their physicians in 1994. Adults had the fastest-rising rate of ADD diagnosis between 1990 and 1994, though they accounted for a very small percentage of the total.

Corroborating findings come from IMS America Ltd., a commercial drug-surveying company.[53] IMS has found the same increases for Ritalin use as shown by Swanson's analysis. By 1996, however, the ratio of boys to girls had dropped to 3.5 to 1, suggesting an increase in the number of females now using the drug. Perhaps most surprising (or alarming) was the IMS report of much-increased use of Ritalin among adults: 25 percent of Ritalin use in 1995 was in the adult population. This not only reflects a big jump in the diagnosis of adult ADD but greatly increases the possibility that Ritalin may be abused, since unlike children, adults can self-administer it.

Rates of Ritalin use within the United States vary widely.[54] Virginia holds the dubious distinction of having the highest per capita use of Ritalin among the states, with rates six times those of the lowest state, Hawaii. After Virginia, the next four states in order of highest Ritalin use are South Carolina, Delaware, Indiana, and Michigan. IMS data confirm that the drug is most widely used in the South and used least in the West. (This was something of a relief for me to learn, since I sometimes have the impression that half the Ritalin in America is taken in my own northern California backyard.)

The ADD-Ritalin boom appears to be primarily a white, middle- to upper-middle-class, suburban phenomenon.[55] Minorities are underrepresented, in proportion to their numbers, in their use of the drug. Several surveys have confirmed that African-American children receive the ADD diagnosis and Ritalin less frequently than Caucasian children.[56] Cultural and economic factors most likely are responsible for this. Many black families lack the financial wherewithal to take their children to medical specialists for behavior and performance problems, and others may not wish to. Crack cocaine has been so injurious to the black community that some parents are apprehensive about using any kind of stimulant for their children. In general, blacks are less comfortable than whites with the use of drugs to treat behavior problems, and are generally skeptical of an educational system they perceive as too ready to fault black children for behavior as judged by a white-dominated society.

The incidence of ADD (and most other psychiatric disorders) is also quite low in the children of Asian immigrants living in the United States.[57] In their methods of disciplining children and their discomfort with the mental health system, Asian-Americans are quite different from their white American contemporaries. No other racial group comes close to the rate of Ritalin use among white fifth-grade boys in Virginia Beach, Virginia: 17 percent, or one in six district-wide, were taking the drug in 1996.[58] Elsewhere, community-wide rates of Ritalin use as high as 38 percent in boys have been claimed, but only the Virginia Beach survey is substantiated.[59]

This explosion in Ritalin use appears to be a uniquely North American phenomenon. The United States produces and uses about 90 percent of the world's stimulants.[60] Ritalin consumption in Canada quadrupled between 1990 and 1996, but it remains less than one half the per-capita use of the United States.[61] Australia is the only other country to note a similar rise in the use of Ritalin in the 1990s, although their rate of usage remains a tenth of ours.[62] None of the other industrialized nations of Europe or Asia has experienced a recent rise in the use of stimulants.[63]

PROFITS AND POLITICS

The ADD-Ritalin boom has created an extraordinary growth industry. Pharmaceutical companies' profits from Ritalin are up an estimated 500 percent since the start of the decade.[64] These drugs are quite inexpensive to produce and relatively low-cost to the consumer, which—given sufficient demand—translates into high volume and high profits. In addition to the two drug companies currently producing Ritalin, generic methylphenidate, or Dexedrine, three more have registered with the DEA to manufacture stimulants, and another four have expressed an interest in putting out their own products in the field. Adderall is a combination of amphetamines, newly introduced and highly promoted by the Richwood Pharmaceutical Company. Its advertisements to physicians boast "over a million prescriptions" for Adderall in its first year of use.

Another type of profit center is the array of physicians and clinics that have responded to the rising demand for ADD evaluation and treatment. Widely varying rates of Ritalin prescribing from county to county suggest that there exist individual and group practices whose financial well-being rests on diagnosing large numbers of ADD patients and prescribing large amounts of Ritalin.[65] In 1995, the most recent year for which such figures are available, 2 out of 1,309 providers in Virginia wrote 26 percent of all prescriptions for Ritalin in the state. (*Providers* here means medical purchasers of Ritalin, which could be a clinic, physician, or pharmacy. The names were not made public.) In Delaware, 9 of 135 purchasers wrote 26.3 percent of Ritalin prescriptions.

Similar patterns were found in other states. The survey of triplicate prescriptions for Ritalin in Michigan found that 5 percent of pediatricians were prescribing 50 percent of the Ritalin.[66] The Virginia Beach survey found a huge blip of Ritalin use and prescription writing in Wilmington, where large numbers of college students live. While not absolutely indicting, these findings imply the existence of Ritalin mills, where everyone gets the same diagnosis and the same treatment.

Not to be left out, nonmedical entrepreneurs both legitimate and dubious have sprung forth to take economic advantage of the ADD-Ritalin boom. Advertisements in professional journals regularly promote tools for assessment and treatment (as does a direct-mail marketer called the ADD Warehouse), along with such information as "How to Set Up an ADD Clinic." Like most behavioral specialists, I am besieged with mail, phone calls, and faxes selling various products and services for ADD treatment. If it's not the latest vitamin or herbal preparation or homeopathic remedy, it's color therapy, or video guides, or computer software to teach organizational skills. There are scores of special camps and schools for ADD kids; there are electronic devices that claim to boost auditory discrimination (and reduce distractibility) or that vibrate gently to remind somone to "stay on task."

These aids range from the possibly helpful to the probably harmless, but it's clearly a case of caveat emptor. A few products are associated with pyramid business schemes that require participants to buy the product in bulk and inveigle others to sell it for a percentage of the profits. The FDA and officials in a few states have investigated several companies for questionable product claims.[67]

THE PUSH FOR DECONTROL

In late 1996 the support group CHADD formally petitioned the DEA to loosen its controls on Ritalin by changing its status from a Schedule II to Schedule III drug.[68] (Among Schedule III drugs are low-dose combination opiates such as Tylenol with codeine, and migraine preparations that combine analgesics with barbiturates.) This change would have meant that manufacturers no longer had to seek approval on production quotas from the DEA; a company's only obligation would be to report its intended production level.

The ostensible reason was to preclude another possible shortage like the alleged one in late 1993. It's understandable that CHADD parents would want to make sure they had access to a drug that helped their kids, but this move to decontrol Ritalin had other implications. If the DEA complied, the states would receive an unmistakable message that Ritalin was not as dangerous or likely to be abused as had been judged, and states requiring the triplicate form might reconsider its use. Triplicates were particularly odious to families using Ritalin and to the doctors writing them. Often it meant a visit to the doctor's office to pick up the prescription, since triplicates can't be called in to the pharmacy, and some doctors charged for the brief visit. Prescriptions could be mailed to the family or pharmacy, but this entailed delays and possible slipups. It was the hassle factor and the stigma associated with triplicates that fueled CHADD members' desire to do away with them.

The professional groups that added their names in support of the petition also were motivated in part by the hassle factor—and by the belief that low-dose Ritalin was quite safe, as well as by some natural aversion to government oversight of their prescribing habits.[69] The American Academy of Neurology was a direct signatory, and other organizations, among them the American Academy of Pediatrics, the American Psychiatric Association, and the American Academy of Child and Adolescent Psychiatry, filed their names in support. Physicians had their own problems with triplicates. Before the Ritalin boom, practitioners might write one or two a week, but as more and more children began taking Ritalin, writing these prescriptions was becoming burdensome to some doctors, who could otherwise have their nurses or administrators simply phone them in. Many sincerely did not see any risk in decontrolling the drug.

I strongly disagreed. I had done some research into stimulants and their history in 1993, and by the time of the decontrol petition, I had learned enough to be wary of any attempt to make these drugs easier to obtain. I had no problem in principle with the concept or use of triplicate prescriptions for Ritalin, though indeed it had become tiresome to me, as well. Moving Ritalin to Schedule III could have had a profound impact on the availability of the drug. When New York State instituted a triplicate prescription for Valium in 1989, sales of the drug dropped by 40 percent; I imagined the reverse happening with the decontrol of Ritalin.[70] I wrote an article about the decontrol issue and also presented my concerns to the American Academy of Pediatrics, which subsequently reconsidered its support for the change in status.[71]

The DEA considered CHADD's petition but found no compelling reason to grant it. If anything, the conditions that had prompted its moving Ritalin to Schedule II in the first place were still in effect, only more so. What had changed was the size of the ADD constituency, and its political and economic clout. The DEA took the usual steps to prepare its preliminary response, in which it planned to deny the petition. In the normal course of things, this would probably have resulted in hearings at the Department of Health and Human Services.

However, before the DEA could officially reply to the petition, a bombshell was dropped. The Merrow Report, a team of investigative journalists, produced a television documentary on the ADD-Ritalin epidemic that aired nationally in October 1995, in which it was revealed that Ritalin's manufacturer, Ciba-Geigy, had contributed nearly $900,000 to CHADD over five years.[72] Moreover, the program reported, CHADD had failed to disclose the existence of this money or its source to most of its own members and to the general public.

This revelation, acknowledged by both CHADD and Ciba-Geigy as accurate, raised grave concerns about whether CHADD's agenda was influenced by the drug company. CHADD denied that the contributions were linked with its petition. That may be so, but the funds certainly aided CHADD's ability to exploit the mass media and lobby for its views nationally. Some watchdog organizations were not satisfied with the denials; for example, the UN's International Narcotics Control Board expressed concern that a financial transfer from a pharmaceutical company to promote sales of an internationally controlled substance could be viewed as hidden advertising. As such, it would violate the provisions of a 1971 narcotics control treaty to which the United States was a signatory.[73]

Whether or not this embarrassment had anything to do with it, early in 1996 CHADD withdrew its petition to decontrol Ritalin. A few months later Ciba-Geigy issued a letter to physicians reminding them about the possibilities of Ritalin abuse and urging them to act responsibly—prescriptions should be limited to a month's supply, and parents should be reminded about the potential for abuse and told to monitor drug use carefully.[74]

A POTENTIAL EPIDEMIC?

In preparing its response to the CHADD petition, the DEA reviewed findings from several recent surveys showing that the illegal diversion and abuse of Ritalin had been increasing, in parallel with the growth of its prescribed use. This and other factors had prompted the agency's concern about the potential for an epidemic of Ritalin abuse in America.

There is an epidemiology to drug abuse.[75] Just as a virus or bacteria in circulation cannot cause an epidemic in the absence of various host factors in the population, so certain conditions must be present for a stimulant drug such as Ritalin or Dexedrine to become subject to widespread abuse. There must be an initial oversupply of stimulants, on both the legal and illegal markets, backed by large-scale manufacturing capabilities. Large numbers of people must be initiated or "inoculated" to the drug, leading to widespread knowledge about the stimulant experience. Eventually there develops a core group of chronic abusers who, as tolerance builds up, take to injecting the drug intravenously.

America first became widely exposed to amphetamine following World War II. Rommel's much-feared North Africa corps reportedly were the first to use it during the war.[76] Eventually the drug was widely disseminated to troops on both the Allied and Axis sides. After the war many soldiers continued to use amphetamine, and the habit spread to civilians. Japan has seen at least three major amphetamine epidemics in the postwar period.[77] In the United States, specific epidemics occurred in the 1950s, the late 1960s, and the late 1970s—the last based on the legal availability of Dexedrine, which millions of people took to lose weight (unsuccessfully in most cases).[78] The FDA withdrew weight reduction as an indication for Dexedrine in 1981; today many older physicians and pharmacists still refuse to prescribe or supply Dexedrine Spansule—the long-acting form of the drug—because of its popularity with abusers.

Amphetamine (or Ritalin) taken orally in high enough doses, snorted through the mucous membranes of the nose, or injected (under the skin or intravenously) makes the abuser feel euphoric and gives him or her more energy or endurance and a sense of power, aggrandizement, and mental sharpness. As the drug wears off, heightened fatigue, poor concentration, irritability, and depression are common—as is a craving for more of the drug. Persistent abuse can lead to psychotic episodes, paranoid delusions, hallucinations, and other bizarre behavior. Sudden death, generally attributed to cardiac arrhythmia, can occur during abuse of the drug, even if a steady abuser has experienced no prior ill effects. By the early 1970s, as America's then-current period of drug experimentation was climaxing, many walls in San Francisco's Haight-Ashbury district bore the legend "Speed kills."

Sweden's experience with Ritalin and other stimulants is instructive.[79] Amphetamine had been classed as a narcotic in that country since 1944, but when methylphenidate and the related stimulant phenmetrazine (Preludin) were introduced in the mid-1950s, they were not controlled and were widely promoted and prescribed for weight loss and certain depressive states. Speed addicts who had difficulty getting amphetamine soon recognized the abuse potential of these new drugs, began using them intravenously, and created an illegal market by buying them up from patients who easily obtained them for obesity problems. News of Sweden's Ritalin abuse problem was among the factors prompting the DEA to designate it a controlled substance in 1971.[80]

But the Ritalin boom of the 1990s has given rise to renewed concern. The DEA has documented many cases of abuse,[81] and there has been at least one report of a death due to nasal ingestion of Ritalin.[82] Abuse of the drug among high-school seniors quadrupled between 1992 and 1994; the DEA has concluded that more of them have tried Ritalin illegally than are taking it under a doctor's supervision. One telling statistic is the rate of emergency-room visits for Ritalin overdoses or intoxications: In 1990 there were forty cases in the ten-to-fourteen age group, and four hundred for the same group in 1995.[83] While this number seems small compared to the total number of children taking Ritalin, it's identical to the same-year figure for cocaine—a drug we take much more seriously. And, of course, it represents just the tip of the iceberg for abuse.

Teenagers and middle-school-age children do not see Ritalin as a serious drug like cocaine or heroin.[84] They think that since their younger brother takes it under a doctor's prescription, it must be safe. Most teens would be surprised to learn that selling Ritalin, even to a friend, remains a federal felony. From some of my high-school-age patients I learned that Ritalin was readily available at their schools; in 1996 ten milligrams went for about three to five dollars a tablet. According to undercover narcotics officers, Ritalin is cheaper and easier to purchase at playgrounds than on the street.[85] That Ritalin isn't more widely abused may be due only to the ready availability of cocaine and methamphetamine. Nevertheless, Ritalin has the potential to be the entry-level pharmaceutical-grade drug—the inoculum, as it were, for a much larger stimulant abuse epidemic.[86]

RITALIN IN THE LONG RUN

Over the past thirty-five years, ADD has been the most extensively studied pediatric psychiatric condition and Ritalin the most extensively studied psychotropic drug in pediatrics.[87] Still, there remains much we don't know about the benefits or drawbacks of taking Ritalin, especially over many years. Does Ritalin "cure" ADD, so that once people stop taking it, they maintain their improvement? What are the long-range prospects for people who took Ritalin as children once they reach adulthood? And does the risk of stimulant addiction for adults increase as a consequence of having taken Ritalin during childhood?

Such questions are problematic because, among the many studies on ADD and Ritalin, very few have followed into adulthood children who took Ritalin.[88] There are good reasons for this; long-term prospective studies—those that follow subjects into the future—are difficult to run and full of logistical challenges.

Nevertheless, what published research does exist has found the long-term value of Ritalin disappointing. Studies beginning in the 1960s showed that children who took stimulants for hyperactivity (the name for ADD at the time) over several years did just as poorly in later life as a group of hyperactive children who took no medication. Compared to children without hyperactivity, both groups were less likely to have finished high school or to be employed, and more likely to have had trouble with the law or to have drug or alcohol problems. A large percentage of the hyperactive group, medicated or not, did relatively well, but overall those in this category wound up struggling much more frequently than their normal peers. These studies also suggested that adolescence was an especially tough time for people with ADD—the subjects had more difficulties during this period than they did after reaching young adulthood.

My own experience with young patients has brought these dry statistics to life for me and has sometimes contradicted the studies. I've been able to follow at least a handful of kids from under ten into late adolescence or early adulthood, and while each child's story is distinct, there are some common themes. Considering only those who continued taking Ritalin, the children showed some immediate improvement after beginning Ritalin therapy in grade school. The amount and persistence of improvement varied, depending on the child's response to the medication and whether the parents (and schools) succeeded in using behavioral techniques and changes in the classroom environment to reinforce the drug therapy.

As the kids got older they began to express clearer opinions and feelings about themselves, their behavior, and the fact that they took medication to help them behave better. Some, as they headed into preadolescence, began to object to taking medication and felt sure they could handle things on their own. This occasionally proved true—with a lot of help from their support systems—but just as often not. Other kids came to regard Ritalin as a kind of security blanket and clung to it even when I judged that they could probably do all right without it. The normal trials of adolescence on top of ADD-related problems brought some teens close to crisis or plunged them into it, and there were episodes of running away, recreational drug use, and outright defiance of parental control. Some barely avoided trouble with the law; others had to be sent away to more tightly disciplined school settings. The father of one young patient believed that his son now and then had sold Ritalin to some of his buddies at school.

The experiences of my patients on reaching young adulthood have been mixed. Some fit the pattern of the published research in having more than the average amount of difficulty in holding down jobs, forming intimate relationships, and steering clear of substance abuse problems. Others have done better than studies suggest; most, in fact, have found jobs, though it seems critical that the job really engage their interest. Several former patients have done well in computer technology or Internet-related work, and others have found the structure they needed by joining the military. Most have been able to manage their ADD symptoms without medication; some have continued to take Ritalin for nearly a decade. Quite a few adults branch out into other medications as they get older, seeking the right one or combination that fits their case—which may be complicated by depression or other symptoms.

A highly controversial issue is whether the use of Ritalin in childhood predisposes an individual to abuse drugs later in life. This has not been conclusively resolved. We know that children with ADD problems go on to abuse alcohol and drugs—including the stimulants—more often than normal children.[89] But studies thus far have reported no evidence of a higher incidence of drug abuse among teenagers and adults who took Ritalin as children than in those with similar problems who did not.[90]

As noted, the ADD diagnosis after childhood is sharply on the rise, with Ritalin increasingly prescribed for teenagers and adults who have problems with attention or performance. It seems to be helpful in the short term, as the few studies of Ritalin use among adolescents and adults do demonstrate improvements in concentration, attention, work completion, efficiency, and organization.[91] It has not yet been shown to produce serious side effects or lead to abuse, though none of the studies has followed individuals beyond several months. Perhaps the only "paradox" about Ritalin is that it is probably safer for children than for adolescents and adults, because children in general do not self-administer the drug—significantly decreasing the risk of abuse.

THE NEW RITALIN MISSIONARIES

Ritalin does not "cure" ADD in the sense that an antibiotic cures an infection or surgery removes a tumor. It can reduce the symptoms of hyperactivity, poor attention, and impulsivity for as long as it remains active in the body; it must be taken continuously for its benefits to continue. In the absence of other forms of treatment, someone who stops taking Ritalin after five years will be in the same place as when he or she began taking it—allowing for developmental changes that may affect ADD symptoms.

But the lack of conclusive evidence that Ritalin actually makes a difference in the long term has not deterred its enthusiastic proponents. The growth in the use of Ritalin continues unabated, despite unresolved questions about its ultimate efficacy, about the public health risks of its increasing availability, and about the ethics of using medication in borderline cases to enhance performance. I hope I've made clear my belief that Ritalin has an important place in treating children and adults with behavior problems—but it does not work miracles, especially when other forms of treatment are ignored, as they all too often are.

The other elements of a multimodal approach to ADD include behavioral training and/or therapy for the child, along with parental training (and sometimes family therapy), as well as special-education services. All of these work slowly and gradually (if they do work) and are costly and time- and labor-intensive. As a result, while such efforts may be recommended as part of a treatment plan, in our overbusy, economically stretched world they are often abandoned or never seriously pursued. Most often a course of Ritalin therapy is the only treatment followed.

Some researchers, such as Russell Barkley of the University of Massachusetts Medical School, now suggest that Ritalin should be the *primary* treatment for ADD, and that in many cases "talk" therapies or special education may not be necessary at all.[92] Barkley and like-minded experts have reassured physicians that they no longer need to feel guilty about not offering a treatment plan that includes psychosocial elements. They cite new evidence that such combined treatment offers no greater benefits than Ritalin alone. I'm in accord with those who feel this finding is preliminary and inadequate.[93] However, both Barkley and Joseph Biederman of Harvard, one of the most widely published people in the field, recommend lifelong treatment with Ritalin for some patients.[94]

But what about the parents, child, or family who may not want to make Ritalin a permanent part of their lives? Alice, Mark, and Joe, once known as "Rocket Boy," were such a family. Grateful as they were for the help Ritalin offered Joe at a critical time, they did not welcome all its effects on his personality. So as he got older and continued to improve, they were encouraged to try weaning him from Ritalin. It took quite a while: He seemed to do well at first, but gradually his schoolwork and overall grip on himself would slip enough that the drug was resumed. This cycle happened two or three times. By the time he was nine, Joe was fully aware of the purpose of his medication, and he told his parents he'd rather not be taking it. Around that time they stopped the Ritalin again, and to my knowledge he hasn't taken it since.

I hasten to note that the parents' role in making such a transition successfully is critical, both in the amount and type of feedback they give their child, and in adapting their styles and schedules to his needs. It's a big commitment and a lot of work. Kids with ADD symptoms vary, too, in the degree to which they naturally mature with age and acquire effective coping techniques; Joe was one of the lucky ones who learned ways of pulling himself together when he noticed danger signs. The point, however, is that the concerns and hesitancies of such families regarding long-term Ritalin use deserve at least thoughtful consideration, and their efforts should have the support of doctors, teachers, and others in the child's world. Yet this is not the message being delivered by the American medical community. In the present climate, families are more likely to be overwhelmed by the surge toward Ritalin.

Chapter 3

$\longleftrightarrow$

ATTENTION DEFICIT DISORDER: IN THE EYE OF THE BEHOLDER

I know it when I see it.

—Supreme Court Justice Potter Stewart,
on distinguishing pornography from art

Among the doctors and other professionals who evaluate and treat patients for ADD, some express great confidence in their ability to diagnose the condition. Following the official guidelines set forth by psychiatry, they take histories, count up symptoms, pronounce their verdict, and (usually) prescribe medication. Doctor, patient, and loved ones go home feeling better, believing that in can-do American fashion a problem has been identified and addressed, if not solved.

But for me and for many others, getting a handle on the syndrome we call ADD is not nearly so simple. In any given week, I may be asked to evaluate an array of patients with an astonishing range of problems:

• a three-year-old kicked out of preschool because he can't play quietly with other toddlers and keeps everyone fussing during naptime

• a five-year-old who isn't talking much, seems withdrawn, shows developmental lag in picking up numbers and letters, and still can't throw a ball any distance

• an eight-year-old constantly in trouble for hitting his siblings and schoolmates

• a prepubescent girl who's socially awkward and shunned by her peers, and who chronically fails to finish her homework

• a teenager whose grades don't live up to his IQ scores, and whose parents see his college prospects slipping away

• a young woman who's had to move back into her parents' home because she can't get it together at a job or keep her checkbook current

• a mother of two whose drinking and outbursts of temper have begun to scare her husband

• a heretofore successful stockbroker who finds that the pace of trading in today's market has outstripped his ability to perform one of his primary tasks: tracking the performance of securities

All of these people are consulting me because they—or their parents, teacher, primary-care doctor, or spouse—have heard about ADD and suspect that this "disorder" lies at the root of their troubles. Some of them may have read about ADD in books such as the best-selling *Driven to Distraction*, by Edward Hallowell and John Ratey. Aimed chiefly at the booming population of "adults with ADD," this book offers a memorable list of a hundred self-assessment questions.[1] The first ten on the list are:

1. Are you left-handed or ambidextrous?

2. Do you have a family history of drug or alcohol abuse, depression, or manic-depressive illness?

3. Are you moody?

4. Were you considered an underachiever in school? Now?

5. Do you have trouble getting started on things?

6. Do you drum your fingers a lot, tap your feet, fidget, or pace?

7. When you read, do you find that you often have to reread an entire paragraph or an entire page because you are daydreaming?

8. Do you tune out or space out a lot?

9. Do you have a hard time relaxing?

10. Are you excessively impatient?

And the list goes on, encompassing nearly every negative that can apply to the human condition (along with a few flattering traits such as "Are you particularly intuitive?" "Do you love to travel?" "Do you laugh a lot?" and "Would you describe yourself as hypersexual?"). While the authors are careful to describe this list as only "an informal gauge," they do say that the questions "reflect those an experienced diagnostician will ask." No guideline is provided as to how many yes answers should cause concern. It's not surprising that this well-publicized questionnaire has brought many people into my office and those of specialists nationwide.

Considerable publicity also has been generated by lists claiming to identify famous people with attention deficit disorder. One such roster included Beethoven, Henry Ford, Louis Pasteur, John Kennedy, and Woodrow Wilson, along with an inspirational message for less-renowned ADD patients: "With perseverance they made it—so can you!" A *Time* magazine feature story added Winston Churchill, Albert Einstein, Ben Franklin, and Bill Clinton, who was diagnosed by an ADD expert as being "one pill away from greatness."[2]

Such lists and questionnaires make easy targets for criticism, providing fuel for doubters who challenge whether ADD exists at all. That's not my purpose, or even close to it. But I do believe that such efforts to introduce ADD to the public have opened a Pandora's box. In attempting to package for public consumption a condition that psychiatry has only recently defined—in fact, is still struggling to define—and for which it has a long list of symptoms but no firm explanation, the popularizers have contributed to widespread confusion about just what ADD is and who can be said to "have" it.

The medical/psychiatric community—the experts who define diseases and write diagnostic guidelines—are themselves confused about ADD. Close to a century after researchers first identified the primary symptoms of the condition, there exists among doctors and mental health professionals a wide range of opinion about how many children and adults are affected by it, what its chief causes are, the best methods of evaluation and treatment, and even how it should be described.

At a 1996 national meeting of the Society of Developmental and Behavioral Pediatrics, a fellow pediatrician remarked to me, "Twenty years ago, I thought I didn't know much about ADD, but about ten years ago I felt like I had a handle it. Now I feel like I don't know anything again!" Another doctor wished (only half seriously) that Ritalin could be available over the counter, so he wouldn't have to be the one to decide which child got it and which didn't. A prominent behavioral pediatrician summed up the situation: "The current status of the ADD diagnosis is an embarrassment."[3]

How did this come to pass? The roots of our uncertainty about ADD reach back to the earliest attempts to scientifically isolate and define behavior problems, and are entwined with the development of psychiatry itself.

WHAT'S IN A NAME? THE EVOLUTION OF ADD

Any definition of ADD involves problems in three major areas of functioning: *attention*, that is, the ability to focus on an activity or task over a period of time; *control over impulses*; and *level of physical activity*. All of the myriad problems shown by my patients, or mentioned in Hallowell and Ratey's hundred questions, can in theory be traced back to these three broad categories—which are like primary tree limbs that support countless smaller branches, twigs, and leaves. Put another way, a person diagnosed with ADD is likely to behave in ways that demonstrate poor attention (or distractibility), poor self-control (impulsivity, also referred to as disinhibition), and excessive activity, or hyperactivity. Leading expert Russell Barkley calls these the "holy trinity" of symptoms.[4]

Each of these three realms of behavior exists on a spectrum or continuum. Everyone has a unique point where they fall on the spectrum of attentiveness, or impulsiveness, or activeness; where each of us falls is part of our basic temperament or personality. If we land too far from the norm in one direction or another, that aspect of our personality is considered to be "maladaptive"—that is, detrimental to our ability to function in a satisfactory way. ADD, then, is a way of codifying certain behavioral tendencies that interfere with people's lives. *To what extent* is a key question; you can already see that we are speaking about something relative. Just how poor is a child's ability to pay attention? How impulsive or active is he compared to others? What do we consider a satisfactory life, and how significantly do aspects of our personality get in the way of our achieving it?

These behavioral tendencies are not new. No doubt there have always been children and adults who were more active, distractible, and impulsive than the norm. But whether such personality traits are perceived as problems surely has something to do with the environment in which a person is functioning. In late twentieth-century middle-class America we are likely to see individuals who are more active, distractible, and impulsive as maladapted, but in other places and at other times those same traits may have conferred advantages.

At least one investigator has suggested that ADD traits are the vestigal characteristics of a "hunter" type, evolutionarily suited for survival in the wild, but less well adapted for modern life. In his intriguing book about the "hunter," Thom Hartmann puts a positive spin on typical ADD symptoms.[5] For example, distractibility can be seen as the tendency to constantly monitor one's environment (for prey opportunities, or to avoid becoming prey). Someone who acts impulsively can be considered decisive and willing to take risks. The person who has trouble staying on task might be called flexible, able to quickly change strategy to take advantage of the instant. And so on. Such theories are interesting but speculative; what is undoubtedly true is that people with the symptoms of ADD today find many aspects of contemporary life gravely challenging.

The first report of children who probably would fit the modern diagnosis of ADD came in 1902, in lectures by the British physician George Still to the Royal College of Medicine.[6] Still described these children, numbering twenty, with terms such as "aggressive," "defiant," "resistant to discipline," "excessively emotional," or "passionate." He noted that they showed little "inhibitory volition"—an idea central to the very latest thinking about ADD, by the way—and believed they displayed a "major defect in moral control," with tendencies toward "lawlessness" and dishonesty. Some of the children had physical abnormalities such as enlarged head size, which at the time was commonly thought to signify inadequate intellect or morals. Some of them came from inadequate (or worse) family backgrounds, but others did not, and Still discounted this as a factor, hypothesizing that the problems he observed were either hereditary or the result of some birth-related brain injury. He also considered them chronic in nature. In some of these ideas, he anticipated much later thinking about ADD.

Further grounds for positing brain damage as the cause of behavior problems was provided by an outbreak of encephalitis (a viral infection of the brain) in 1917–18. Children left with behavioral and cognitive impairments after their illness were studied by several researchers, who found, among other symptoms, evidence of hyperactivity, failure to control impulses, and impaired attention—the same trio of symptoms that now de-

fines ADD. By the 1930s this collection of behavioral problems was sometimes called "organic drivenness" or "restlessness syndrome." Through the
1940s more severe manifestations of this kind were believed to result from
some kind of brain injury, while milder forms of hyperactivity were attributed to poor child-rearing practices or "overstimulating" classroom environments.

In the 1950s the term MBD (standing at first for "minimal brain damage") served as an umbrella for a large group of loosely related behaviors
thought to originate in defects of the central nervous system. The behaviors included "excessive restlessness, poor ability to sustain interest in activities, aimless wandering, and excessive appetite." Later MBD was revised
to "minimal brain dysfunction." Proof (anatomical, chemical, or electroen-
cephalographic) of any brain damage remained elusive in the vast majority
of children.

By this time, however, the evidence that stimulants mitigated hyperactivity in children was fairly well established, and research began to focus on
how these drugs operated. This was the start of a trend away from attempts
to identify the source of the problems—which was proving so difficult—
and toward a more pragmatic approach: simply sorting out and describing
symptoms in detail, and learning what did or did not lead to improvement.

During the 1950s and 1960s hyperactivity came to be seen as a fairly
common behavior problem in children—one that could be related to brain
mechanisms but not necessarily caused by brain damage. Researchers
shifted their focus to milder forms of overactivity and invented new terms
to describe it, including "hyperactive child syndrome," "hyperkinetic reaction," and "hyperkinetic impulse disorder." Influential studies proposed
that overactivity was the defining feature and that this was often resolved
by puberty. By the early 1960s it was held that the best treatment would
combine stimulant medication, psychotherapy, and parent counseling.
This was the era when Freudian ideas held sway; therefore much emphasis
was placed on parenting dysfunctions and the use of traditional psychotherapy.

By the 1970s hyperactive child syndrome had become more strongly
linked with other symptoms such as distractibility and short attention span.
During this decade the concept of MBD faded away: There was still no
neurological evidence to support it, and it was felt to be overly inclusive
and not useful in prescribing treatment. Work had begun to focus on teasing out specific child developmental problems from earlier broad charac-
terizations like MBD. Learning disabilities such as dyslexia and language

disorder were identified. This work constituted a kind of sharpening of the scientific lens through which children's behavior problems could be viewed. As noted in Chapter 2, this was also a time when the public was reacting against stimulant therapy for children.

An event took place in 1972 that, looking back, was a watershed in the emergence of what we now call ADD. Virginia Douglas, the leader of a research team at Montreal's McGill University, delivered a paper to the Canadian Psychological Association about a group of children that she and her team had been studying for years.[7] Though they'd been diagnosed with hyperkinetic syndrome, their problems, Douglas claimed, centered more on deficits in sustaining attention and controlling impulses. Many of the children showed serious problems in functioning without any signs of hyperactivity, and when physical hyperactivity *was* present, it could often be traced to problems with impulse control. (A distractible child who reacted impulsively would move quickly from one thing to another.) In other words, the importance of hyperactivity was deemphasized in favor of the other two symptoms in the "trinity."

The discoveries of the McGill team were reinforced by other research, and from this rethinking was born a new name for the condition—attention deficit disorder, or ADD—and a new, much larger, group of patients: those with problems of attention and/or impulsivity without any hyperactivity.

This new focus, especially on attention deficit, helped to officially distinguish ADD from other psychiatric conditions where hyperactivity also could occur, such as autism or anxiety disorders. In related developments, Douglas and others found that hyperactivity was more likely to subside as children moved into adolescence, while problems of attention and impulse control tended to persist beyond puberty. And like George Still nearly a century earlier, Douglas noted strong links between ADD symptoms and children's failure to develop a moral sense, leading to the likelihood of problems with the law during adolescence.

Growing professional acceptance of Douglas's view climaxed in 1980 with the introduction of the name "attention deficit disorder" in the third edition of psychiatry's bible—the *Diagnostic and Statistical Manual of Mental Disorders*, or DSM.[8] Published by the American Psychiatric Association (APA), this was and is a book that affects thousands of American mental health professionals and millions of their patients, directly and indirectly. A condition acknowledged by the DSM as a disorder can be the basis for a specific treatment, the rationale for a research project or a researcher's career, the justification for a disability claim, a legal defense, or a political stigma. The DSM's impact reaches beyond the realm of academia and medicine to American society at large—and so it has proved with ADD.

THE GOSPEL ACCORDING TO DSM:
PSYCHIATRY'S BIG SHIFT AND ITS IMPACT ON ADD

Over the course of DSM revisions since 1980, the tide of professional opinion about the importance of hyperactivity in the ADD recipe has continued to ebb and flow. In response to concerns that it had been deemphasized too much, the 1987 revision, DSM-III-R, changed the official name of the syndrome to attention deficit/hyperactivity disorder (ADHD), and so it has remained ever since. However, most people continue to refer to it as ADD—perhaps because that is simply easier to say, or perhaps because it more accurately reflects the growing number of children and adults who demonstrate problems only with attention.

What the ADD entry in DSM-III *didn't* have was any suggestion of possible causes for the behaviors and symptoms. Looking back over the history of the syndrome, none of the proposed causes—from brain damage to unspecified nervous system dysfunction to dysfunctional families—had ever been confirmed by research. So perhaps it's not surprising that the experts finally retreated to a position of simply describing the symptoms they saw. In fact, this official deemphasis of causality is consistent with the overall approach of DSM-III. And this is where we see a great change in psychiatry as a whole.[9]

By the 1970s many researchers and academicians had begun to seriously doubt whether psychiatry really qualified as a branch of medicine. Medicine, after all, was based in science, and it was difficult to see much hard science operating in psychiatry at the time. The problem for clinical practitioners was twofold. First, the diagnostic system in the first two editions of DSM was greatly influenced by descriptions and causes of conditions rooted in the still-prevalent Freudian model. These guidelines were sufficiently ambiguous or open to interpretation that one patient's history and set of symptoms could lead several clinicians to several different diagnoses. Further, it was questionable whether the primary form of treatment used—psychoanalysis—actually improved the condition of most patients. The two difficulties compounded each other: Treatment outcomes could not effectively be assessed because researchers could not agree on exactly what was being treated.

The situation came to a head with the preparation and publication of DSM-III, which returned to a pre-Freudian classification scheme. The authors chose to follow the lead of Emil Kraepelin, a German psychiatrist of the late nineteenth century, who classified his patients' signs and symptoms into meaningful groups called "disorders" or "syndromes" without ascribing to them any specific cause. In returning to this model of description-without-cause, clinicians and researchers hoped to be able at least to agree on what was being seen. (For ADD, eleven possible symptoms of inattention were described, and five signs of hyperactivity: the patient was required to demonstrate a certain number of those behaviors to receive a diagnosis.) Subsequent revisions of the DSM—the most recent, DSM-IV, was published in 1994—have retained the same approach.[10]

The DSM-III announced a definitive power shift away from the Freudian old guard. Said Gerald Klerman, then one of America's most prominent psychiatrists, "DSM-III represents . . . a significant reaffirmation on the part of American psychiatry of its medical identity and its commitment to scientific medicine."[11] No matter that the new definitions were in some ways as subjective as the previous ones—basically, the "experts" who authored them relied on their judgment and experience and the few epidemiological studies available to justify their opinions. Still, there was much excitement and hope that the new approach would provide a gold standard for diagnosis and research, and thereby restore luster to psychiatry's tarnished image. Certainly it has succeeded beyond its authors' hopes in becoming the official lingua franca not just for doctors but, as one writer notes, "for the entire culture and economy of a mental health establishment made up primarily of nonphysicians: clinical social workers, psychologists, and counselors."[12]

THE DSM IN PRACTICE:
HOW A DOCTOR USES IT (OR NOT)

When I first began evaluating adults for ADD, I wanted to find out how other doctors dealt with this new group of patients, so I consulted with a fellow ADD specialist nearby. It was no big deal to him: "Just count the symptoms," he told me, "and if they meet criteria, you can treat them"

(with medication, it was implied). The subtleties and contradictions of behavior and emotions, the interactions of relationships and environment—
none of this seemed important to him. It made me wonder why a doctor
was needed, if this was all an evaluation required.

Before 1980, front-line practitioners like myself barely gave DSM a nod;
it was primarily intended for researchers. That situation has changed vastly,
due largely to the rise of managed health care, which requires doctors to
hew closely to official guidelines in making diagnoses. But what goes on
the insurance paperwork and what really goes into an understanding of a
patient and her case is something like the difference between a frozen pizza
and a subtly seasoned, long-simmered stew.

Take for example the Gordon family, introduced briefly in Chapter 1.
The process of evaluating a patient starts with the first phone call: the one
in which six-year-old Steven's mother, Sheila, related with such distress the
problems he was having at school. If her report was correct—that he was
having trouble "staying on task," "keeping up with group activities," and
"keeping his hands to himself"; that he was fidgeting with pencils and wandering off—and if I were simply counting symptoms, we would already be
more than half way to a diagnosis.

To meet criteria according to DSM-IV, Steven must show at least six out
of nine symptoms of inattention *or* at least six of nine behaviors indicating
hyperactivity-impulsivity.[13] (See Figure 1.) Other criteria that must be met
are:

- Symptoms must have begun before age seven.

- The child or adult must demonstrate the problem behaviors in at
least two situations (school, home, or work).

- The behaviors must cause significant distress or impairment in
functioning.

- Finally, the behaviors cannot be better explained by other diagnostic conditions (a list of examples is provided).

I knew Sheila had the idea that an ADD diagnosis might fit Steven. But
I was much more interested, during this first interview, in her and Frank's
detailed descriptions of the problems he was having. I asked them to describe his behavior in a variety of situations: at home, at school, in after-
school activities, and with friends. Chiefly, it was detail and specificity I was

Figure 1: DSM-IV Criteria

Inattention

(a) often fails to give close attention to details or makes careless mistakes in school work, work, or other activities

(b) often has difficulty sustaining attention in tasks or play activities

(c) often does not seem to listen when spoken to directly

(d) often does not follow through on instructions and fails to finish schoolwork, chores, or duties in the workplace (not due to oppositional behavior or failure to understand instructions)

(e) often has difficulty organizing tasks and activities

(f) often avoids, dislikes, or is reluctant to engage in tasks that require sustained mental effort (such as schoolwork or homework)

(g) often loses things necessary for tasks or activities (e.g., toys, school assignments, pencils, books, or tools)

(h) is often easily distracted by extraneous stimuli

(i) is often forgetful in daily activities

Hyperactivity

(a) often fidgets with hands or feet or squirms in seat

(b) often leaves seat in classroom or in other situations in which remaining seated is expected

(c) often runs about or climbs excessively in situations in which it is inappropriate (in adolescents or adults, may be limited to subjective feelings of restlessness)

(d) often has difficulty playing or engaging in leisure activities quietly

(e) is often "on the go" or often acts as if "driven by a motor"

(f) often talks excessively

Impulsivity

(a) often blurts out answers before questions have been completed

(b) often has difficulty awaiting turn

(c) often interrupts or intrudes on others (e.g., butts into conversations or games) after, not whether the answers fit the criteria. However, as noted above, the occurrence of problems in multiple settings is one of the DSM's diagnostic criteria for ADD. Here we ran into the first potential roadblock: Steven's problems seemed to be centered on school, and Sheila had so far reported no difficulties at home. Perhaps Steven's core problem was a cognitive one—some minor learning disability—rather than ADD. But in the doctor's office, with parents desperate for help, pragmatism tends to rule, and the two-or-more-environments rule often gets fudged so that medication can be offered.

As the interview went on, Sheila and Frank's accounts of how Steven acted matched up well enough with some of the official behaviors listed in the DSM-IV. His persistent playing with pencils could be interpreted as "often fidgets with hands or feet." He sometimes wandered to the window in class, that is, "often leaves seat in classroom or in other situations where remaining seated is expected." His teacher's report that he had trouble "staying on task" is another way of saying "often has difficulty sustaining attention in tasks or play activities." And so on. Yet what often strikes those encountering DSM criteria for the first time is how common these symptoms are among children of Steven's age. Don't all kids at one time or another fidget with their hands, not listen when spoken to directly, and avoid boring tasks ("reluctance to engage in tasks requiring sustained mental effort")?

That the diagnostic criteria include so many common behaviors leaves the DSM open to easy ridicule by critics who accuse psychiatry of manufacturing mental illness out of normal coping behavior. The DSM's defenders are quick to retort that it's not the behavior per se but its frequency, intensity, and degree of impairment that tip the scales in diagnosis. Clearly, all those famous, accomplished people (Edison, Benjamin Franklin, JFK, and so on) were not impaired *enough* to fail in life—even though they may have displayed symptoms we associate with ADD. But the way things are going, even some of these notables might be offered Ritalin by today's diagnosticians.

In my interviews I also want to get a sense of the parents: their opinions and personalities, how they get along, what shaped their ideas, and whether they can account for their child's problems in other ways besides ADD. I try deliberately to avoid yes-or-no questions, which often lead to dead-end exchanges. Questions asking how, what, or why generate a richer response and much more information. To give a few examples: What happens when you tell your son to put away his toys? How do you know his teacher is concerned about his schoolwork? How large is his class? How does the teacher try to interest the children in what's being taught, and how does she maintain discipline? Why do you think he's not getting along with his friends? Does Steven have a brother or sister, and how does their behavior compare to (or affect) Steven's? I also want to find out whether the parents agree on their observations of and responses to their son, and whether there are other stressful factors in their lives.

Nothing in DSM-IV says that I shouldn't conduct interviews in this way, but there's little to support it, either, other than a statement in the introduction about "the use of clinical judgment."[14] The trend—unfortunately, as I see it—is to rely more and more on the DSM checklist alone as the primary diagnostic tool. In that case, the interviewer's job is to proceed through the list of symptomatic behaviors, checking off any that a child is reported to demonstrate, along with their frequency and intensity. Does Steven "not seem to listen when spoken to directly? Always, sometimes, seldom, or never?" No elaboration, no telling detail is called for, and the potential richness of the interview is lost. The need, then, for a doctor's experience and insight becomes moot: A clerk or a computer program could take down the yes/no, always/sometimes/seldom/never responses prompted by the DSM symptom lists. Are families ready to have their child evaluated so mechanically, and given medication on this basis? In trying so hard to make diagnosis a science, the DSM diminishes the fact that medicine is also an art.

THE PROTEAN DIAGNOSIS: PROBLEMS WITH TODAY'S VERSION OF ADD

In drawing attention to problems with the ADD diagnosis, I must emphasize that neither I nor any mainstream physician who treats children would deny the existence of a core group of patients who have significant problems that can be associated with inherent overactivity, attention deficit, or impulsivity. A diagnosis of ADD can help both the children and their families understand that these problems are not just willful bad behavior. If nothing else, we've learned that in dealing with "problem personalities," the line between "he won't behave" and "he can't behave" is very hard to draw. Though it happens less today than in the past, I've met parents who were convinced their difficult child's angry, deceitful, and irresponsible behavior was the irrevocable outgrowth of a bad character. When such children are shown to meet criteria for ADD, it allows the parents to reenvision the situation as something that can be remedied and to see their child in a more humane way.

That said, I'll briefly outline what I see as the most troublesome aspects of how ADD is currently framed in official psychiatry:

The process of establishing "objective" diagnostic standards for ADD has itself been quite subjective.   The people in medicine's academic circles who define disorders are inevitably influenced by the biases and sociopolitical interests of their time. For example, the DSM classified homosexuality as a sexual disorder until 1974, when pressure from gay advocates within and outside the profession lead to removal of the "disease" label. Similarly, a new category, post-traumatic stress disorder, was developed in response to work with veterans of the war in Vietnam.

The professionals who create or revise DSM categories are recruited by the American Psychiatric Association, and political considerations, as well as professional relationships and rivalries, inevitably enter into the selection process. In essence, various experts, primarily from academia and research, choose one another. Clashing factions on a disorder may sit on the same committee, and decisions are sometimes made for reasons other than strict science.

A case in point involves the evolution of ADD criteria. When the diagnostic standards were being revised for DSM-IV, the committee instituted a series of field trials in an attempt to correlate the number of symptoms to the degree of a patient's impairment.[15] A study group of some nine hundred children was chosen, and information was collected from parents, teachers, and children through interviews and other means. In each case, an experienced clinician ultimately determined the diagnosis after reviewing this information. These diagnoses in turn were used to determine which symptoms, and how many, were key to the diagnosis.

Yet even after all this earnest effort, politics prevailed. The main study group had determined that only five of nine symptoms would be required to qualify for a diagnosis of "ADHD: hyperactive/inattentive subtype" (that is, a "combined" version of the disorder). But then the supervisory DSM-IV task force astonishingly overruled this decision and increased the number of symptoms required to six! Presumably, they were concerned that five criteria were too few and might result in too many children being diagnosed with this type of ADD, but the arbitrariness of their action has little to do with science.

Such episodes have raised doubts even within the inner circle of the profession. Herman van Praag, who once headed the psychiatry department at the Albert Einstein College of Medicine (and was instrumental in helping rewrite DSM-III), comments: "Today's classification of the major psychiatric disorders is as confusing as it used to be some thirty years ago. All things considered, the present situation is worse. Then, psychiatrists were at least aware that diagnostic chaos reigned and many of them had no high opinion of diagnosis anyhow. Now, the chaos is codified, and thus much more hidden."[16]

Official guidelines for evaluating ADD symptoms are vague and open to interpretation—yet they lead to an all-or-nothing diagnosis. In all the behaviors listed by the DSM under ADD, the word *often* is used to describe behavior that has become a problem. How useful is this? In thinking about Steven Gordon, for example, I wonder how the term applies to his playing with pencils. Does it mean, perhaps, three times in an hour? Or just often enough to be noticed? And is it the frequency that makes it a problem, or something else? What precisely does he do with the pencil—is he tapping it, gnawing on it, rolling it in his fingers? (One of these might suggest overactivity, another might indicate anxiety, yet another just boredom.)

A certain kind of absurdity begins to enter this process. Careers are now based on measuring and quantifying children's levels of activity, and there exists a commercial device called the Actometer that purports to monitor the activity rate of the child wearing it. No doubt we've all been stumped at one time or another when asked to answer questions about whether we do something "always," "sometimes," "seldom," or "never." It has been shown that when parents are first presented with such measures—rather than asked simply to describe the behaviors in detail—they often choose one that sounds more serious, perhaps to reinforce their own feeling that a problem indeed exists. This would be natural enough.

Another fact becomes apparent on close scrutiny of the DSM symptom lists: Certain behaviors reiterate others. For example, "often loses things necessary for tasks and activities" sounds an awful lot like "is often forgetful in daily activities." If counting symptoms is the point, this produces two "yes" answers to fundamentally the same question.

Despite the vague, general, and repetitive nature of the DSM's symptoms, however, and the difficulty of judging their frequency, the evaluator finally is required to make an all-or-nothing decision. Patients either meet the criteria for the diagnosis or they don't. If their symptoms meet the criteria, then they "have" a psychiatric disorder. This has important consequences for the people diagnosed, for suddenly they're not just experiencing significant coping problems; rather, they have a disease. (I'll explore the implications of this further as we proceed.)

In contrast, many clinicians (and parents) recognize that a spectrum of problem behavior exists, from relatively "normal" activity and distractibility at one end to major acting out at the other. But what if a child demonstrates only five of the nine qualifying behaviors instead of the six required for a diagnosis? Does he have "mild" ADD or "near" ADD? How serious is his problem? A categorical approach to diagnosis surely is useful in research, but in a clinical setting a dimensional model[17] (reflecting the spectrum of impairment) or a needs-based model[18] (emphasizing what the child needs in treatment) would be more useful. The present ADD diagnosis falls short in this regard, and thus offers only limited help to a doctor's real-life decision making.

The ADD diagnosis has no definitive medical or psychological marker, and so it is often made exclusively on the basis of a patient's history. In seeking a diagnosis for any medical condition, we look for some kind of marker, a reasonably sure sign that we're heading in the right direction. In physical medicine, we're often looking for a bacterium that can be cultured and identified, and if we find it, we prescribe a medication known to combat that bacterium. In psychology, certain kinds of learning disabilities have fairly specific markers: If someone performs normally on most sections of a standard test but poorly on its block design or coding portions, this strongly suggests the presence of a visual processing problem. As yet, however, no such marker exists for ADD. Researchers naturally are looking under every rock, and some claim to be able to use brain scanning techniques to identify specific abnormalities associated with ADD. But there is nothing conclusive.

In the absence of this—whether we call it a marker or a cause—we are left with a disorder whose diagnosis is based solely on symptoms. In the past, those symptoms would have to have been demonstrated by the patient in the presence of a doctor (or other qualified evaluator). The DSM, however, now states that "symptoms are typically variable and may not be observed directly by the clinician." Instead, the clinician is encouraged to lean heavily on history—usually reports from parents and/or teachers—to make the diagnosis.

Once again, subjectivity enters the picture. The circumstances and biases of those reporting a child's behavior are seldom taken into account. If Sheila Gordon, for example, were depressed, as moms of troubled kids often are, she would be likely to overreport Steven's problems. If Steven's teacher in a regular classroom is feeling overwhelmed by too many kids and unable to cope with a few who are disruptive, he or she might well say that he wandered to the window "often" rather than "sometimes." (It's been shown that general-education teachers tend to overreport compared with special-ed teachers.) And if Steven's dad felt helpless to control his son's problem behavior, he too would show a bias toward overstating it. In all probability, none of them do this deliberately, but it happens—and that being so, the current trend toward diagnosing without ever seeing the child is all the more troublesome.

Sir Michael Rutter, one of the most influential figures in child psychiatry in recent decades, observes that any diagnosis, in order to be useful, should be distinctive from other disorders in its causation, natural progression, or treatment.[19] Rutter feels that ADD as currently defined does not meet these standards.[20] First, there is no identified cause specific to ADD. Second, its progress and likely outcome are very hard to differentiate from certain other childhood disorders. (We don't know, for instance, whether Steven's behavior is traceable to ADD or if his anger and acting out are primarily a response to inconsistent feedback from his parents. In any case, whether or not his behavior is labeled ADD may not matter in how things turn out for him.) And finally, the effects of the usual treatment for ADD— Ritalin—are not specific to the disorder. The drug potentially improves the performance of anyone—child or adult, ADD-diagnosed or not. Whatever the source of Steven's problems, if they are the kind that improve on Ritalin, that treatment will probably work.

In short, with ADD, the symptoms *are* the disease.[21] We are left with the possibility that ADD may be a catch-all condition encompassing a variety of children's behavioral problems with various causes, both biologically predetermined and psychosocial. And the fact that Ritalin helps with so many problems may be encouraging the ADD diagnosis to expand its boundaries.

The ADD diagnosis is overly focused on the individual and doesn't take sufficient account of family systems and other environmental factors. The DSM in general does not directly take note of "systemic" issues such as family dynamics.[22] For my work with children and families, I would prefer a more holistic diagnostic system—one that gives more emphasis to relationships. Examples might include the feedback links between inconsistent parenting and children with difficult personalities, or between a failing marriage and depression. In the DSM's handling of ADD in particular, the demands and responses of environment are not perceived as critical to the diagnosis, except perhaps in extreme circumstances (for example, abuse or neglect, which might prompt an alternative diagnosis for a child). This failure to allow for the role of environment seems especially important when the patient is a child; by virtue of their size and level of development, children are especially vulnerable to environmental influences.

I came across a telling comment on this situation in the letters column of a 1995 issue of the journal *Pediatrics*. New York pediatrician Daniel L. Zeidner writes:

> It has become increasingly apparent to me, and perhaps to other pediatricians, that a new syndrome exists among adults who teach our school-aged children: Teacher Deficit Disorder, or TDD. I have observed that this diagnosis should be made on the teacher when the following classic signs and symptoms exist among one or more of his/her students: students who fidget in class constantly moving their fingers or legs, who do not pay attention, who frequently daydream, who do not complete their homework or classwork, and who frequently get out of their seats. When students exhibit these manifestations, the teacher should be diagnosed with TDD and, of course, should be medicated immediately with amphetamine or other drugs that should speed him/her up, thus making him/her . . . more dynamic and interesting to his/her students.[23]

This of course is satire, but Zeidner's observations and logic are as impeccable as those in any real DSM diagnosis.

In its current phase as a "disorder for all seasons," ADD has become too inclusive. It has lost relevance to the age-related, developmental nature of some core problems.   The effect of all the diagnostic and interpretative changes around ADD in the last two decades has been to greatly increase the number of children and adults receiving the diagnosis. In the mid-1970s, a child pretty much had to demonstrate some signs of hyperactivity or impulsivity in the doctor's office. Today, children can behave and perform quite normally in the doctor's office yet meet the criteria for ADD by reports of difficulties at home or school.

Normal performance in many situations is not a disqualifier as long as underperformance occurs in critical areas. A child may concentrate well on any number of subjects or activities—for example, building with Legos or doing artwork—but if he is struggling to complete schoolwork and home chores, he could still qualify for ADD with "selective inattention." He might even overconcentrate on, say, television or the Internet and not respond to requests to shift his focus. This behavior, too, gets interpreted within the ADD framework as "attentional inconstancy."

The ADD subtypes are related to age and developmental issues, yet the DSM does not acknowledge this. Younger children generally aren't presented with situations in which long-term focus is an issue, so they are not likely to be diagnosed with inattention problems; however, hyperactivity can cause problems for their families and preschool teachers. Attention deficits and impulsivity, if they exist, become highlighted when the demands of school and peer relationships grow in importance. And they are the issues around which adults diagnosed with ADD have problems. Prior to 1980 adults were not considered candidates for the disorder, because few still show signs of hyperactivity.

One consequence of the greater number of adults seeking evaluation for ADD today is a further weakening of the diagnostic criteria. Recall that DSM requires that the patient have a history of symptoms beginning before the age of seven. Many adults, not surprisingly, don't have access to such history of their early life, or can't remember back that far. So for quite a while this criterion has been quietly overlooked in making diagnoses for adults; as of late 1997 the leading experts have called for its elimination altogether.[24]

ADD as officially described can look a lot like certain other childhood psychiatric disorders. And many children meet criteria for some, but not all, of the symptoms of several different conditions.   I want to discuss this problem by talking about a young patient of mine in some detail. I hope this will provide a vivid sense of how hard it is to pin down some people's problems by means of a diagnosis and, more important, to do anything about them.

DUELING DISORDERS: THE CASE OF SAM

When Sam Maynard first came to see me, he was ten years old and in pretty bad shape. Sam had been having problems since first grade. He tended not to finish his work at school, instead switching his attention to things he liked doing, such as building with Legos or working on art projects. His grades weren't bad—B's and C's—but he was clearly bright and capable of more. Mildly impulsive, he was less of a problem at home, though often he would not do as his parents asked unless his father became quite stern or even physical. He generally ignored his mother, though not in a mean or spiteful way.

About four years before we met, Sam had developed a throat-clearing habit that would wax and wane but never go away completely. It seemed to worsen when he became tense—if his parents were fighting with each other or yelling at him. He also sometimes demonstrated repetitive hand-wringing; this also increased under stress. Both habits greatly annoyed his parents. Sam struck me as rather a sad child. In our early meetings, when we would mostly talk and play, his eyes would dart around, never meeting mine directly. In time we talked about this; he knew that his failing to look at people directly gave them the impression he was uncomfortable (which he was, but couldn't admit to) or that he wasn't listening or didn't care. As we got to know each other, I'd sometimes ask him to look at me, and he would—but it took effort.

Sam complained—mainly to his mother but also to me—about some vague, confused, and troubling thoughts that he couldn't get out of his head. They might be what he called "bad" ideas or even inoffensive words that somehow disturbed him. He called these his "patterns," and rated them on a scale of zero to ten. Zero was the worst; ten represented absolute freedom from intrusive thoughts. He rarely reached a ten and said he'd never been at zero—but even a two or three meant nearly total preoccupation with thoughts that "told" him literally to take one step back for two steps forward, or to make circles with his hands. He "complied" with these instructions but felt miserable. Sam was not psychotic: He made it clear these were thoughts, not voices, that directed him.

Where Sam's problems most interfered with his life was in making and keeping friends. Though his language skills were okay, he was socially awkward and often misread social cues. His poor eye contact didn't help. He could usually latch on to one or two kids in his class who were also "different," but he ached for more friends. He had begun to spend more and more time alone in his room, and his parents, seeing his self-image deteriorate, had become deeply worried. I was not the first doctor they had consulted; rather, I inherited Sam from several other physicians. By the time I met him, he had already been diagnosed with ADD and another psychiatric disorder, and was taking three medications simultaneously. In fact, this was one of the things that made it hard to know what was really going on with Sam. He was always under the influence of some medication or other and often seemed lethargic in addition to his other troubles.

Sam was a classic example of a child whose symptoms seem to span several different disorders of childhood. Psychiatrists informally divide child behavior problems into "externalizing" and "internalizing" categories. ADD falls into the former category, along with conduct disorder (CD) and the quite similar oppositional defiant disorder (ODD). "Internalizing" disorders include anxiety problems (pronounced fears, phobias, separation anxiety, and psychosomatic symptoms), as well as depression and obsessive-compulsive disorder (OCD). OCD is defined by the DSM as recurrent and persistent thoughts, impulses, or images that are experienced as intrusive and unwanted, or cause anxiety or distress. Sam's "patterns" did sound related to OCD symptoms, and indeed that was the second diagnosis he'd received after ADD. He was already on Ritalin, and at that point began taking large doses of Anafranil, a drug originally developed to treat depression but now used most often for OCD.

Still another doctor felt Sam might be suffering from Tourette's syndrome, a condition of uncontrollable muscle and vocal twitches. Tourette's sufferers are infamous for their bouts with coprolalia (literally, "shit coming out of the mouth," referring to explosions of swearing without apparent provocation). While Sam's behavior clearly wasn't this extreme, the doctor who suspected Tourette's added to his regime a drug called clonidine (Catapres), originally developed to lower blood pressure and now used for children's psychiatric problems.

Observing the way Sam acted with his parents, I thought he could meet criteria for yet another DSM diagnosis: oppositional defiant disorder. The official symptoms of ODD are likely to raise the eyebrows of anyone skeptical of psychiatry's tendency to turn behavior into disease. A child with ODD

1. often loses his or her temper

2. often argues with adults

3. often actively defies or refuses to comply with adults' requests or rules

4. often deliberately annoys people

and so on, through another four symptoms. In lay terms, this might describe a tough, bratty kid who probably is also quite unhappy. The DSM's almost exclusive focus on the individual strikes me as especially myopic when considering this "disorder"; it would seem critical to know what or whom the child is opposing. I'm thinking of parents and teachers, and their rules and responses. (Sam's parents, Tom and Susan, had some problems providing consistent and immediate rewards and discipline in response to his behavior, which we worked on in counseling to some extent. But Tom and Susan seemed more committed to finding a chemical solution to Sam's problems.)

And we're still not done with Sam's diagnostic smorgasbord. His social problems seemed more severe than the usual childhood struggles to keep friends. This might be attributed to Asperger's syndrome, a communications disorder that is much milder than autism, and that was first officially recognized in DSM-IV. It is yet another behavioral condition whose causes are thought to be inherent, neurological in origin, and not necessarily learned behavior. No medications are specifically indicated for Asperger's or for ODD, which may partly explain why other avenues were explored first for Sam.

If it was decided that Sam in fact met criteria for more than one of these conditions, he would be described technically as "co-morbid" for ADD with ODD (or whatever). In plain language, co-morbidity means someone can have more than one mental disorder at the same time. The concept of co-morbidity is supposed to address the problem that one diagnosis alone may not fit all of a child's specific symptoms. Like a valid single diagnosis, the diagnosis of co-morbid disorders is supposed to shed light on disease mechanisms, suggest a progression, and direct treatment. A common progression or prognosis, for example, for a child with ADD or ODD is that he or she may later develop antisocial behaviors such as those labeled conduct disorder or antisocial personality disorder—especially if a child is co-morbid for both ADD and ODD.

Sam's case is not particularly unusual, because the rate of co-morbidity for ADD with other externalizing disorders is astonishingly high. A 1997 article by two distinguished child psychiatrists found that ADD occurred together with ODD or CD in anywhere from 43 percent to 93 percent of the sample populations used in various studies.[25] ADD co-occurred with internalizing disorders less frequently, but the rate was still high: between 13 and 50 percent.

What do these numbers really mean? They reinforce my suspicion, and that of many others, that it's very hard to distinguish among some of these childhood disorders using DSM criteria. Most people, including children, just don't fit into diagnostic pigeonholes that readily. Behaviors associated with one condition may lead to symptoms of another—for example, poor impulse control can cause trouble in relationships—and this often becomes the rationale for trying another medication, or a combination of several.

Speaking of treatment, let me briefly bring Sam's story up to date. Concern about Sam's sleepiness led me to recommend discontinuing his Anafranil. In response to considerable pressure from Susan, who read up on the latest medical wonders and would roam the Internet looking for helpful herbs and vitamins, we replaced it with Prozac. This hugely popular antidepressant also had a reputation for helping OCD, but the results here were inconclusive. Sam continued to slide downhill, and at age thirteen he hit bottom. For the first few months of seventh grade he tried hard, but he was soon failing in several subjects and admitted to me that he'd given up. The work was harder in middle school, but more than that, he was overwhelmed by the increased need for self-responsibility and the intense seventh-grade social scene. I started seeing him every week and he made it through the school year—barely.

It was clear that school was destroying Sam, but by law he had to be educated. And he actually could learn pretty well at times; he was an avid reader and explored the Internet on his own. His parents' situation wasn't suited for home schooling, but another possibility emerged. Sam's older brother had successfully attended a small Christian school known for its strict rules and high academic standards. Sam wasn't their usual kind of student, but the director was sympathetic and willing to give him a try, with some special accommodations to his needs.

Tom and Susan worried that the school's behavior and academic requirements might be impossibly hard for Sam to meet. Would he respond to its greater structure and intimacy or buckle under the increased demands? I found it hard to advise them, and it was Sam who finally declared he wanted to go. He didn't clearly state his reasons, but he may have welcomed the chance to follow in his successful brother's footsteps. A month after Sam started at the new school, he and his parents came for an appointment, and the change in him startled me. He sat straighter and spoke enthusiastically about how well he was doing. The routine of daily homework, with next-day checks and immediate consequences, helped him get his work done, he said. And he got along better with the kids. They were more his type, and they didn't try to be as hip or cool as the children in public school. I think he really wanted to succeed and was thriving off the pride of attending this rigorous school.

His parents and I held our collective breath for a few months, hoping the change wasn't just a honeymoon. But Sam continued to do well, leading to less frequent visits with me and a renewed discussion about his medication needs. He was still taking Ritalin, Prozac, and Catapres; I thought he could at least stop the last, as he'd had no throat-clearing or other Tourette's-type symptoms for more than year. His parents were open to the idea, but Sam would have none of it. As usual, he couldn't explain his feelings, but perhaps he believed he'd found just the right chemical mix and didn't want to rock the boat. I rather suspected his improvement had more to do with the new school and growing emotional maturity, but I didn't push the issue. Sam needed more time to live with success before addressing his psychological dependency on prescription drugs.

As Sam's situation illustrates, the diagnostic categories set forth in the DSM permit much leeway in interpreting behavioral problems and directing treatment—to the point where a diagnosis can be of questionable use. These categories can, however, have tremendous influence on how a child is perceived by others in his world and what kind of treatment is offered by the medical, educational, and insurance bureaucracies. Lest I be accused of diagnostic nihilism, I accept that some system of categorizing behavior problems is needed. But from a practical standpoint, I'd rather describe children's strengths and weaknesses, how they compare to their peers, and what help may be necessary. Such descriptions are more useful to me than the current system of psychiatric diagnosis.

How Common Is ADD?
Many Views from Many Beholders

The actual prevalence of ADD is the subject of considerable controversy. Doctors do not report their diagnoses to any central database, so estimates are made on the basis of study populations and figures for the production of Ritalin. Various estimates are regularly offered; the one most frequently quoted (which uses DSM-III criteria) is based on a 1987 study done in New Zealand. It found that ADD occurs in 6.7 percent of the general population of children.[26]

A more recent (1996) survey of nearly thirteen hundred children in four different areas in the United States (including San Juan, Puerto Rico), using later DSM criteria, found ADD prevalence rates ranging from 1.1 to 4.1 percent in "mild" cases down to 0.3 to 1.9 percent for "severe" cases.[27]

One thing is evident: As the ADD criteria have changed and the diagnosis has expanded over the years, the total population of those diagnosed has grown. Mark Wolraich, professor of pediatrics and director of the Child Development Center at the Vanderbilt University Medical Center, attempted to show how teacher reports of ADD were affected by changes in diagnostic criteria from the 1987 revision of DSM to the current DSM-IV.[28] His study showed that the number of children thus "qualified" rose from 7.3 percent in DSM-III to 11.4 percent in DSM-IV—which translates as a 57 percent increase in the overall number of children meeting ADD criteria!

The influential Joseph Biederman at Harvard has estimated that as many as 10 percent of American children have ADD.[29] If the usual ratio of four or five males to one female remained constant in this equation, then between one in six and one in seven boys between the ages of five and twelve would be diagnosed with ADD. Dr. Biederman is the head of a prestigious department of pediatric psychopharmacology and most of the ADD children he sees probably fall into a category called "ADD-plus": children with more complex or severe symptoms compared with those seen by pediatricians or family doctors.[30] This might explain why Biederman and his colleagues also find an extraordinarily high rate of co-morbidity in his ADD population: for example, an astounding 23 percent also meet criteria for juvenile-onset bipolar disorder (the new name for manic-depression).[31]

All of these estimates, of course, are only as reliable as the method used to diagnose the disorder. And I hope it's apparent by now how much the eye-of-the-beholder effect is operating in diagnosis, despite strenuous efforts at standardization. Furthermore, DSM criteria are regularly ignored in making the ADD diagnosis in real-world situations where doctors are facing pressure to prescribe medication.

This was shown in another study directed by Mark Wolraich, which examined the diagnosis and treatment patterns of ten pediatricians and family physicians whose practices encompassed the entire care of children in two small midwestern towns during 1987.[32] The investigators found that more than one quarter of the children diagnosed with ADD by their doctor failed to meet the diagnostic criteria, compared with the results of more formal evaluations involving structured psychiatric interviews with the parents. The proportion increased to half when compared to structured interviews with the children's teachers.

The study concluded that an ADD diagnosis quite often connoted the physicians' *perception of the severity* of a child's behavior problems, rather than specific symptoms of attention deficit, hyperactivity, or impulsivity. Further, the researchers did not consider that the overall use of medication to be unacceptably high in their view. Rather, what caught their attention was that Ritalin was being used for a wide variety of children's behavior and performance problems. It's worth noting that this study took place before DSM-IV widened the parameters of the diagnosis, and before the 700 percent rise in Ritalin use began; one wonders what the investigators would find today.

The issue of who meets the exact criteria for ADD may be academic in the end. Peter Kramer, the author of *Listening to Prozac*, describes many patients who fall within the "penumbra," or shadow, of a psychiatric diagnosis—a vivid metaphor.[33] Many are squeezed or fudged into a diagnosis for purposes of treatment, or insurance and disability coverage. Kramer also uses the term "diagnostic bracket creep" to describe the process by which growing numbers of people receive psychiatric diagnoses.

Most experts share my perception that in the current environment it takes less-severe behavioral problems to qualify for an ADD diagnosis than was true a decade ago. Some feel that this is a very good change. They make an analogy between higher standards for behavior and performance, and modern improvements in public health and nutrition that resulted in greater growth rates for children. A child whose growth may have been normal a hundred years ago might now be considered as suffering from "failure to thrive" and receive an evaluation and possible treatment. Growing awareness of the condition we call ADD, rather like the heightened recognition of child abuse, has led to increased frequency of diagnosis. It has also led to much greater use of Ritalin.

RECENT IDEAS ABOUT ADD AND RITALIN

Attempts go on apace to create or refine a conceptual framework that encompasses all facets of ADD, or that identifies some irreducible, indispensable characteristic at its root. Among the most unsettling and controversial ideas proposed in the last decade or so is that the syndrome may include constitutional deficits of *motivation*. In many ways it is an intriguing notion, and it could help account for aspects of behavior not well explained by other theories—for example, the uneven performance exhibited by many inattentive-type children. But such a notion also presents a Pandora's box of moral and philosophical issues. For example: Is this an appropriate target for medication? Joseph Biederman, among others, has suggested that if a person's IQ (as a measure of potential) is higher than his level of academic performance, then Ritalin is indicated. One of the symptoms of ADD (inattentive type) since DSM-IV is the "reluctance to engage in tasks that require sustained attention." Reluctance is a quite different matter than inability, in most people's minds; it can boil down to the difference between "can't" and "won't." If medicine takes the step of deciding they are somehow one and the same, the implications will be far-reaching and profound.

Russell Barkley, arguably the leading theoretician about ADD, has been in the forefront of those talking about ADD as a disorder of motivation, and has brought forth other, related ideas.[34] Barkley felt that inattention and distractibility were so variable that they should not be cornerstones of the diagnosis. For several years around 1990 he suggested that "deficits in rules-governed behavior" best account for the behavioral and performance problems of ADD. Simply put, the person with ADD has a neurological or temperamental tendency to disregard the known consequences of his behavior. For example, Johnny tells himself: "I know I'm not supposed to hit Susie and will get grounded for it, but I'm going to hit her anyway."

In more recent writings, Barkley has shifted his emphasis away from these ideas. Instead he has refined the concept of impulsivity, that core feature of ADD, to mean the relative inability to utilize one's knowledge of delayed consequences. In other words, Johnny's hitting Susie shows not a general insensitivity to rules, but an insensitivity linked to the *time delay* in the consequences for breaking them. According to Barkley, then, ADD is most accurately described as a deficit *not* in attention, but in "behavioral inhibition." In his view, this is what makes things so difficult for a person with ADD. Given his influence in the professional and lay worlds of ADD, we may see yet another name change in future DSMs: to behavioral inhibition disorder, or BID.

Perhaps the most significant observation to make is that *all* the behaviors that have been embraced in the ADD diagnosis—inattention, impulsivity, hyperactivity, undermotivation, and insensitivity to rules—respond to some extent to stimulants. Furthermore, we know that such response is not restricted to children diagnosed with ADD; Ritalin acts on "normals" as well. So do we have a disease that meets the criterion of responding to specific effects of a drug? This can be a theoretical way of defining a disorder, but one that most researchers would reject. Nevertheless, the Ritalin response remains the only provable constant among all the versions and symptoms of ADD.

Seen in this way, it begins to make sense that many physicians are prescribing Ritalin for children who don't meet specific ADD criteria, but who do improve short-term on the drug. And Ritalin's across-the-board effects have surely influenced the thinking of those who construct the DSM's models. From a front-line clinician's viewpoint, the history of this disorder may be seen as a case of putting the cart before the horse: The diagnosis has evolved and expanded, I think, partly to account for all the problem behaviors and performance deficits that respond to stimulants.

Chapter 4

←——————→

Coping with a "Living Imbalance": ADD-ogenic Forces in Families, Schools, and Society

American society tends to create ADD-like symptoms in all of us. We live in an ADD-ogenic culture.

—Edward Hallowell, M.D., and John Ratey, M.D.,
Driven to Distraction

Johnny Hester, just thirty-nine months old, is awakened by his mother, Patty, at 6 A.M. weekday mornings. She and her husband have already been up for a half hour. Patty also wakes up Johnny's brother, Kevin, who is five years old, and his sister, Amanda, almost two. All three children have to be dressed and out the door with their dad, Jim, by 6:45. Both parents work, and Jim has the shorter commute: only twenty-five minutes to the lab where he works as a chemist.

Patty leaves the house before them because she must drive the infamous "Corridor" every day to her job in Silicon Valley. When there are no traffic problems it takes her about an hour and a half each way. She has a "good" job, which means about $70,000 a year with benefits and some stock option bonuses if the company is doing well. There is virtually no job security, however, at this wireless communications company that's tied into the software industry in San Jose. Intense competition and rapid changes in technology and corporate structure keep people working very hard, as the ground is constantly shifting under them (this being California, no pun intended).

On this Monday morning Johnny and Kevin fight over a toy they each want to take to day care. Jim, who is shaving, tries to ignore them until the yelling gets so loud he can no longer stand it. "Cut it out! Can't you guys share for once?" He distractedly attempts to mediate, while thinking that it's getting late. The kids continue to argue. Jim grabs the toy truck, saying, "Forget it. It's mine, because you guys can't decide." Both kids start crying and Jim mutters, "Oh, great. Now we'll definitely be late."

He pacifies both kids with the promise of a candy bar before they leave. He knows his wife wouldn't approve, but he just doesn't have time to work it out another way, and he's tired of hearing them whine. He's also feeling a little emotionally raw and rebellious toward Patty; they've just reconciled after a separation she insisted on, and he's upset with her for turning their lives upside down. Little Amanda is trying to get dressed by herself. Jim, still with shaving cream on his face, helps her with pants and socks, then returns to the bathroom to finish getting ready himself.

The kids will eat breakfast at their day care center. They arrive only a bit late (for Jim) at about 7:15. All three will spend the next nine and a half hours at Wee World until Jim picks them up. Sometimes when their dad has to work late, Patty tries to make it home by 5:30. She can do it if her trip home isn't delayed by traffic. She knows that steep additional fees are charged if she picks them up after 6 P.M., and the kids always seem extra cranky when she gets back that late. On the other hand, her feelings about getting home are ambivalent, because the kids are at their worst at the end of the day, Jim has been giving off resentful vibes, and by comparison her office sometimes looks like a refuge.

Wee World is considered a good day care center, providing preschool activities as well as child care. Most of the classes have a waiting list for spaces. There are ten other three-year-olds in Johnny's "Dolphin" class; Miss Annie is their teacher. After breakfast, Johnny and the others are sent to play outside. Before nine o'clock, one child is already crying, claiming that Johnny pushed him off the slide. Annie gives Johnny a warning and sighs. She foresees another long day for herself and her most difficult charge.

During morning circle time, Johnny squiggles away from his place near the teacher—where she put him so she could literally keep a hand on him if necessary—to sit next to his pal, Marc. Annie doesn't think this will work but hopes for the best. Within moments they have distracted each other and are giggling and rolling around. The other kids soon become distracted, too. Annie yells at the boys to stop, and when they persist, she gets up and pulls them apart. Johnny takes a swing at her. She firmly grabs his arm and, as he protests with cries, takes him over to the time-out desk in the corner of the room and tells him to stay there. Marc also is given a time-out on the other side of the room.

Johnny has trouble just sitting on the chair. He climbs on it. He lies on it. He crawls underneath it. He leans back on the chair and it falls over with him, at which he and the other children laugh. Annie doesn't. She goes over, yanks him back firmly onto the chair, and says sharply, "Stay there now, or I'll have to take you to Miss Gloria." Gloria, the director of Wee World, knows Johnny and his family well. She's had Johnny in her office regularly and often helps monitor him in the yard or in Annie's classroom.

Briefly chastened by Annie's flash of anger, Johnny sits in the chair for about two minutes, then gets interested in the cord that controls the window blinds. He begins flicking the cord back and forth. Annie notices but lets it go because it doesn't seem to be bothering anyone. After another minute or two, Annie tells both boys they can rejoin the group. Johnny bounds up and nearly runs over two little girls to get back to his place next to Marc. "No, Johnny," Annie intervenes. "Sit next to me." Johnny moves quickly next to the teacher, who holds his hand for the rest of the fifteen-minute lesson.

During free play, when various classroom groups mingle, Johnny doesn't spend much time with any one toy. This doesn't trouble the teachers as much as his tendency to hurt the other children. Sometimes it seems unintentional: He'll start by hugging one of his friends but wind up squeezing so tightly that the other child pushes Johnny away or cries. It looks to the teachers as though Johnny thinks this is fun. Other parents have complained. The school is aware that all is not well in Johnny's home. Gloria and Annie know about the separation, and they feel Patty is terribly overburdened. She tries to set limits for the children, but Jim is more inclined to placate them. Kevin, the older boy, is a bit of a bully but backs off quickly when admonished. But Johnny, the teachers feel, is an extreme case. They think he may "be ADD," and Gloria has been fairly direct with Patty. Unless Johnny gets evaluated, the preschool may not let him continue to attend. His aggressiveness with the other kids is threatening their enrollment.

Johnny is an intense, high-energy kid, no doubt about it. Whether or not he meets criteria for ADD, his temperament could safely be described as "difficult." And for such personalities, how well their environment suits them can be critical in determining whether inherent personality problems expand into full-blown clinical disorders. Twenty years ago this particular scenario of trouble in Johnny's life would have been much less predictable, but cultural, educational, and economic shifts have made today's world especially challenging for toddlers like him.

Today, we expect more *for* our children, and we expect more *of* them. At the same time, the network of social supports for them and their families has been undercut. A ten-year-old patient of mine, upon hearing about the idea of a "chemical imbalance" underlying ADD, produced this insight about his own situation: "It's not a chemical imbalance, Dr. Diller—it's a *living* imbalance." The phrase has stuck with me, because it seems clear that life imbalances of various kinds can cause trouble for that large group of children within the penumbra of the ADD diagnosis.

PRESCHOOL AND DAY CARE: ACADEMICS AT A TENDER AGE

Young children today typically spend their days very differently from toddlers of a generation ago. Major socioeconomic shifts are part of the reason why. And two specific phenomena, emerging in America during the 1960s, revolutionized ideas about what children could learn before age five, encouraging both parents and educators to believe that you couldn't start a child's education too early.

The first was public television's delightful *Sesame Street*, which demonstrated that educational TV could be as captivating for kids as Saturday morning cartoons. Many parents, came to believe that exposing their children to *Sesame Street* was a critical part of preparing them for the primary grades. Today, more than thirty years later, the first "school" for most American children is still *Sesame Street*.

The year 1966 saw the establishment of the Head Start program, one of the most successful components of President Lyndon Johnson's Great Society initiative. This nationwide effort to provide publicly funded prekindergarten programs, primarily for disadvantaged children, had great impact on making preschool education more acceptable to the country at large. Interestingly, it has been shown that Head Start's positive effects were largely limited to children from impoverished environments. For such kids, the preschool experience correlates with improved long-term performance in school and with less delinquency during the teen years.[1] It appears that what such kids gain from Head Start programs, more than anything else, is learning how to relate to teachers early on—a skill that serves them well throughout the school years.

Among children not from disadvantaged backgrounds, however, the gains realized from Head Start—or any preschool program—are far less consistently demonstrable. Children from middle-income families have not shown significant long-term benefits from a preschool education. This makes sense if interaction skills vis-à-vis teachers are the chief benefit of such programs; most middle-class children start out better-equipped in this area by their families and culture.

As for *Sesame Street*, studies show that many young viewers come away with significantly improved recognition of letters and numbers—but it's arguable whether this translates into long-term academic benefits. Certainly there's a widespread public perception that very young children (say, age two) can get a jump on school from *Sesame Street*. In contrast to Head Start, the show seems to be more successful with children from *higher* socioeconomic groups, because its positive results are dependent on adult involvement and encouragement.

In fact, this is what Head Start and *Sesame Street* seem to have in common. While they chiefly benefit different socioeconomic groups, in both cases interaction with and reinforcement from adults (parents and teachers) are key to success. In other words, the result has less to do with *what* is learned (the content) than how and *with whom*—the process. And this is true in a broader sense as well.

The child's unique developmental pace is critical in this mix. Educators and child development specialists know, though many parents do not realize, that not all children are ready to learn their numbers or alphabet at age three or four. There is a natural spectrum of ability, and by that age some children are ready to learn such information, through visual and sound associations, while others are not. Their developing brains are simply not ready to process such information. Because it is too difficult for them, they are not engaged or lose interest. Some of them, particularly the boys, can look at that point as if they have attention deficit disorder.

However, these kids are not necessarily abnormal. Parents would do well to keep in mind that for the fairly large group of children—perhaps 20 percent—who cannot learn numbers and letters at preschool age, the long-term outcome can be as good as for the other kids.

Unfortunately, anything perceived as below average (or even below the median) is cause for great concern among middle- and upper-middle-class

American families today. Humorist Garrison Keillor gently mocked this preoccupation in his signature line about the fictional Lake Wobegon, "where all the children are above average." Many parents now believe that for their children to be ready for kindergarten and succeed in elementary school (read: succeed in life) they must attend a preschool that offers academic teaching. They seek any opportunity to give their kids a leg up, sometimes overlooking real costs or disadvantages of this path to their particular child or family. In the late 1990s middle-class suburban parents are bucking the social norm if they don't send their kids to preschool by age four.

Why are we seeing such a drive among parents to position their children for academic success? Why so many stories about fierce competition for spaces in the best schools? The segment of parents who feel this concern most keenly were themselves children of the baby boom, raised in relative affluence in an America that promised a rosy future for anyone who worked hard in school and on the job. Now, however, they are caught in an economic squeeze that seems to be moving the American dream—home ownership, job satisfaction, retirement security—ever farther out of reach. And like all good parents, they want to do whatever it takes to make life better for their children, or at least as good. As James Atlas noted in his 1997 *New Yorker* article "Making the Grade," "The parents of the nineties are the children of the sixties. We have insanely high expectations, and our kids represent another sphere in which to achieve."[2]

Of course, not all families are concerned about putting their children on the academic fast track. Many just need a place to put them. Preschool can be regarded, and in many cases serves, as just an enhanced form of day care. How much it is enhanced depends on the quality of the program and whether the child is ready for structured learning. But day care in the broader sense is ubiquitous across the socioeconomic spectrum. It reflects our era's most fundamental changes in family life: Usually there is no one home to watch the kids, because both parents are working and Grandma lives three thousand miles away. Among married mothers in the United States with children under six, the number who work outside the home has doubled since 1960, from about 30 percent to more than 60 percent in 1994. Nearly 70 percent of *all* married women with children worked in 1995.[3] (The percentage of single mothers working outside the home has risen, too, though not as dramatically, since more of them have always had jobs or else manage on public assistance. New welfare rules will undoubtedly drive more of these women into the workforce.) In 1970 a little over a third of all American children attended preschool; now it is more than half.

Many children in fact thrive in quality child-care programs. But the potentially long day in a structured day-care setting, the intense interactions with other children, and the compliance required from the child are stresses for all who attend. Low-end programs—characterized by a high ratio of children to caretakers and overuse of TV as an electronic pacifier— are the bane of children's advocates such as pediatrics guru T. Berry Brazelton. But the spirited or very sensitive child may struggle even in a quality program.

Routine and structure are generally considered good for all children, and they can be especially useful for the child with ADD-type behavior. Even if a preschool has basically sound rules, however, they may be monitored and enforced inconsistently. This becomes a treacherous environment for children struggling with self-control, who need immediate and consistent attention to help rein in their activity and spontaneity. If they do not get it, they may look hyperactive and impulsive and wind up with an ADD diagnosis.

Rules alone are not the answer. If a child cannot be closely monitored and helped to comply, then a more flexible environment may result in fewer problems, less stigmatization, and a better experience for the child. By their very nature, child care centers must be less flexible and more structured than the child's home, or even day care in someone else's home—perhaps a better option for some ADD-type children.

Remarkably, no study exists to my knowledge that has tried to correlate referrals for ADD evaluations of children under five to those who attended structured day care versus those who stayed at home. If such a study were to demonstrate fewer problems for the children looked after at home or in home day care, parents might have greater psychological and political support for those choices. In my own experience, most referrals for ADD in very young children do involve those who attend large day care centers— but preschool for young children is so ubiquitous in my community that it would be hard to find an equally large sample of children who stay at home with a parent.

One large prospective study followed more than thirteen hundred children in a variety of day care settings, and its findings sound mostly reassuring.[4] Overall the study showed that very young children who attended a quality day care program full time showed the same levels of cognitive and language development as those who stayed at home. ("Quality" meant that the child-to-caretaker ratio and language stimulation offered were adequate.) Somewhat worrisome, however, was the finding that full-time day care did tend to negatively impact the quality of the mother-child relationship. The effect was small compared to the inherent strength of the relationship, but it was statistically significant. This tendency, while certainly not true for all young children who attend day care, could produce additional stress for the family already coping with a temperamentally difficult child.

It's quite possible that even if Johnny Hester had never attended Wee World, thus avoiding preschool's pressures, his kindergarten teacher would have noted and complained of the same behavior when he entered primary school. There is some evidence that children identified as ADD at age three or four continue to show problems later in childhood; this suggests that ADD is a "stable" characteristic. Attending preschool merely facilitates earlier identification and treatment of an inherent biological problem—or so the argument goes. However, I'm not so sure that biologically driven behavior is the only problem in this scenario; sometimes being labeled as having a "disorder" can contribute to ongoing negative behaviors. Sad, angry children who feel bad about themselves act out their confusion and insecurity. Being tagged as "troubled" or a "troublemaker" two years before kindergarten can worsen their negative feelings about themselves. Adults may feel better for having a diagnosis, but, short of taking Ritalin, it may not do much for the child.

THE TROUBLED CHILD IN A TROUBLED FAMILY

The Hesters' family doctor was not comfortable giving Ritalin to a child as young as Johnny, and referred them to their managed health care company, where a mental health counselor saw Johnny once and referred the family to me. By the time I met with Patty and Jim, they'd already decided Johnny "had" ADD. They had read a book about the disorder and felt he had all the signs. Very early in the initial interview, they asked me if I thought Ritalin would help their son. My internal reaction was, Whoa, slow down—lots of three-year-olds are active. How different could Johnny be?

They did tick off a list of Johnny's misbehaviors that fit an ADD profile; for example, other than TV or video games (he started early on these), he rarely spent more than a few minutes with any toy or activity, and he always ran instead of walked, it seemed. But his hyperactivity was less problematic for them than his intensity and defiance. "It's never easy getting Johnny to do something *he* doesn't want to do," Patty noted. This and his frequent, prolonged tantrums were pushing the whole family to the edge, and everyone blamed Johnny. I noticed how intense and driven Patty seemed, and I asked Jim how he helped his wife when she was feeling stressed. He looked blank and then said weakly, "Well, I try to get her out of the house." Even though the parents were back together, this household still seemed tense and unhappy. The parents, by the way, said they noticed no difference in Johnny's behavior during or after their separation.

I asked Patty and Jim to bring all three children to our next appointment. Whenever possible, I like to observe how the whole family interacts. I learn much more when I see a child's behavior in the context of his primary relationships; also, young children are more comfortable meeting me for the first time if their parents and siblings are present. When I opened the door to the family interview room, Johnny and his older brother, Kevin, dashed in without pausing and made straight for the toy bins, their parents with little sister Amanda trailing behind. I good-naturedly asked Patty and Jim if they didn't think the boys should at least wait to meet the person whose toys they were going to play with. They agreed and tried to call their sons over to the couch where they'd sat down. Neither kid budged, and after several verbal tries, Patty got up and pulled Kevin back with her, at which Johnny followed.

Johnny was dark-haired and small even for a three-year-old, but his air of barely suppressed energy filled the room, like a firecracker waiting to explode. He moved abruptly and didn't smile much; he seemed like a child who found life a struggle and wasn't comfortable in his world. He would pop up and run to the next activity while his brother walked. During the forty-five minutes we were together he hardly acknowledged me, throwing me a fleeting glance when I joined the play or issuing terse commands like "Gimme" or "Here." Language development clearly wasn't the issue, as I heard him speak freely with his parents and siblings. Kevin was more at ease, with direct eye contact and conversation. Johnny tended to grab toys, not take them, and once literally ripped a toy out of Amanda's hands—to which his parents did not react at all. Some of his behavior was simply an exaggeration of normal three-year-old activity, but he definitely bore watching more than most.

His parents, who seemed tired, mostly looked on as the kids played, occasionally yelling, "Don't throw that toy!" or "Kevin, share that with your brother." Patty at least made an effort to play with them, but it seemed forced: She would pitch her voice oddly high, as if exaggerating her enthusiasm or interest. I think Kevin, the oldest, already found this a bit lame. Jim just sat on the couch and observed, looking alternately depressed or overwhelmed. When I coached the parents to structure the play so that the kids knew in advance they would lose the desired object if they couldn't get along, they actually shared quite well. I noticed that Johnny could stay with a toy for several minutes at a time, much like any other boy who had just turned three. Little sister Amanda was pretty easygoing, whereas Kevin was no slouch in the bossiness department. But as long as there was immediate parental supervision, they did okay.

I didn't think it would be easy helping Johnny gain more self-control, but it certainly was possible. I'd seen children this young act quite hyperactive from either basic temperament, stress, lack of an appropriate parental response, or a combination of the three. Many kids improved sufficiently without the use of medication, just by working with the family and the school. Despite the family problems (especially in the marriage), I thought it was worth a try with the Hesters.

Patty didn't like the idea of deferring medication, but she grudgingly agreed to work with Jim on a new time-out procedure. Jim promised he would try some structured play-wrestling with the kids, who needed some playtime with their dad. We established some clear rules about starting and stopping to keep the roughhousing from getting out of hand. Then it was time for the school. I called Wee World and spoke to Gloria, who talked of chemical imbalances and children's reactions to sugar. However, she did agree, at least over the telephone, to try a more consistent and immediate reinforcement schedule with Johnny and to limit his unsupervised activity in the playground. She was willing to work with him for a few more weeks.

Three days later Patty phoned. The school had called her to pick Johnny up early. He had bitten one of the children in the yard—a cardinal sin in preschool, the one most likely to enrage other parents and put a child beyond the pale. She was angry and wanted an appointment for Jim and herself right away. She felt she had been "jerked around" by several doctors, she told me, and that no one was ready to help. "You're not getting it, Doctor," she declared when they arrived. But she also felt stuck with me; to go see someone else meant starting over again and perhaps having to pay more money for the visits.

It was hard to decide whether to prescribe Ritalin for Johnny or offer Patty medication to calm herself—not that it would have been a solution. Her evident strain had to be affecting the children's behavior, but whenever I tried to acknowledge her difficult situation, she felt blamed by me and became defensive. I faced the probable loss of both parents' support unless I medicated Johnny. While I still thought that behavioral approaches alone could work, they obviously would need more than just a three-day trial—so I wrote the prescription for Ritalin. On the way out the door, Patty and Jim mentioned that they were having some success with the time-outs and the wrestling.

I monitored Johnny's response to the Ritalin by having the school fill out feedback forms. Ten milligrams in the morning produced a clear response: Johnny wasn't as active and could focus better on his toys. He still had episodes of fighting, but they were less intense. At this point, Patty and Jim thought they were done with me; they were surprised when I asked them to come in again with all the children. A few follow-up sessions and some behavioral counseling were important to Johnny's treatment and were part of my standard approach, as I'd told them, but Patty agreed only with great reluctance.

When they finally came for a session, three weeks later, our meeting started uncomfortably and went rapidly downhill. When the children began to squabble, Patty lashed out at me: "You know, they're just fighting because they have to come here. If they didn't have to come, there wouldn't be any problems." Though I knew this reproach came from her feeling of being burdened beyond bearing, I felt my anger rising. The tightness in my voice when I replied betrayed my own frustration: "Patty, I know you feel this is all unnecessary, but I'm not prepared to simply prescribe medication for a three-year-old when I feel there are other factors involved in his troublesome behavior." Patty needed no further excuse—she stormed out of the room with the kids in tow. Few sessions end so dramatically.

Jim stayed a few minutes longer and apologized for Patty's behavior. I felt bad, too. I told Jim I was worried about Patty and about the family, even though the medication had helped Johnny. Jim said he would talk to Patty, but I wasn't optimistic about their returning. I believed these parents' domestic issues were hindering their ability to provide consistent affection and discipline for their children, but they seemed unready to deal with this factor.

The next day I received a fax requesting that I send information on Johnny's medication to their family doctor. The parents had gotten what they came for. But rather than just a brief note on the medication intervention, I wrote at more length to the doctor (whom I knew) describing my interaction with Johnny and his family, and the family's difficulties, and urging him to find another counselor for them. I didn't believe that Ritalin alone would solve Johnny's or his family's problems.

The Elementary Years: Making the Grade

The grade-school years are prime time for Ritalin. For the first time in most of their lives, kids encounter real performance demands when they enter first grade, and falling behind can have serious consequences. Attention problems generally don't show up in younger children because they've not been faced with tasks that demand prolonged attention.

When I first met Michael Sturdevant, he had just turned eight and was in the second grade at Commoner School, a public school in his neighborhood. His parents, Jon and Marci, called me in the state of stunned anxiety parents enter when they've been told for the first time that something is wrong. Midway through the school year, Michael's teacher called them in for a conference; they were further disturbed to learn that she had asked the school psychologist to observe him without their knowledge. Such informal observation doesn't require the parents' permission, but it bothered them.

I quickly learned the basics about Michael's school environment, which was fairly typical of grade schools today. There were thirty-two children in his class. The teacher, Mrs. Gray, had been teaching at the elementary level for ten years. She worked alone in the classroom, without an aide, though when she had first started teaching, she had about twenty-five children in her classes and a part-time paraprofessional helping her. Both the physical arrangement of her classroom and her teaching style have changed over the years, reflecting new educational theories. The children's desks and chairs were no longer in parallel rows, nor was the teacher's desk at the front of the class. Indeed, there was no "front" or "back" in this classroom, which was a wedge-shaped space in a circular building where all the classrooms opened to a central community area. The desks and chairs were arranged in "pods," clusters of four desks placed throughout the room. The teacher kept her materials at several "stations" in the room.

The chief goal of such physical arrangements is to encourage interactional-cooperative learning between the children; according to this theory, children can learn best when they interact with and help one another. It also allowed Mrs. Gray to teach from several points in the room, so that no one group of children had the "favored" position of being nearest the teacher all of the time. Mrs. Gray's curriculum guides discouraged a didactic approach to teaching. Instead of primarily talking or writing on the chalkboard, she was encouraged to emphasize "experiential" learning, in which the children can leave their seats to "experience," touch, play, and work with what's being taught. This approach is supposed to make learning more fun and effective.

However, Mrs. Gray's curriculum and the school principal also made it clear that certain subjects must be taught and standards of performance met by the children. Such standards reflect the belief that children can learn more at an earlier age, as well as pressure on educators to get back to basics and produce results (that is, improve students' performance on standardized tests). Mrs. Gray regularly assigned her class twenty minutes of homework on weekday nights. Some school authorities have concluded that even children in kindergarten should be given some homework to prepare them for more rigorous assignments to follow, and to get their families into the habit of overseeing the homework.

Michael's parents didn't recall having to do homework in the second grade. Nor did they remember experiencing the heavy emphasis on academics that prevailed in Michael's class at Commoner, and even earlier. By the end of kindergarten, Michael was supposed to know all his letters and consonant sounds, and be able to blend sounds, because in first grade he was expected to "hit the ground running" in learning to read. Jon and Marci's kindergarten memories were mostly of playing games and singing the alphabet with their friends. In first grade Michael was in the lowest reading group in his class, but while his first-grade teacher noted his behavior as "exuberant," she did not draw attention to it as a problem. In hindsight, his parents felt that this teacher placed minimal demands on him.

A year later, however, the combination of a flexible classroom along with more rigid academic requirements created a double whammy for Michael. At the first conference with Jon and Marci, Mrs. Gray noted that Michael was having trouble staying on task with many of his academic assignments. He would talk to his pod mates, sometimes disturbing them. If they refused to talk or play with him, he might distract himself with his pencils or doodle. During class discussion, "when he isn't fooling around," she related, "Michael has trouble waiting his turn. He'll blurt out an answer or wave his hand and get so excited and impatient that I feel compelled to call on him."

He seemed bright enough, Mrs. Gray thought, and when she would quiz him individually or insist that he finish his work—which required frequent monitoring on her part—the final product was quite good. Michael had some friends among the boys, but many of the children, especially the girls, gave him a wide berth, especially on the playground. During lunch recess there were 150 children outside with two parent volunteers on yard duty. Michael would race around the yard in chase games with his buddies and get "benched" on a regular basis when his activity level became too much for another child or the adults.

In conclusion, Mrs. Gray told Jon and Marci that she thought Michael might have ADD. Children in some of her previous classes had been diagnosed with the condition, and she had seen Ritalin's positive effects on their focusing ability and self-control. Currently two other boys in her class were taking Ritalin, she told them, and on the days when they forgot to take their pills, she could tell the difference in their behavior almost immediately. She was pretty sure Michael had ADD, too, which was why she'd had the school psychologist observe him. The psychologist concurred, and both recommended that Michael be tested for an official diagnosis. His pediatrician referred the family to me.

Sandy-haired and blue-eyed, Michael acted like a friendly, happy child in my office. He seemed almost too comfortable in this new setting, sprawling on the stuffed chair, sometimes strolling around as we chatted (and he could chat!). He talked to me about Bill Clinton and the Goosebumps books, which he really liked. (Not bad, I thought, for a kid supposed to have reading problems.) He changed topics almost too quickly to follow, and rattled off in rapid-fire order a list of reminders he'd been taught for controlling his temper at school: "Get a drink of water. Blow the fire out. Walk away. Tell the teacher to tell me to stop. Count to ten . . ." and so on.

He did fidget a lot, but Michael's parents handled him in exemplary fashion, combining strict discipline with humor. He was their only child. Jon observed, "I was just like him when I was a kid. Hell on wheels sometimes. I don't know how my parents stood it." He and Marci demonstrated a nice balance, letting Michael bounce around at times, yet firmly reining him in at moments when they needed his attention. Having adapted so well to his behavior, they didn't experience it as a problem at home, but they acknowledged that he was having problems at Commoner. They wanted their child to feel successful; they did not want him to take Ritalin. I thought their position was reasonable. Perhaps another kind of classroom might work better for Michael, if one could be found.

Commoner's interactional-cooperative style of learning is currently an educational vogue. While this system offers advantages to most children in the classroom, it may be counterproductive for the child who is sensitive to stimuli and tends toward spontaneity. This child finds it harder to stay focused on the assignment when his neighbor is within arm's reach and his teacher is speaking from somewhere behind his back. If Michael's class setting allowed him to sit in the front of the class, in a first-row seat right next to the teacher's desk, it would probably be easier for both of them. He would have her intensity, which is what he needed to stay focused, and he wouldn't have the distraction of classmates sitting right next to him. Mrs. Gray would have easier access for monitoring his work. She could provide the needed immediate reinforcers—perhaps an admonitory look or a light touch on his shoulder—that would remind him to stay on task.

As it was, Michael's only opportunity to learn in a less stimulating, more controlled environment came at the cost of being stigmatized in his class, when he was sent to sit in one corner of the room after he'd gotten into trouble or didn't do his work. It was quieter there and he had fewer distractions. He was also less bothersome to the rest of the class. Paradoxically, though, this made it even harder for Mrs. Gray to monitor his performance.

After meeting with me, the parents scheduled a conference at the school, which I attended. Mrs. Gray and her colleagues listened politely to their feelings about what was best for Michael, which I supported, but there was an undertone that indicated the school's decision was already made. They subtly suggested that Michael was an ADD kid who could benefit from medication. Jon and Marci soon decided to look for another school; luckily, they found one within the district whose principal was quite sympathetic to working with the family on its terms. His parents tightened up the rules some for Michael around the house, and as of my last contact with them, he was doing okay.

For the ADD-temperament child, today's typical American elementary school can be a minefield. I've thought a lot about why this is so—why so many kids between the ages of six and twelve are lining up for their noontime Ritalin dose—and while I don't have conclusive answers, a few observations make sense to me. A hundred fifty years ago ADD per se did not exist, though the temperament or biological predisposition for it surely did. Among the reasons why it did not manifest as a serious problem was, no doubt, the ironic fact that children's environments offered more alternatives than is true today. Then, if it was too hard for a child to sit still in school, he or she could go back to helping on the farm, for example, or work in the family's store, or help care for younger siblings.

The twentieth century brought compulsory education to the industrialized world—certainly a good thing in general—and for the first time, children en masse *had* to function in this environment for about six hours a day. This was a new evolutionary challenge for all children but especially for those with the specific temperament type we label ADD. In the bad old days, there was a ready response to children who misbehaved in school—they were likely to be beaten into submission. Rejecting that option, as we've rightly chosen to do, has created a double bind that I believe feeds into the ADD-Ritalin boom. We're no longer willing to intimidate children into compliance, but we might just be willing to drug them into it.

More recent changes in the school setting have been a factor, too. Michael Sturdevant's second-grade class is an all-too-common example of how pupil-teacher ratios have been creeping up; thanks to tax-cutting measures such as California's Proposition 13, many classrooms have more than thirty children per teacher. Large classes produce more distractions, permit less flexibility, and make it hard for a teacher to attend to each child's individual needs. As I've pointed out, ADD-type children require close monitoring and immediate reinforcement for good or bad behavior, but the teacher in a classroom of thirty-plus simply does not have the time or energy to be effective with the more demanding children.

Amazingly, there are no studies that specifically address the relationship of class size to the incidence of ADD. Such studies are difficult to design because it is hard to isolate the effects of class size from other confounding cultural and socioeconomic variables (for example, wealthier school districts tend to have smaller class sizes). Though not specifically looking at ADD, both Indiana and Tennessee funded studies to determine the effects on children's performance when the pupil-teacher ratio was reduced from twenty-five to one in kindergarten through third-grade classrooms to fifteen to one.[5] Not surprisingly, children in the smaller classes performed better on standardized tests for academic and cognitive growth, and gains were noted for those children over several years following the experiment, which lasted from two to four years. They had fewer referrals for behavior problems as well.

An unusual opportunity to study changes in class size has emerged in California, where in the summer of 1996 Governor Pete Wilson suddenly made special funds available to school districts that could create first- and second-grade classrooms with twenty children or less. Class sizes had been averaging twenty-eight. By December 1996 virtually every district had managed to meet the requirement.[6] As of May 1997, with California's economy looking up, the program was extended through grade four.

It would be very interesting if a researcher took advantage of this abrupt change in class size statewide and examined the number of referrals for special-education or ADD evaluations. I suspect the data would confirm what's intuitive. Special kids who need more attention do better when they get it.

Children prone to ADD symptoms also are especially vulnerable to the impact of rising academic competitiveness at the elementary level. Subjects such as multiplication and division are introduced a year earlier than in the curriculum of twenty-five years ago. After-school work for a fourth-grader at Commoner (Michael's old school) averages about an hour nightly. Parents tend to be ambivalent about the increased workload, because they've been told that academic success is the best guarantee of economic success later in life. The prospect of a child's falling behind causes more anxiety than ever. At the same time, their children complain, and everyone feels hurried much of the time.[7]

THE SCRAMBLE FOR SPECIAL EDUCATION

While schools have made life tougher for families and children in many ways, one kind of assistance has become *more* available since Michael's parents went to school. Twenty-five years ago, learning disabilities and special-education services to address them were virtually unknown, but identifying and treating such problems has become a prominent feature of education in the 1990s. A child is assumed to have a learning disability when he or she displays average or above-average intelligence and adequate skills in most areas but is markedly weaker in one aspect of information processing or academic skill.[8] Dyslexia is the best-known example. A dyslexic child has otherwise normal intelligence but cannot read at the expected level. Recent theories suggest that the dyslexic brain struggles to process and utilize the basic structural units of reading, called phonemes, as encoded by the letters of the alphabet.[9]

Special-education techniques and services arose in recognition of the facts that not every child learns in the same way and that children can be taught compensatory techniques for their weakness—and/or the standard curriculum can be modified for them. Federal law now establishes that each child is entitled to his or her own optimal educational plan.[10] Unfortunately, it doesn't always work out that way in practice.

Jenny Carter was a young patient of mine who was struggling in the fourth grade at a public school. One of thirty-three children in her class, she often had trouble finishing her assignments and would have to miss recess to make up the work. A family friend suggested to her parents, Susan and Peter, that Jenny's problems might be related to ADD, but they didn't see any signs that she was hyperactive or impulsive at all. Nor was her conduct a problem, at home or school. In fact, she was well liked by her friends, showing kindness and warmth and an "emotional intelligence" that isn't reflected on report cards or standardized tests. She did have a tendency to daydream and even seemed to move physically more slowly than other kids, as if her inner clock was set at a more leisurely pace. It took her longer to get things done—even things she liked—and she was tardy in completing chores at home, though her parents felt they could handle that problem.

Jenny had been evaluated at the end of third grade and demonstrated some reading and comprehension weaknesses. However, school officials told her parents that her reading problems were not severe enough to qualify her under state criteria for the school's special-education services. Ms. Cronin, the special-education teacher, explained that five years earlier she might have been able to squeeze Jenny into her tutoring program, but with continued funding cutbacks from the state, spaces were fewer. The school could not apply for more money because Jenny did not meet the criterion of performing two grade levels below her fourth-grade peers. Ms. Cronin felt badly that she could not tutor Jenny herself during school hours. She volunteered to advise the regular classroom teacher on ways to modify some of the curriculum for Jenny, and offered Susan and Peter some ideas for improving her reading. She also advised them to find after-school private tutoring for her.

Susan and Peter felt in a bind. They didn't have the money for regular after-school tutoring, but it was clear to them that Jenny needed help of some kind. Her problems in school were brought home to them, literally and vividly, by the ordeal that completing her homework had become. What should have been taking thirty minutes, according to her teacher, usually dragged out to an hour and a half or two hours. Jenny was supposed to start her assignments in the afternoon after a short play period, but she always found excuses for putting it off or would ask for just a little more time with her dolls. Susan often had to resort to threats merely to get her to the dining room table. She'd let Jenny start with the work that was easiest for her (math or art), but then they had to face the harder tasks—book reports and similar analyses were especially tough for Jenny—after they were already worn down. If Susan left her daughter alone, she'd return to find that Jenny had been daydreaming and gotten no further. Susan would get more and more on edge; Jenny would get quieter and quieter and finally burst into tears, declaring, "I can't do it!"

By the time Peter got home from work, he'd find mother and daughter grim-faced and/or tearstained, both looking to him for rescue. Facing that scene over and over after a long workday, Peter told me, was enough to make him turn on his heels and flee. He couldn't, of course, because Susan, by then depleted, was depending on him to finish up with Jenny. He was able to keep more emotional distance while working with her, but the rewards were scant, as she was too tired by then. He'd often wind up dictating some answer for her to copy—knowing this wasn't the best way for her to learn but lacking the heart to push her further.

Susan and Peter were noticing signs of sadness creeping into their otherwise mellow child. I noticed it, too, when I met Jenny: a round-faced ten-year-old who spoke softly and favored skirts over the usual unisex kid style. She would come to life and sparkle, though, when she played with her dolls or told make-believe stories. Her imagination and empathy really shone through at such times, and I could understand why she was well liked. When it came to making a clinical diagnosis, though, I was hard pressed to come up with anything definitive. Depending on what evaluation tools one used, she could possibly meet DSM criteria for the inattentive form of ADD. But symptoms of attention deficit can strongly resemble those of a learning disability; the conditions can and do coexist. I was inclined to believe that Jenny's learning problems predominated—whether her ADD-type inattentiveness followed from or contributed directly to those problems was difficult to sort out.

Susan and Peter were pretty desperate in wanting help for their daughter and were willing to try Ritalin if it could enable her to cope more successfully. Jenny herself was open to a medication that "would make school easier"; in general, she was quite compliant. The pressure I felt to prescribe Ritalin was subtle but hard to resist, given their circumstances, and we did put her on a trial. The drug seemed to improve her concentration and tolerance for sticking with difficult material, both during school hours and in getting through her homework. The parents were satisfied, while my reaction was mixed: I was concerned that Jenny's underlying learning problem was not being addressed. While Ritalin might help in the short term, it couldn't substitute for tutoring in how to compensate for her learning weaknesses. Beyond that, Jenny made me wonder about the expectations we uniformly have for middle-class children today. Here was a girl who was successful and well adjusted in many areas of her life, but who had to be medicated because she couldn't keep up academically. Did it make sense?

HIGHER GRADES, HIGHER EXPECTATIONS

Leaving the security of elementary school for the larger world of high school is like getting kicked out of the womb. And with more and more schools moving to a middle-school system for grades five or six through eight, more and more kids are facing this transition earlier. Children as young as eleven and twelve suddenly no longer have one teacher in one classroom; like their older peers in high school, they rotate through subjects with different teachers. Even simple tasks such as learning to operate a locker can be a major hurdle. It's no wonder some kids become nervous wrecks at the start of middle school or junior high—and the process is even more daunting for temperamentally challenged students.

Moving from the close personal relationship with a single teacher to a more anonymous experience with several teachers, each handling five different classes and 150 students, is stressful for young adolescents, as educators and psychologists recognize.[11] Some schools, in an attempt to ease the transition, offer "core" classes for the sixth-graders, in which English and social studies typically are taught consecutively in one classroom by one teacher. Even so, many youngsters continue to need the personal connection that comes with a single-teacher, one-classroom arrangement.

One of the key ways in which ADD manifests during these years is an apparent lack of motivation, though it's a bit more complicated than that. Current thinking describes core ADD behavior as a "failure to utilize delayed consequences." When the consequence of not finishing one's work is a poor grade given weeks later by a teacher she barely knows—rather than, say, an on-the-spot assist from a very familiar teacher—a student with ADD tendencies is more likely to ignore those delayed consequences, that is, display less motivation.

Overlarge classes create special stress for children struggling with distraction in the upper grades. Aside from the obvious difficulty of focusing on work when there are too many kids with too little supervision, there's a more subtle impact in that an underperforming child can more easily "hide out" in a large class, as long as his or her behavior is not disruptive. As ADD-type children grow into adolescence, symptoms of hyperactivity and impulsivity often disappear. Problems with inattention, motivation, and organization may be less disruptive but can have deadly effects on performance in high school, where students are expected to take increasing personal responsibility for getting their work done.

High-school-age kids are likely to feel stepped-up pressure from their families to perform, because grade-point average is seen as key to one's future. Getting into a good college is perceived as critical by many middle- and upper-middle-class families, and their ambition makes economic sense. A child whose grades are B's and C's, but whose potential is judged as higher by parents or teachers, may well become a candidate for ADD evaluation and treatment, especially when he or she shows problems with concentration, motivation, and boredom.

Of course, there are students whose talents simply are not geared to a higher-education degree. What alternative tracks are available today that are not stigmatizing or demoralizing? Meaningful vocational or artistic electives have been virtually eliminated at most public high schools, due to funding cutbacks or at times a kind of educational snobbery. The cookie-cutter approach to education that begins in preschool continues right through the first twelve years of education in this country. Whether a child is a round peg or a square one in terms of personality or talent, he or she must fit into the identical round educational hole.

Melvin Levine, one of the nation's preeminent pediatric specialists in learning disabilities, has noted there are really only two arenas where a child can feel successful in the early years of life: in school or on the athletic field. I often counsel families that if they can help their kid through the first ten years or so of school and nurture a degree of self-esteem, more opportunities for success will open up to them later. In the upper grades of high school, meaningful electives such as drama or yearbook offer the special child new chances to demonstrate interest and excellence. Employment experiences become available, sometimes in the trades (there are probably more unemployed Ph.D's than electricians these days). Still, I appreciate how parents and kids can worry about a future that's not founded on academic performance. I also know that Ritalin can enable some square-peg kids to fit in more smoothly until good alternatives arise.

INTO THE FIRE: DEMANDING JOBS AND DEFERRED DREAMS

The insistent drumbeat of competition only gets louder for young people who pursue higher education and postgraduate work. In publicly funded higher education, cutbacks continue to diminish the resources available to students. In the top private colleges and universities, spaces for admission are highly coveted, and a market for SAT and GRE/MCAT/LSAT tutoring thrives.[12] With the step into legal adulthood, young people can choose, if they wish, to get off the academic fast track. But not only is parental pressure hard to resist, it is reinforced by messages from society. This is unfortunate, to say the least, for many people with ADD-related and learning problems, whose personalities and gifts aren't suited for the most academically competitive fields. If they can find a comfortable niche, they can often do without medication. Some, however, continue to pursue goals that are admirable but much harder for them to achieve. Matching goals to gifts is discussed further in Chapter 12.

Working life today is characterized by high stress, long hours, and a perform-or-else mentality. This not only affects parents but also trickles down in the amount of attention they can give their children and in their responses to their children's behavior and performance. A not-infrequent response, it turns out, is avoidance. In her book *The Time Bind: When Work Becomes Home and Home Becomes Work*, Arlie Hochschild describes an odd reversal in which the work environment is experienced, by both mothers and fathers, as calmer, more structured, more reassuring, and more rewarding compared with the complex, sometimes intractable problems they may encounter at home.[13] Johnny Hester's mother, Patty, was showing signs of this syndrome: even though her job had a lot of pressure, it was predictable and fairly safe in comparison with the minefield she faced at home, with three young children (one of them with borderline ADD symptoms), a shaky marriage, and a fellow parent who had to be coaxed to do his share of parenting. "Honey, I'm stuck at the office" used to be a man's line; what's new in the 1990s is that women are now resorting to the same excuse. However understandable this response on the part of working parents may be, it's one more factor in the fragmenting of children's lives, and one that may be ADD-ogenic.

The effects of stiff competition and low job security surely figure in the soaring rates of diagnosis for adult ADD. There are plenty of reasons for people to feel they are performing inadequately at their jobs—increased workloads due to layoffs, industries that are changing too fast to keep up with, managers who manage to make things harder instead of easier—and most of the possible solutions don't lie in an individual's hands.[14] Sometimes it's simply a case of the right person in the wrong job—but when jobs are scarce, moving on is scary. Thus some find reassurance in the idea that their problems can be explained by a medically identified syndrome (one that's not stigmatized as a mental illness) and "fixed" by taking a well-proven drug.

Karen McCormack, the architect mentioned in Chapter 1, felt that she had ADD and, after reading about it on the Internet, that Ritalin might be the answer. Karen worked for a large, publicly held engineering firm that had experienced a significant downturn in business in the late 1980s and early 1990s. After surviving several rounds of layoffs, she was left with the responsibilities of what had been two architects' jobs. Barely managing to cope with her new workload, she was given a big new project but lost her secretary and the partial use of one draftsman. This particular experience, which left her tense, overwhelmed, and drained, was what led her to seek me out. Her lack of concentration and efficiency, which she believed had always held her back, now proved grossly inadequate to the task.

Karen's restrained demeanor belied a stubborn forcefulness when it came to pressing her agenda. Changing jobs or careers seemed out of the question to her, and that made her angry at herself as well as at her situation. I imagined she was scared, too, but reluctant to show it. She had described to me in detail how difficult it was for her to read through all the material she needed for her job, and I suspected that her biggest problem might be a weakness in processing information. However, she had no interest in pursuing my suggestion that she get tested by a specialist. She seemed strongly motivated to see her problem as ADD and the solution as Ritalin, and when I pressed her to try something else before trying medication, she sought help elsewhere.

More pressures, society-wide, and fewer supports: This has become a formula for encouraging the emergence of problem behavior, for persuading some teachers that their best hope for a sane classroom is more kids taking Ritalin, for bringing more families with children to see doctors like me, and for leading thousands of adults to seek evaluation and treatment for ADD.

Is Ours an ADD-ogenic Culture?

In general, researchers in the ADD field have paid much less attention to the context of children's lives than to the wiring of their brains. Of more than a hundred articles and chapters in books published by Harvard's Joseph Biederman and his colleagues exploring the nature and treatment of ADD, only two studies analyze in any detail family and environmental risk factors for ADD in children.[15] One study looked at the stressors of "severe marital discord, low social class, large family size, paternal criminality, maternal mental disorder, and foster care placement." The researchers found a strong association between all these stress factors and the risk of ADD.

The second study pinpointed exposure to family conflict and maternal mental illness as the most significant factors associated with ADD. The study concluded that "while previous work suggests that genetic influences may be operant in ADHD, the present results indicate that psychosocial risk factors may be equally relevant to its expression." I strongly agree with the authors here, but I remain disappointed that they did not choose to pursue this line of investigation further. All their other work has been directed toward biological factors and medication.

Children living in the lowest socioeconomic class, frank poverty, were excluded from both of the above studies "to minimize the potential confounds of social chaos." Even though such children are brought to doctors for ADD evaluations less often than kids from middle-class backgrounds, for a host of economic and cultural reasons, their life circumstances put them at very high risk of developing ADD behavior. This is one of the disturbing ironies of the ADD-Ritalin phenomenon. In 1996 one in four children lived in poverty, and the situation is likely to get worse for such kids when recent welfare reform legislation takes full effect.[16]

So far in this chapter, the psychosocial risk factors discussed have been those in the child's immediate environment—that is, the family and school. An "ecological" view of ADD would extend the circles of influence beyond family and school to encompass other cultural factors that might affect rates of diagnosis. For example, many casual observers presume without question that "television causes ADD." Or substitute any of a dozen ubiquitous features of life in our fast-paced technological society: video games, MTV and other electronic or film images, rock music, ambient noise in general, excessive visual stimulation (loud colors, screaming billboards, our whole message-laden surroundings), urban crowding, and so on. Some also lump under this general heading of environmental agents the child's diet and exposure to environmental toxins or allergens. (Diet is such a popular notion of causation that I address it at some length in Chapter 6.)

Way back in 1977, long before MTV or Nintendo, psychologist Gerald Block proposed that the "cultural tempo" of society had speeded up in the previous half-century, giving us "a more stimulating existence in comparison to that of an urban dweller 100 years ago."[17] (His use of the term *tempo* is not accidental; Block draws a parallel with the demonstrated acceleration of musical tempos since Bach's time.) "As a result of the increased level of excitement that permeates our society," he wrote, "more children who in the past may have been *prone* to hyperactivity, now *are* hyperactive" (his italics). Block did not claim this is the sole or even primary cause of hyperactivity (the term ADD was not yet in use), but he did suggest that it can lead to its "expression," that is, cause latent symptoms to appear. Further, he attempted to show how "cultural tempo" complements other theories of causality: genetic, biochemical, emotional, and trauma- or development-related.

The effects of culture on ADD are difficult to demonstrate scientifically. The chief criticism of a "presto tempo" theory of ADD genesis comes from data showing that its prevalence varies widely among industrialized countries. If fast-paced urban living promotes ADD, then why do Tokyo and London, for example, show rates of Ritalin use so much lower than those for major U.S. cities? Nevertheless, many share an intuitive perception that "everyone's hyperactive these days."

At least one large factor in our technoculture—television—has been the target of hundreds of scientific studies aimed at resolving arguments about its pernicious effects on children. Pediatric authorities (including the American Academy of Pediatrics) are quite explicit in stating TV's negative effects on children's behavior, which include increased aggression and acceptance of violence, difficulty in distinguishing fantasy from reality, distortions of the world, passivity and disengagement, and negative effects on cognitive learning.[18] Other studies show a mutually reinforcing effect between excessive TV watching and sedentary, emotionally disturbed children, who tend to watch more than the average child.[19] It's hard to pinpoint the chicken and the egg here: Do such children watch more because they are disturbed, or does watching make them more disturbed? Again, the effect is thought to be bidirectional, but in its own right TV has been shown clearly to contribute to antisocial behavior over the long term.

Only a few of the many studies of TV watching have specifically tried to relate it to kids diagnosed with ADD (most have looked at children's aggressive behavior). One of these studies suggests how TV and ADD behavior may have become linked in the public perception.[20] Its findings showed that, in a controlled laboratory situation, ADD kids acted more distracted than normal kids while watching TV (for example, playing with other toys at the same time). However, it turned out that the ADD subjects retained just as much information about the TV program; they just *looked* as though they weren't paying attention.

This feeds into the interesting notion that TV and video games constitute a strange sort of good-fit situation for distractible children. These activities are among the few things they *can* concentrate on well. Because this is the case, they do watch or play such games a lot; therefore, people are led to think that TV causes hyperactivity or ADD. In television we have a source of input and stimulation that is almost custom-designed—with its rapid editing and quickly digestible bites of information—for the distractible child in all of us. My own opinion is that excessive watching of TV or use of other electronic media may amplify preexisting temperamental tendencies toward ADD but are not causative.

Earlier, in speaking about the potential for an epidemic of Ritalin use in America, I noted that for an epidemic to take hold, certain "host factors" must be present in the environment. The social and economic conditions outlined in this chapter—economic stresses that produce two-career families and restrict the time parents can spend with young children, exposing kids to the demands of preschool education when some might not be ready for it, funding pressures on educational resources at all levels, and (as we'll see) changes in the health care system—are the host factors that will encourage continued spiraling growth of Ritalin use among both children and adults. All these factors are interlinked: With less real time and energy to give their children, parents understandably look to schools and teachers, and other social institutions, to fill the gap. Teachers, as a result, are feeling beleaguered, constrained by funding cutbacks to offer less, yet expected by families (and the rest of society) to offer more.

There are signs that things finally may be improving on the funding side. Voters are approving more new education bonds—a fairly predictable response to the anxiety level of American society at large. It's been observed that whenever Americans feel insecure about how well we are doing, we look to education both as scapegoat and potential savior. The Soviet Union's Sputnik triumph in 1957 sent shivers through our collective psyche and propelled massive funding for education, directed primarily at the sciences. Now, with the dimming of America's post–World War II preeminence, again the anxious call has gone out to educators that our youth must be geared up to a higher standard of performance. This call is being heard from the president's cabinet down to the child entering preschool.

It will take some time, however, for the effects of renewed support for education to relieve America's performance anxiety—if it ever can. In the meantime, there is Ritalin.

Chapter 5

<———————>

Blaming Johnny's Brain:
The Power of the
Biological Paradigm

If ever any country badly needs a sobering dose of science about ADHD to temper overenthusiastic diagnosis and treatment, it is the United States. Those of us who helped start it [the ADD boom] look at their out-of-control American progeny with something akin to the horror of the creator of Frankenstein.

—John S. Werry, M.D.

From time to time I attend local meetings of CHADD, the largest and most influential ADD support and self-help organization. One that I witnessed early in 1997 offered striking insights into a belief that prevails within this organization and in the public mind as well—that ADD symptoms are caused solely or overwhelmingly by some malfunctioning of the brain.

The audience gathers in a suburban Elks hall around seven in the evening. Numbering about seventy-five, they are all middle-class and white. Some are accompanied by children about ten and up, who seem responsive and affectionate toward their parents, and who follow the presentation alertly.

The evening's speaker is a doctor who runs a clinic with a vaguely soothing name, and it's quickly apparent that the audience is in the hands of a master. He wins their loyalty by describing his own struggles with his ADD child *and* spouse, sharing horror stories leavened with a brand of mordant humor that's a hallmark of ADD sufferers and their families. His stories clearly are aimed at exculpating parents from any complicity in their children's behavioral symptoms. Then he gets down to the business of "proving," through slides and persuasive (if unsupported) theorizing, that ADD is due to any of several kinds of neurological problems, including congenital defects in particular zones of the brain, infant trauma, or an inability to produce enough of the right kind of brain chemicals.

Among other plausible-sounding notions, he asserts that ADD behavior demonstrates a kind of biological "craving" for stress. His delivery is dramatic and his language vivid and compelling as he describes ADD kids as "addicted to turmoil," claiming they actually seek an extreme reaction from their parents as a "stimulant substitute." "Biologically, these kids love to be yelled at," he says. Then comes a very effective punch line, in terms of pushing a parent's guilt button: "Withholding medication from these children is a form of neglect." As if to drive this point home and emphasize his own faith in stimulant medication as the treatment of choice, he adds, "I probably write more triplicates than anyone in the state of California."

The presentation winds up with a series of slides advertising the doctor's ability to "locate" ADD via pictures of the brain created by a radiological scanner used by his clinic. The slides, with their bright (enhanced) colors denoting various parts of the brain and showing comparisons between normal and "ADD brains," are mesmerizing, and his assurance that this high-tech hardware can accurately diagnose ADD is surely appealing. His audience is people who are likely to feel frustrated by the ambiguity of the ADD criteria, or angry at skeptical reactions they've encountered from friends, relatives, or others ("Does this ADD thing really exist?"). Its reality is very present and compelling in their lives, and they take the slide show as hard, visual evidence: So *this* is where Johnny's problems lie. The brain scans being touted are an expensive brand of reassurance, however—about $1,800 a pop—and once a diagnosis is made, the treatment offered is the same as ever: Ritalin or one of its close relations, often in combination with another drug or two.

During the question period, one parent, the mother of a nineteen-year-old who has been in serious trouble with the law, is clearly near the end of her rope. She's made an appointment for her son to have a brain scan at the facility used by the speaker, but her first problem, she says, is getting him there. She's not sure she can even locate him when it comes time for the appointment.

This mother's exhausted air compels sympathy, and I am impressed by her persistence in rescuing her son, but given her son's age and apparent lifestyle, I find it difficult to believe that they would find salvation in a brain scan, an ADD diagnosis, and a Ritalin prescription.

Yet her response clearly illustrates the power of brain-based explanations of ADD for people whose lives are profoundly stressed by their child's behavioral symptoms, or their own. They badly want answers, and most are frustrated by suggestions that their lives may be out of balance, or their kids' schools are understaffed, or their responses to a child's acting out are ineffective. It's much simpler to call it a neurological problem.

The current emphasis on biological causation has transformed the nature of the ADD diagnosis. What should be construed, according to formal psychiatric guidelines, only as behavior meeting criteria for a diagnosis of ADD has in the 1990s come to mean "having" ADD, a neurological disorder. The effect of this has been implicitly to diminish the significance of learning disabilities and emotional problems, family dynamics, classroom size, and economic and cultural issues that may be relevant to ADD, in favor of genetic and neurochemical factors.

The biological-origins theory of ADD has been embraced by physicians and patients alike. Physicians generally are more comfortable prescribing medicine than spending time with patients; certainly it is quicker and less costly. Most parents of children with ADD also have welcomed the notion that brain chemistry is to blame. For many years psychotherapists had implied to parents—especially mothers—that it was their fault their children were having problems. Thanks to the biological explanation, now *it's nobody's fault*—a phrase that is also the title of a recent popular book on ADD and other emotional problems of children.[1] Further, less stigma is attached to a medical or neurological diagnosis of ADD than to a psychiatric one. "Medicalizing" ADD behavior brings insurance reimbursement for treatment up to parity with that for treatment of other medical conditions, whereas psychiatric disorders until recently were covered at much lower rates. Finally, a diagnosis of ADD opens doors to special services and disability rights extended to those with medical conditions.

BIOLOGICAL PSYCHIATRY: MAGIC BULLETS FOR THE MIND?

How did all this come about? Over the last several decades the theory and practice of psychiatry have been redefined by the rise of biological psychiatry. This has been defined as "the investigation of the constitutional de-

terminants of psychological disorders, with a goal of devising correspond-
ing preventive or remedial measures for whatever may be amiss in the human organism."[2] In America today, it has become the dominant model for
understanding and treating mental disorders.

This revolution began in the 1950s, partly in reaction to the demonstrated inadequacies of Freudian psychotherapy but chiefly because of the
introduction of new medications that dramatically improved patients'
symptoms and outcomes. These included the tricyclics, used to treat depression—for example, amitriptyline (Elavil) and imipramine (Tofranil)—
the phenothiazines (Thorazine is best known) to treat psychosis and
schizophrenia, and lithium for the treatment and prevention of the symptoms of manic-depression. Over time, serious problems became associated
with all of these drugs, and the early sense of total triumph faded when
long-term outcomes and side effects were closely scrutinized.[3] At the time
they were introduced, however, their actions were immediate, dramatic,
and measurable compared to the "talk cures." Researchers, physicians, *and*
patients all found advantages to treatment in the form of pills, which could
be counted and standardized. Whatever their shortcomings, the medical
and entrepreneurial promise of safe, effective psychotropic drugs led to
continuing research and efforts to develop better and better ones.

Biological psychiatry went hand in hand with rejection of the Freudian
model in the making of DSM-III. Describing pathological behavior without attempting to address its causes was an explicit rejection of Freudian
thinking. However, even though the DSM's authors resolved to describe
conditions without reference to cause, a biological basis for most DSM
classifications soon became implicitly assumed.[4] Informally and practically,
a paradigm based on biological psychiatry, heredity, brain chemistry, and
neurology came to replace the conflict and trauma of the psychodynamic
model.

Along the way to its ultimate triumph over Freudianism, biological psychiatry developed its own orthodoxy and shibboleths. Today, to question
biological psychiatry is to be considered unscientific, unscholarly, or naive.
Early in my career as a behavioral pediatrician, trying to talk with committed Freudians often made me wonder if we spoke the same language or
were treating people on the same planet. Nowadays I feel a similar gap in
communicating with psychopharmacologists, especially the academicians.
While I'm trying to figure out a child's learning capacities, how he is affected by and affects his family's dynamics, and what things are like for him
in the classroom, they are likely to be wondering if his symptoms are most

suggestive of ADD, ODD, OCD, or MR (mental retardation)—the latest alphabet soup of child psychiatry, where each condition or combination thereof calls for a different medication recipe. "Let's try Adderall for the ADD component," they might muse, "but maybe Norpramin (a tricyclic) might be better because he does seem a bit anxious. On the other hand, we should consider Prozac because he can be quite irritable." And so on.

This communication gap is serious, because it tends to polarize those who are in the profession of helping adults and children cope with emotional and behavioral problems, as well as those being treated. Some who favor counseling and other psychosocial approaches feel fearful or hostile toward those they perceive as mere dispensers of drugs, while those who believe medication to be more effective often dismiss other approaches. This conflict does not serve patients and their families, who can benefit most from a thoughtful, individualized treatment plan that combines various elements.

But in America today, biological psychiatry has essentially co-opted the market. Even people coping reasonably successfully with their lives are now seen to have "shadow" disorders that can be treated with medication. In his 1983 book *The Shrinking of America*, psychologist Bernie Zilbergeld described how psychotherapy was sold to the American public.[5] His analysis is just as valid when applied to the promotion of biological psychiatry.

- Continue the psychologization of life—that is, call attention to symptoms people might otherwise ignore and create unwarranted anxiety by labeling such problems as "disease."

- Make problems out of difficulties and spread the alarm.

- Make it acceptable to have a problem and to be unable to resolve it on one's own.

- Offer salvation in the form of [*a pill*]. [*psychotherapy* in the original]

Pills have replaced psychotherapy as the "hot" and effective treatment. And when it comes to ADD, psychiatry has moved from blaming Johnny's mother to blaming Johnny's brain.

How Do Psychotropic Medications Work?

Ritalin, like other medications used for behavioral and emotional problems, is thought to work its therapeutic effects by altering neurochemical function in the brain in some way. With all these drugs, we know only a limited amount about how they specifically work—more in some cases, less in others.

We now know that brain function is based on the transmission of electrical impulses among nerve cells. Impulses are sent when certain chemicals are released or absorbed at the nerve endings, and we have identified several of those chemical agents, or neurotransmitters. Most of the neurochemical pathways discovered so far were traced through the effects of certain drugs on the nervous system. These drugs work in two primary ways: They prevent the reabsorption of the neurotransmitter into the nerve cells, or they cause more of the neurotransmitter to be released. Thus, working backward from effect to cause, we know about the role of epinephrine (adrenaline) and norepinephrine in depression because antidepressant drugs such as imipramine increase the overall availability of these chemicals.

Other neurotransmitters found to be affected by the use of psychoactive drugs include dopamine, serotonin (the one affected by Prozac), and acetylcholine. Still other important chemicals may remain undiscovered. Indeed, none of the clinical conditions in psychiatry is completely explained by any of the known neurotransmitters. But in the darkness, one can search for a lost key only under the light of a street lamp, and psychotropic medications have been our street lamp for understanding the brain's chemical mechanisms.

Several neurotransmitters—epinephrine, norepinephrine, and dopamine (known collectively as the catecholamines)—are thought to be implicated in ADD symptoms.[6] Efforts to pinpoint an anatomical site for Ritalin's activity have been unsuccessful, though current research has focused mainly on the prefrontal cortex.[7] This part of the brain is believed to control behavior inhibition; that is, it enables us to say no to many of the impulses surging up from the more primitive parts of the brain, and it enables us to select which of many stimuli to focus on. Because Ritalin is known to increase levels of dopamine in the brain, a popular theory posits that ADD is caused by a dopamine deficiency in the prefrontal cortex. Dopamine suppresses the responsivity of neurons to new inputs or stimuli; therefore, the theory goes, someone with too little dopamine will respond too impulsively in situations where pausing to process the inputs would work better. Research does not fully support this idea, however. For one thing, not all the drugs that improve ADD symptoms have the same effect on dopamine levels.

Other theories zero in on a different part of the brain: the locus ceruleus, located at the base of the brain with connections to the frontal area and the spinal cord. It's thought that in this area of the "ADD brain," the levels of epinephrine (adrenaline) and norepinephrine may be set too high. These chemicals are normally released in response to a need to pay attention (such as focusing on a math problem). But if the neurotransmitter levels are already high, the increase evoked by the stimulus is not large enough to focus attention, as it would be in a "normal" brain. In this fairly convoluted hypothesis, Ritalin at first raises the levels of these neurotransmitters still further, which, through a series of feedback loops, leads to a long-term *decrease* in their activity. At that point the ADD brain can respond more normally to a stimulus requiring attention.

Various neurological factors surely are associated with ADD symptoms or have a role in instigating them. But the conflicting findings to date, along with the breadth of possible ADD symptoms and the frequency of their co-occurrence with other behavioral problems, may mean that no single biological breakthrough will ever explain the genesis of every case of ADD, or even most cases. Researchers won't stop looking and the public won't stop hoping, but the current fuzziness of the picture should persuade all of us that this is not a disease with a simple chemical cure in its future.

The path this brain research has followed—that is, tracing the positive effects of a drug back to the brain chemistry involved—has encouraged one of biological psychiatry's most dubious assumptions: that if a patient responds to a psychotropic medication, it "proves" the problem is biological in origin. Thus if someone responds, say, to an antidepressant, his or her depression must be the result of a chemical imbalance or deficiency, probably inherent in nature. But in fact such improvement on medication says nothing definitive about the cause of a person's problems. If aspirin relieves a headache, we do not necessarily conclude that the headache was engendered by an "aspirin deficiency."[8] With regard to ADD, this fallacy was demonstrated long ago, in Judith Rapoport's studies showing that stimulants affect both symptomatic and asymptomatic subjects. (See Chapter 2.) Nonetheless, many parents remain persuaded that if their child improves on Ritalin, it means the problem is strictly organic.

PAVING THE WAY WITH PROZAC

It is no accident that the Ritalin boom that began in 1991 followed the Prozac explosion by just a few years. Prozac and its sister drugs (primarily Zoloft and Paxil) have revolutionized medically prescribed drug taking for emotional problems in this country and much of the world. In just the few years since its introduction in 1987, a mythology also has developed around Prozac—a mythology that strongly reinforces the belief that behavior is genetically and biologically based, and is most appropriately and effectively addressed by a chemical agent.

Prozac acquired a certain mystique from the start because of the systematic (and highly touted) science that went into its development. Researchers at Eli Lilly in 1971 targeted one of the known neurotransmitters, serotonin, as a possible mediator in severe depression. They then went about systematically testing hundreds of compounds, searching for one that could selectively increase levels of serotonin around the synaptic connection between the nerves (hence the formal name for this class of drugs: selective serotonin reuptake inhibitors, or SSRIs). In less than two years they discovered fluoxetine, which Eli Lilly trade-named Prozac.

The first clinical trials and patient experiences with Prozac suggested only minimal side effects. Prozac's safety was another selling point—that is, it was much safer in intentional overdoses (not uncommon in people with depression) compared to the antidepressants most used previously, the tricyclics. Later it was revealed that up to a third of the patients taking Prozac experience some sexual dysfunction, which caused many to stop using it. (On the other hand, early reports about a so-called Prozac reaction syndrome—episodes of psychosis or violence while taking the drug—remained unproven.) More important, as results were observed over time, rates of recovery from moderate and severe depression were no higher in patients taking Prozac than for those using other medications.[9]

However, the vast majority of patients seeking treatment for emotional problems are not severely depressed by DSM criteria. They tend to be described as "dysthymic"—a less well-defined condition of chronically feeling low or down. The SSRIs, with their mostly deferred side effects and high short-term safety record, were much easier to take and keep taking than the tricyclics. Prozac was the ideal drug, not for the severely depressed but for the "walking wounded." By the early 1990s more than six million people in the United States had been prescribed the medication. Recently its use has expanded to disorders ranging from OCD to bulimia—it's the panacea of the nineties. In 1997, the *Wall Street Journal* reported, twenty-eight million Americans were using Prozac or one of its SSRI sisters.[10]

Prozac's enormously rapid growth cannot be explained solely on the basis of its effects, or even by Lilly's intensive marketing to physicians. The greatest impact on the consumer came from the mass media. The major talk shows and national news magazines all featured Prozac, and Peter Kramer's book *Listening to Prozac* became a tremendous influence thanks to its provocative ideas and perfect timing.[11]

Kramer himself overtly states that he is less interested in describing the full ramifications of taking Prozac than in speculating about the meaning of personality and behavior changes in the dysthymic patient. But the publicity around his book made making over a person's psyche sound relatively simple and painless, without side effects and available to anyone. By extension, it had the effect of promoting psychotropic drugs for everyone, adults and children, the severely dysfunctional to the mildly maladjusted. More than any other single factor, the Prozac phenomenon has made Americans familiar with the metaphor and model of biological psychiatry, and comfortable with the idea of using medication to improve personality and enhance performance.

The Quest to Make ADD Biological and Genetic

Establishing a genetic connection is a major milepost on the road to defining an emotional and behavioral condition. There is good evidence that some psychiatric conditions are genetically linked and inheritable to some extent. Studies have shown that disorders such as schizophrenia, bipolar illness, and ADD cluster in families. The most convincing work, in terms of teasing apart genetic and environmental factors, has focused on identical twins separated at birth, who exhibit remarkably similar traits and life patterns, though raised in very different environments. Despite some theoretical flaws, studies of both identical and fraternal twins strongly support the likelihood that an "ADD personality" is inherited. It was more likely that both twins would meet ADD criteria in a set of identical twins than was the case with fraternal twins; the proof rests on the fact that identical twins share exactly the same genetic material.

The genetic contribution to any personality or physical trait is expressed as a percentage. For example, height in humans is thought to be about 90 percent inherited. Rather remarkably, Russell Barkley currently claims that

ADD is almost as heritable as height: he says the factor is about 80 percent.[12] Other experts in behavioral genetics offer estimates ranging from 50 to 70 percent. "Putting the findings together," says Robert Plomin, an international leader in this field, "a heritability of about 70 percent seems to be a reasonable estimate. This value implies that the genetic component is stronger for this disorder than for most other types of childhood psychopathology, other than autism. In an especially interesting contrast, conduct disorder (in the absence of overactivity/inattention) does not show much genetic influence."[13]

These kinds of findings about behavior and genetics don't capture the public imagination as much as the prospect of discovering a particular gene for ADD. Despite great efforts, however, no specific "ADD gene" has been identified. In 1996 newspapers announced that researchers had found an abnormal gene associated with hyperactivity;[14] closer examination of the findings reveals that half the ADD children studied had a particular genetic sequence, compared to 20 percent of the normal children.[15] This result is no doubt interesting and grounds for further investigation, but a long way from determining a specific gene for ADD behavior. Scientifically, the hope in seeking an ADD gene is that it will serve as a marker or prototype protein for better drugs to treat the disorder; realistically, such a breakthrough is years away. Further, any such work will be plagued by the same factors that confuse all biological research about ADD: the difficulty of defining the disorder[16] and the variety of causes that go into the making of any behavior.

That personality in general, and ADD personality in particular, has a genetic component is highly likely, and important. The error of biological psychiatry is in making too much of this connection. Most of the studies that show these links suffer from methodological flaws that make it difficult to entirely separate the effects of family heredity from those of family environment.[17] In fact, Robert Plomin and fellow researcher Alison Pike have declared that, if anything, "genetic research provides the best evidence for the importance of environmental influence" in the generation of mental disorders.[18] More important in any clinical decision about ADD and its treatment is a different question: To what extent does this genetic component determine an individual's destiny? The social and cultural implications of accepting a purely biological view of behavior are profound and will be explored in the last chapter. Finally, there's the issue of medication. It's an easy step from accepting that ADD is genetic and biological to accepting Ritalin (or other drugs) as the sole form of treatment, but this is a fallacy. Just because a condition has biological and genetic associations doesn't mean that its treatment must or should be limited to medication.

Other efforts to prove ADD's biochemical origins include anatomical and physiological studies aimed at showing differences between normal and ADD brains, through the use of radiological techniques. The study cited most frequently was presented in a lead article in the *New England Journal of Medicine* in 1990, which made the front pages of many newspapers.[19] Alan Zametkin and colleagues at the National Institute of Mental Health (NIMH) used the new technology of positron emission tomography (PET) scanning to evaluate the glucose metabolism of the parents of children with ADD. (Scientific ethics precluded the use of this technique on the children themselves because of significant radiation exposure from PET scanning.) This study found that certain parts of the frontal and prefrontal cortex of the parents' brains underutilized glucose, compared to the brains of the controls. (As reported by popularizers, this translated into underfunctioning of the "just say no" center of the brain.)

A series of follow-up studies was undertaken, using both adolescent boys and girls diagnosed with ADD as a way to get closer to the target population of children.[20] While the results varied, they failed to confirm the strength of the original finding. Furthermore, in later short- and long-term studies of adults with ADD, treatment with Ritalin did not change these patterns of glucose underutilization—leaving one to question whether the disparity really has anything to do with the disorder.[21] And if so, then how *does* Ritalin work in the brain to improve the condition? Typically, biological psychiatry attempts to explain these discrepancies and inconsistencies in the data by suggesting that there are different subtypes of ADD. One group is said to have a "familial and persistent" type of ADD, while another group does not. Once again, the later disconfirming studies were hardly noted in the popular press.

A California physician claims to have used another radiological device— single photon emission computed tomography, or SPECT scanning—on more than two thousand patients over a seven-year period. This machine uses less radiation than PET technology. According to its chief proponent, Dr. Daniel Amen, the technique can indicate variations in blood flow (and, indirectly, in biochemical activity) in the brain and thus diagnose ADD and other psychiatric conditions. However, little has been published that would enable other researchers to evaluate the usefulness of SPECT scanning. In 1997 Dr. Amen and Blake Carmichael published an article reviewing their data on fifty-four children and adolescents with ADD, purporting to show a connection between the disorder and "decreased blood perfusion" in the prefrontal cortex.[22] Zametkin at NIMH has criticized this study for its lack of reproducibility.[23] Yet within the lay ADD community locally, SPECT scanning is hailed as evidence of ADD's biological nature.

JOEY'S BRAIN SCAN: A CAUTIONARY TALE

I became involved with Joey Brinks and his family when I was asked to serve as an expert witness in a court case they had brought. When Joey was twelve, he'd been horsing around with some neighborhood kids and got hit in the eye with a mud ball containing a small rock. Joey may or may not have started the mudslinging, but in any case the kids stopped when he screamed in pain. He received both emergency treatment and appropriate follow-up care, but still was left with about a 70 percent loss of vision in that eye. His divorced parents, Jeff and Carol, were suing the family of the boy who had thrown the rock—I was brought in by *their* homeowners' insurance company—but the basis for the suit was more than just his physical injury.

Joey had been mostly a happy, compliant, well-behaved boy for his first ten years, but had seen some trouble lately. Joey, the third of four children, was the only one to stay with his mother after the divorce. (She had been diagnosed with cancer; though it was in remission, she couldn't care for all the kids.) When he entered sixth grade in private school, his grades began to fall a bit, and he got a little more difficult at home. Still, this was nothing out of the ordinary for a boy his age, until the eye accident. After this, his behavior deteriorated markedly. He began cutting classes as soon as he started seventh grade (now in a public middle school) and became overtly angry, defiant, and withdrawn at home. He challenged Carol constantly, and his father more than once had to get physical with him to maintain order.

For a few months Joey saw a psychologist weekly, but things kept getting worse. He was getting into fights frequently; his parents suspected he was using drugs and were panicked. A social worker who specialized in adolescents met with Joey once, told Jeff and Carol he might have ADD, and suggested they consult with "ADD experts" at the Center for Effective Living in Fairfield, California, about a half hour's drive away.

Upon Joey's third visit to the center, Dr. Pincus (not his real name) prescribed Dexedrine for him and also ordered a SPECT scan. Both recommendations indicate that he had diagnosed ADD. Two days after the scan, which purportedly showed some decreased blood flow in the cortex, Joey returned to the center for a second scan, called an Intellectual Stress SPECT Study, during which he was "stressed" with a series of random math questions. Meant to confirm the evidence of the first scan, this showed "a drop-off in prefrontal activity in response to an intellectual challenge." Joey's parents were billed $1,800 (which their medical insurance did not cover) for the scans and their interpretation. A month later Dr. Pincus wrote a to-whom-it-may-concern letter stating, "Joey has a neurological condition as shown by his SPECT scan where his frontal cortex is unusually hypoactive. This causes severe impulse control and other cognitive problems which are greatly affecting his life and family."

When Joey didn't improve noticeably on Dexedrine, Prozac was added to his regimen, then discontinued in favor of two other drugs: Effexor, a newer antidepressant, and clonidine (Catapres). The latter, which acts on the central nervous system, is chiefly used to treat hypertension but more and more often is given to children diagnosed with ADD who are also oppositional. Therapy was recommended but not pursued. Dr. Pincus wondered if Joey was even taking his medications; the boy had told his parents that he didn't want to. His downward spiral continued: He threatened to kill another child and was admitted to a psychiatric hospital for ten days. In desperation, nearly a year after the accident Jeff and Carol (who actually did a pretty good job of co-parenting despite the divorce) sent Joey away to a very strict Christian school for troubled teens in Utah. At about the same time they initiated their lawsuit, claiming the eye injury had caused additional "pain and suffering" because it had aggravated Joey's ADD.

Joey spent six months at the school and told me about it when we met. Conditions were harsh, he said, and discipline unforgiving. If a boy acted up, his whole class was made to run laps to exhaustion, and the offender was predictably beaten up by his classmates. He'd pleaded with his parents to be allowed to come home, and they finally relented. Five months later, when I met him, he was a strong, handsome blond teenager with an easy smile, who spoke forthrightly and looked me straight in the eye despite his one bad one. He was now getting A's and B's in high school, and his parents reported his behavior to be exemplary; they were happy to have him home. We developed a rapport, oddly enough, since I was working for the defendant in their suit.

When I asked Joey what he thought had happened to him after the accident, he replied without hesitation, "I thought my life was over, and it was my fault." The injury had left the pupil of his right eye permanently dilated, and "every time I looked in the mirror, I thought people would blame me. I shouldn't have started the fight." "What was going on when you were doing so poorly in school and were so angry?" I asked. He replied, "I felt, like, what's the point? I was angry and sad and just wanted to be left alone. I felt like everyone was bothering me." His parents had earlier described Joey as intense, passionate, and a perfectionist; it made sense that this young adolescent would see his situation in unforgiving black and white.

In response to my question about whether his medications or therapy helped him, he answered, "Nah—the psychologists were wimps and the psychiatrist was weird. The medication just made me feel sleepy—I was using some methamphetamine myself at that time." He spoke of hitting bottom at the Utah school, and of how grateful he felt to have his own life back: "The injury's bad, but now I realize it's not the whole thing with my life."

During a court deposition, Dr. Pincus testified as to the nature of the SPECT scan performed on Joey, and that its findings had been "abnormal," indicating ADD. However, by this time the parents' feelings about the Center for Effective Living had soured. "We were desperate," they said, when I asked about this. "We felt Joey was going down the tubes, and when they told us he had ADD and started the drugs, we had some hope. Now we feel like we were exploited. Especially that brain scan." I asked all three of them if they felt Joey had ADD now, and they laughed. Joey added, "No way." Shortly after meeting with me, Jeff and Carol decided to settle the case. I never had to appear in court after all.

It is all too easy, as this story demonstrates, to create pseudoscientific yet convincing connections between biological findings and the behavior of children. Even granting that SPECT scanning can show abnormal brain activity, its use in this case to confirm an ADD diagnosis must be seen as a "false positive." No one knows how many such false positives there may be, because the findings of this type of scan are subject to interpretation. They are also more difficult to reproduce and compare than PET scans. Even more important, there's a logical fallacy to the whole brain scan approach to clinical diagnosis and treatment. We don't know if the identified "abnormality" was inherited or acquired, a real cause of the behavioral condition or merely associated with it. In the end, this approach is simply part of the greater readiness by many doctors to leap from such associations to the conclusion that biochemical imbalances cause ADD, and the readiness of parents to follow them.

THE RUSH TO MEDICATE

The message that behavior and emotional problems are biological in origin is affecting every medical practice in America today; certainly it has affected mine. Parents come primed with the vocabulary of biological psychiatry. They speak easily of "chemical imbalance" or tell me they think their child might be "bipolar" or has a "mood disorder." They describe their child's behavior as "obsessive" instead of telling me what he is or isn't doing that's a problem. Even while striving for a broader assessment of behavior, I must start from a position the parents can relate to, just to get their attention.

At times the pressure for me to medicate a child is intense. Referrals are made and consultations are sought specifically with medication as the goal—why else see an expert with a medical degree who can legally prescribe? There are more internal, personal pressures as well. I sometimes wonder, if I don't immediately prescribe medication, whether I am old-fashioned, or timid, or less well informed than my brethren.

The great majority of the prescriptions I write are for Ritalin and other stimulants. However, I've written prescriptions for antidepressants, major tranquilizers, and mood stabilizers, despite my general uneasiness and lack of conviction that nonstimulant medications are especially useful for children. I have not been overwhelmed by their success but feel that to refrain from trying such medications in difficult cases is to neglect a potentially helpful intervention. Even without the evidence of controlled studies, journal after journal and conference after conference send this message.

The medical model of psychiatric illness is built on studies using treatments that are standardized and easily measurable (how many pills), and where only one variable changes at a time. Such studies do not come close to approximating the realities of clinical psychiatric practice. Rarely do patients demonstrate just one "pure" diagnostic category, and practitioners seldom employ only one kind of treatment. Real-life techniques in psychotherapy, for example, are individualized to each patient. By their very nature, then, they are difficult to quantify and standardize, and therefore suffer in comparison to the measurable effects of a pill.

But while the "talk therapies" have been maligned as less effective, a unique survey published by *Consumer Reports* in November 1995 found that 54 percent of patients believed their psychotherapy treatment was "very helpful" and 90 percent found it "somewhat helpful."[24] This study not only challenged the prevailing wisdom about psychotherapy's relative ineffectiveness but also questioned the methods that biological psychiatry uses to establish its superiority.[25]

And for all the success stories about medication therapies publicized during the past decade, the sobering bottom line of psychiatric illness has not been much improved. The suicide rate continues to rise in this country and throughout much of the Western world. Ironically, a primary agent for suicides has been the tricyclic antidepressants. Hailed as the first really effective treatment for major depression, the tricyclics also have replaced the barbiturates (sleeping pills) as the primary means of suicide by overdose.[26]

NATURE VERSUS NURTURE REDUX

I certainly accept that a person's biological makeup, in its expression as personality, influences his or her behavior. However, I believe that environment also plays a critical role in the determination of behavior and the creation of mental illness. Indeed, nearly all reputable biological psychiatrists, if challenged, acknowledge the role of environment in either the genesis or persistence of psychiatric disturbances. But in scientific presentations and papers, and in communicating with the public, their emphasis is clearly on genes and brain chemistry.

When environment *is* invoked as a cause of ADD among researchers, they are usually talking about the environment of the fetus. Maternal smoking and subtle intrauterine infections associated with the winter season are thought to increase the likelihood of ADD in offspring.[27] This case aside, the persistent search for a biological cause of ADD over the past decade has led me reluctantly to conclude that psychiatric academia appears more interested in the environment of the synapse than in the environment of the child.

In fact, the role of environment in shaping behavior begins at birth and continues throughout life. Current research indicates that brain biochemistry and personality may be more plastic than has been generally believed—that environmental influences can actually alter brain function, especially in very young children.

The medical model does not exclude environmental factors from influencing the development of biological disease. For example, weight gain has been clearly and causally linked with both hypertension and adult-onset diabetes. Losing weight and handling stress more effectively are the first treatments suggested in these diseases. Another kind of environment-modifying therapy is practiced with babies who have amblyopia, a condition in which one eye is markedly weaker at birth. Left untreated, this can result in near-total atrophy of the optic nerve in the weak eye. So the good eye is covered, thus encouraging the other to develop; it's the great neural plasticity of the young that makes this possible.

A study of obsessive-compulsive disorder in adults using PET scanning offers compelling evidence that biological disturbances associated with psychiatric syndromes can be affected by behavioral interventions.[28] In this study, patients who met strict OCD criteria had PET scans that showed excessive activity in the parietal lobes of the brain (the area above the ears). The subjects were divided into two groups, one receiving only medication as treatment, the other only a form of psychotherapy known as behavioral densensitization. (In desensitization patients are exposed in ever-larger increments to an anxiety-provoking situation, such as touching a "dirty" doorknob, and over time learn to control the anxiety repsonse.) Both groups improved clinically with treatment, and—lo and behold—when the brain scans were repeated, both showed a "cooling" of their parietal hot spots, indicating their brains had returned to normal. This was a remarkable demonstration of the power of both environment and medication on the visible workings of the brain.

With regard to ADD, some studies have demonstrated that preschoolers who showed ADD symptoms continued to exhibit them into the second grade, when they were officially diagnosed with ADD.[29] This is taken as evidence that the ADD personality is biologically determined and persistent. But other research has found parenting styles to be more influential than the inherent temperaments of preschoolers. One study, following a group of sixty children from birth to about age eleven, found that "maternal and contextual factors" were more accurate than personality assessments at predicting ADD problems.[30] Specifically, where mothers were found to be "intrusive and overstimulating," isolated and with few emotional supports, children were more likely to appear distractible around age three and hyperactive around ages six through eight. These findings suggested to the researchers that one type of ADD may be more biologically based, while others are quite responsive to environmental influences—another exercise in subtyping.

Further evidence that the brain remains very plastic in young children, and subject to environmental shaping, may come from recent work with autistic children. In contrast to theories that prevailed during the 1950s about "refrigerator mothers" producing autistic children, autism now is believed to be a classic neurodevelopmental disorder, hardwired at birth and resistant to therapy (indeed, earlier psychotherapy efforts achieved minimal results). And, as in ADD, no single biological cause or marker for autism has been found. However, a very rigorous, intensive form of behavioral training has recently produced remarkable improvement in very young autistic children.

I witnessed such change in a young patient named Aftim, who was twenty-five months old when I first met him and his parents, North African émigrés Ahmed and Christiane. My heart sank as I watched this toddler wander aimlessly around the room, touching objects only briefly, neither speaking nor responding to his parents' words and gestures. His regular pediatrician was worried that he wasn't speaking yet, and my observations confirmed that he met criteria for autism.

In giving his parents the distressing news, I mentioned a relatively controversial new program of treatment for autistic children developed by Ivar Lovaas, a psychologist at the University of California, Los Angeles. Approaches based on Lovaas's ideas use the powerful tools of behavior modification in massive amounts to alter behavior and "teach" more adaptive functioning to the autistic child. "Massive," for a two-year-old showing signs of autism, means working a minimum of five hours a day, six or seven days a week, with a trained therapist. The training goes on for months, and if improvement is observed, potentially for two or three years.[31]

Ahmed and Christiane seemed galvanized by this shred of hope, and, to shorten a long story, they did pursue this intensive behavioral treatment for Aftim. When I saw them six months later, the change was extraordinary: Aftim sat down on the floor with his parents and they played together! The parents' participation is crucial in how well these techniques work, and I saw evidence of this: When Aftim tried to get up and wander, Christiane or Ahmed would grab him and force him to reengage, going so far as to physically direct his face toward themselves or the object at hand. Aftim was now using about ten words and developing that vital aspect of communication called the pragmatics of language (for example, making eye contact when in conversation). His interaction with his parents was vastly better, and I had to believe that much of the change was due to the parents' commitment to this intervention.

These behavioral interventions call into question the presumed stability of personality characteristics. Reporting on two children who recovered fully from pronounced autism after intensive behavioral intervention, two psychiatrists noted, "The brain is in a state of maturational flux before and after birth. . . . Review work demonstrates how experiences shape the brain's neural circuitry at critical stages of development. . . . One can hypothesize that in those autistic children whose condition is as yet modifiable, rigorous behavioral therapy modifies the neural circuitry before the condition becomes permanent."[32]

As yet no studies have examined the effects of such intensive behavioral training on children with incipient ADD or other behavioral disorders. This may be partly because ADD does not usually manifest as a serious problem warranting full-scale intervention in children as young as two. Yet it's just at this time, while the brain is still malleable, that such massive environmental influence can be most effective. Perhaps by waiting until a child is five or six—the usual age when ADD symptoms are first noted—it is too late to make permanent alterations in the child's personality.

I believe that efforts to determine whether nature or nurture causes ADD are ultimately futile. Clearly the hardwiring of a child's brain affects his or her behavior, but is itself altered by stresses on the child. Environment affects a child's behavior and the child's behavior affects the environment, in true cybernetic fashion. To argue that the 700 percent increase in Ritalin use is due only to the recent discovery of a neurological disease not only flies in the face of social reality but ignores the most sophisticated current thinking about brain-behavior feedback cycles.

American psychiatry lost its nerve in the 1970s. With the fading of Freudianism and the truly revolutionary discoveries in psychopharmacology, an opportunity existed to reconfigure the broad understanding of mental illness according to a "biopsychosocial" model.[33] This model posits that several factors—including a person's biology, emotional status, and environment—all interact in maintaining health and generating disease. In this model, there is no false dichotomy between mind and body: The physical brain affects emotions and behavior and is affected chemically by the person's experiences. The path between mind and body is seen as a two-way street. Instead, driven by its insecurity as a branch of medicine, American psychiatry chose to copy the categorical and restrictive medical model of illness and diagnosis.

RECONCILING TEMPERAMENT AND ENVIRONMENT

When parents ask, "Does he have ADD?" often what they really want to know is whether their son's problem behavior occurs because he "can't" or because he "won't." Is some malfunction in the brain putting the desired behavior outside his control? ADD's implied neurological basis suggests "can't" and thus diminishes the importance of willful conflicts with parents and teachers. "Won't" carries implications of problems that are more emotional or relational in nature—or, if one thinks in terms of larger systems, problems for which parents and teachers are partly responsible. In reality, behavior is never 100 percent either "can't" or "won't." There's a circularity to the dynamic: If you find a task particularly difficult, you are less likely to want to perform it, but at the same time, your attention is more likely to wander.

These days a patient may go from one psychiatrist to another in search of a precise fix on his or her "chemical imbalance" and the ideal drug to treat it, when it might be more useful to reframe the problem as a collision of life circumstances that puts contentment or peace of mind out of reach. Of course, in other cases, the persistent search for a psychological cause or resolution can be unrewarding, and seeking a biological propensity for the problem may be more appropriate. Psychiatry should allow room for both possibilities.[34]

A model that strikes a middle ground between psyche and biology was first elucidated in the 1950s by Stella Chess, Alexander Thomas, and Herbert Birch, child psychiatrists who were dissatisfied with strict psychoanalytic descriptions of early childhood behavior.[35] These doctors reintroduced and formalized what grandmothers have always known intuitively: that children are born with their own distinctive temperaments, which Chess and her colleagues saw as inherent, genetic, and reflected by a constitutional biochemistry.

Their work following a cohort of children for many years led to their identifying three types: children whose temperament could be characterized as "easy," another group characterized as "difficult," and a third group they described as "sensitive."[36] The easy children were adaptable and flexible in coping with stress or change, were easy to console when upset, and generally had a sunny disposition. The difficult children got upset easily and were difficult to console, persistent, and intense; their mood was often negative. Children in the third group were easily overwhelmed by stimuli and tended to withdraw from new situations; their parents would call them shy.

Not surprisingly, the latter two groups showed more behavior problems. The difficult kids tended to act out with "externalizing" behaviors (including some of the ADD type). The shy children had more "internalizing" or anxiety-type problems. However, temperament is not destiny. Chess and colleagues insisted that the well-being of children depended less on innate personality types than on what they called "goodness of fit" between the child and the family. This was the happy result when the child's environment, including expectations and demands, fit with his or her innate temperament. A good fit was, in essence, a harmony between the needs, desires, and understanding of the parents—within the values of a given culture—and the personality of the child.

Naturally enough, the constellation of qualities that makes for a difficult temperament also tends to make a good fit harder to achieve, and this can become a negative cycle. Difficult children challenge parents, and if they are a poor fit with the parents' capabilities and needs, this is likely to make their behavior even more problematic. Certain temperament risk factors have been identified as predisposing children to a poor fit—an incompatible relationship—with their environment, and thus to excessive stress and conflict in their interactions with caretakers, and ensuing clinical problems.

Cross-cultural surveys reveal fascinating differences about what constitutes a good or bad fit for families in different situations. It turns out that no single set of traits is maladaptive in all cases. In a study of African babies and children during famine, for instance, the children with a difficult temperament—those who fussed and cried more—tended to get fed more than the easy babies and so had a higher survival rate.[37] Another survey, in New York City, found that babies with the classic difficult-temperament traits (negative mood, irregular biological rhythms, intense responses) caused serious problems for middle- and upper-middle-class New Yorkers, disrupting schedules, creating interpersonal tensions, and so on. But the same personality traits were less problematic in working-class Puerto Rican families, who had fewer expectations and demands—for example, that their children develop regular feeding or sleeping schedules or early competency in getting dressed. Interestingly, the most problematic quality for the latter families was a high activity level, probably reflecting the smaller living spaces these families had to occupy.[38]

A temperament-fit model of ADD would say that some children have a genetic tendency toward greater activity and distractibility along with less inhibition than others of comparable age. If their environment cannot adapt to or meet the needs of the child's personality, problems for the child and the family will develop. "Adapting" to such a personality does not mean giving in to or permitting all of the child's behavior. One key element of a successful fit with an incipient ADD child might be that the parents provide very structured, consistent, and immediate limits. In studies that pursued the ideas of Chess and her colleagues with larger numbers of children, Michel Maziade and his colleagues found that among many of their subjects, extremes of temperament were not in themselves risk factors for problem behavior, *unless they were associated with dysfunctional family discipline.*[39]

Providing ideal responses to an ADD child's behavior is far from easy, especially since many parents of ADD-type children may themselves have personalities that lead to inconsistent parenting. In any case, this formulation is not parent-blaming. Indeed, many temperament experts argue that the child's personality plays a crucial role in the kind of parenting he or she gets. A person's behavior not only expresses innate biological and psychological traits, but helps to create an environmental niche that regularly calls forth those traits. "A highly reactive, intense, difficult child," notes behavioral genetics researcher Sandra Scarr, "requires specially calm, undemanding and accepting parents to achieve good outcomes."[40] Some children may need a degree of parenting that few families could deliver.

Beyond the circle of the family, the child's environment includes the demands made on (and support offered to) families and schools by the larger society. If the demands are excessive and the support minimal, the stresses on both the child and the caregivers make it less likely that the children will behave or perform up to expectations. Alternatively, the caregivers probably won't respond optimally when challenged by kids acting up or tuning out. These are factors that lead us back to Ritalin—which may improve behavior problems and performance in the short term, regardless of the causes, but addresses the issues only at the chemical level of the child's brain. The best that can be said for the drug is that it offers symptomatic relief that may help both the child and the caregivers to cope more effectively.

The fact that an ADD personality may be genetically determined is moot to a certain extent. ADD traits may indeed be heritable at a very high rate, but it's not a biochemical abnormality that brings children to my office for treatment; it's their oppositional behavior at home or their failure at school. Just as a person's height is not perceived as a problem unless society says it is, so with an ADD personality.

This is why, for me and many others (especially pediatricians), a temperament-fit model is so much more congenial in helping to explain behavior and set goals for treatment. Ironically, these ideas, originally set forth by psychiatrists, have been largely abandoned by academic psychiatry in its urge to emulate the medical-pathological model of disease. Yet they could prove most helpful in our search for the possible sources, besides the brains of children, for the epidemic of ADD diagnosis and Ritalin use in America.

Chapter 6

Welcome to Ritalin Nation: An ADD Culture Arises

This private world of loony bins and weird people that I had always felt I occupied and hid in had suddenly been turned inside out so that it seemed like this was one big Prozac Nation, one big mess of malaise.
—Elizabeth Wurtzel, *Prozac Nation: Young and Depressed in America*

Instead of thinking of myself as having a character flaw, a family legacy, or some potentially ominous "difference" between me and other people, I could see myself in terms of having a unique brain biology. . . . In fact, I would much rather have ADD than not have it, since I love the positive qualities that go along with it—creativity, energy, and unpredictability.
—Edward M. Hallowell, M.D.

Sometimes the ADD-Ritalin phenomenon hits very close to home, as when friends of the family approach me at a holiday party. Richard was an electrician—he had once done some work for us. He had heard that I was working on a book about ADD, and he wanted to share the amazing discovery that had recently changed his life. "I'm ADD," he declared, with a note of relief and even excitement. He went on to describe the attentional and organizational problems that had plagued him throughout life, and his feeling that he'd never been able to achieve up to his potential, either in school or in business. "I always felt like a failure. Like it was my fault for not being better-organized or trying harder. Hearing that I had ADD was a relief—I felt like a burden had been lifted. And Ritalin has made life so much easier."

I listened with interest, recalling that his work habits on our small project might have suggested ADD symptoms. He was late a few times and the work took longer than promised—still, that's not unusual in the contracting business. Richard usually had a reasonable explanation, and was so contrite and polite that we overlooked the delays. When I asked him about his understanding of ADD, he replied matter-of-factly, "It's a problem with my brain. I have a chemical imbalance there's little I can do about, except take Ritalin. I'll have the problem for the rest of my life." Asked about how he coped before his diagnosis, he told me that he kept elaborate lists (but often lost them) and relied on his wife Shelley to keep him organized.

Around that time Shelley wandered over. "He's really different on the Ritalin," she offered. "He's way more focused and efficient. I like that." Was there anything about Richard on Ritalin she didn't like? I asked. "Well, he's not as soft." I assumed she was referring to Richard's gentle, deferring nature. "But he goes back to being that way in the evening, when the medication has worn off. Overall, I'd say he was much happier. Wouldn't you agree?" She turned to Richard, who nodded. "The diagnosis has been such a relief to him. He used to beat himself up over his mistakes."

THE CULTURE OF ADD

Richard is far from the only person to have greeted his ADD diagnosis with a sense of relief and unburdening; in fact, it's a pretty typical reaction. Edward Hallowell, the coauthor of *Driven to Distraction*, writes, "When I discovered in 1981 that I had . . . [ADD], it was one of the great 'Aha!' experiences of my life. Suddenly so many seemingly disparate parts of my personality made sense. . . . It was a pivotal moment for me."[1]

The idea that their problems are not of their own making but controlled by skewed brain chemistry and genetics represents salvation from a sense of failure many people carry, and it allows them finally to make sense of their confused, chaotic, frustrating responses to the world. More and more, as the "ADD-positive" population swells, it also provides a place to belong, a community, a culture in which people whose behavior typically has made them outsiders, struggling for acceptance, can feel accepted, understood, and supported.

If language is destiny, the way people talk about ADD affects how they deal with it, or how it deals with them. At the very least, it reveals how people come to identify with the condition, and sometimes even regard it possessively:

"He has ADD. . . ."

"My ADD made me do it."

"She is ADD and so am I."

"I've been an ADDer for ten years."

There's nothing really wrong with using such shorthand for convenience—I sometimes do so myself in the interest of economy and readability. But each time the phrase "I am [have] ADD" is repeated, the slippery nature of the diagnosis is ignored and its validity as a medical disorder is confirmed; it gets easier to forget that the name "ADD" is a metaphorical construct, not the reality itself.

Saying "I have ADD" or "I'm ADD" also reinforces a person's identification with the condition. But overidentification is a danger, with the potential to encourage a victimlike passivity or to psychically ghettoize the ADD community. And I think a distinction must be made between an adult's choice to identify him or herself with a "disabled" group and assigning a child willy-nilly to the same fate. Adults are better able to put on or shed an identity at will and usually have developed some capacity to resist societal pressure. Self-image for children is highly dependent on peer opinion, starting at a young age, and once labeled, it may take them until well into adulthood to learn that they have a choice in the matter—if they ever do believe so.

Most kids under ten years old, in my experience, don't seem to "get" having the ADD label or strongly identify with it, on a conscious level anyway. When a young child says, "I'm ADD," he or she is often parroting parents or teachers. Some, of course, may learn to use "It's my ADD" as an excuse—studies have shown that children diagnosed with ADD tend to hold themselves less accountable for their behavior than other kids. The fact of taking medication also produces varying reactions in children, with a substantial number saying they don't like it. Others will tell me that they don't care or that "it's okay"—but children often will say one thing to a doctor, while their parents report something quite different. (See Chapter 11.)

Some people who decide to accept "their" ADD go further and embrace it. In addition to "creativity, energy, and unpredictability." Hallowell speaks of "an indefinable, zany sense of life" that is somehow different from that displayed by non-ADD people, and describes a boy he treated thus: "Like many ADDers, he was intuitive, warm, and empathic."[2] Thom Hartmann, in his popular book *Attention Deficit Disorder: A Different Perception*, goes further still. He claims that "ADD is neither a deficit nor a disorder. It is instead an inherited set of skills . . . which would enable a Hunter or warrior to be eminently successful" but happen not to be as well suited to the "Farmer" society we currently inhabit.[3] Among ADD sites on the World Wide Web currently is one created by an "ADD minstrel" named Jerry Mills, described by a reviewer as "a composer, guitar player, singer, lecturer, teacher and all-around poster boy for some of the best aspects of being ADD." Another Web page is described as "a celebration of ADD creativity," and so on. This again resembles what has happened in other "disadvantaged" communities, from "black is beautiful" to "gay pride" to resistance by deaf activists against efforts to make them more like hearing people.

It's possible both to applaud the desire of ADD folks to see themselves in a positive light and to worry about a subculture that emphasizes its differences from the general population or credits a disorder for positive traits that may simply coexist in the same personality. All of these attitudes are rooted in the desire to see ADD as a biological abnormality that relieves all except fate of blame, and disinclines people to look beyond the brain for explanations (or solutions) to the problem. Such a culture must give central place to biological interventions, in the process devaluing other treatment modalities and ignoring the greater social circumstances that create "living imbalances." In other words, it becomes a culture of Ritalin.

I'm not sure what to make of the fact that several doctors who are in the forefront of spreading the word about ADD and Ritalin are themselves diagnosed with the condition, or it seems to run in their families. Both Edward Hallowell and John Ratey are self-admitted ADD sufferers who have taken medication (whether Ritalin or some other drug isn't specified). At least one other member of CHADD's professional advisory board, Theodore Mandelkorn (a Seattle-area physician), says he has ADD. Closer to my home, Daniel Amen, best known for his work with SPECT scans, does not claim to have ADD but announces regularly at CHADD meetings that his wife and son do. (He doesn't say who diagnosed them.)

There's nothing inherently unethical about a physician with a disorder—physical or mental—treating patients with the same problem. Indeed, it could enhance his or her understanding of and empathy with the patient. Seeing the world through ADD-colored vision might also, however, blur the boundaries between the problems of the doctor and those of the patient. Certainly it seems possible that such practitioners could offer ADD as an explanation for every patient with problems of attention, focus, or task completion—perhaps too readily.

SHAMANS OF THE BRAIN

ADD culture has caught the current upbeat mood of psychiatry regarding science's potential to unlock the black box of the brain. There is a sense in some quarters that, just as it's been proven we can shape up our bodies with the right combination of diet, exercise, and attitude, we can bring to bear all of our present-day arsenal of techniques to shape up (take control of) our emotions and behavior. John Ratey, director of a Massachusetts research hospital and Edward Hallowell's coauthor, is quoted in a 1997 *Psychology Today* article: "From dyslexia to depression, we're beginning to understand the ways we can help balance our brains through everything from medication to therapy to behavioral coaching." Says Ratey, "That's magic. People start re-framing their entire lives."[4]

On the face of it, this sounds great. The reality, however, is that far more mental illness can be traced to adverse social conditions than to chemical imbalances in the brain, and so far neither medicine nor society has shown the will or leadership to attack these causes at their roots. The powerful ideology that supports and perpetuates this state of affairs is the model of biological psychiatry. The true common denominator of the ADD culture is a drug—and beyond that, a belief that brain chemistry is the fundamental thing that separates ADDers from others, that the medical model for mental health is the right one, and that research eventually will target the exact gene or piece of the brain "responsible" for ADD.

Psychiatrist Peter Kramer, whose book about Prozac firmly planted the brain chemistry model in the popular consciousness, is quoted in the same *Psychology Today* article. He says that today you can alter "your temperament with medication, or by choosing your challenges wisely, or through talk therapy, which has its own biological impact."[5] Kramer's comment about "talk therapy" is revealing. How does it work? At least in part, by having "biological impact": today's litmus test for any treatment of value.

ADD culture also echoes the current enshrinement of diversity in the larger culture in the idea that everyone has a unique brain biology, no better or no worse than any other. The fact that there are so many different kinds of brains becomes admirable in itself; no qualitative distinctions are made. Again quoting Hallowell: "Our old distinctions of 'smart' and 'stupid' don't even begin to describe the variety of differences in human brains."[6] My reaction to this kind of thinking is to ask: If ADD as an expression of diversity is a good thing, why are so many people taking Ritalin to better fit into the mainstream world?

CHADD's WORLD

The largest of the ADD self-help groups, with some thirty-five thousand members, CHADD has grown phenomenally in less than a decade, in membership, level of activity, and influence. Local chapters sponsor monthly meetings and other events, and an annual national meeting draws fifteen hundred people and features talks by leading researchers on ADD. An official newsletter called *Chadder Box* is published monthly and mailed to the entire membership, and its glossy magazine, *Attention!*, is also free with membership. Larger chapters also have their own newsletters.

CHADD's professional advisory board includes most of the prominent academicians in the ADD world, a veritable who's who in research. Besides Hallowell, Ratey, and Mandelkorn, it currently includes Russell Barkley, Judith Rapoport, James Swanson, and Alan Zametkin, all introduced elsewhere in this book. CHADD today represents the mainstream, the central current of ADD culture.

A smaller national organization, the Attention Deficit Disorder Association (ADDA), focuses on dissemination of information and lobbying efforts. It does not have local chapters or provide local support activities, though its national conference is apparently popular within the ADD culture. I concentrate on CHADD because its influence is greater.

Unquestionably CHADD provides a very useful information and support network for families struggling to raise children with ADD-related problems. In local communities, its chapter representatives often know where to find help for families, from expert evaluators to treatment facilities. They teach parents how to advocate for their children in schools, go to bat for them on issues of insurance coverage, and work to enlighten teachers and school administrators about ADD. *Attention!* magazine publishes accurate reports about medical, legislative, and legal developments of concern to ADD sufferers—though not surprisingly, with CHADD's own spin on the facts.

From the start, CHADD adopted a strongly biological view of children's problems. This is understandable, since the experts they have relied upon promote that view. References to ADD as a "neurobiological disorder" appear throughout CHADD's literature, a representation they claim is based on Alan Zametkin's 1990 study for the National Institute of Mental Health (NIMH) showing variations in glucose utilization by the brains of ADD children's parents (see Chapter 5).[7] They do not mention later studies of his that do not as strongly support such a biological link. A citizen gadfly, Michael Parry of Washington State, shared with me his correspondence with Peter S. Jensen, M.D., chief of the Child and Adolescent Disorders Research Branch of the NIMH, in which Jensen states that "NIMH does not have an official position on whether ADHD is a 'neurobiological' disorder."[8] (In his own writings, Jensen uses the term "behavioral disorder.") It appears that NIMH is not ready to accept CHADD's unequivocal statement of biological certainty.

CHADD has become a powerful player in influencing the national perception of ADD and official policies on the condition. Its lobbying and letter-writing campaigns have resulted in major changes to federal laws that give children access to special-education services and other educational accommodations and that recognize ADD as a potential disability. The most recent national guidelines on mental disabilities in the workplace also reflect the work of ADD activists. (Details are in the next chapter.) In these and similar battles, the neurobiological model clearly has had strategic value—the more "medical" a disorder, the better the chance for official disability status.

CHADD's commitment to the biochemical explanation of ADD has created a widely held perception that the organization strongly promotes Ritalin for the treatment of ADD. Some parents, after attending a few CHADD meetings, have called me to ask if I know of an organization for families who don't want to give medication to their children with ADD. They feel there is little tolerance for this point of view within the organization. CHADD's leadership will dispute this, and its literature seems to advocate a multimodal model of treatment—but close reading will reveal an emphasis on medication that's predictably similar to the professional literature of academic psychiatrists and psychologists, on whom CHADD has depended upon for advice.[9]

Reliance on these experts also led CHADD to pursue its ultimately embarrassing effort to loosen controls on Ritalin production and prescription, which I described in Chapter 2. The DEA's negative response to the petition was predictable, supported by considerable evidence of historical abuse and disquieting new evidence of recent increases in abuse. A battle royal was in the making, only to be short-circuited by the Merrow Report's revelation of Ciba-Geigy's undisclosed funding of CHADD—which at minimum had the appearance of hidden advertisement by Ciba and a major conflict of interest for CHADD.

The extent to which CHADD had become the "voice" of ADD was further revealed in another finding of the Merrow Report.[10] Earlier in 1995 the U.S. Department of Education Office of Special Programs (OSEP) had produced an educational videotape called *Facing the Challenges of ADD*, advance copies of which were sent to members of Congress, participants in the production, and relevant associations. The Merrow Report journalists noted some interesting facts: Nearly all of the parents and spokespeople interviewed for the government's video were CHADD members, yet this was not mentioned in the video, nor was there any mention of CHADD's receiving funding from the manufacturer of Ritalin. When the director of OSEP, Thomas Hehir, was asked on camera whether he was aware of these facts, he appeared visibly startled and denied knowledge of either. In October 1995 the OSEP video was withdrawn from distribution.

CHADD clearly intends to extend its reach still farther. A 1997 fundraising letter opens with a blast against media reports that "still get it wrong" about ADD, that is, discount its medical credibility.[11] The letter quotes from what it describes as "savage attacks" in the *Wall Street Journal* and *Forbes* magazine and seeks the reader's help in "fighting these battles of misinformation, innuendo, ignorance, and outright hostility toward children and adults who have a neurobiological disorder." An enclosure summarizing CHADD's 1998 goals and objectives is headed by the following items:

- to disseminate accurate, authoritative information about ADD to national media outlets, and conduct a proactive media relations program

- to challenge negative, inaccurate reports that demean or undermine people with ADD

This suggests that CHADD these days sees a primary purpose, if not its central mission, as one of public relations, nurturing ADD's image as a medical condition. The mere fact of a single organization being the primary source of information on such an issue isn't bad in itself. But one can justifiably wish that an organization with such ambitions embrace a bona fide range of views, make serious efforts to address the broad social roots of a problem such as ADD, and weigh carefully the promotion of Ritalin as central to its position.

ADD Culture Online

For a lot of people involved with ADD and Ritalin, a favorite meeting place these days is the Internet. ADD-type individuals are drawn to cyberspace like salvation seekers to the revival tent. For one thing, it's the perfect distraction for those with "attentional inconstancy"—that quality of attending too closely to something attractive while giving insufficient attention to important but boring tasks, such as one's job. The Internet's content and format seduce the disaffected, the rebellious, those drawn to notions of conspiracy. Finding someone to listen to your problems is easy, and neither party is under any obligation to sustain the relationship. If you get bored or don't like what's being said, you can sign off with little concern for having broken a social contract or a therapeutic commitment. If you're just browsing and not interacting, it's easier still. "Computers are good listeners," observed one participant in an ADD chat room.

Quite a few of my current and former patients with ADD are major computer and Internet junkies, and when I want to get a sense of what's new on the Net, I often call on them. One of them, Harvey, helped with this chapter. When I first met him, Harvey was living in an upscale suburban neighborhood with his wife and two children, doing pretty well as an insurance broker but (as it turned out) hating the work and living close to the financial edge much of the time. He acknowledged that he'd had lifelong problems with authority, which he attributed to an alcoholic yet demanding father, and described himself in other terms common among people diagnosed with ADD. Harvey claimed that his patterns of operating, which were heavy on denial and procrastination, often sabotaged him. He drove for six years without a license and wound up in jail briefly "once, when I was caught." "I've always been able to talk my way out of trouble," he'd say, "but I get real anxious in the process."

Harvey first sought me out because he was convinced, after reading *Driven to Distraction*, that he had ADD and that it was the central force behind his myriad problems. Not only had he read the book, it seemed he had virtually memorized it; he could recite symptoms chapter and verse. At certain times, especially with adults and certainly with Harvey, it can become difficult to sort out the symptoms a patient actually displays—the genuine experience—from his or her recitation of a list absorbed from a book or article. Practically speaking, it may be somewhat moot: When someone comes in believing she or her child has ADD, it's almost impossible to address the problems without taking that self-diagnosis into account.

I hadn't seen Harvey for a while when I called him to ask him about ADD and the Internet, but he seemed glad to hear from me. "Hold on a minute," he said. "I'm multitasking." Indeed, as we spoke on the phone he was logging onto the Net and proceeding to check out various sites. "Multitasking"—computerspeak for the newer hardware's capability to perform more than function at a time—is a metaphor that's been enthusiastically adopted by the ADD community. Harvey was one of those who took pride in being able to do several things at once, or at least switch back and forth between them quickly and repeatedly. Thom Hartmann, in his quest to redefine ADD as a creative adaptation, has even proposed that so-called normal people can be seen as suffering from task-switching deficit disorder (TSDD), which forces them to "plod along on one job at a time."[12]

According to Harvey and my own informal searches, there are currently hundreds of sites on the World Wide Web related to ADD, and a request for keyword matches to "attention deficit" turned up 18,720 matches! Many of the sites are personal home pages created by individuals or parents of children who "have" ADD. CHADD's national office maintains a Web site whose information appears, for the most part, to be accurate and responsible. So does ADDA, whose annual conference has occasioned a lot of buzz on the Net. America Online has its own proprietary feature for the ADD audience, called "ADD on AOL" and hosted by an M.D. who goes by the name of "Dr. ADD." ADD chat groups also can be found in AOL's "Personal Empowerment Network." And several other online information clearinghouses link together many ADD-related Web sites; an example is the ADD WebRing.

To give just a sampling of the range, one can visit ADD News for Christian Families; ADDult Recovery (a twelve-step approach); the ADD Dragon Web Page (for teachers and parents of kids in school); BRAKES: The Interactive Newsletter for Kids with ADD; Brandi Valentine's ADD Pages (which support "alternative" treatments); ADD in Bermuda; and—of course—the ADD Warehouse, an online catalog of products and literature for sale.

It's common for newcomers to ADD chat groups to say they've "finally found a place where people understand." Another frequent remark is "Everything you've just said is true of me, too." The combination of an empathic audience and virtual anonymity opens the floodgates, so that those who sometimes describe themselves as wallflowers in their non-digital lives are anything but that online. Behavior quirks are confessed and compared, funny/awful stories of forgetfulness and disorganization are shared, ADD jokes are exchanged, and coping methods suggested. Thus, to a considerable degree, is the culture of ADD transmitted these days.

On one level, it's hard to find anything wrong with such a lively community. The usual criticism of online social life could be made: that it's not a satisfactory substitute for face-to-face relationships. A possible further risk for parents of ADD children may be that in spending a lot of time online learning how to deal with their kids' problems, they have that much less time to interact with the kids. However, the most significant problem with ADD coverage on the Net is simply that vast amounts of information are available, with little or no way to distinguish the reliable from the fantastic.[13]

Alternative, nonmainstream information and ads for ADD-related products abound on the Net. Not just the ADD Warehouse but scores of obscure but popular Web sites offer products for sale. While the Net is becoming increasingly commercialized, most of the ADD vendors retain a mom-and-pop approach. Often someone who has created a Web site sells space on a monthly basis to a distributor of products for ADD. Some sites at first appear informational but are designed ultimately to attract referrals or sell products.

Thus patients come to their doctor with requests for new drugs or drug combinations, health products, or treatments that they've seen mentioned on the Net or promoted by not-always-scrupulous entrepreneurs. Hardly any of these have been studied in a rigorous fashion; virtually all medications are promoted for "off-label" use; that is, the FDA has not approved them to treat ADD. (Admittedly, off-label use is common in child psychiatric practice, as few drugs have been developed just for children.) CHADD warns against many of these fringe treatments.

Even online enthusiasts more committed to the ADD mainstream seem suspicious of conventional treatment practices—a manifestation of the conspiracy mind-set. For example, it is taken as gospel on the Internet that generic methylphenidate is not as effective for treating ADD as the more costly brand-name version of the drug, that is, Ritalin. The Food and Drug Administration (FDA) insists that approved generic medications contain the identical version of the drug produced by the trade manufacturer. Aside from anecdotal reports of some individuals responding differently—perhaps, as with a placebo effect, due largely to stronger belief in the brand-name version—there is no evidence that the generic version works any differently. Yet many remain convinced of Ritalin's superiority.

It should also raise concern, I think, that there exists within many Internet chat rooms (even more than in CHADD) a certain party line about ADD and Ritalin that approaches cultlike rigidity. If you raise questions about the integrity of the ADD diagnosis or the value of Ritalin in these parts of cyberspace, you are quickly challenged, made to feel unwelcome, or simply dismissed. On such sites, the whole world is seen through ADD glasses, and participants exchange ideas as if their very identities are wrapped up in viewing themselves as ADDers. Therefore, even raising any questions is perceived as threatening and usually dismissed with responses like "You just don't understand." You may even get "flamed"—receive a slew of hostile, anonymous postings—which is the ultimate insult in Net society.

MEDIA HYPERACTIVITY

The attention paid to ADD by the media since the early 1990s has undoubtedly contributed to the boom in diagnosis and Ritalin use. News reports tend to exaggerate the positive findings of scientific studies while downplaying studies that demonstrate negative results (for example, no risk of cancer or no long-term drug benefit).[14] Journalists favor simple story lines with easily identifiable heroes and villains, good and evil sides, black and white answers. Ritalin as a miracle cure has obvious appeal—that the drug has some critics only adds to the drama.

Here is a snippet from the voice-over of Nancy Snyderman on *Good Morning America* from 1992:

> ADD symptoms tend to show up in the classroom, and teachers are often the first to notice a problem. Both Stefan and Hans are intelligent youngsters, but *their brains are affected by a chemical imbalance.* In a landmark study two years ago, researchers found that *brain activity of hyperactive adults was significantly lower than in normal people.* [Italics added]

It is very unlikely that the program followed up on these comments by reporting the same researchers' failure to find consistent differences among adult brain scans in later published studies of ADD.

Another segment from the same year, from the newsmagazine *20/20,* dramatized the miraculous nature of the Ritalin "cure" and the possibility that many may suffer from the disorder without knowing it.

NARRATOR [*voice-over*]: Hannah [*Oreste, parent of Devorah*] refused to accept the school's assessment and didn't give up until finding the proper diagnosis: attention deficit disorder. Devorah began treatment, which included taking Ritalin, one of the same medications originally found to be effective in treating hyperactivity.

HANNAH: The second day she was on it, she was watching a movie, and she came into the kitchen and she started telling me about the movie, start to finish. She'd never done that before.

NARRATOR: Then a report came back from the school. Devorah was a new child in the classroom. Amazed by the turnaround in her daughter, Hannah decided to find out all she could about ADD.

HANNAH: The first thing I did was I got out a book and read on what it was, and the first article I read described her to a T. And I read this article and I sat there thinking, "This is me. . . ." [And after she tries medication]: It was just—it was actually like—you know, when your TV has snow on it and you need to tune it in? That's, in essence, what it was like [before medication]. Having the feeling of fuzziness, but then all of a sudden somebody tuned it in.

Hannah was describing the nonspecific effect that would be experienced by anyone taking low-dose Ritalin. Nevertheless, it had a profound effect on her beliefs and "confirmed" that Devorah had ADD. Later in the same program, we learned how Ritalin saved a marriage.

REPORTER CATHERINE CRYER [*voice-over*]: Mary and Bill were at the breaking point, and neither understood why their marriage was failing. . . . After a careful evaluation and diagnosis, Bill began treatment.

BILL: The first day of Ritalin was—that was—that was unique. That Friday I was able to go to work. I solved problems in the morning, I solved problems in the afternoon. I still had time left over in the day. And it was like everything was measured, there was a sense of order that all of a sudden came to light. And I got home at night and sitting down, and I even—actually sat with the kids and they were near me, we were watching TV, and Mary came in and we were talking, and I was just calm.

MARY: It's very emotional. I'm thinking, "My goodness, it's like we have been released, we have been freed." We have a totally new lease on life, and we like each other. It's unbelievable.

In an exception to the general rule, program host Hugh Downs went on to muse how others in the TV audience may *incorrectly* believe they have the disorder, and suggested how people might properly go about getting diagnosed. Still, it's no wonder that for several weeks thereafter my telephone rang off the hook.

More recently the media has attempted to highlight the controversy over Ritalin—all too often oversimplifying these complex issues. The usual formula is to begin with the reporter commenting on the "new" diagnosis of ADD and the explosive growth in Ritalin use, followed by the provocative question: Are children being overdrugged in our classrooms? Two families will be presented: one with a child whose "life was saved" by Ritalin, contrasted with another whose child experienced intolerable side effects or underwent an undesirable personality change on Ritalin.

Next appear the "experts" in front of impressively filled bookshelves in their offices, or striding down a hospital corridor. Each expert (usually two) gets about fifteen to twenty seconds for a statement. Then the camera cuts back to the children—one happily playing in the schoolyard, apparently cured of his malady, the other at home, lovingly protected by his parents from the vagaries of medical science. The segment closes with the reporter solemnly intoning, "ADD and Ritalin—cure or curse? Make sure you check with your doctor." Finally, the news anchor may ad-lib a remark to colleagues in the studio that may reflect insensitivity, misunderstanding, or worse.

Most physicians, experts or not, recognize that collaborating with the media carries risks—both to the integrity of the message and to their professional standing. It's a Mephistophelian Pact that most, myself included, are willing to make in order to reach a wider audience. However, the response to such publicity may not always be to their liking. Alan Zametkin was pleased when his research on PET scans of the parents of ADD children (see Chapter 5) was chosen in 1990 as a lead article by the *New England Journal of Medicine* and relayed by major news outlets to the general public. But he was shocked by the level of passion the media coverage generated and has expressed discomfort with the ADD audience's uncritical embrace of conclusions not consistently supported by further research.[15]

The reductionistic view of ADD as a neurological disorder has obvious appeal for reporters and editors, because it's easy to grasp on a superficial level, and also because brain science is "sexy" these days. Studies showing the results of behavioral training in the home and school, for example, just aren't perceived as newsworthy compared with so-called hard science. By choosing to report on ADD research that focuses on brain activity and biochemical processes, the media becomes part of the whole constellation of factors that are pushing research and public perception in this direction.

Media coverage can cut both ways on an issue, of course. Ironically, one of the best-documented studies of its effects on treatment concerns a temporary downturn in Ritalin use. Baltimore researcher Daniel Safer and his colleagues have been tracking Ritalin use in their county for nearly twenty years. In a study published in 1992, they demonstrated rather conclusively that Ritalin use, which had been doubling every four to seven years locally, dropped by 39 percent between 1989 and 1991 from its peak in 1987—coinciding with highly negative publicity around lawsuits against doctors and clinics initiated by alleged Church of Scientology activists.[16] It took several years for the local rates to rebound. The Baltimore episode follows the usual sequence of media effect: at first, stories exaggerate the drug's positive effects, ignoring perceived minor negatives, until a sufficiently large negative is raised. Then the media overdoes it and frightens the audience with alarms.

I think it's likely that ongoing media attention, along with rising skepticism about making behavior problems into diseases, may feed a backlash against the ADD-Ritalin boom in the not-too-distant future. It might be triggered by the release of strongly negative research—for example, very preliminary data from animal research seem to suggest that children who take Ritalin are more prone to become addicted to stimulants as teenagers or adults.[17] When I heard this reported at a conference, I envisioned headlines shouting, "Ritalin Addicts Children to Speed." Even more damaging to Ritalin's reputation would be a personal tragedy such as the death of a well-known politician's or entertainer's child linked with a Ritalin overdose. Overreaction to such an event would heighten the already tribal mentality of the ADD community, causing it to circle the wagons against all outside critiques. This would be unfortunate, to say the least.

CONSUMER ALERT: DRUG ADVERTISING
AND ALTERNATIVE TREATMENTS

Enterprises with a profit motive have had a strong hand in shaping the culture of ADD. One phenomenon that demands attention is the enormous growth of direct advertising to consumers by pharmaceutical companies. Among the first prescription drugs to be advertised in the popular media were Rogaine, for baldness, and other elective treatments such as oral contraceptives. More recently, medications for blood pressure, ulcers, and allergies have been featured. Most disturbing, however, are the print ads for psychiatric medications. The most ubiquitous markets a drug called BuSpar, used in anxiety disorders. The ad presents consumers with a questionnaire that begins, "Does your life have signs of persistent anxiety?" and goes on to detail the symptoms—many of which, of course, could be experienced by the average person under stress. It's a similar approach that people take when self-diagnosing ADD: checking off items on a list of symptoms.

Until recently, consumers were shielded from the full force of the pharmaceutical industry's powerful public relations and advertising efforts, which were limited to "informing" physicians about their products. But the trend toward direct consumer advertising is mighty: Companies spent an estimated $610 million on it in 1996, compared with $44 million in 1990.[18] It may be only a matter of time before we see ads for Ritalin, Dexedrine, Cylert, or Adderall in the parent-oriented magazines that litter the waiting rooms of pediatricians and family doctors.

If big pharmaceutical companies represent the mainstream, the growing list of "alternative" treatments for ADD delineates a counterculture. Information that differs sharply from what most experts maintain is accurate abounds on the Internet and in the popular press, as well as in schools and wherever parents meet: the mall, soccer field, or supermarket. In general medicine, consumers' growing suspicion of conventional Western medical practice and its drugs has been accompanied by growing interest in Eastern traditions, bodywork, and "natural" remedies of all kinds. It's not surprising to find a parallel trend in mental health. And entrepreneurs have discovered there is much profit to be made in offering ADD evaluations and treatment.

Medical or mental problems that are ill-defined, chronic, and lacking in clear solutions—this describes ADD, of course—are especially fertile ground. Simple explanations and alternative cures are very attractive to people struggling with problems like ADD behavior that are, in reality, quite complex and resistant to change. While wildly different in form and origin, all such alternatives tend to be as reductionistic, in their way, as the mainstream model of brain chemistry and Ritalin they oppose. "Do this, take this, and you'll be better," they promise.

Here I can only touch on a few of the best-known alternative treatments—they are far too numerous for me to analyze in detail.[19] Indeed, there are activists for each approach who would take me to task for not devoting more attention to their favorite in a book that purports to question Ritalin use. But one central point holds across the board: While any of these treatments might produce results for a particular child, when studied in large groups of children they have not proven valuable. Proponents of any alternative treatment can usually point to one or two studies that ostensibly demonstrate its effectiveness, but in general those studies are flawed or their results are not replicated by further work.

Megavitamin therapy.   Taking large doses of certain vitamins and minerals has been claimed to help children with behavior and learning problems. While some studies have noted improvements, these did not qualify as fully controlled trials, and others that did use placebo and double-blind controls found no benefits. Very high doses of some vitamins can even be harmful, so despite the intuitive appeal of using vitamins to treat ADD, this approach can't be recommended.

Anti-motion-sickness medication.   An intriguing theory proposed that ADD symptoms are linked to the vestibular receptors that control balance in the inner ear, and how these receptors communicate with the brain's cerebellum. Treatment with anti-motion-sickness medications such as Dramamine is used in this method. Despite an observed association between poor balance or coordination and learning difficulties in kids, however, no scientific proof supports the role of the cerebellar-vestibular system in learning and attention problems; the evidence is all anecdotal (again, true for most of these ideas.)

Antifungals and the role of candida.   *Candida albicans*, a member of the yeast family that lives in the human body, can cause infections when its growth gets out of hand. Some claim that it can weaken the immune system and thereby instigate psychiatric symptoms, including ADD, as well as a huge range of physical ailments. The chief proponent of this theory recommends treatment that includes a controlled diet, elimination of environmental toxins, nutritional supplements, and antifungal medication, especially for children with a history of antibiotic use. Scientific support is lacking.

Essential fatty acids and amino acids.   Both of these nutrients are important building blocks for healthy cells—amino acids are also components of neurotransmitter chemicals—and deficiencies have been blamed for a variety of ills, from allergies and skin disorders to ADD. A concentrated essential fatty acid (EFA) derived from the oil of the evening primrose plant is a popular (but expensive) remedy and has been studied in England for its effect on ADD, though not in a controlled way. Amino acid supplements such as tryptophan and phenylalanine have also been tried, with disappointing results.

Other medications.   A drug called Piracetam (pyrrolidine acetamide), related to the neurotransmitter known as GABA, has been marketed in Europe and tested on reading-disabled children in the United States with initially promising results. This was in the 1980s, however, and follow-up work apparently has not proven its value. More recently a hot item in health food stores and on the Internet is Pycnogenol, a pine-bark extract that's said to work as an antioxidant, neutralizing free radicals in the body— the latest culprit in a vast range of ills, from Alzheimer's to varicose veins. Pycnogenol is touted for ADD treatment because of its claimed power to cross the blood-brain barrier (which does in fact prevent many oral medications from affecting the brain). The attractive-sounding but vague claim made for it is that it protects brain cells from damage by free radicals.

Dietary theories.   Besides being a component of treatments that feature other items from this list, corrective diets form the centerpiece of several theories of ADD causation and treatment. Eliminating foods that contain refined sugar, food additives and/or dyes, or salicylates (the acidic component that gives many fruits their tang)—or all the above—has led to improvement in many cases reported anecdotally. These ideas originally gained notice in the 1970s and remain current, despite repeated studies showing that dietary interventions work with only a very small percentage of children.

The popular Feingold diet of the 1970s addressed ADD symptoms specifically, claiming that by eliminating refined sugars, food dyes, and salicylates—all common in the typical American diet—ADD behavior could virtually be cured. Feingold's diet was popularized by a best-selling book and became a fad.[20] However, it was backed up by only one uncontrolled study; repeated attempts consistently failed to replicate the findings.[21] By the mid-1980s enthusiasm for this diet had waned, yet the rumor of refined sugar's effects on child behavior refuses to die.

In 1994 Mark Wolraich published a convincing refutation of sugar's alleged effects on children.[22] His study recruited, for a six-week trial, families who felt strongly that their children's ADD behavior was sugar-related. In the double-blind experiment, each family ate three different diets at varying times: one used refined sugar as the sweetener; the second, saccharin; and the last, aspartame. Neither the doctors nor the families knew which they were getting when. The mothers kept detailed daily records of their children's activity and behavior. At the end, neither the parents nor the researchers could determine from the reported behavior which families ate which diet during which weeks; no pattern or consistent effect was found.

This and a similar study debunking the role of sugar in ADD behavior received prominent media attention—yet only a few months later, another scientific journal reported that nearly 80 percent of twelve hundred schoolteachers surveyed in the United States and Canada believed that diet made a difference in problem behavior.[23]

Only a few studies demonstrating any dietary effect on children's behavior have survived the scrutiny of medical journal peer review. One from 1980, authored by James Swanson and Marcel Kinsbourne (highly respected names in the field), showed the effects of giving very large doses of a blend of artificial food dyes to a group of children who had previously responded to Ritalin, and to another group that had had adverse reactions to the drug.[24] After ingesting the dyes, the children who were Ritalin-responsive performed worse on some concentration tests, while the colorings had no effect on the Ritalin nonresponders. The researchers noted no *behavioral* changes in either group of children and did not attempt to extend their conclusions beyond what they found in the laboratory. Swanson today feels that diet may play a small role in the behavior of children under five, but that otherwise its contributions to behavior are not measurable.[25]

Another well-run study by Australian researchers showed some limited effects—signs of irritability, restlessness, and sleep problems—on hyperactive children from the food dye tartrazine.[26] However, most of the children did not meet full criteria for hyperactivity, and the symptoms most affected by the test were not primary for ADD. These two studies are the best of the few that have been published on the effects of food additives or sugar on ADD behavior. Although numerous other studies have failed to confirm these findings, concerns about diet were so widespread in the 1970s that a national three-day meeting was convened by the National Institutes of Health to reach a consensus on the effects of diet on children's behavior. Its conclusions, published in 1982, confirmed the lack of scientific evidence to support the connection.[27]

Still the concerns persist, though these days I hear more from parents about sugar as the culprit than about food colorings and natural salicylates—the offenders of the Feingold diet. One explanation for the belief in the power of sugar (or any other substance) to cause ADD may come from the belief itself. In other words, if a parent *believes* that sugar affects a child's behavior, it may well do so—but the true cause is the parent's expectations and behavior. An ingenious 1994 experiment tested this hypothesis.[28] Daniel W. Hoover and longtime ADD researcher Richard Milich recruited thirty-five pairs of five-to-seven-year-old boys and their mothers, who had reported them to be behaviorally "sugar-sensitive." In one of two groups, the boys were given Kool-Aid that their mothers were told was sweetened with sugar, when in reality the drink contained aspartame (NutraSweet). The other mothers were correctly told that the Kool-Aid was flavored with aspartame; in other words, both groups drank the identical concoction.

The mothers who thought their sons were drinking sugar-sweetened Kool-Aid rated their children as more hyperactive than did the mothers who knew the drink was artificially sweetened. This confirmed the study's main hypothesis: that expectation affects perceived behavior. However, the researchers' blind viewing of videotapes of the mothers and kids produced a big surprise. The children in first group, whose mothers thought they were ingesting sugar, actually were *less active* than those in the other group—possibly because the mothers in the first group acted more critical and controlling, and stayed in closer physical proximity to their children, compared to the other mothers. The children of these moms, who worried and hovered, responded with more controlled behavior. But that's not how their mothers *saw* it—they believed them to be *more* "hyper."

My personal belief is that any diet in moderation will not cause harm to children or significantly affect their behavior. That's been the case with kids I've evaluated and treated, and I have heard from very few families that diet has made a big difference in their child's behavior (though that silence may partly follow from my skepticism). I provide information about various diets to parents who really want to pursue them. However, for any one particular child, I cannot absolutely say that eliminating sugar from the diet or treating an alleged yeast infection will not make a difference.

I share with many parents a discomfort with today's standard medical approach to ADD—especially its emphasis on the use of Ritalin for their children's problems—and understand the attraction of more "natural" approaches. Such theories and treatments seem to offer an escape route from a medical system that many people increasingly find cold, confusing, and inordinately cost-driven. Unfortunately, there is also a cost or downside to pursuing alternative treatments for ADD: the time, energy, and financial expenses they can consume. There is also a possibility (though usually small) of harming the child. But the chief argument I would make is that efforts directed toward alternative treatments may detract from efforts more likely to yield results. It's not easy, for example, to maintain a child on a restricted diet that denies him or her many attractive and tasty foods. The discipline required might be better directed toward an effort that yields more provable results: picking up the toys on the floor, say, or finishing the night's homework.

No one can legitimately claim that they have the right answer for every child with behavior problems. Regarding alternative treatments, I generally offer an opinion to families only if asked, refer them to other sources of information (national CHADD offers sensible recommendations),[29] and leave it to them to decide which avenues to pursue. If they are inclined to purchase products or equipment based on a pitch on the Internet or elsewhere, I might remind them that the profit motive operates in much the same way among small-scale entrepreneurs as among pharmaceutical giants. For the most part, those who explore "natural" alternatives represent a dissenting minority, many of whom return to Ritalin when other methods fail.

Chapter 7

←——————→

MAKING ACCOMMODATIONS:
ADD IN AN AGE OF VICTIMS' RIGHTS
AND MANAGED CARE

Well people are disappearing. . . . If the behavior of doctors and the public continues unabated, eventually every well person will be labeled as sick.
—Clifton K. Meador, M.D.,
"The Last Well Person," *New England Journal of Medicine*

Sensitivity to the needs and concerns of others is the mark of a civil and civilized society. . . . [but] if everyone is a victim, then no one is.
—Charles J. Sykes, *A Nation of Victims*

How else can I get help for my son unless he is labeled with ADD?"
The question was put to me just that starkly at the end of a talk I gave in 1996, shortly after I had begun to speak publicly about my misgivings regarding the ADD-Ritalin epidemic. My questioner said that she appreciated my perspective on ADD, but that getting help for her son took precedence over any larger social issues. She went on to describe how for years she had watched him struggle in school, seen his self-image erode and his behavior turn disrespectful both there and at home. The school had been unresponsive to her requests to have him evaluated, so she finally paid for a private evaluation, to the tune of $800. Armed with a report saying he had ADD (plus some weakness in language comprehension), she pushed for the full educational benefits he was entitled to by law. Her son did receive some accommodations, spending one class period each day in a smaller classroom with extra help. He still struggled but seemed happier, she thought.

"I wish I didn't have to do it that way," she concluded. "I'm not thrilled that he's stuck with a label. But I'm a taxpayer, and the law says he's entitled to services. I *know* that having the diagnosis helped make the school respond and do something for my son. What do you think?"

This mother's question captured in a nutshell the dilemma we are currently facing now that ADD (and other hard-to-define behavioral conditions) have joined physical disabilities as officially designated reasons why people can receive special treatment—in education, employment, and elsewhere.

Very real stresses on children and their families force them to seek help in any way they can. An ADD diagnosis can open doors otherwise closed. CHADD activists have told me that nothing infuriates them more than educational psychologists or psychiatrists who question the basic validity of ADD as a medical condition. They sense an implication that they are somehow to blame for their children's problems, that their parenting was flawed, and that their pain somehow is not entirely justified. I need no convincing that trying to raise a child with severe ADD symptoms can be hellish, frustrating, and tremendously burdensome. I understand why parents want schools to share the load.

Yet the expansion of legal rights for those who qualify as disabled due to ADD or related learning weaknesses has opened several large cans of worms. It has helped create a special-interest group eager to take advantage of the accommodations such rights confer on themselves or their children—assistance that may mean the difference between success and failure in our competitive age. It has created extra stresses on already underfunded and understaffed school systems, and made employers fear that complying with the law may force them out of business. It has tended to polarize Americans, with some favoring such widened rights and benefits, others viewing them as a burdensome form of government interference.

And it has contributed directly to the dramatic rise in Ritalin use. In 1991 ADD for the first time was officially included as a disability under two key federal laws (I'll review the background below). It was also in 1991, the data show, that Ritalin production and use took off in the United States. Jim Swanson is the director of the Child Development Center at the University of California, Irvine, a principal researcher on ADD, and one of the smartest people in the field—politically adroit but unafraid to call things as he sees them. Swanson has observed—and I have independently reached the same conclusion—that the rate of diagnosis and treatment of ADD stepped up markedly once it became a diagnosis that made people eligible for special services.[1] More ADD means more Ritalin, and the move to official disability status provides the most persuasive explanation for the huge increase in Ritalin use over the past decade.

SOMETHING ELSE TO BLAME: THE ENABLING SIDE OF DISABILITIES

Jennifer Conrad was seventeen when she and her family sought help for symptoms they felt were holding her back in school. Except for some conflicts with her parents over schoolwork and boys, Jennifer had made it to her junior year of high school without major academic or social problems. She wasn't crazy about school—she was generally a C student who got occasional B's and a rare D—but she wanted to go away for college. Her psychometric test scores placed her overall performance within the average range of intelligence, but she showed a weakness in math ability (and, not surprisingly, hated the subject). The psychologist who tested her was struck by how long it took Jennifer to complete several subtests and thought it likely that she might be distractible beyond the norm.

Her parents were aware of ADD and wondered if Jennifer might be affected by it. Then they discovered an urgent reason to find out: Her mother heard that Jennifer might get unlimited time to take her Scholastic Aptitude Test (SAT) if she could get a doctor's note saying she had ADD. Soon they arrived at my office for an evaluation. Jennifer and her parents agreed that she performed academic tasks very slowly; she told me she often got distracted—not by external goings-on but by own thoughts. However, when I sat with Jennifer as she worked, I couldn't tell whether it was distractibility, anxiety about getting an answer wrong, or some combination of both that caused her to proceed very slowly and to go over material repeatedly. I certainly didn't want to harm Jennifer's chances for getting into college, yet I doubted if I could support an ADD diagnosis for her. (We'll return to Jennifer shortly.)

As it turned out, a positive diagnosis wouldn't have helped Jennifer get unlimited time for her SAT in any case. The tests were just around the corner, and the Educational Testing Service, which administers the SAT, requires a longer history for a student's disability status. Still, the number of students both requesting and receiving such accommodations has risen sharply in recent years. While it may seem paradoxical that parents would seek to have their child categorized as disabled in order to further his or her education, it is an ever more present fact of American life.

How did it come to pass that federal law requires the ETS and other national testing organizations to adapt to persons with special needs? The civil rights and other social movements of the 1950s through the 1970s spawned another kind of activism: a belief in victim's rights that led various groups to seek remuneration and redress based on their disadvantaged condition. In *A Nation of Victims: The Decay of the American Character,* Charles J. Sykes notes this country's long tradition of sympathy for the downtrodden and compassion for the less fortunate.[2] But he detects a change in the American character and society over the last twenty-five years, one that is brewing "a formula for social gridlock: the irresistible search for someone or something to blame colliding with the unmoving unwillingness to accept responsibility."[3]

A laudable quest for heightened consciousness of the needs and rights of disabled people led to action on many legal and legislative fronts to "level the playing field," so that today there are few situations outside of family and private life in which people with disabilities are not protected. Statutes governing the rights of the disabled, introduced beginning in the 1970s, apply to schools, universities, local and state governments, and businesses large and small. Though originally intended to help those with physical handicaps, these initiatives have been expanded more recently to include mental illness, plus people with learning disabilities or ADD.

Today there are two primary federal laws under which children diagnosed with ADD can receive special help in school. The first of these is Section 504 of the Vocational Rehabilitation Act of 1973, which covers anyone with a physical or mental impairment that limits a "major life activity." Under the current provisions of this law, learning is a major life activity and ADD may cause such an impairment.[4] The other law—and the more powerful one, in part because it confers funding for special services—is the Individuals with Disabilities Education Act (IDEA), passed by Congress in 1990 (PL 94-142). The IDEA mandates that eligible children receive access to special education and/or related services, and that this education be designed to meet each child's unique educational needs through an individualized education program, or IEP.

Section 504 is a civil rights law; it requires only that schools (or any program receiving federal assistance) not discriminate against children with disabilities.[5] The IDEA, on the other hand, sets out specific criteria for eligibility, provides guidelines for creating an IEP, and guarantees parental participation in the process. Section 504 has looser eligibility requirements than the IDEA, and thus potentially covers more children with ADD, especially those with less severe symptoms. Only IDEA-eligible children can qualify for placement in a special-education classroom.

Schools often prefer that a child be served under Section 504 because it allows them more leeway in determining what services may be offered, in administrative procedures, in degree of parental involvement, in economic cost, and, significantly, in disciplinary actions. On the plus side, notes an attorney writing in CHADD's magazine, Section 504 can provide "a faster, more flexible, and less stigmatizing procedure for obtaining some accommodations and services."[6] Nevertheless, most savvy parents prefer to win IDEA eligibility for their child; it offers a wider range of options, access to special-education classrooms and programs that are guaranteed funding, and stricter procedural safeguards.

THE FIGHT TO INCLUDE ADD

While the IDEA was being drafted in 1990, a fierce debate raged behind the scenes over whether to include ADD in the list of disabilities that would qualify people for services. The self-help groups CHADD and ADDA, as well as some professional organizations (notably PGARD, or the Professional Group for Attention and Related Disorders, a network of academic researchers and medical clinicians), lobbied for its inclusion. On the other side, various educational and teacher organizations, including the National Education Association and the National Association of School Psychologists, joined with the NAACP Legal Defense and Educational Fund in trying to keep ADD off the list.

The teacher groups asserted that the special needs of children with ADD were currently being met by services offered to children with learning disabilities. They also claimed that the ADD category was too ambiguous (in this they were prescient) and that the increased number of children it would make eligible for services could overwhelm an educational system already straining to meet the needs of previously identified special-education students.[7] The NAACP for its part expressed concerns that the ADD label might be applied excessively to African-American children and "invite abuse for the black children, especially black males, resulting in the disproportionate referral to special education."[8] Reflecting its critique of standard intelligence tests, the NAACP also pointed out that culturally biased concepts of appropriate attention and activity levels would unfairly suggest that black children, as a group, tended to be neurologically impaired.[9] In its view, social conditions and racism were responsible for poor performances, not brain dysfunction.

Phyllis McClure, who represented the NAACP Legal Defense and Educational Fund for twenty-four years, recalls the persistence and vigor of the parent groups during the IDEA hearings. Their lobbying of her verged on harassment, she told me: "They followed me all the way out to the airport once. They just wouldn't let go."[10] Nevertheless, the groups opposing the inclusion of ADD prevailed, and the IDEA of 1990 passed without mention of it.

What followed, however, was unique in the annals of education legislation.[11] A massive letter-writing and lobbying campaign, mounted primarily by CHADD, generated four thousand letters (to members of Congress and their staffs, key committees, and the Department of Education)—a large number for such an issue. Influential legislators were persuaded to exert pressure on the Department of Education to reconsider ADD's status. In September 1991 the department issued a Policy Clarification Memorandum directing schools immediately to include ADD as a covered disability under both the IDEA (in the category "otherwise health impaired") and Section 504.[12] Children diagnosed with ADD could now (a CHADD handout reminds parents) "qualify for special education and related services *solely* on the basis of their ADD when it significantly impairs educational performance or learning."[13] This policy change was, I believe, the spark that set off the decade-long explosion in Ritalin production and use.

When the IDEA came up for congressional reauthorization in early 1997, the battle lines were drawn much as in 1990–91, with parents and disability groups on one side and school administrators on the other. Meanwhile, the number of children classified as disabled had grown to an eye-opening 10 percent of the total school population, issues of safety and discipline in schools had come under the media spotlight, and a popular backlash against continual broadening of rights for the disabled had begun to set in. While the reauthorization was approved, *The New York Times*, reporting on Congress's actions, noted that "no issue has been more knotty or more illustrative of the conflict between individual rights and group protection."[14]

SPECIAL ACCOMMODATIONS FOR ADD: WHAT SCHOOLS CAN PROVIDE

If a child is having problems with schoolwork or behavior in school that the parents or teacher suspect may be related to ADD, either may request that a child be evaluated by a multidisciplinary team to determine whether special services are needed, and what kind. A screening evaluation must then be provided at no cost to the parents, including under some circumstances the medical component of the evaluation—even if the parents have insurance. Where the school denies the need for evaluation, of course, parents are on their own.

Following the evaluation, students who qualify for special education under the IDEA are supposed to receive an individualized education plan tailored to their needs. An IEP may include teaching a child alternative ways to learn required material (either in a separate classroom or with extra staff in the regular classroom), allowing him or her more time to take tests or complete assignments, and grading that's based partly on effort as well as results. The IEP is reviewed annually and necessary changes made, subject to the parents' approval. It is legally binding on the school.

Some of the same accommodations may be available through Section 504, with variations from district to district. In general, however, the more expensive services—such as a separate special-ed classroom, a learning specialist, and individual classroom aide, or special equipment—are available only through an IEP.

Many adaptations can be made in the general classroom to accommodate ADD and learning-disabled students. The Department of Education's 1991 Policy Clarification Memorandum specified some of those modifications, to which students covered under either Section 504 or the IDEA are entitled. As listed in a CHADD handout, they include:

• tailoring homework assignments

• providing a structured learning environment

• simplifying instructions about assignments

• supplementing verbal instructions with visual instructions

• using behavioral management techniques

- modifying test delivery

- using tape recorders and computer-aided instruction[15]

These can be helpful techniques and suggestions for all children, by the way, not just those with an official diagnosis. Indeed, in defending special accommodations for ADD and learning-disabled students, parents and some teachers and school administrators say that such classroom innovations and adaptations can result in better education for all students. (One teacher had the smart idea of naming an area in the back of her classroom "the office." Just as mommies and daddies went to their offices to work, she explained, her kids could have their own office if they needed less stimulation to get their work done. In another local classroom, a teacher obtained a pre-fabricated study carrel—essentially, a three-sided box—designed for ADD students to decrease distracting stimuli. Ironically, the carrel became a much-coveted item that all the children wanted to use.)

Under both the IDEA and Section 504, schools also must develop a plan to address a child's behavior problems. One school in Ohio was found in violation of Section 504 because it failed to address the situation of a student who, though previously diagnosed with ADD, was repeatedly sent out of the class because of disruptive behavior.[16] Expelling such a student would have been in violation of the law. Court actions have upheld these interpretations, and schools that don't comply may face legal costs and even damages from suits brought by parents.[17]

CHADD goes to some lengths to make sure that parents of ADD children are aware of their rights under the law. Its handout warns that "many children with ADD continue to be denied access to . . . special education and/or related services. Myths and ignorance about ADD abound, *even though scientific research has documented ADD as a neurobiological disease*" [my italics].[18] CHADD advises parents to meet regularly with teachers, take an active role in preparing the IEP, and appeal the decisions of school officials if they disagree. Complaints about a school not complying with IDEA requirements can be filed with the state education agency or the U.S. Department of Education. Parents may also complain to the Department of Education about alleged violations of Section 504. The courts may be used as a last resort, though they usually require parents to pursue all administrative remedies first.

Over the past twenty years I have attended a few hundred IEP meetings for children I have evaluated, to ensure that my recommendations were properly addressed and the child's needs were being met by the school. All but a handful of these meetings with parents and school personnel have proceeded amicably and concluded with agreement on the services to be provided. In cases where I have already made an ADD diagnosis, participating in these meetings is a useful component of the integrated approach to treatment I espouse. Certainly it can strengthen the parents' case to have a physician present, and the fact that a child may already be taking medication helps to reinforce his status as "disabled."

However, as the ADD diagnosis has grown more elastic and has been extended to more adolescents and adults, I have grown uneasy in my role as the "expert" who determines whether ADD constitutes a disability. In Chapter 3 I raised the hypothetical situation where a person demonstrates only five of the nine designated behavior symptoms, when six are required for an ADD diagnosis. What if the five symptoms are all quite severe? Or what if a patient shows eight symptoms, but all are mild? Should either qualify for a disability? In the absence of any definitive biological or psychometric test for ADD, this falls to the judgment of the evaluator. My uneasiness grows stronger when I sense that parents or adult patients want me to rubber-stamp a diagnosis in pursuit of a specific goal. I have declined opportunities to evaluate for this reason.

DISCIPLINARY ACTION: A HOT POTATO

The 1997 bill to reauthorize the IDEA passed by huge margins in both houses: 420 to 3 in the House and 98 to 1 in the Senate. The landslides were hailed as evidence of unanimous support for special treatment of disabled students. However, the media failed to dwell on one telling detail. Because the lobbying was so fierce, leaders of both parties had actively discouraged any attempts to amend the bill. Even so, Senator Slade Gorton (R.-Washington) introduced an amendment that would have made disabled students subject to the same disciplinary policies applied to all others.[19] He succeeded in bringing it to a vote, where it lost by the narrow margin of 51 to 48—highlighting the divisiveness of this particular issue.

Disciplinary policy is one of the key differences between Section 504 and the IDEA. Under Section 504, school officials may remove children from special programs or suspend or expel a child for serious conduct problems, especially if they feel other children or staff are endangered. Under the IDEA, however, parents may request an impartial hearing if the school proposes any disciplinary action, and the child must remain in the then-current educational placement until all administrative and legal proceedings are concluded. A committee that includes the child's parents must determine that the misconduct was *not* related to the disability in order for the school to carry out disciplinary action.

During the 1997 reauthorization school officials did realize some gains on the disciplinary front. Previously they had felt hampered by the IDEA in protecting the general student body and teachers, because of lawsuits resulting from attempts to discipline students with disabilities. (In one well-reported case, four students had been found to be selling drugs at a high-school campus; the only one not expelled had disability status.) The new bill allowed schools to impose a forty-five-day suspension in cases where a child is accused of bringing drugs or a gun to school. Also, court hearings on family-school disagreements were replaced by an administrative procedure, because court costs had been a factor inhibiting schools from taking action against a student. However, advocates for the parents beat back other proposals to equalize disciplinary treatment. This will remain a hot topic for the foreseeable future.

In a case that bears directly on this issue, I was contacted by the frantic mother of sixteen-year-old Laura, who had been accused of selling drugs to two girlfriends on their high school campus. The two friends were found with marijuana and claimed Laura sold it to them; when confronted, Laura admitted her culpability. It wasn't her first problem at school; she had been cutting classes and doing poorly academically. The penalty for selling drugs on campus was automatic expulsion. However, if it could be shown that Laura had a disability that wasn't being addressed by the school, expulsion was not automatic; lesser penalties might be invoked.

Laura had already been diagnosed with ADD by doctors at a well-known Ritalin mill. (I use this pejorative advisedly, because I know the practice in question fairly well.) Even so, Laura's mother needed a second opinion because, based on its own evaluation, the school had refused to accept the diagnosis. She was desperately seeking a confirming verdict so that Laura could continue at her local high school, and I was the means to this end.

Just from talking on the phone with Laura's mother, I knew that this case was complicated. (Practically speaking, there is no such thing as "uncomplicated" ADD by the time one reaches adolescence—see Chapter 12). Laura might meet ADD criteria as well as those for a host of other vaguely defined disorders. Since it was so clear what they wanted from me, and I was relatively sure I could not deliver it, I didn't think it fair to invite Laura and her mother in for even one consultation—they had to travel some distance. I explained that because of my uncertainties about defining ADD as a disability, I thought they would be better served by finding an M.D. more comfortable in this role.

Privately, I felt that the mother's quest was not the best use of her energies toward helping Laura in the long run. Recall that some degree of insensitivity to consequences is part of the ADD profile; this calls for intensive, consistent, long-term work on the parents' part to encourage the child's awareness that her actions do have consequences. Expulsion from school is a harsh punishment for a teenager—therapeutically speaking, the ideal consequences are more immediate and less severe. But it was far from the worst that could happen, and perhaps it was serious enough to get both Laura and her parents to notice their pattern and confront her behavior.

GETTING INTO AND OUT OF THE VICTIM MENTALITY

Laura's case bears comparison with that of Jennifer Conrad, the girl whose mother hoped she could qualify through ADD to take an untimed SAT. In evaluating Jennifer, I was concerned by her apparent passivity in dealing with her problems. Beyond her difficulties with math and test taking, I sensed that she coped with adversity by avoidance, denial, and procrastination. Inevitably she would offer a reason or excuse for her failures, and I feared that an ADD diagnosis would add to her list of "I can't" reasons. Unintentionally, the family dynamics—especially between Jennifer and her mother, Elaine—may have reinforced her sense of helplessness. Elaine, a powerful personality, tended to take over problem situations rather than let Jennifer develop her independence by working them out for herself. At one point Elaine suggested that her daughter write a college admissions essay entitled "ADD and My Life." This may have seemed to Elaine a way for Jennifer to face her problems openly, but encouraging close identification with a "disabling" disorder is not what I would have prescribed for this particular teenager.

I did prescribe a three-month trial course of Ritalin, with equivocal results. Jennifer's failure to improve significantly didn't rule out attention deficit as a factor, just as improvement with Ritalin doesn't prove that ADD exists. The family's response to my other efforts was not encouraging: They canceled or postponed several appointments and generally ignored attempts to talk about the larger issue of Jennifer's passivity. I think their preconceived reason for seeing me—did she have ADD and should she be on medication?—kept other messages from getting through; not finding what they came for, they eventually drifted away. I never learned whether Jennifer took the untimed SAT or how she did in college.

A very different stance toward life was taken by eighteen-year-old Stephanie. Already on her way to a small private college, she and her father (with whom she had lived since age five) came to see me, curious about ADD and medication. Like Jennifer, Stephanie had long struggled academically and taken extra time to finish assignments, though her GPA hovered around the 3.0 range. She worked heroically, according to her father, except for a period during her sophomore year when she became angry with her family and school (her father and stepmother were fighting and eventually divorced); she started breaking curfew and smoking cigarettes, and her grades fell. Stephanie went into counseling at that time, and just before seeing me she had received a thorough psychoeducational evaluation that suggested previously undetected dyslexia and a possible attention deficit.

Stephanie found some emotional relief in learning that her academic difficulties might have sources other than laziness and lack of effort, to which her stepmother had attributed them. On the other hand, she was quite uncomfortable with the idea of asking for special accommodations at college for her attentional and reading problems. She wasn't so much worried about being labeled ADD, but rather ambivalent about getting priority for a single dorm room because of her disability status. She felt that getting this special privilege was somehow "cheating," to use her own word.

I reassured Stephanie that she was entitled by law to have some adjustments made for her education and even in her future employment. I was less concerned about imparting the legalities of her position than about giving her permission to be nice to herself. This young woman had persevered through much adversity and was actually quite tough on herself; I guessed she would continue to work hard and would benefit as well from any accommodations made for her disability. Not that Jennifer didn't have to struggle, too—but her and her family's response to stress seemed diametrically opposed to Stephanie's. Sure, ADD makes it much harder to cope with many aspects of life. But giving up and looking outside for salvation—from parents, spouse, school, or government—is the dangerous dark side of the disability movement for an individual. Even most die-hard ADD advocates would discourage adopting an "I can't" attitude based on an ADD diagnosis.

In the face of my occasional reluctance to diagnose ADD for disability status, many parents would probably respond: "Where's the harm?" If a child can be helped by the classroom and testing accommodations made available, what's the problem with stretching the diagnosis a little? In fact, there can be good reasons why some children (or adults) may not be better off labeled as disabled. The contrasting cases of Laura and Jennifer, on one hand, and Stephanie, on the other, demonstrate some of these. The pattern of rescuing a troubled child can all too easily become entrenched in families under stress, especially when the parents' personalities tend to be controlling.

Such families face a heightened version of one of the most fundamental dilemmas of parenting: finding the right balance between helping and demanding performance, between protecting and setting limits, between giving the child every advantage and encouraging him or her to develop independent resources. Problems arise when rescuing goes on too often or too long, because the stakes get higher as kids get older. At some point parents can no longer protect them from the demands of their environment (school or job) or from conflicts with friends, loved ones, or the law. And sooner or later, most children will reject such protection, interpreting it as controlling—an essentially healthy reaction that can be destructive if too long delayed.

TEACHERS AND SCHOOLS: DISABILITY CUTS BOTH WAYS

What does the growing number of children classified as educationally disabled mean for schools and teachers? As with so much else about education these days, a lot of it comes down to funding. Special services are costly, and while the IDEA provides some federal funding for special education, only a certain amount is available in a given year, to split so many ways. Section 504 carries no funding of its own; services obtained under its provisions must be paid for out of general education funds in most states.

As noted earlier, tax revolt measures and other funding cutbacks in many states have hit schools hard. California, for example, has over the past decade gone from being in the top ten states in per capita funding for education to among the last ten states. Teachers have been asked to do more with less and have been held more strictly accountable than ever in their use of public funds. California public school districts receive funds based on their total student enrollment. Included is an amount based on a calculation that 10 percent of that population is getting special-education services. If fewer students actually qualify for special education, then more money is left for the district's general education fund. But if more than ten percent of the students qualify for special education, then administrators must draw funds from general education to pay for federally mandated services. The result: larger classes, and less money for library books, or athletics, or arts programs.

This has made some school administrators reluctant to devote what they see as a disproportionate amount of money and resources to serving disabled students, claiming that the general student population suffers as a result. Some have resisted, in particular, accepting ADD as a disability, believing that the broad category of learning disabilities (LD) covers most children with significant ADD-type symptoms. Indeed, even some experts believe there is little distinction between ADD and LD, especially when the primary problems are attentional.

Teachers are caught in the middle, compelled to economize but directed to make accommodations for disabled students. In the absence of funds to hire additional staff, purchase equipment, or provide courses in behavior management techniques, existing teaching staffs must stretch themselves to comply with requirements. Teachers in this fix have a dual perspective on ADD as a disability: on one hand, they may be reluctant to see yet more children qualify for special services. On the other hand, once a child is diagnosed with ADD, he or she is likely to start taking Ritalin, which can make the child easier for teachers to manage. Alternatively, shifting an ADD-diagnosed child into special education can relieve some of the teaching and disciplinary headaches caused by overcrowding in regular classrooms.

Despite federal mandates, programs for disabled students vary considerably from district to district. Some rely chiefly on segregating a limited number of children into special education classes. Others, in addition to modifying lesson plans and classroom environments, are using peer counseling, classroom aides, and extensive parental assistance in the classroom and at home to help ADD students along. CHADD and other parents groups see it as chief among their missions to educate the educators and to push for ever-increased commitments. CHADD official Lynne Castellucci, the parent of two ADD children, works closely with California's Department of Education to disseminate advice about teaching and treating ADD students; interestingly, she feels that "overwhelmed teachers" are sometimes too quick to recommend stimulants for children they believe may have ADD.[20]

As usual, we come back to Ritalin. It's not hard to see why, in the present circumstances, it's so often seen as a solution, and why doctors who raise questions about Ritalin use are not always welcomed by teachers and school administrators. A personal acquaintance is assistant principal in an upscale suburban school district, where the average classroom has a student-teacher ratio of thirty-two to one. Upon learning that I was writing this book, she exclaimed to a colleague, "Oh, great! He's going to write a book saying bad things about Ritalin, which will make our jobs that much harder." She sincerely believed that Ritalin was helping many children in her elementary school. I'm well aware of the pressures she and her teachers were feeling, and it's quite true that Ritalin can help many students (and their teachers) cope with larger class sizes. So, too, can the classroom and curriculum modifications dictated by the IDEA and Section 504 for learning-disabled kids—only these involve vastly more work for teachers, and more money.

This anger that many teachers are feeling these days is understandable. They are asked to share responsibility for the performance and behavior of children from all kinds of backgrounds, with all kinds of problems, and to make adaptations that they feel are difficult or impossible "for the sake of the child." Like the family in which both parents must work to make ends meet, teachers and school systems under pressure find that giving Ritalin to the symptomatic child can help ease the strain. One cannot medicate a school system, however, and it is the child who gets the drug.

How the Snake Eats Its Tail:
The Dilemma of Too Many Disabled

To those who ask what's the harm in offering a diagnosis to gain special services for a child, I would also answer that there's a social price to be paid: a phenomenon I call "the snake eating its tail." There are plenty of specific examples; the general principle dictates that granting disability status more and more freely cannot but harm the nondisabled majority of kids, and eventually society at large, in the long run.

This phenomenon reached crisis proportions and made headlines in New York City in 1994.[21] There the budget for special-education students—13 percent of the total student population—accounted for 25 percent of the total funds available for education. While spending on students system-wide was fairly high in New York compared with other states, the $18,700 spent on each special-education student left only $3,500 to $5,000 remaining per child in the regular classroom. This amount put the regular classroom student on a par with those from the poorest states in the country.[22] (The alert reader will note that the dollar amounts and percentages do not tally. The figures reflect different political interests, but no one disagrees about the trend.)

Nationally, public school spending rose 28 percent from 1991 to 1996, but because most of the increases went to special education, the amount per student grew only by 0.7 percent.[23] Less money for the regular classroom translates into larger classes, higher student-teacher ratios, and fewer educational supports (teacher's aides, computers, materials, and so on). These are the very conditions that push borderline symptomatic ADD kids and learning-disabled kids into frank failure. This phenomenon is occurring not just in New York or California but across the country, as more and more families try to help their children succeed by obtaining special services. With less funds per child available for general education, more children in the regular class become problems. The system for helping children with disabilities becomes overwhelmed as more children are referred and more funds are drained from general education. And around it goes. No one can get extra help if everyone becomes a special-education student. The rush to seek special help is turning into an educational pyramid scheme. If you can get in at the beginning, before the system gets overburdened, you have a good chance of getting some help. But if you are at the bottom of the pyramid, there may be nothing left except empty promises.

As the criteria for ADD broaden and many more individuals attempt to qualify for special services, those with the most severe and persistent attentional problems may not get the help they need. The condition already has become trivialized by the growing numbers of cases being diagnosed. Treatments (other than Ritalin) are diluted as funds and services are more thinly distributed to a larger and larger group.

There is increasing skepticism on many fronts about the educational disabilities movement. The parents of children in regular classrooms are complaining that special education is draining too much money from their children's education. In New York, only one in twenty children who go into a special-education class is ever fully returned to the regular classroom. Government officials are recognizing that the large amounts of money being spent aren't necessarily leading to improved outcomes.[24] At the Dalton

School, an elite New York private school, a special-education fund created for the evaluation and treatment of learning problems led to so much over-diagnosis and treatment (which pushed up fees paid by parents) that the program was abandoned.[25]

REASONABLE ACCOMMODATIONS?

In higher education, the ADD or learning-disability status is no longer accepted as readily as it once was, due to perceived abuse of the diagnoses and the increased costs of providing for the special needs of the learning-disabled. In the past many schools simply accepted a letter confirming the diagnosis from a "qualified" professional. The ADD student could then be eligible for benefits such as a private dormitory room and unlimited time for taking tests. Now the University of California, Berkeley, and other schools require the professional to document the evaluation process by detailing which of ten methods and psychometric tests were employed to reach the diagnosis of ADD. The university's own disability psychologists may do their own evaluation in real-life settings (for example, studying for an exam or taking a test) to determine specifically how the disability interferes with the student's performance.[26]

Students who have won accommodations under the disability laws have strenuously resisted attempts to roll them back, as a recent court case involving Boston University illustrates. In the late 1980s and early 1990s Boston University was in the forefront of universities actively adapting to the needs of learning-disabled students, and even courting them. It created an Office of Learning Disability Support Services that became nationally known. Then in December 1995 the school suddenly announced new, more stringent eligibility criteria for special-education services, including full-scale retesting of students with LD and ADD every three years.[27] As a result, many students who had chosen Boston University because of its reputation for accommodation had to be reevaluated in order to continue their status. In justifying the revised policies, university officials—led by President Jon Westling, who had formerly run the Support Services office—questioned the validity of some of the qualifying diagnoses and cited the university's right to set academic standards.

In 1996, 10 of these students (on behalf of the other 440) filed a discrimination suit against the university in federal court, charging violations of Section 504 as well as the Americans with Disabilities Act (ADA).[28] For a time CHADD and several other disability groups joined the suit as organizational plaintiffs. According to the evidence presented in the case, President Westling had said that students with learning disabilities were often unmotivated or disingenuous and that they undercut academic standards. He had earlier described, in arguing for stricter policies, a student whom he called "Somnolent Samantha" but in testimony acknowledged that he had invented her. Another Boston University official was quoted as saying, "Some of the things that pass for learning disabilities used to be called stupidity."

In August 1997 a federal district judge found, in part, for both sides. The court ruled that the university had violated the civil rights of six students in the manner in which it implemented its change of procedures, and awarded them in total $30,000. The court also ruled, however, that the university's foreign language and mathematics requirements could be retained for all of its students.

In other recent cases, the courts have upheld an institution's right to set criteria for access to mandated accommodations.[29] In one instance, three medical students sought an injunction to compel the National Board of Medical Examiners to grant them additional test time and a private room for their medical licensing test. All three students claimed they had ADD, and two also said they had reading or writing disabilities. Here the court found for the board, based on their finding that these students were not "substantially limited"—they'd had a prior history of adequate achievement without accommodations—and therefore not disabled under the ADA.

Testing—whether for college or graduate school admission, or professional licensing—is a key area of concern over disabilities. When I was looking into Jennifer Conrad's situation, I contacted the Educational Testing Service (ETS) in Princeton, New Jersey, the private company responsible for developing and grading the SAT, and spoke with June Zumoff, coordinator of testing of students with disabilities. It was she who told me that Jennifer would have been unlikely to qualify for the unlimited-time privilege. ETS screens such requests fairly closely, especially claims for disability allowances where the evaluation and diagnosis are made just weeks or months before the exams. They prefer to see several years of disability status. They also seek confirmation that the student's school recognizes the disability and has already made the legally required adaptations. A certified diagnosis from an appropriate professional is required, but they do not insist on further documentation if the school acknowledges the disability.

All in all, Zumoff feels there has been little abuse of the disability exceptions for the SAT. She notes that the number of teenagers gaining the unlimited-time allowance doubled in the five years between 1991 and 1996, from seventeen thousand to about thirty-five thousand, yet remains a small fraction of the two million who take the test annually. While the disability status includes more severe physical and visual handicaps, 87 percent of the exceptions made are for learning disabilities, including ADD.

Zumoff questions whether, ultimately, unlimited time is such a great deal for the ADD student. The test score is flagged, and colleges know that it cannot be directly compared to the scores of those who had to complete the test with a time limit. Nevertheless, unlimited time for the SAT is featured as one of the main entitlements for the ADD adolescent in materials prepared by CHADD.[30] (Based on published speculation, I recently checked back with Zumoff to see if ETS planned to do away with flagging of unlimited-time test scores, but she denied that this was being considered.)

Not all observers share Zumoff's benign view. The statistics alone are noteworthy: Besides the four-year doubling in the number of kids taking untimed SATs, graduate-level exams have shown similar rises.[31] In the 1996–97 school year, 160 students were specially accommodated in taking the Law School Admission Test (LSAT), sixteen times the number five years earlier. And in 1995 there were 645 nonstandard Medical College Admission Tests (MCAT), a fivefold increase over the preceding five years. Seven out of ten of these exceptions were made for those with learning disabilities or ADD.

But the consequences are more important than the numbers. Even though the test scores are marked "nonstandard administration," the specific reason (whether untimed, or given in Braille, large print, or so on) is not provided. If school admissions offices request such specifics or challenge the test results, they may risk being sued or losing federal funding. Yale and Harvard say that they treat nonstandard test results like any other, citing their legal obligation "to make reasonable accommodations." To date, the performance of students admitted to colleges and graduate schools after nonstandard testing has not been tracked extensively, though a study by the Law School Admissions Council found that all testing-accommodated students did worse than predicted by their LSAT scores during their first year (the only year for which results existed at the time).

We've seen the beginnings of a backlash against special entitlements for those who are not obviously disabled. There's nothing really wrong with them, goes the simplistic argument—it's just a matter of proper effort or discipline. The media's tendency to focus on disciplinary cases in reporting on educational disability issues and the tight congressional vote on a discipline-related amendment to the IDEA are also symptomatic of some negative reaction. At least in education, however, the pendulum has yet to settle. Americans have agreed, through acts of Congress, to try to give young people with varying degrees of disability the best possible chance at success, and clearly it will take more time to sort out how the ultimate effects of these laws on the rest of society will be absorbed and accepted.

ADD and Other Emotional Disabilities in the Workplace

A 1996 article in *Forbes* magazine harshly criticized the use of ADD as an educational disability and raised the scenario of an emergency-room physician who had received unlimited time to take his MCAT.[32] Would such a doctor get extra time in real life? the article asked. This scenario seems unlikely, but many Americans today do hold jobs in the regular workforce despite various kinds of mental and learning-related disabilities, and their rights are protected under the Americans with Disabilities Act of 1990. Currently all private employers with fifteen or more workers, and all state and municipal governments, are prohibited from discriminating against a broadly defined disabled population estimated at forty-three million Americans.[33]

Originally the ADA was invoked in employment situations mainly to protect workers with physical disabilities. But as the definition of disability expanded to encompass psychiatric and emotional conditions, a clear need arose for better guidelines in this area. Neither employees nor employers had a firm sense of what kinds of conditions made a worker eligible for accommodations under the law, or what those accommodations should be. This confusion prompted the federal Equal Employment Opportunity Commission (EEOC) to issue a compliance guide for employers. Appearing in early 1997, the guidelines received front-page treatment around the country.[34] It was news to many people that of all complaints over alleged job discrimination filed with the EEOC, nearly 13 percent concerned psychiatric impairments. Only complaints about mistreatment of back problems were more frequent.

The key concept set forth by the EEOC guidelines was that traits normally considered undesirable in employees—chronic lateness, poor judgment, or hostility to coworkers, for example—"may be linked to mental impairments." If the impairment is significant enough to meet criteria for a mental disorder, and so long as it does not substantially interfere with job performance, accommodations must be made. Several examples were provided; one cited a warehouse worker who loads boxes and has little contact with employees. His company's handbook states that employees should look neat at all times and behave courteously to each other. This worker often appears disheveled and is sometimes abrupt or rude with fellow employees. But he loads his boxes efficiently, so according to the EEOC, his company would be in violation of the ADA in taking disciplinary action against this worker if his conduct was caused by a mental impairment.

The new guidelines also stipulated that employers may not ask a prospective employee if he or she has a mental disorder; and if accommodations are made, other employees may not be told the reason, but are simply told that the company is acting for legitimate business reasons or in compliance with federal law. Further, any records involving a mental disorder must be kept separate from the employee's regular medical file.

The guidelines met with a wide range of reactions.[35] The mental health community of patients and doctors was pleased in general, and big corporations found that the guidelines were for the most part helpful. Small-business owners and their associations were much more leery. They voiced concerns about the lack of staff or resources to verify claims and make required accommodations. A common objection to the guidelines concerns the difficulty of drawing the line between ordinary personality traits and mental illness.[36]

While ADD is not among the psychiatric disorders specifically listed by the EEOC, people diagnosed with ADD may meet the guidelines if they can show that their symptoms significantly impair their ability to perform "major life activities" such as learning, concentrating, and interacting with others. If so, they can request accommodations such as:

- time off for treatment or recovery related to a disability

- modified work schedules

- physical changes to the workplace or equipment, such as workspace dividers, devices that address distracting background noise, and procedures to assist with organization, such as color-coding files

• modifying workplace policies; for example, permitting someone to take notes in situations where that is normally discouraged

• adjusting supervisory methods for maximum effectiveness; for example, increasing communication with supervisors, or assigning someone a "job coach"

CHADD regularly publishes news about workplace guidelines and test cases, and literature that advises members of their legal rights.

While some employers are supportive of these moves to integrate disabled workers of all kinds into mainstream jobs, many worry they will find themselves caught between the law and an employee whose performance they simply consider unsatisfactory. Why should they make efforts to accommodate a worker who is frequently late, excessively disorganized, and highly inclined to procrastination? (These patterns often are associated with ADD.) What are the potential economic consequences of making requested accommodations? And what are the possible legal consequences if they fail to comply with the guidelines? These concerns may blind employers to the very real talents and contributions of an employee who seeks to exercise rights based on a disability.

Some employees who feel they are being discriminated against because of their ADD are testing the strength of their protection under the ADA, or at least are thinking about doing so. One woman whose case was reported in the *Wall Street Journal* could not convince her company of six thousand employees to restructure her job to accommodate her difficulties with concentration and handling interruptions.[37] She was told there were no other positions for which she was qualified, and she was given the choice to stay at her current position, subject to the same standards as the other employees, or to quit and receive three weeks' pay. She chose to leave but was consulting an attorney to determine whether legal action was warranted.

Not long ago I was contacted by a fifty-five-year-old woman named Sandra, who had worked in the box office of a performing arts company for fifteen years. She'd been told that her employer was planning to fire her for unsatisfactory job performance, citing frequent mistakes and her denial of them. Sandra acknowledged that she was a nervous person but was naturally upset over the prospect of losing a job that was her sole source of income. She had done some reading about ADD and felt that she had it, but after talking with her by phone, I chose not to get involved with her case. I take on adult ADD cases carefully. Most have evolved from relationships

I've formed with people while treating their children. I was also uneasy with the prospect of addressing the full spectrum of psychiatric disorders it seemed that Sandra might display. Further, given the ambiguities of the ADD diagnosis and the potential for a dispute based on a disability claim, I felt that her case would be stronger with the imprimatur of a university-based psychiatrist. So I referred her to the one psychiatrist at the University of California, San Francisco, who works with ADD adults; as of this writing I haven't learned the outcome.

While disability laws cover a wide range of employment situations, there are a few cases in which exclusions can apply to people being treated for ADD. Currently, for example, the ADD diagnosis does not disqualify a person for military service, but the use of medication does. Similar rules apply to airline pilots in the civilian sector. I am not aware of any cases where ADD patients taking Ritalin have tried to challenge these policies, and this doesn't seem likely to happen in the near future.

I tend toward the view that while adhering to the new disability rules may be cumbersome for employers, and some employees will try to take unfair advantage of them, serious abuses are likely to be few. But problems are bound to arise over the difficulty of distinguishing between disabling conditions and quirks of the human condition—especially in the case of ADD, where the spectrum of severity is so wide. I also find it interesting that proponents of parity for mental disorders don't object to the EEOC rules that specify confidentiality procedures and prohibit questions about mental illness. If parity with medical illness is truly the goal, this seems counterproductive, in that it perpetuates the mystery and stigma associated with mental illness. Such precautions may be seen as necessary to preclude unofficial discrimination; however, I think they carry the risk of encouraging further backlash by a tolerant but strained society against yet another group of victims.

It Pays to Medicate: Managed Care in a Nation of Victims

Over the past decade, managed-care companies have become the primary vehicle for delivering health care in this country, and this trend has intersected with the rise of disability rights in ways that should concern doctors, patients, and all of society. The bureaucratic nature of managed care has reinforced the dominant biological view of mental illness. The medical model seems well suited to the managed-care environment; it suggests discrete entities that can be targeted, billed, and cost-controlled.[38] Procedure codes lend themselves to quality control and utilization review. Biological psychiatry proposes a pharmacological solution for nearly every condition, and such drugs are less costly than psychotherapy or special education. Leon Eisenberg, a nationally respected professor of social medicine at the Harvard Medical School, has warned about new drugs for children, "Managed care and psychotropic drugs are a Satanic mix."[39]

In practical terms, categorizing ADD and other behavioral problems as neurological disorders has been a useful way to maximize reimbursement within health maintenance organizations (HMOs) and managed-care plans that provide less-than-equal coverage for treatment of "purely psychiatric" conditions. Parity for the treatment of mental illness has been the goal of recent federal legislation on health insurance, but it is not yet a reality.[40] Pressure from business groups created several loopholes, and it may turn out that parity simply will lead to companies' reducing or eliminating mental health benefits entirely.[41] This has been my experience locally. As more families have sought evaluations and treatment for ADD, local physician groups that contract with the major national HMOs elected first to decrease benefits and then entirely eliminate ADD as a covered diagnosis— another example of the snake eating its tail.

ADD as a disability may also be contributing to the crisis in disability insurance. Premiums for disability insurance have been driven sky-high—if coverage can be obtained at all—by the increased claims for "soft" medical conditions such as carpal tunnel syndrome, chronic fatigue, back pain, and psychiatric problems including ADD.[42] Insurance companies are offering reduced benefits in order to stay in the business.

As a doctor, I'm equally concerned about how managed care affects the individual families I treat and the kind of care they can receive. There's no doubt it has intensified pressure on physicians to prescribe a drug rather than spend time with a patient or his family. Even before managed care, insurance reimbursement schedules paid physicians more for "cutting" or "zapping" than for talking with the patient, otherwise known as "cognitive time." Especially for primary-care doctors—pediatricians, internists, or family practitioners—whose overheads routinely run above 60 percent of their gross income, the economic incentives to ascertain and treat problems quickly are immense.[43] In health coverage today, the overriding principle is value for money, and for the mental health community, this means an overwhelming emphasis on the use of medication in preference to other treatment.

The story of one young family is fairly typical. When his parents brought seven-year-old Todd Foster to see me, they acknowledged they were in conflict over how to deal with their son, who wouldn't listen to their instructions. After meeting them twice, I found Todd a bit impulsive and quite intense and determined when he didn't get his way or was frustrated. Still, I thought his family might manage without Todd's taking Ritalin if they could work out their parenting differences and practice their approach with their son. This would involve further "talk therapy," but they could not afford to pay for more sessions with me. Unfortunately, their HMO permitted doctor visits for mental health problems only if medication was being considered or offered to the child. Though few other providers in their health plan could offer the range of treatment and experience I had with ADD-type children and their families, the Fosters would have to turn elsewhere for help unless I prescribed medication.

The trend in coverage is to provide for less and less access to specialists. ADD specialists—child psychiatrists and behavioral-developmental pediatricians—have seen payment for services slashed and restrictions placed on patients' access. Most managed-care plans require that a patient be referred by a primary-care doctor. Many insist that any ongoing care be reviewed and approved by a nurse, or sometimes a clerk. The primary-care doctor is given a preset amount of money (called capitation) to handle all of a patient's problems. Primary-care doctors already were under economic pressure to treat quickly; under capitation, they suffer direct economic loss if they refer a patient to a specialist. Under many plans, the specialist—myself, for instance—is allowed only one full visit of about fifty minutes and two twenty-minute follow-up appointments to monitor the results of medication. If medication is not prescribed, the patient is returned to the primary-care physician.

Under such circumstances, the attraction of a quick-fix solution is powerful. The failure of Ritalin as a sole treatment in long-term studies of ADD doesn't diminish its rapid and dramatic effects in changing a child's short-term behavior. Logic suggests that the rate of medication with Ritalin is higher among families with managed-care plans, compared with those using other forms of payment. Surveys focusing on the use of psychotropic drugs in managed care certainly confirm this tendency.[44]

One of managed care's selling points is that it can offer care equal in quality to traditional fee-for-service systems. But there has been little agreement on how to determine the quality of care.[45] Regarding ADD, for instance, there is an ongoing debate in the professional community as to what constitutes a basic or complete evaluation. While no studies have documented the advantages of spending more time and resources beyond a thirty-minute interview with a parent and brief examination of the child, my experience indicates that the briefer the evaluation, the more likely it is that medication will be the only treatment offered.

It is with some chagrin, even anger, that I look at my own schedule of patients and note how few of them I will see for more than five or six visits. As recently as three years ago, I could develop longer relationships with children and families. Some I would see weekly for two or three months, until they had established more productive patterns of interaction, then less frequently for several more months—rarely more than twenty sessions a year. After the first year, the family might continue to check in two or three times a year, or if a relapse or crisis occurred.

Today, I seldom develop this kind of relationship with a family, and there's a painful irony in my role. Because I am an M.D. and can prescribe medication, some people turn to me only in situations where medication is being considered for a child. Once a patient is stabilized on medication, I may see them once every six months. If they need counseling, they may be out of luck, or they may get six to eight sessions with a non-M.D. therapist. At least I've managed to insist on a minimum four-session evaluation process; some companies want me to perform an evaluation in a single one-hour visit. However, those I work for have agreed to my standards—I'm not sure why, but guess it's because they find me cost-effective despite the higher start-up cost.

I miss the opportunity to know many children and their families better. And I believe they lose out by forgoing the holistic skills of a physician well versed in addressing the whole of a child's biology, emotions, and environment. This situation saddens me.

It has also occurred to me that I could be busier (and make more money) if I were more aggressive about prescribing medication. Consultations on medication often end with my recommending that the family or school try a different approach and give it time to work before resorting to medication; with a few exceptions, this approach is appreciated by parents. And not surprisingly, it often succeeds in improving the problem enough that medication is not prescribed, at least for a time. That's one less patient for me to follow up and a loss of income. Thus, for me, it pays to medicate. I'm uncomfortable with the thought that money could influence my decision to prescribe psychotropic medication for a child but realistic enough to believe that in borderline situations it could.

ALL ROADS LEAD TO RITALIN

The managed-care industry's efforts to reduce or eliminate benefits for ADD reflect a society-wide unwillingness to pay for what has become a public health issue: the underperformance of children. The schools aren't properly funded and say it's a medical problem. The medical industry and insurance companies contend it's an educational or psychiatric matter. Few parents have the funds to pay for additional tutoring, private school, or the comprehensive testing or follow-up required for treating a complex neurobehavioral problem. Ritalin is an economical solution to this dilemma, and one that enables us to ignore its social basis. But in relying on it so heavily, we fail to pursue opportunities for prevention and long-term cures.

At least part of society's current reluctance to support nonmedical treatment for ADD or special services in the schools and workplace follows from the rush toward victimhood. Americans in general perceive that there's something wrong with an I'll-get-mine-however-I-can attitude, and we get especially annoyed when it seems to be promoted by federal policy. Yet when such chances are offered to us, we're likely to seize them. The seesaw struggle between our impulses to help ourselves versus helping each other seems to be in an especially volatile phase. We should keep a few things in mind: that one's take on such issues has everything to do with one's perspective and position; that for every case of abuse reported in the media there are thousands of children who probably get a better shot at education through disability accommodations; and that the best-intended helping policies sometimes go too far, especially when political pressure is a factor.

Aiding those with special needs can usefully challenge us and broaden our perspective; it should be part of the social contract. Yet the continuing clamor for special services seems certain to continue straining society's resources, thus deepening the division between those seeking extra help for their or their children's ADD, and the rest of us. Even more than other mental disorders, ADD's diagnostic ambiguity creates problems in deciding who truly qualifies as disabled, and makes it a special target of those who criticize disability policies.

Chapter 8

←——————→

THE POLITICALLY CORRECT PARENTING TRAP:
HOW COPING WITH DIFFICULT KIDS GETS HARDER

A lot of my friends feel insecure in their role as parents, and they don't let the child know, "I am the boss, you are the child." They want to be friends with them. I think they don't want to relive their parents' [style of parenting], when it was too structured and disciplined. And they have guilt for leaving the kid in day care all day and running off to work. So it's "We can't tell them no."

—A Denver mother, quoted in *Kids These Days: What Americans Really Think About the Next Generation*

I'm always intrigued that parents who fail to exert even a modicum of control over their children at ages 1 through 4 seem surprised when teachers tell them that their child is "out of control" at age 5.

—Daniel L. Zeidner, M.D., *Pediatrics*

Emory Hoffman's mother called me a few weeks after his kindergarten teacher had called her, complaining that he was disrupting the class on a regular basis and needing too much of her time. It wasn't the first complaint about Emory from a teacher. In preschool, Emory's behavior during group time and with other children had been right on the edge of acceptability. His parents, Julie and Harold, had more than once considered getting some help for their son but always hoped he might "outgrow it." Now that he was five and in "real" school, his behavior seemed to be getting worse, if anything. The teacher's concern prompted Julie to consult their family doctor, who referred them to me.

In my first meeting with Emory's parents, I learned that Emory had been a challenge almost from day one. He had colic, that ill-defined malaise of early babyhood. "He cried for hours on end," Julie recalled with a shudder, "and it seemed like nothing I did could calm him." Repeated trips to the doctor failed to uncover any serious medical problem. Ultimately the pediatrician resorted to giving Emory a weakly sedating antihistamine so Julie could get some relief; even this barely worked. The experience seemed to have left a permanent impression on both parents. Julie admitted, "I still dread hearing him cry."

After babyhood, Emory grew up generally healthy and vigorous, if perhaps too active and intense. Since he was their first child, it was hard for his parents to know whether Emory's development and behavior were "normal." His developmental milestones (when he first walked, talked, played with certain toys), seemed within average range, but the behavior patterns they described sounded worrisome. "When he got his own way, he was this funny, delightful kid," recalled Harold. "But he was incredibly stubborn. If we said no to him, he'd get real angry—clench his fists, stamp his feet, throw himself to the ground, and sometimes hit us." While I tend to use (in preference to the word *stubborn*) more neutral descriptions of personality—such as *determination*, *persistence*, or *emotional intensity*—it was clear they were describing more than the usual toddler tempestuousness.

When I asked about Emory's attention span, again the parents had trouble deciding whether it was too short or normal. "Sometimes he can play with his cars for a half hour," said Julie, "but it's hard to tell because there's usually so many toys dumped on the floor. I know we should have him put some of them away, but it doesn't seem worth battling over." He didn't seem especially hyperactive, they said, but Harold added, "Our main worry is that he's been getting more defiant. We used to be able to get him to apologize, but lately he won't—he just stays so angry." Both parents acknowledged that dealing with Emory had caused them to think long and hard about having a second child. But nine months earlier, Julie had given birth to Alison, who seemed like a different species of baby. "Of course, she's a girl, and also she didn't have colic—I was ready to join a convent if she did," noted Julie. "But her level of intensity is totally unlike his."

Our own experience of growing up is our basic education in parenting, so as usual I made a point of asking about Julie's and Harold's upbringings.

Harold's clearest memories were of his father taking a belt to him on occasion—"I was rebellious but nothing on Emory's level, at least according to my mother"—and father and son clashed frequently. "We have a much better relationship now," Harold reported, "but I've never told him how I felt about his hitting me—how angry it made me. I vowed that I'd never get physical with my own kids." Thus it bothered Harold tremendously when, in rare circumstances and when all else failed, he spanked Emory. (In any case, this only temporarily quieted him.)

Julie's memories were quite different. The second of four girls, she could barely recall getting into trouble or being disciplined. "It makes me wonder how my parents *did* discipline us. It seemed like we all just listened. Partly because my dad was such an authority figure—even a nasty look from him was enough to wither any of us girls." Both of Julie's parents worked, and she remembers wishing her mother had been more available to her. "There was love in our family but not a whole lot of physical affection." Julie was determined to be much closer to her children, and on one level she felt she had been successful. Emory would come to her with his boo-boos and hurt feelings. "But it seems like no matter how much time I give him, he always demands more." Not only had Julie had given up her job to be at home with the kids, but Harold apparently made real efforts to spend time with them and to give his wife some time off.

Harold and Julie had gotten contradictory advice from relatives: they needed to be stricter, or to devote more time to their son. A year earlier they had consulted with the family doctor, who thought Emory might be somewhat hyperactive but didn't want to medicate a four-year-old. Julie had accumulated a library of parenting books, some of which she found interesting (including ones about ADD) and had urged Harold to read as well. But at critical moments with Emory the books failed her. "We feel like we've tried everything and nothing is working," Julie lamented—a nearly universal plaint from parents I see. They could go on coping with him at home, they felt, but were at a loss to address his problems in school. Like many parents, they had come to wonder if his angry, defiant behavior could be caused by ADD.

Then it was time to meet Emory with his parents and sister. A really cute little guy with bright blue eyes, apple cheeks, and neatly combed brown hair, Emory caught my eye for the briefest instant as I opened the door, then pulled away from his mom and made a beeline across the room. He'd caught sight of the plastic bins filled with toys and immediately began trying to remove their lids. Julie repeatedly and ineffectually called him: "Emory, please come back to the couch," where she and Harold were sitting, with Alison at her mother's feet. Emory ignored Julie and managed to unlatch one of the bins, dumping a bunch of Lego blocks onto the floor with a loud crash. "You *need* to come back to the couch now, Emory." Julie's voice took on an edge. "I mean *now*, Emory!" The boy didn't even glance up; his obliviousness seemed almost intentional. When I asked Harold, silent so far, if he would try to get Emory to come to the couch, he called in a rather flat tone, "Emory, please come over here now." Emory at least looked at him, but went on playing. At that point Harold resignedly rose and picked up Emory, who squirmed and struggled in his father's arms all the way to the couch. I said hello to Emory and introduced myself, but he continued to squirm, and so after thirty seconds I told Harold he could let him go. Emory popped out and went back to the toys. Alison remained quiet throughout this minidrama, seemingly content to explore her mother's shoes. I felt that I had seen a lot in just five minutes.

Toward the end of the session, when it was time to clean up, Emory's parents politely tried to get him to help. They promised a trip to Yogurt Barn; they threatened not to let him watch Power Rangers on TV. Harold actually took his hand and moved it toward the toy bin, but Emory pulled away, yelling, "No!" and continued to play. Julie and Harold took turns putting away the toys. When it was time to leave, Emory again gave me a brief glance (was he uncomfortable with transitions?) and dashed out of the room with his father in pursuit, leaving Julie and me to make the next appointment. After forty minutes with them, I felt tired and could well understand how all of them (except maybe Alison) might be worn down by this kind of behavior. They needed some help.

What's Wrong with the Kids?

The kind of interactions the Hoffmans displayed are not at all unusual in my daily practice. Emory's behavior may be more extreme than most, but the fact of a child not listening to his parents is an everyday occurrence in my office. Julie and Harold clearly love their children and have arranged their lives so as to spend as much time as possible with them. They don't seem to have significant marital problems that would affect their parenting. In my practice, I don't see a lot of physical or sexual abuse; the children I see are not acting out as a result of trauma. So what could account for a plague of ineffectual parents and acting-out kids?

I know I am not alone in my experience. Colleagues regularly lament the monotonous necessity of reciting to parents the mantra about setting proper limits for their children. Conservatives and the Christian right are not the only people who rail about the failures of parenting in our society and the lack of moral values in America's children. Generally the issues raised are not drug use and violence, but far more mundane matters such as picking up toys, doing homework, using bad language, or simply acting "unfriendly." National newspapers run headlines like "When Parents Decide to Take Charge Again," and bookstore self-help sections are filled with guides to restoring discipline at home or getting children to sleep through the night.[1]

This trend was resoundingly confirmed by a 1997 report from the opinion-research organization Public Agenda titled *Kids These Days: What Americans Really Think About the Next Generation.*[2] This survey of two thousand Americans reveals a high level of dissatisfaction with, even antipathy toward, our young people. Much of this is directed at teenagers—not surprising, since a generation gap has existed at least since its mention by writers in ancient Rome. The surprise is that so many people now feel negatively about preteen and younger children, finding them poorly behaved, obsessed with material things, and lacking in moral development. The respondents viewed children's behavior as a crisis that threatens our nation's future, and while they acknowledged mitigating circumstances such as economic pressures, outside threats, and disorderly schools, they tended to place primary responsibility for this crisis on the failure of parents to instill values and exercise proper discipline. What's more, parents themselves seemed to agree. "Many parents," says the report, "seem tentative and uncertain in matters of discipline and authority, and many believe that society is increasingly likely to question their judgment in this area."[3]

The ADD-Ritalin epidemic is a further sign of America's perception that things are "out of control" with our kids. Some theorists would (and do) argue that the decade-long surge in ADD diagnoses is just a process of catching up with the true rate of the disorder's occurrence—that a large group of kids who act out can't help themselves because of the disorder. But even if this is partly true, the phenomenon is much broader than any clinical diagnosis can account for, especially in the kind of upper-middle-class communities represented by my clinical practice. The scale on which Ritalin is currently being prescribed, and being demanded by parents, must reflect society-wide unhappiness with children's behavior and performance, and a grasping at any apparently effective, safe, convenient solution.

Certainly some misbehavior reflects the stresses on children, parents, and teachers that I've already discussed. But I've also become convinced that a good deal of it stems from the currently dominant form of socially approved parenting, which I have come to call "politically correct parenting," or PCP.

There have always been children whose personalities, apparent since birth, made them difficult to raise. The constellation of qualities labeled "difficult temperament"—extremes of determination, intensity, sensitivity, negative mood, and inconsolability—calls for levels of parental confidence, consistency, and support that in some cases may be impossible to deliver. However, this hypothetical "impossible-to-parent" group is quite small compared to the legions of children giving their parents grief in America's suburbs. Emory Hoffman, in my opinion, falls into the much larger difficult-but-not-impossible-to-parent group.

His parents, however, are thwarted by the ideals of psychological political correctness and reluctant to deliver the combination of affection and discipline that would work best with their child. For example, it might have been appropriate at the start of the session in my office for either parent to hold Emory by the arm until greetings had been exchanged or he had been invited to use the toys. And they needed to take action sooner when he ignored their requests to come back to the couch. Not that this is as simple as it sounds: With a child like Emory, the parents must be prepared for any firm action to precipitate an embarrassing and upsetting public tantrum. That parents choose to tolerate defiant behavior in preference to such scenes is understandable.

THE ROOTS OF POLITICALLY CORRECT PARENTING

Politically correct parenting became the dominant style in America sometime after World War II, and can be attributed to the influence of Sigmund Freud and his disciples, including Dr. Benjamin Spock. The age-old adage "spare the rod, spoil the child" came to seem authoritarian as American society, in its postwar affluence, placed its faith in psychological science. Too, in our postwar mood of horrified reaction against totalitarianism, Americans may have been attracted to notions of a more "democratic" and tolerant family. By the 1950s Freud's psychoanalytic theories—such as the primacy of the unconscious and the idea that unresolved childhood conflicts (or thwarting of childhood drives) lead to neurosis in adults—became the unchallenged scientific dogma in child psychiatry and psychology.

Freud's own work was primarily with adults, though his observations and theories relate to infancy. His followers soon began working with children. By the 1950s an unfortunate misinterpretation (at least according to Freud's daughter, Anna, considered the first child psychoanalyst) led Freudians to urge that children be reared in ways that *avoided* the conflicts they believed led to neurosis or worse.[4] Gratifying a child's primal needs, such as nursing and excretory functions, was seen as necessary in order for them to develop into secure adults; so feeding on demand was encouraged and late weaning and toilet training tolerated. The child's immediate needs for gratification took precedence over instilling the discipline required for adult life. Both at home and at school, self-expression and freedom of choice for children were the goals.

The child psychiatrist, advocate, and author Robert Coles, who knew Anna Freud personally, reiterates her perspective on how the foundations of politically correct parenting were laid:

> When the new instinct theory gave aggression the status of a basic drive, tolerance was extended also to the child's early and violent hostilities, his death wishes against parents and siblings, etc. When anxiety was recognized as playing a central part in symptom formation, every effort was made to lessen the children's fear of parental authority. When guilt was shown to correspond to the tension between the inner agencies, this was followed by the ban on all educational measures likely to produce a severe super-ego [Freud's term for the controlling, repressive part of human consciousness].[5]

Anna Freud makes clear how misguided she believed these initiatives to be: "Above all, to rid the child of anxiety proved an impossible task. Parents did their best to reduce the children's fear of them, merely to find that they were increasing guilt feelings, i.e., fears of the child's own conscience. Where in its turn, the severity of the super-ego was reduced, children produced the deepest of all anxieties, i.e., the fear of human beings who feel unprotected against the pressure of their drives."[6]

Julie Hoffman thought she was being loving and open by acceding to Emory's demands. This is what she believed, based on her own temperament and experience, to represent the ideals of parenting. My opinion was that unless Julie and Harold revised their views of parenting and changed their actions, the course they were taking with Emory was a prescription for major trouble (and probably for Ritalin, too).

The single individual who had the most profound impact on parenting in postwar America had practiced as a psychiatrist during World War II and was much influenced by his reading of Freud. As a pediatrician, Benjamin Spock brought psychoanalytic sensitivities to American child rearing in a readable, accessible form. His first book appeared in 1946, just as families were moving to the suburbs, away from the grandparents, relatives, and neighbors upon whom previous generations relied for advice. It's hard to imagine these days just how revolutionary Spock's advice to feed a newborn on demand must have seemed. Previously, "expert" notions had emphasized getting the infant on a regular schedule as quickly as possible. In retrospect, Spock's influence was probably useful and inevitable, providing a counterbalance to the more rigid views of prior generations. Spock's own background is interesting: He himself experienced an authoritarian upbringing by his mother.[7] This personal history may have predisposed him toward a more open, permissive style of parenting (though, curiously, Spock's own children say he was authoritarian and rigid at home).

Spock's views changed somewhat over the long history of writing and revising his classic *Baby and Child Care*, which remains one of the best-selling books ever published. As late as the 1968 edition, he was still saying:

> We have learned . . . that children need the love of good parents more than anything; that they work hard, all by themselves, to be more grown-up and responsible; that many of the ones who get into trouble are suffering from lack of affection rather than lack of punishment . . . that too harsh a repression of aggressive feelings and sexual interest may lead to neurosis; that unconscious thoughts are as influential as conscious ones.[8]

But he had also become aware of the problems such a stance can engender. In the 1957 edition he noted, "Nowadays there seems to be more chance of a conscientious parent's getting into trouble with permissiveness than strictness."[9] He went on to say (in 1968), "The parents who have had more trouble with the new ideas [that is, with psychoanalytic ideas] are usually those who haven't been too happy in their own upbringing. . . . They have often read meanings into them that went beyond what the scientists intended—for instance, that **all** children need is love [his boldface]; that they shouldn't be made to conform, that they should be allowed to carry out their aggressive feelings against parents and others; that whenever anything goes wrong it's the parents' fault; that when children misbe-

have the parents shouldn't become angry and punish them but should try
to show more love. All of these are unworkable if carried too far."[10]

Still, the Spock zeitgeist continued to emphasize a high degree of
parental permissiveness and a sense of fragility about the child's emotional
development. Parents were supposed to talk to their children, and listen to
them, before taking action or making decisions about them. Feelings were
very important, and it was critical that children understand why they were
being disciplined or denied. Children were born, it was felt, as blank slates
of psychological health on which parents could all too easily leave damaging marks.

Another writer who helped set the stage for politically correct parenting
was Selma Fraiberg, a social worker strongly influenced by psychoanalytic
principles. I remember reading Fraiberg's *The Magic Years*—still considered
a classic on child development—as a college student and thinking it was
wonderful. About ten years later, as a behavioral pediatrics fellow, I read it
again and was struck by how strongly the current of child fragility ran
through the text: the idea that children's emotions were made of glass and
it was the parents' paramount responsibility not to shatter them. Childhood was a scary and vulnerable place that parents had better not make any
scarier. Fraiberg writes in her preface:

> But the magic world is an unstable world, at times a spooky world,
> and as the child gropes his way toward reason and an objective world
> he must wrestle with the dangerous creatures of his imagination and
> the real and imagined dangers of the world, and periodically we are
> confronted with his inexplicable fears or baffling behaviors.[11]

While this imaginative, empathic view of the young child's mind offers
some wonderful insights, the conclusions to which it led Fraiberg are questionable today. My experience as a behavioral pediatrician belied the notion
that children are blank slates at birth, all with the same degree of sensitivity to the world's "dangers." As I learned to perform the neonatal assessments developed by T. Berry Brazelton, I recognized more and more
clearly that some personality traits are obvious from birth onward. And
some babies (like Emory) were going to be pretty tough to raise from the
moment they left the hospital.

Over time I developed a deeper but different kind of sympathy for the
challenges of parenting, one that recognizes there is no set recipe for every
parenting situation. Sometimes in dealing with a "difficult" child, the best

approach is to sit her on your lap and whisper sweet nothings in her ear. Unfortunately, this tends not to work well when the goal is to set limits for a determined, intense child who is prone to tantrums. Many children's personalities are neither well suited nor especially responsive to a cognitive style of parenting, which assumes that if you discuss things with your child and she understands, she will make the rational choice. The difficult child in the grip of anger often simply cannot attend to her rational side.

These are the children who often become candidates for an ADD diagnosis, but whether they truly "have" ADD is beside the point in terms of how parents deal with them. Despite the best efforts to separate children with "pure" ADD behavior (only the qualities of inattention, impulsivity, and hyperactivity) from those with other "externalizing" problems (oppositional and defiant children), expert recommendations on setting limits are the same for both.

PERSONALITY-APPROPRIATE STYLES OF PARENTING

At the zenith of Dr. Spock's influence and of permissive parenting in general, an important and sensible new voice arose in the field of child development. This was Diana Baumrind, now a professor of child development at the University of California, Berkeley. In 1966 Baumrind wrote courageously (for the time) about temperament and fit, about the value of setting limits on children, and about the need for different styles of parenting. Her long-term studies on discipline provided solid, scientific evidence that had long been lacking in this field.

Baumrind characterized three distinct parenting styles, which she called permissive, authoritarian, and authoritative.[12] The permissive parent:

> attempts to behave in a nonpunitive, acceptant and affirmative manner toward the child's impulses, desires, and actions. She consults with him about policy decisions and gives explanations for family rules. . . . She presents herself to the child as a resource for him to use as he wishes, not as an ideal for him to emulate, nor as an active agent responsible for shaping or altering his ongoing or future behavior. She allows the child to regulate his own activities as much as possible, avoids the exercise of control, and does not encourage him to obey externally defined standards. She attempts to use reason and manipulation, but not overt power, to accomplish her ends.

The authoritarian parent, the other extreme on Baumrind's spectrum,

> attempts to shape, control, and evaluate the behavior and attitudes of
> the child in accordance with a set standard of conduct. . . . She values
> obedience as a virtue and favors punitive, forceful measures to curb
> self-will . . .where the child's actions or beliefs conflict with what she
> thinks is right conduct. She believes in keeping the child in his place,
> in restricting his autonomy. . . . She regards the preservation of order
> as a highly valued end in itself. She does not encourage verbal give and
> take, believing that the child should accept her word for what is right.

The authoritative parent falls somewhere in the middle. This type of
parent:

> attempts to direct the child's activities in a rational, issue-oriented
> manner. She encourages verbal give and take, shares with the child
> the reasoning behind her policy, and solicits his objections when he
> refuses to conform. Both autonomous self-will and disciplined con-
> formity are valued. . . . Therefore, she exerts firm control at the point
> of parent-child divergence, but does not hem the child in with re-
> strictions. She enforces her own perspective as an adult, but recog-
> nizes the child's individual interests and special ways . . . affirms the
> child's present qualities, but also sets standards for future conduct.
> She uses reason, power, and shaping by regime and reinforcement to
> achieve her objectives and does not base her decisions on group con-
> sensus or the individual child's desire.[13]

As with any typology, Baumrind's is meant to suggests a range of possibilities. Few parents fall entirely into one group or another, but ideally
would find a place on the spectrum that allows them to interact most effectively with their child's personality. The authoritative parent sounds to
me (and others, I'm sure) like the perfect parent of the 1990s—but this
ideal is, in reality, almost impossible to achieve when dealing with the "difficult" or ADD-type child. The behavior of a hyperactive, intense, determined child is likely to thwart parents' more rational, give-and-take
initiatives, making them inappropriate in many situations. My sense, borne
out by recent studies, is that ideal parenting for such children actually falls
somewhere between the authoritative and authoritarian styles. "Do this because I said so" isn't always a bad thing to say to a child.

Harold, for instance, told me that if he didn't hold Emory when he wanted to talk to him, Emory would run out of the room (or down the street if they were outside). For a child like Emory, actions are more effective than words. Most such children respond best to consistent, immediate, and tangible reinforcers from their parents. This is the basic principle of the behavior modification techniques that are discussed at some length in Chapter 10. But such an approach runs counter to the "psychologization" of children that is a hallmark of politically correct parenting.

From Permissive to PC

At around the same time that Dr. Spock was starting to temper his views and Diana Baumrind was articulating her ideas about parenting styles, new discoveries were being made about an old social ill—child abuse—that were to have widespread public impact. C. Henry Kempe, a professor of pediatrics at the University of Colorado, had worked since the early 1960s to alert the country to a hidden epidemic of physical child abuse.[14] Kempe's influence was mainly in the professional realm; he helped crack the unwitting conspiracy of silence that led many doctors to ignore evidence of child abuse and accept parents' stories about how injuries happened. Others, such as Jonathan Kozol in his moving book *Death at an Early Age* and novelist Pat Conroy, who fictionalized his abusive Marine father in *The Great Santini*, helped arouse the entire nation's consciousness. By the 1970s, family-education programs were proscribing physical forms of parental discipline, and new laws mandated professional reporting of suspected abuse. Retrospective analysis of the families where child abuse took place had also shown that the abusive parents often had been abused themselves as children.

The rising flames of emotion over child abuse coincided with the growth of the recovery movement, which made "adult child" and "dysfunctional family" part of the American vocabulary. This reinforced the old psychological cautions to the nth degree. Psychoanalyst Alice Miller, a chief theorist of the movement, paints an extreme picture of child vulnerability, claiming that nearly all children have been emotionally abused by their parents, and that unless they can fully exhume this "repressed truth" as adults, they are doomed to do the same to their own children.[15] Miller's idea of abuse extends to parents refusing to share their ice cream bars with their two-year-old—an example from one of her books, which have been influential since the early 1980s.[16] Around the same time, the issue of physical discipline also became conflated with the even more inflammatory issue of sexual abuse, to the point where many parents became fearful of touching their children in almost any way.

The furor over child abuse, unquestionably important in protecting many children truly at risk, has had some unfortunate side effects. First and foremost is the confusion and uncertainty it has promoted among parents over how to discipline their children, raising the fear of social opprobrium (or even of a call to child protective services). From the fact that abused children often become abusers as parents, the illogical conclusion has been drawn that physical discipline in all situations is bad. Just because there is a high incidence of corporal punishment in families where abuse occurs does not mean such discipline and abuse should be invariably equated, or that in families where spanking is used it will inevitably lead to abuse.

The controversy over physical punishment, centering on spanking, has by now raged on for two decades. On one side are children's rights advocates, feminist groups, and many mental health providers (child psychologists, psychiatrists, and social workers). On the other side, religious groups until recently have been the main supporters of the right of parents to discipline their children by physical means.[17] Under these circumstances, it's not hard to see how parenting choices have become politicized.

This debate shows no signs of ending soon, but clearly there is widespread dissatisfaction with how today's dominant style of parenting is working.[18] This may result in more support for parents who want and need a greater range of choices in discipline. T. Berry Brazelton, who replaced Spock as the pediatrician-spokesperson for the baby boomer generation, and Stanley Turecki, a child psychiatrist and author of *The Difficult Child*, take a much more balanced, temperament-fit approach to child rearing, and acknowledge that certain children do better with less talking and more action.[19]

The results of some anti-corporal-punishment legislation may have an effect as well. Sweden, for example, in 1979 passed what is called the *aga* law, banning both corporal punishment and verbal abuse of children. Current statistics do document the hoped-for reduction there in the use of physical punishment. Contrary to expectations, however, the same studies report a fourfold increase in child abuse and a nearly sixfold increase in teen violence. "Thus," notes Diana Baumrind, "a strong endorsement of the ban against spanking and a non-confrontational and lenient approach to child-rearing has not reduced abusive violence by children brought up under the *aga* law."[20]

The PC parenting of today basically matches Baumrind's "permissive" type: responding to a child's behavior in a "nonpunitive, acceptant and affirmative manner" and attempting to use reason alone to produce the desired behavior. On top of this, it imposes a layer of guilt and fear. Guilt because there just isn't enough time to enjoy parenting fully, because the child's environment is not as safe and/or enriching as parents would wish it, the available schooling may not be top-quality, and because children are mostly deprived of the benefits of extended families—in other words, all the external factors that make parenting harder today. And the fear takes several forms: that children may be psychologically damaged by almost any kind of discipline—the legacy of the Freudians—as well as worry for their safety, which can hinder efforts to nurture independence, and that parents themselves may be cast as villains if they do exercise firm control.

Even if someone's natural style of parenting tends to be less permissive, the PC message may persuade a parent to temper his or her response to a child's unwanted behavior. When the lesser response doesn't work, frustration sets in and the fuse grows shorter. In the worst case, the parent may lose it—screaming, exploding over a minor infraction, hitting back when a child hits, or taking away TV "forever!"—or, as Stanley Turecki describes it, "descending to the level of the child." Such meltdowns inevitably leave children with a sense of confusion and inconsistency.

LET THE DISCIPLINE FIT THE CHILD

The challenge of raising a temperamentally difficult child is great enough; it becomes nearly impossible if parents are deprived of the only tools that will work in certain situations. Diana Baumrind has spent her career researching and advocating the position that, within the context of a warm, loving family, controlled and methodical punishment is not bad for any child and, indeed, may be quite necessary. Appropriate forms of punishment can span a wide range, from the time-out to what I call the "emphatic no" to more physical actions when warranted—and when the stage has been properly set for an escalated response. All these methods are described fully in Chapter 10.

But there remains great pressure on parents not to punish. Spock wrote in 1968,

Is punishment necessary? The only sensible answer is that a great majority of parents feel that they have to punish once in a while. On the other hand, many parents feel that they can successfully manage their children without ever having to punish. A lot depends on how the parents were brought up.[21]

The last sentence can be seen as a guilt-inducing (if unintended) judgment, leaving parents wondering about their own adequacy—have their backgrounds handicapped them for parenting?

Spock went on to say, "The best test of a punishment is whether it accomplishes what you want without having other serious effects. If it makes a child furious, defiant and worse behaved than before, then it certainly is missing fire."[22] On the contrary, I know of no punishment that leaves a child feeling happy at the time. In fact, I often counsel parents of difficult children that the methods that will work best in the long term probably will make things worse before they get better. It can be a critical moment: When parents take a firm stand, things may become quite unpleasant for a while, leading the parents to back off from a potentially useful strategy. If they could manage to persist a bit longer with their intensely reacting and determined child, the technique is likely to succeed.

Selma Fraiberg's views on physical discipline—as something to be avoided at nearly all costs—again emphasize the child's psychological fragility:

> Whenever reality reinforces a child's fantasied dangers, the child will have more difficulty overcoming them. This is why, on principle, we avoid any methods of handling a child which could reinforce his fantasies of danger. So, while parents may not regard a spanking as a physical attack or an assault on a child's body, the child may regard it as such, and experience it as a confirmation of his fears that grown-ups under certain circumstances can really hurt you.[23]

Instead, Fraiberg favored the use of guilt as a way of discouraging problem behavior:

> It is probably true that my friend preferred the mother's swift smack to her father's reproach ... for the father's reproach left the child feeling that she had not measured up to his good opinion of her. . . . Father's reproach was matched by the little girl's self-reproach,

accompanied by guilt feelings. We will grant that these feelings are uncomfortable, even painful, but they play a crucial role in conscience development. On the other hand, "Mother's smacks" left no residue of guilt feelings . . . "I was naughty; I paid for it; now we are all square. The slate is clean." It clears the air . . . but leaves little behind that can be used in the building of an effective conscience.[24]

I have no problem with anything that works between a particular parent and child, including a measure of guilt. But for the overactive, impulsive, insensitive-to-consequences child, this approach is generally ineffective. First and most important, it doesn't sufficiently discourage him from repeating the offending act. The difficult temperament responds best to immediate, short-term actions. Second, such verbal, cognitive punishments often leave a child who has trouble controlling his behavior feeling even worse about himself. ("Why can't I behave right if I'm a good and smart child? I must be bad and stupid.") With such children, it is precisely the "square and clean" response that will most likely keep the bad behavior from recurring and lead to more positive responses from the parents—thus helping to validate and improve the child's self-esteem.

"But aren't you teaching the child that violence is okay?" parents ask me. My response is that the *context* in which physical discipline takes place is all-important. Children need to know that their parents understand them, that mommy and daddy love and enjoy them, that they are the apple of their parents' eyes. But as Anna Freud argued, children also need to be protected "against the pressure of their drives." Or as we might say today, steadiness of discipline contributes to a child's sense of security. As long as the parent's response is methodical, preplanned, controlled, and limited to the intensity (in terms of power and duration) needed to effect a change in the child's future behavior, the physical nature of the act isn't necessarily bad.

Children understand context from a very early age: even at six months, they "get" the game of peekaboo—they know you haven't really disappeared. Likewise, a two-year-old understands the difference between an out-of-control, angry adult (or child) striking someone (which is very frightening and potentially damaging), and a parent who has announced in advance that leaving a time-out before the timer has gone off will result in the child's being returned to the time-out area along with a smack on the bottom. In Chapter 10 I describe in more detail the method of escalating a parent's physical response in a way that's tied to her previous words or actions. The intent is to get past the child's anger or impulsiveness or distractibility so that he is able to consider his choices at that moment. Otherwise, his impulses—especially anger—can override his cognitive understanding ("I shouldn't do that"). The parent's goal is to inhibit the defiant action, leading to less frequent need for a physical response.

Developing conscience is very important, and for some kids it is enough. But the ADD-vulnerable child, by virtue of his temperament, simply cannot do it himself. It is precisely his insensitivity to delayed consequences (or his distractibility and impulsivity) that makes outside control crucial. A behaviorist model is less concerned with psychological subtleties, rather seeking ways (safe and ethical ones) to change the child's behavior—from which much else will follow. A good conscience in a perpetually acting-out child will only create a poor self-image with a lot of guilt.

SPANKING: THE LIGHTNING ROD OF PCP

For years, children's rights advocates from outside and within the American Academy of Pediatrics (AAP) had been pushing the organization to issue a formal statement proscribing the use of corporal punishment, particularly spanking. Corporal punishment in public schools and most private schools had already been banned in this country. The advocates hoped that a stand by the AAP, representing organized medicine's experts on children, would propel nationwide changes in law and practice as applied to other settings, such as the home—similar to laws already existing in Sweden and Norway.

But the majority of pediatricians—around two thirds—have not supported a total ban on spanking. Surveys of AAP members indicated that most had themselves used corporal punishment as one method of disciplining their own children. After years of waffling, the AAP in 1996 convened a special conference to decide the issue. Clinical and personal experience was discussed and compared, and a vast range of research was studied and analyzed.

The findings, published in a special supplement to the journal *Pediatrics*, concluded that there was not enough "credible evidence to support a blanket condemnation of carefully defined disciplinary spanking."[25] In fact, the best designed studies demonstrated *better* outcomes—for example, improved compliance without lowered self-esteem or greater delinquency—for children who experienced physical discipline from their parents.[26]

There were more specific findings: The child's age was important in the outcome (the results were more negative when physical punishment was used with teenagers). And, once again, the overall context of parenting emerged as critical. The children who did better when spanking was used came from families where parenting overall was evaluated as loving and consistent. These children actually had better outcomes than those with equally supportive parents who never spanked.

The conference organizers were somewhat surprised by their results. "Although we attempted to achieve 'neutrality' we must confess that we had a preconceived notion that corporal punishment, including spanking, was innately always 'bad.' During the conference, we became increasingly impressed with the interactive nature of corporal punishment, and that the issue of whether spanking is harmful or beneficial to a child must be viewed within the total context of a child's life and environment."[27] A call for more research was issued, as usual.[28]

The last word, for the moment, should go to Diana Baumrind, whose career studying children and discipline now spans thirty years. In May 1997 I met with Baumrind in her small, journal-stuffed office on the Berkeley campus of the University of California. A spry, feisty woman who has experienced in her time various waves of hysteria over corporal punishment, she approached the topic of spanking with both wariness and disdain. "The fuss about spanking is a sideshow," she concluded. "If parents choose to use limited physical punishment with their children, they shouldn't be made to feel guilty, that they've done something wrong, or that they are 'bad' parents or failures."

Parenting Styles and the ADD-Vulnerable Child

I hope it is clear that my criticisms of PC parenting are focused chiefly on its inefficacy with the difficult-temperament child, and are in no way meant to be parent-blaming. Such children are very tough to raise. Their personalities can wear down a parent's resolve and elicit inconsistent responses. And the economic stresses that create two-parent working families do not help matters. One of the last things a parent wants to do, when he has only two hours at the end of the day with his kid, is to spend that time disciplining him. However, in the best case, consistent, action-oriented limit-setting actually frees up more time for love, affection, and plenty of play. Most of the parents I see with their incipient-ADD chil-

dren love them very much, but ineffective parenting renders their interactions much more stressful than necessary (their child is constantly challenging them) and ultimately makes the expression of their love much
more problematic.

The evidence that PC parenting may be contributing to the ADD-
Ritalin boom is mostly anecdotal and suggestive. Any study that attempts
to determine such a contributing effect is stuck in the old nature-nurture
conundrum. Does inappropriate parenting lead to ADD-type behavior in a
child, or does the child's inherent personality wear down the parents and
lead to their acting inconsistently and ineffectively?

A systems model of family behavior would suggest the effects are bidirectional and circularly reinforcing. Where the cycle begins is arbitrary.
Say a child with a "difficult" temperament elicits inconsistent parenting,
which leads to more behavior problems, and so on. In an opposing
scenario, appropriate parenting decreases the child's problem behavior,
leading to her improved self-image and sense of self-worth, which in
turn allows the parents to have an "easier" job parenting. In still another
version, wrongheaded if well-meaning leniency forces a parent to try
the same unsuccessful approaches over and over, inevitably culminating
in the blowup—that dreaded loss of control that is the ultimate sin of
PC parenting. Having lost control, the parent feels guilty and vows never
to do that again, consequently permitting the child even more leeway.
And so the cycle continues. Ritalin for your child becomes attractive
when you've "tried everything" for several years and nothing has worked.
The idea that the problem must be biochemical then takes on great appeal.

Some of the best (and only) evidence on the effects of parenting styles
on ADD-type children comes out of studies of children's peer relationships. In a 1987 review of the literature, Jeffrey G. Parker and Steven R.
Asher investigated how children's peer relations at the elementary-school
age level correlated with their later social and academic success.[29] Peer relationships turned out to be a strikingly good predictor: in essence, children who were better-liked by their peers in grade school were more
likely to do well in high school. Those who were less well accepted as
young children had higher dropout rates and poorer performance generally. Children who were perceived by their peers as aggressive showed
higher rates of juvenile and adult criminality later on. Parker and Asher's
review also looked into whether low peer regard was a factor in adult
mental illness; rates were higher for adults who had less peer acceptance

along with perceived aggression as children, though the links were not as strong.

What do these findings have to do with parenting? Simply put, parenting style has a major influence on children's peer relationships. Psychologist Stephen Hinshaw has made a special focus of family, peer, and social influences on ADD. One of the principal researchers currently evaluating different treatment modalities for ADD, Hinshaw runs an ADD treatment program at the University of California, Berkeley. Within this program he has set up a summer day camp for both ADD-diagnosed and normal kids, at which children spend about eight weeks. In part because it operates in "real time"—behavior is observed as it happens, and the responses to questions are fresh—rather than retrospectively, like most studies, this is close to an ideal setting for learning about ADD children and their peers.

Early in the session, the parents of the ADD children complete a questionnaire aimed at determining their primary style of parenting, according to Baumrind's categories: permissive (or rational), authoritative, and authoritarian. Children and their parents also are videotaped in planned situations, and the researchers observe their behavior and interactions without knowing whether any given child has ADD. At the end of the summer, the children are asked to rate each other on qualities of friendship.

In Hinshaw's results to date, the ADD children who were rated most highly by their normal and ADD peers had parents who were authoritative in style.[30] As noted earlier, my feeling is that they probably showed some authoritarian qualities, as well—the line between these parenting styles is not hard and fast. Interestingly, Hinshaw's work thus far has assessed the attitudes only of the mothers of children at his camp. He could not assemble a statistically significant cohort of fathers because many of the kids had single mothers, or the fathers weren't available to participate.

More attention to fathers will be important, because it is often observed that ADD-type children act better around their fathers, and men in general. This has never been formally studied, but stereotypically in American culture, men are more comfortable giving orders and taking action, and women are better at listening and nurturing. In the cases where Hinshaw was able to videotape fathers with their children, a very interesting result emerged.[31] The ADD children whose fathers gave more critical, negative, and even hostile responses to misbehavior demonstrated less antisocial behavior with their peers compared with children whose fathers were overtly supportive. This applied only to the ADD kids, however. The effects of restrictive paternal parenting were just the opposite for children without

ADD symptoms, in these cases "interfering with mastery and independent functioning."[32]

This is not to suggest that every interaction between such children and their parents should be characterized by negativity or hostility—far from it. The vital basis of parenting difficult children is not only clear, firm limits but a loving warmth that conveys the parents' real enjoyment of their role. However, it becomes impossible to enjoy parenting if you're constantly being pushed to your limits. Parents who are comfortable acting with authority do much better at coping with the consequences of a difficult personality.

My personal experience includes a friendship with a father and son with whom my sons and I sometimes do things. My kids love their friend Evan because he's bold and daring; he's also extremely intense and hard to reach at times. But his dad deals with him beautifully, with a combination of humor and sharpness. His barked commands to Evan actually have startled me and reminded me a bit of an alpha wolf disciplining its young—but they penetrate Evan's intense focus and get his attention. There are, as well, some families I see professionally who have very challenging kids but manage them in ways I can only marvel at, getting on their case at the slightest sign of trouble. Again, this would be counterproductive with many kids but is appropriate for these.

Politically correct parenting for ADD-type children only adds to the challenge of raising them. Though it's very difficult to prove through research studies, leading experts agree that effective parenting is critical to coping with ADD symptoms.[33] It can be a key turning point when parents finally acknowledge that their best efforts to cope with their child's behavior don't seem to be working—when they realize they're stuck and in need of some professional help to get them and their child unstuck. What should happen after that, during the course of a complete evaluation for ADD, is described in the next chapter.

Chapter 9

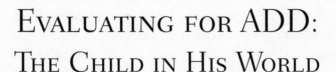

Evaluating for ADD:
The Child in His World

Right now, we are like blind men describing an elephant. The elephant is there—this . . . collection of people with varying attentional strengths and vulnerabilities. However, generating a definitive description, diagnostic workup, and treatment plan . . . still poses a challenge.

—Edward M. Hallowell, M.D.

It takes a lot for most families to decide that they need help from an outsider to solve a child's emotional problems. For each family and person, that point of frustration and desperation is different. Usually the problems have been going on for some time when some event—a call from the teacher, a suspension, an argument, a terrible report card, an allusion to suicide—pushes parents over the edge.

Families usually have tried other resources before they contact me. Sometimes there has been no clear crisis; it's just time. Life is tolerable for most people if the problems they face vary from day to day. When it's the same darn problem day in and day out (and it happens to center on your child), it eventually becomes too pressing to ignore, and ADD may sound like an explanation parents can live with. Over the telephone I'll be asked, "Do you think our problem is serious enough to start an evaluation for ADD?" Unless I sense that a child may be in physical danger, I do not directly recommend that the family see me, nor do I hazard guesses about diagnoses before seeing a child. Rather, I acknowledge the parents' concern and tell them that by bringing their child to me they may get a better understanding of his problems and help in developing a plan to deal with them.

In asking about a specific diagnosis such as ADD, parents hope to gain a better grasp of, and learn to cope more effectively with, their child's situation.[1] This desire for a clear-cut explanation is entirely understandable. A diagnosis can be a form of telegraphic communication. Naming a problem can provide reassurance that something tangible is going on, that it's not just a parent's subjective fears. People who share a common diagnosis can come together for information and support. And diagnosis clearly is useful in dealing with bureaucracies: institutional categorizing, research, insurance reimbursement, and disability claims.

However, as I've pointed out, the broad and ambiguous nature of the symptom complex called ADD limits the value of a diagnosis. Self-defined by its symptoms, the diagnosis alone may do little to guide decisions about treatment. Conferring a diagnosis can have other disadvantages as well. It can turn into a label or a stigma. It can lead to feelings of hopelessness or resignation, if the condition is believed to be chronic, or to a sense of victimization and entitlement. In general I prefer to describe a child in terms of his or her specific strengths and weaknesses, though I certainly understand why a diagnostic label is appealing or needed at times.

When parents ask, "Does he have ADD?" often what they really want is to resolve the "can't" versus "won't" dilemma. Is some malfunction in the brain putting the desired behavior outside the child's control? ADD's implied neurological basis suggests "can't" (as does a learning disability) and thus diminishes the importance of willful conflicts with parents and teachers. "Won't" implies problems that are more emotional or relational in nature—or if one thinks in terms of larger systems, problems for which parents and teachers are partly responsible. In reality, behavior is never 100 percent either "can't" or "won't." There's a circularity to the dynamic: If you find a task particularly difficult, you are less likely to want to perform it, but at the same time, your attention is more likely to wander.

Parents who think their child might meet the criteria for ADD have their own opinions about how much of their child's misbehavior or underperformance is under his control. They may also have heard a teacher's opinion, a school nurse's, or a pediatrician's. In a sense, by coming to see me they get another view on the percentages.

WHAT MAKES A GOOD EVALUATION:
THE DRIVE TO STANDARDIZE

The continuing controversy over what constitutes good treatment for ADD extends backward to the question of determining what is a good evaluation. Much effort recently has been focused on developing ways to standardize evaluations and to make them shorter. The impulse behind this comes largely from research, where ideally you want a consistent method of establishing a subject group to study, and where time and cost pressures encourage attempts to streamline the history-taking process. Pressure to reduce the time and cost involved in diagnostic evaluations comes also, of course, from administrators of managed-care plans.

This means that evaluators in both research and clinical settings are relying more and more on the use of standardized questionnaires and child rating scales to diagnose ADD.[2] Another part of the overall push to develop a consistent method of evaluation is an emphasis on standardized intelligence and performance tests, used at a later stage of the evaluation. The chief rationale behind all such diagnostic tools is that they are said to lend greater objectivity to a process inherently fraught with subjectivity.

Questionnaires generally ask the raters—most often parents and teachers and occasionally the child himself—to determine the frequency of dysfunctional, problematic, or "bad" behaviors from a list provided.[3] Frequency is assessed with phrases like "not at all," "just a little," "pretty much," or "very much," and an overall score or profile is developed from the answers. Scores will range from "normal" to "abnormal," which clearly reflects the dimensional nature of ADD problem behaviors. But nearly all the scales have a cutoff point where the behaviors are deemed sufficiently abnormal to fit the diagnosis of ADD. Sometimes statistical analysis is used to locate that point.

The cutoff concept has clear value for the categorical diagnoses of DSM—either you've got it or you don't—and specifically for research efforts aimed at delineating and treating ADD. However, such cutoff points on a scale, despite vigorous attempts at statistical and clinical correlation, remain arbitrary by definition.[4] Their reality ultimately depends on the opinions of observers, professional and lay, starting with the views and judgments of parents and teachers. It will always be a matter of opinion as to how many fidgets constitutes "pretty much." Special-education teachers generally are more tolerant of ADD-type behavior compared to regular classroom teachers.[5] And parent opinion is affected by many factors. Mothers tend to overreport, compared with teachers,[6] and mothers with problems of their own (depression or other psychiatric disturbances) tend to report more behavior problems in their children, problems not independently confirmed.[7] It's known that children in families under stress have a higher incidence of ADD, but it's impossible to distinguish the direct effects of family stress on a child from its effects on how the parents *experience* the child's behavior.[8] Both probably are operating, whereas the ADD diagnosis aims the sole focus on the child.

A 1996 study led by Mark Wolraich contained a telling finding about the variations between raters.[9] Some of the research data came from teacher questionnaires, and children who were identified as ADD by the research teachers in the first year of the study were followed into the next school year. When their new teachers were asked to rate the symptoms, only 52 percent of the same children met ADD criteria. The researchers could not account for this drop by the children's treatment with Ritalin or anything else—it seemed clearly to indicate the varying views of the teachers.

A further reason to treat standardized questionnaires and behavior rating scales with skepticism is their possible cultural bias. Most are not "normed" for other than white middle-class children, and a criterion such as "talks excessively and fidgets" means different things to different communities.[10] Were such diagnostic tools widely used among nonwhite ethnic groups, children from those groups (especially African-Americans) would likely be overrepresented when evaluated by whites.[11]

Diagnosing ADD over the telephone is a growing trend in child psychiatry research. In some recently published studies, children were diagnosed with ADD after evaluators spoke only to their mothers on the telephone.[12] More usually an evaluator will meet in person with parents, but often the child is not seen at all—in part because he is deemed (especially if he is under age twelve) an "unreliable" historian. The fact that a child can act "normal" and perform well in a doctor's office yet still "have" ADD is also invoked to justify not interviewing the child.

No one has yet suggested that in real, clinical situations—as opposed to research studies—ADD diagnoses should be made or Ritalin prescribed over the telephone; the ethical and liability issues are obvious. But with rising pressure from managed care to control costs, doctors are spending less and less time in direct contact with the children they evaluate. I see this as a trend that cannot help but increase reliance on Ritalin. Without a more intimate knowledge of the child and his or her situation, the family and its dynamics, the clinician is ill equipped to work out alternative or complementary strategies.

Within academic child psychiatry, the use of standardized tools and the streamlining of the ADD evaluation are hailed as progress. In my dissenting view, the quest for an totally objective evaluation is a bit like seeking the Holy Grail—a noble but illusory endeavor. The condition is simply too broad, too heterogeneous in its causes, too dimensional, and too subjective in its interpretation. Because questionnaires and standardized tests produce a number on a scale, they lend an aura of scientific objectivity to the ADD diagnosis, but they do not tell you anything about the attitudes and opinions of the raters. Whether that is a parent, teacher, or third party, some degree of subjectivity must operate. Moreover, they fail to address the child's competencies, strengths, or good coping behaviors. Thus they tend to emphasize problem behaviors and encourage a mind-set of pathology.

My own approach relies less on standardized tools than on forming a detailed picture of the child and his or her situation. In order to thoroughly understand the case and feel confident in my ultimate recommendations for treatment, I feel the need to spend a considerable amount of time with both parents and child, as well as gathering information from other sources: family doctors, teachers, siblings, and the results of previous assessments.

Typically, the evaluations I perform involve three or four fifty-minute sessions in my office, both with and without the child present. The total amount of time and the structure of the meetings vary slightly according to the child's age and other factors; every evaluation should be tailored to the unique circumstances of a child and family. Yet there are certain basics I try to cover most of the time. I've chosen a young patient named Bobby Hall and his family to illustrate the unfolding of a typical evaluation.

WHEN PARENTS SUSPECT ADD: THE HALL FAMILY'S STORY

Bobby Hall was almost eight the first time his mother, June, called me. Only in the second grade, Bobby was having a terrible year and had already been suspended five times for using bad language, spitting, and losing his temper. The previous year he had been given a full psychoeducational evaluation by the school psychologist, who felt he had some of the hallmarks of ADD but also had emotional problems. She had recommended that Bobby be moved to a special class for children with severe emotional disturbances, but the Halls had resisted the idea of putting their child in such a restrictive environment. I collected this information over the telephone;

usually I limit these first conversations to about ten minutes, or stop after I've filled a small sheet of paper. (If a parent is still bursting to convey more, it's probably time to do so face-to-face.) At that point I asked that both parents come in for a first visit, without Bobby. Her husband was a very busy man, June replied. When I gently insisted that it was important to meet with both of them and offered to call Bill directly at work, June said that wasn't necessary. We set up a tentative appointment for both parents.

The Halls had gotten my name from their pediatrician, Jane Garrison, who knows my position on ADD and agrees with my approach to evaluation and treatment—an approach based on the belief that ADD exists as a problem between the child's brain (or inherent strengths and weaknesses) and the demands and responses of his environment. Dr. Garrison would prefer to refer nearly all children she suspects might meet ADD criteria, feeling that she literally cannot afford to spend the time for a proper evaluation. However, with primary-care doctors under ever greater pressure from managed care *not* to refer, she currently finds herself evaluating more than she'd like. When she can refer to me, she takes back management of relatively straightforward cases after my evaluation.

We both know of doctors who "evaluate" children in twenty minutes and then prescribe Ritalin. However, we (and others) believe that a twenty-minute evaluation portends an almost inevitable recommendation for one treatment alone—medication. Neither Dr. Garrison nor I are comfortable with settling for just medication for most of the kids we see.

Bobby's parents are lucky. They can choose from at least three behavioral-developmental pediatricians within a half hour's drive of their home. Each has a different perspective and reputation, which allows a family to choose the approach they feel most comfortable with. Also within reach are several child psychiatrists and a host of psychologists, social workers, and other therapists—many of whom profess some expertise in working with children and ADD. In the nearby cities of San Francisco and Oakland, several medical centers have multidisciplinary teams for the evaluation and treatment of ADD. Finally, there are freestanding clinics that specialize in child and adult ADD. Some of these have the reputation of being "Ritalin mills": Everyone gets the same diagnosis and at least Ritalin, if not a second medication.

But an hour or so away, in some of the smaller towns and cities of California's Central Valley, families with concerns about their children's behavior do not have as many choices. Indeed, for many families distant from large urban areas, there are no local experts, or there may be one who has an unvarying approach to diagnosing and treating ADD. These families may be stuck with that practitioner's approach or the need to travel a long distance to obtain another opinion. It is worth asking an evaluator over the telephone what approaches to diagnosis and treatment he or she employs. A family's primary-care doctor may have his or her own ideas about the best referral resource (that is, specialist) for ADD. For most children with behavior problems, the pediatrician or family doctor will be the overall manager of the child's health care, especially under managed care. His or her comfort with an evaluation and treatment plan from a specialist is also important.

Meeting with the Parents

When evaluating children younger than thirteen or fourteen, I meet first with the parents, without the child. I find it easier to ask certain questions if the child is not present, and they can give me their full attention. I get more out of later visits with the child when I've been able to get a complete history at the start. Parents are sometimes taken aback by this preference, having formed the idea that I should see their child immediately. But most agree, and in fact find it a relief to get acquainted without the distraction of hands-on parenting. They may feel freer to speak candidly—and they get to evaluate me before involving their child. In cases where the parents are separated or divorced, depending on how they get along, I may have each parent (with his or her new spouse, if there is one) come separately, or, if they are comfortable with each other, have all of them come in together for the first meeting.

When it's unavoidable that parents bring a child to the initial visit, his sensitivities must be addressed as we talk about his problem. Sometimes a concerned parent will talk about a child's problem as if he weren't in the room at all—another reason why, the first time, I prefer that he not be. The kid may look as if he's not paying attention, but he's picking up most of what is said about him. If he is not asked what he heard or understood, he could be left with a lot of confusing and bad feelings.

Teenagers are invited to a first meeting with their parents if they want to come, to let them know they are active participants in the decision-making process (which begins with the asking of questions). If there seems to be any risk of a runaway or suicide attempt, the teen should definitely come the first time. Later I'll need a separate meeting with the parents, assuming the teenager is agreeable. When I evaluate adults for ADD, I ask that they bring their spouse, significant other, or parent (if one lives in the area) to the first or second meeting.

I cannot overemphasize how important it is to have fathers involved from the start. (Thus my persistence with June Hall about getting her husband to the first meeting.) This is even more vital if the parents disagree, as they often do, about the severity or management of the problem. Mothers often report, "Oh, his father doesn't think the problem is that serious. That's why he doesn't feel like coming in." I reply that this makes it even more important that he come at least once, to give me his point of view. I keep to myself, at that point, a preliminary hypothesis that at least some of the child's problems are caused or aggravated by disagreements between the parents. When I talk to a father by phone, I tell him the likelihood of my being helpful to his child will be greatly increased by his input and participation in the evaluation. This is not just a pitch; it is true. Whether it's a testament to my persistence or to the fathers' genuine interest, over the more than sixteen years I've practiced, only four or five available fathers have refused to participate.

At the first meeting, parents tend to launch into a long, oft-recited history of their child's problems from birth onward. I prefer to ask present-oriented questions. "What is Bobby doing or not doing at this time that presents as a problem or concern to you?" I asked June and Bill Hall. There would be time for more history later, but first I wanted to get oriented to what was happening currently. June reiterated the behavior problems Bobby was having at school: "He seems to have an incredibly short fuse. Kids tease him, and no one at the school tries to stop them, as far as I can tell. The teachers and other folks at the school just seem real negative toward Bobby." She and Bill were understandably feeling under attack. They had declined the recommendation of a special class for Bobby, which may have left the school personnel feeling frustrated and impotent, translating into a negative response toward Bobby.

In contrast, the parents thought things with Bobby at home were "great." "He's our only child," offered Bill. "We'd been married quite a while and tried to have kids, but it didn't happen. Bobby finally arrived when were both thirty-eight." Clearly, both he and June were very devoted to their son.

I asked if they had any theories about what was causing Bobby's problems. "Well, last year the school psychologist suggested he might be ADD," June replied. June had done some reading that led her to think some of Bobby's behavior was caused by "genetics, a chemical imbalance.

I'd been feeling really bad about what a hard time he was having and how it was probably my fault. Reading about ADD made me feel less guilty." Bill remarked that from the time Bobby was a baby, "he always needed a ton of attention." As we went on, I learned that getting Bobby to do things required tremendous effort. He was simultaneously messy and a perfectionist (he'd get angry with himself and others about the messes). "Some days, it just seems like he wakes up on the wrong side of the bed," June said, "and by the end of those days, I'm exhausted and feeling beat down." Apparently, things at home weren't all *that* great.

Neither parent, however, clearly identified symptoms of ADD—inattention, hyperactivity, or impulsivity—in their son. When directly questioned, they said he could be distractible but could also work for long stretches of time on things he liked. He wasn't hyperactive, but he could act impulsively—he had recently hit another kid in the playground.

The kind of testing done by Bobby's school is generally quite reliable in turning up learning weaknesses. His tests had involved the psychologist as well as a speech/language therapist and a special-education teacher, but had revealed no such problems. The possibility of a learning disability is always considered in ADD evaluations for children older than six because they so often overlap. An estimated 10 to 25 percent of children diagnosed with ADD also have learning disabilities, and the latter frequently masquerade as ADD. Relatively speaking, it's easier to objectively diagnose learning problems than ADD through psychometric testing.

I always ask about a child's strengths as well as his weaknesses. As they told me about Bobby's wonderful artwork (he spent hours drawing, coloring, and building) it was clear how much they loved him and respected his abilities. "And we really enjoy his sense of humor," June added. I was reassured that they still took pleasure in being around their son. Asking about exceptions to problem behaviors is also useful: What are the times or situations when things go better? In the Halls' case, I learned, things went much better when Bill was around. When it was just Bill and Bobby, his father reported few problems. He could be more effective in getting Bobby to do things, but his standards were lower than June's. And he just wasn't around as much, because he worked an average of sixty to sixty-five high-stress hours a week at a law firm. Based on what I would see later of the parent-child interactions, Bill's responses were more intense than June's; he was much more apt to grab Bobby's arm and make him do what was wanted (often to June's discomfort).

I also asked each of the parents if they thought they had significant marital problems or had ever been separated, or if they thought either of them had an issue with alcohol or drugs. Over the years I've learned to address these matters explicitly, because they can greatly influence a child's behavior, yet parents often do not bring them up. I've listened to couples calmly discuss their child's problem in my office, only to learn the following week that the father has moved out of the house. I've met with families for several months before a mother confides to me privately that her husband is drunk once a week. So now I always ask. The Halls understood my reasons and weren't offended at all. They assured me there were no major problems in their family other than Bobby.

I asked June and Bill a few more general questions, about Bobby's overall health and what the family does together for fun. They granted me permission to call Bobby's teacher, Mrs. Martin, and we wrapped up after making the next appointment, when I would meet Bobby.

REVIEWING OUTSIDE INFORMATION

In addition to interviews in my office, I may obtain information about a patient from a variety of sources. I always review previous evaluations or testing, especially workups done within the prior three years. Report cards offer a quick take on the school's point of view: They usually contain little practical information such as details or causes of poor performance (for example, a processing problem), but they do provide a sense of where the child stands in relation to his peers, academically and behaviorally. When I ask parents what they understood and gained from previous evaluations, they often seem confused or uncertain about the results—not surprising, as professional explanations of psychological data are often atrocious. In Bobby's case, however, my review of testing done the previous year corresponded to June's version of it.

I informed the pediatrician, Jane Garrison, that the Halls had been to see me. She reported that they had struggled for years with Bobby, and, anticipating worsening problems, she had tried unsuccessfully to refer them to me two years earlier. I checked to make sure he'd had a general physical examination, with vision and hearing screening, within the past year. Bobby's eyes and ears were normal. Most kids' usually are, but on rare occasions an evaluation uncovers vision or hearing problems that could explain much of the inattention. Because there is no definitive biological marker for ADD, other laboratory blood work or tests generally are not useful for an ADD evaluation in an otherwise healthy child. The only exception is if the child lives in an area where lead paint is endemic or lead processing industries are located, in which case a blood lead level may be worth getting.

My conversation with Bobby's teacher took place after I'd met Bobby. (Often I prefer to let my own impressions form before I've been influenced by the observations of others.) A twenty-year veteran, Mrs. Martin currently had thirty-one children in her classroom and no aide. Bobby was doing all right academically, she told me. While he often didn't complete assignments—which she attributed to his being easily distracted—he made up for this in his class participation and performance on tests. But his behavior was a serious problem. She had put Bobby on a "behavior contract" that was barely working. He would bring toys into school, contrary to rules, or make noises and mutter in class. His use of foul language, usually with peers, was disturbing. Despite all this, she still had some positive feelings about Bobby. She mentioned that he could be caring and demonstrative, and she felt he had a good mind. She sounded open to any suggestions I might have and said she looked forward to the IEP meeting, at which we would discuss a teaching plan tailored to his needs.

MEETING WITH THE CHILD

I learn a great deal about a child and his world by interviewing the child himself. This may seem obvious and natural but, as noted, the trend in ADD evaluations is to spend less and less time with the Bobbys of the world. All told, I would spend about two hours evaluating Bobby, alone or with his parents. My time alone with him would include lots of talking and playing, along with some academic and developmental screening.

The first time I meet with a child, his parents may or may not participate. Young children are generally more comfortable meeting a stranger if parents and siblings are on hand. Since Bobby had already had encounters with professionals in the past, his parents and I thought he could handle a first visit with me alone. He and his mother arrived together, and after a brief introduction June left Bobby with me.

Bobby was average in size for an almost-eight-year-old, with longish blond hair and nothing very remarkable about his appearance. His level of physical activity seemed quite high; from the moment we were alone, he fidgeted, bounced, and squirmed, sometimes just barely maintaining con-

tact with the chair. He was also pretty distractible, abruptly changing subjects as we talked. Or he'd look outside the window at the traffic on the
street or up at the ceiling vents when the air-conditioning came on. Although he talked a lot, his way of speaking was oddly constricted: The
phrases were rapid and clipped, almost mechanical or robotic, with little
variation in tone and expression.

He was quite forthright, telling me he didn't like Mrs. Martin—and neither did his mother. (June had implied as much in our earlier meeting.)
The teacher wasn't fair, he said; he hadn't been allowed to go on the last
field trip. Then, extending his middle finger upward, he said, "I'm going to
stop doing this. I get into trouble. Kids bug me and I give them the finger."
Once he started on this topic, a lot of conflicting thoughts tumbled out.
"I've got a lot of anger sometimes." (Bobby had been encouraged to "use
his words," today's parenting code for getting children to verbalize rather
than act out.) "I use swear words and now I swing at the kids. I try and tell
the yard duty but she doesn't do anything. It's no big deal getting suspended. My parents don't like it." I scribbled furiously to keep up with his
torrent, thinking that this kid was in touch with his anger. But while there
was bravado in his tough talk, I also heard pathos behind it. It sounded as
though he felt rejected and couldn't stand being teased; both probably
made him still more angry and impulsive. I imagined that it could be a
challenge to see beyond his defiant lashing out, but to me he seemed like a
lonely and quite unhappy child.

Not all my patients are as forthcoming as Bobby. Very occasionally a
child is so uncommunicative (responding only in monosyllables) or so hyper (literally trying to climb the office walls) that attempts to converse are
fruitless. In such cases I may move right on to the play period, or call the
parents in—something I've had to resort to only a handful of times in the
course of my practice.

When I asked Bobby what he liked to do for fun and what he thought
he was good at, he mentioned playing with one friend but didn't elaborate—I wondered if possibly there was no such friend. He liked coloring
and playing with his toy dinosaurs, loved Nintendo but also was good with
K'Nex, a fairly sophisticated building toy for his age. Then he abruptly re-
verted to his earlier manner. When his father got sharp with him, he told
me, "I say, 'Shut up, jerk, shitface!'" He was getting pretty worked up; considering our limited acquaintance and his age, I told him that swearing in
the office was not a good idea. At that he apologized immediately and
seemed to settle down some. Finally I asked: If he had three wishes, what

would he wish for, or wish could happen? He asked for more Nintendo games, more friends at home and school, and a jet plane "so I can blow up stuff." Again, this seemed to capture Bobby's social isolation and the hostile way it found expression.

After we'd talked for a half hour nonstop, I said it was time to play, and we moved to a part of the room where there's a sandbox and lots of small toys. I told Bobby: "Find things you like on the shelves and put them in the sand. If you want to arrange them into a scene and make up a story, you can, but you don't have to. Maybe I'll join in if you want me to, but you start first." I added that playing was a way I could learn more about him, and that it was fun.

Bobby's play was surprisingly sparse and simple for his age. What I was seeing could reflect delayed development—though he didn't seem at all retarded in our conversation—evidence of emotional damage, or perhaps ADD (if the child can't focus long enough to create more detailed play scenarios). At first he put a few cars, sharks, and dinosaurs in the sandbox. He would abruptly pick up a toy he had placed in the sand and replace it with another, but this pattern slowed when we were talking. He couldn't really develop a story about his figures; rather, they simply crashed, killed, or ate one another. Frequently he asked me to join him, and eventually I did, playing on his level. He seemed to enjoy this, asking me if what he was doing was okay, seeking my approval. He was careful to keep the sand inside the tray, as I had asked, and when it came time to put the toys away, he did it without protest. He seemed a bit happier when he left my office with his mother.

ASSESSING THE CHILD'S NEURODEVELOPMENT

At the next appointment, Bobby bounded in expecting to play, despite having been told we'd be doing some work. Although he had been tested the previous year, I wanted to assess for myself his developmental strengths and weaknesses, and where his current skills placed him nine months later. I also wanted to see how he coped emotionally with academic tasks that were not immediately pleasant.

I do not use full-scale intelligence tests in my practice. While many of these, such as the Wechsler Intelligence Scale for Children III (WISC III)[13] or the Pediatric Examination of Educational Readiness at Middle Childhood (PEERAMID),[14] correlate well to learning abilities in school, for screening purposes in an ADD evaluation a complete test (which may take one and a half hours) is not necessary. I do use portions of such tests, the goal being not so much to report an IQ score but to describe how the child is functioning overall, and to rule out any specific developmental disabilities. With this method, however, I can easily project an IQ score approximate to one derived from full-scale formal testing.

A child's IQ can be important when it appears that he or she may be genuinely slow or truly gifted and it hasn't been noticed. More typically, the child's abilities and skills average out within the normal range but can show substantial unevenness—for example, she may understand information she sees much better than information she hears. If such discrepancies are noticed in my evaluation, the child is referred for a more complete psychoeducational evaluation, which by law the school must perform in order to develop an IEP (individualized education plan). Sometimes parents elect to have a full psychometric evaluation done privately. In that case, I direct the psychologist to areas I am concerned about, which can limit the amount of time and money involved.

Nor do I employ Continuous Performance Tests (CPTs), much favored by some as another way to standardize ADD diagnostic procedures. These tests present children with repetitive, boring information—a series of letters, symbols, or numbers, on paper or a computer screen. Every time the child notices a change or error in the sequence, he is asked to mark it on paper or press a button; he is scored on how many anomalies were missed, or how many mistakes he made in noting a change when there wasn't one. However, the interpretation of CPT scores is not always a reliable indicator for ADD.[15] An abnormal score says only that the child's performance was poor on that test, and may also suggest a visual or auditory processing or learning problem separate from or compounding ADD. Also, performance on these tests doesn't always reflect or predict real-life performance. A child may do well on tests in the doctor's or psychologist's office yet experience problems with comparable tasks at home or at school, due to more distractions, less individual attention, or emotional factors in those settings; or she may perform better in real life than on tests.

Unless a child has a history of neurological problems or shows clear physical signs of such disturbance, a full neurological examination—which includes evaluation of the cranial nerves, muscle strength and tone, sensation, balance, and normal and pathological reflexes—is unnecessary and usually doesn't add practical information to the learning assessment. A great deal has been made of the significance of eliciting "soft" neurological signs in children with learning, behavior, and attention problems. A "soft" neurological sign differs from a "hard" sign in that its presence does not suggest a specific neurological or brain lesion (as might weakness in a limb or a very vigorous knee reflex). A typical soft sign might be the relative inability to rapidly touch each of one's fingers to each other, or some stereotypic posturing of the tongue or hands when performing a physical task that requires concentration.

There has been much effort to link such signs with ADD, but the links do not show up consistently in studies.[16] Some children who have these signs meet ADD criteria and others don't. Conversely, some children diagnosed with ADD have these signs and some don't. I find it more useful to assess an eight-year-old's practical skills, such as tying shoes, writing the alphabet, being able to skip, or being able to throw and catch a ball. On the other hand, a full neurological exam confers the dignity of a medical examination, pleases some parents who believe their child's problems to be brain-based, and may lead to increased insurance compensation.

Most of my time in this developmental screening session is spent assessing the child's everyday school skills: having him read, write, spell, and do math with material both above and below his grade level. Bobby made it clear how he felt about doing work—"You're pretty lucky I'm doing this." Yet he worked more carefully and methodically than I expected. "Any brat can do this," he declared as he finished copying some shapes and sentences. After just five minutes, however, he asked to take a bathroom break; when he returned, he began wiggling on the chair as he continued to work. Only a second-grader, he could decode and comprehend material on the fourth-grade level in both oral and silent reading. When I suggested he sound out harder words, he was able to use phonics. Recalling what he saw (a series of shapes or letters) was slightly easier for him, compared to remembering a series of spoken commands, but neither his visual or auditory memory was significantly impaired. His spelling abilities were closer to grade level. Bobby knew his basic math concepts and operations, and he'd found a clever way to add and subtract by putting dots on the number signs, rather than relying on memorized math facts. When the work was done, we had time left to play a board game, in which he handled the rules pretty well.

Overall, I agreed with the psychologist's earlier assessment. If anything, I found Bobby's reading, comprehension, and language skills to be above average. He had no learning disabilities. Bobby actually coped better—was more focused, less impulsive, and more cooperative—when I provided a structure that allowed him to move quickly from one task to the next. He could accept a compliment when he had done well. However, when he made a mistake or wasn't sure about an answer, he tended to fixate on it and wouldn't move on to the next problem unless he got the answer (or I gave it to him). His perfectionism and intensity came through in this way. Inattention and distractibility were not very problematic in this one-on-one situation, where there were minimal distractions. For similar reasons—he wasn't being teased by other children, and he had an adult's full attention—his anger didn't surface often or strongly with me. Bobby seemed pleased with himself when we parted that day.

THE FULL FAMILY INTERVIEW

Now it was time for the family interview—perhaps the most useful and at the same time the most neglected aspect of a typical ADD evaluation. Seeing for myself how family members interact in "real time," even for fifty minutes, is vastly different from hearing a situation reported secondhand. Countless times parents have assured me that there were no problems at home, only to watch helplessly as their children's behavior went out of control in my office. Granted, there's an artificiality about the setting that can affect how both children and adults behave. Family tensions may play out differently at home. However, I am invariably confident that what parents and children reveal about their relationship in my office sheds light on their problems in other settings.

Bobby was an only child, but in other cases I consider it important to have all the siblings—at least those living at home—at the meeting. The roles that various siblings take within the family structure are always revealing, and these may not be reported by the parents or be apparent when one or more siblings aren't present. Further, parents may have their reasons for focusing on one child as a "problem," rather than seeing each child's role in the family as part of a larger picture. For example, one family was concerned about the possibility of ADD in their nine-year old-son, Steven. But Steven sat quietly with his hands folded on his lap during the family interview while his parents chased his hyperactive four-year-old sister, Susie, around the room. Earlier, when I had taken the history from Steven's parents, they barely mentioned Susie's behavior! Girls tend to be reflexively perceived as less problematic even if this isn't the case. More to the point, Susie wasn't in school yet, so her problem hadn't "gone public." Nevertheless, it was draining the parents' energy and leaving them less time for Steven, who also resented his sister's heedless trampling on his space and his stuff.

The family interview is the single most useful instrument available to me in forming hypotheses about the sources of children's behavior problems. It also helps me to bond with parents and children, making my later advice and suggestions more powerful. Parenthetically, most families report that they really enjoy the process and get a lot out of it.

When I opened the door of my waiting room to greet the Hall family, a rubber ball came flying at my head. I ducked, and Bobby said he was sorry. (The act seemed more impulsive than aggressive, not that it matters much.) They all came in and sat together on one of the couches. Following my standard practice, I began by asking June and Bill, "Would one of you ask Bobby why he thinks we are all here today?" This is a tried-and-true technique of family therapy that accomplishes much. It gets family members speaking to each other directly, allows me to observe how they go about discussing a sensitive family issue, and sometimes elicits an interesting response from the child.

June obliged, but Bobby immediately changed the subject, got up, and began wandering around the room. When Bill issued a firm order to return to the couch, Bobby obeyed. This pattern repeated itself several times: When the parents tried to engage Bobby with serious questions or conversation, he would distract them, usually physically—getting up, playing with his clothing, or the like. Bill, at least, was much more effective in setting limits, while Bobby ignored or openly made fun of his mother.

After about twenty minutes I said we were going to play a game. Producing some markers, I asked them to do a drawing together without talking. At first they all started drawing separate pictures. Then Bill, following the assignment, tried to connect his drawing to Bobby's, at which his son screamed out in anger. Bill got the message and immediately backed off. Instead he joined his drawing to June's, and the parents drew together while Bobby drew his own picture without incident for a full five minutes. Later, when they talked about it, Bill told Bobby he thought they were supposed to do a drawing together. Bobby, still mad, shot back, "I didn't want you to ruin my picture!" Both parents looked sad at this, and the session ended with our setting up an appointment for me to share my observations.

This meeting provided a glimpse of how ineffectively the parents coped with Bobby in many cases, as well as further insights about Bobby himself. Clearly he could concentrate pretty well, even with his parents around, but was very sensitive to "space" violations. He needed for things to be very clear and to feel safe about any invitation to share, whether it was drawing or other activities with adults and his peers.

FOLLOWING UP

I usually communicate my findings with parents in another meeting without their child present. As with the first session, it's easier to speak openly without worrying about how much the child understands, and this precludes the possibility of his feeling ignored. I also want to make sure the parents understand and are in some agreement with my ideas before presenting them to the child, his teacher, or anyone else. At some future time I would talk to Bobby directly about my impressions of him, with his parents present. Parents typically are both eager to hear my opinions and apprehensive about what I am going to say, so I try not to spend much time on preliminaries. However, I often ask how they experienced the evaluation—had they learned anything on their own? And I try to begin with some positive statements about the child's strengths or what I enjoyed about meeting him.

With the Halls, I tried to get right to the point and to keep things simple. Often I've seen parents overwhelmed with too much information and technical data, particularly at IEP meetings. The main point I wanted to get across to Bill and June was how sad I thought Bobby was and how poorly he felt about himself, especially in his dealings with other kids. Over the course of the evaluation things hadn't gotten any better at school—reports were coming home nearly every day about his bad behavior, and Mrs. Martin was again suggesting that he be assigned to a special class. I sensed that Bobby's self-esteem was close to bottoming out. In our meeting I used the word *depressed* for emphasis, though he didn't meet classic psychiatric criteria for depression.

Hearing this made a big impression on Bill. "You know," he began, "I'd never really considered it that way. I guess I was just seeing anger more than sadness in the way he acted." Bill mentioned that the intensity of Bobby's reaction to the drawing incident had surprised him. He went on, "I suppose if I thought about it, his acting out might have been a way of showing he felt lousy about himself and what was happening with him."

Then Bill shifted his posture, as if coming out of deep thought. He looked at his wife and said with an air of determination, "So what are we going to do about it?" Without fully understanding the process of his son's unhappiness, Bill was already trying to fix things—a typical male response. As I was about to check in with June, she spoke up herself, saying that she actually felt relieved in a way. "I'd been sensing for a while that he felt pretty bad." Turning to Bill, she said hesitantly, "But it seemed like you always downplayed things." To which her husband responded, "I just didn't want to make it a bigger deal than necessary, honey. I kept on hoping, 'He's just a boy.' I didn't want you or him to feel worse." June: "I didn't take it that way. It just seemed like you weren't hearing that I was really worried." At that, Bill told her he was truly sorry. Their candor and closeness at that moment moved me.

Bobby easily met ADD criteria. Using the DSM-IV's list of eighteen signs of inattention, hyperactivity, and impulsivity, Bobby displayed all of them except "often has difficulty playing or engaging in leisure activities quietly." (His ability to be absorbed by artwork or Legos eliminated this one.) I didn't frame his problem in those terms, however. "Bobby's brain is at least as good as that of the next kid his age," I told his parents. "He's up to his grade level or beyond in academic skills and abilities. But he is more distractible and acts more impulsively than the other kids." I explained my belief that both biological and emotional components were driving his behavior, and that a multilevel intervention should be set in motion without delay. My first recommendation was to schedule a meeting at Bobby's school to coordinate a plan for his progress; this seemed essential, and I told them I would attend. Second, I strongly suggested that the parents needed further professional help to improve their effectiveness and connection with their son. Individual therapy for Bobby was a possibility but could wait, pending the result of changes in his interactions with his family and at school.

Finally, I told Bill and June that I thought Ritalin could help Bobby better utilize the additional structure and care we were arranging for him. It wasn't simply the number of ADD behaviors Bobby demonstrated that led me to offer Ritalin early in his treatment. It was my sense that his problems were poisoning every part of his life, and that even his tolerant parents were close to their wits' end. While I never tell a family they *must* give their child Ritalin, this was one of the times when I felt it could be helpful in jump-starting a treatment program. Other interventions would be more important in the long run: Bill needed to get more involved; both parents' style of discipline had to change; Mrs. Martin and other school personnel would have to consider more effective strategies for dealing with Bobby's behavior.

But all these would take time—and while I couldn't precisely say why, I felt Bobby didn't have that much time. His low self-image was like high-octane fuel for his impulsivity; each was feeding the other daily. If the Ritalin worked, it would work quickly. He might immediately start having more success in school and in restraining his angry reactions to his peers.

This would help him feel a little better about himself. His taking medication might delay or prevent his imminent transfer to a special class. And it might help the other planned interventions proceed more smoothly, as it often does. Much more than Ritalin would be needed to turn Bobby around, but I believed it could help halt his slide.

After they'd had some time to reflect on this discussion, I concluded by recommending one more meeting without Bobby to discuss these interventions in more detail—adding that I would prepare a brief written summary of my findings and recommendations that they could take to the school. Most parents find this helpful, since, like Bill and June, they are tired and a bit dazed after this fifty-minute session. But the Halls also seemed satisfied that progress had been made. When I asked how she felt about my assessment, June said, "I feel sad but relieved that we have a plan. And I'm really glad Bill was here," turning toward him. "Me too," he said, and they agreed to come back in a week.

I had spent about three and a half hours in direct contact with the Hall family, and another fifteen minutes of telephone time talking with Bobby's pediatrician and teacher. A brief report would take about twenty minutes to compose. For families with children age five and under, I might eliminate or shorten the time spent with the child alone. If a very recent learning evaluation existed, I could potentially skip that part of my evaluation. But in the majority of cases, a sound and ethical evaluation takes about this much time. In total, this one cost $520, of which the Halls' insurance wound up paying half—an above-average reimbursement. Sometimes insurance companies pay nothing. Five hundred dollars is a lot of money for most families. The Halls had decided to spend the money; only several years later would they know if it was well spent.

THE ELUSIVE "STANDARD EVALUATION"

As I trust this chapter has conveyed, I am far less interested in arriving at a particular diagnosis (whether of ADD or of any other categorically defined disorder) than in finding out what I need to know to help a patient improve his or her relationship with parents, peers, school, or the larger world. I am uneasy with heavy reliance on standardized questionnaires and testing procedures (though both can help to provide basic data), preferring to rely more on my clinical judgment through a series of different kinds of encounters with the child and his or her environment.

Even when I do conclude that a patient more than adequately meets the criteria established by DSM-IV for ADD, I tend not to emphasize making a diagnosis for its own sake. Some parents (or teenagers or adults) will find the label useful or comforting. If it makes sense clinically—that is, if it will help the overall situation—I am even comfortable saying "He 'has' ADD." But that tends to be the exception. I generally find it more useful to describe what the problem behaviors are, why are they happening, and what can be done about them.

I haven't been entirely free of doubts about my approach to evaluating for ADD. Perhaps my ideas were too idiosyncratic, my procedures not "scientific" enough. However, I was reassured by the findings of a 1996 survey of doctors' decision-making practices concerning ADD and Ritalin.[17] In this survey, more than 500 behavioral-developmental pediatricians, psychologists, and general pediatricians were asked how they conduct evaluations. While many used DSM criteria quite frequently (the specialists more so), only 9 percent listed DSM criteria as the only set of rules they employed. In making an ADD diagnosis, the great majority were far more influenced by aspects of the co-morbid behaviors (acting out, learning problems) associated with ADD.

The most striking result was that while most of the doctors felt they relied on "a consistent set of criteria" to make an ADD diagnosis, only 8 percent of them provided responses specific enough to allow their criteria to be reliably used by other doctors. This is powerful evidence that among both general pediatricians, who perform most of the evaluations for ADD and prescribe most of the Ritalin, as well as specialists, the diagnosis of ADD remains very much in the eye of the beholder.

Rather than devote enormous effort to chasing the grail of "objective evaluations," I believe, we are more likely to attain a consistently higher level of good and useful diagnosis through educating both professional evaluators and the public in the complex biopsychosocial nature of ADD: that organic, emotional, and social factors all interact in its genesis and expression. Through this kind of effort, ADD evaluation and treatment could serve as a paradigm for other disorders now artificially divided between the organic and the emotional. In pursuing this path, psychiatry could move beyond its mimicry of the "disease" concept of current Western medicine, and perhaps even take the lead in creating a broader perspective on the true dimensions of illness and health.

Chapter 10

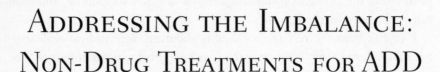

ADDRESSING THE IMBALANCE: NON-DRUG TREATMENTS FOR ADD

Comparing various treatments for ADD is complex because of the hetero-geneity of children and adolescents with the disorder, the inconsistency of treatment effects on different domains of functioning, and the complexity of patients' family, school and peer social environments.
>   —Official practice parameters on ADHD,
>   American Academy of Child and Adolescent Psychiatry, 1997

I don't care what causes it. I just want to help my child.
>   —Mother at an ADD conference, 1996

The last time I scanned the self-help/mental-health section of the San Francisco Bay Area's biggest independent bookstore, I counted at least twenty books on attention deficit disorder. Amazon.com, an Internet book-seller, currently lists 153 titles, and the World Wide Web boasts literally hundreds of sites that offer how-to advice on ADD treatment.

A plethora of published advice usually suggests several things about a problem—it is common, it isn't easy to deal with, and there's no one clear way to solve it. I certainly don't claim to offer the final word on treatment for ADD. What I do know, however, is that on the level of an individual child, his family, and his school, it's very important to take action immedi-ately to deal with ADD problem behavior, because such behavior is proven to have long-term negative effects on a person's self-image and future suc-cess.

The negative impact of unchecked ADD-type behavior starts early: by the time a kid like Bobby Hall (from the previous chapter) reaches high school, his constant experience of alienation in school is likely to lead him to consider giving up, dropping out, and hanging with other kids who feel unsuccessful. Trying to avoid his painful feelings may also lead him to use alcohol and drugs, or perhaps shoplift a few CDs for immediate gratification. At the very least, he is sure to have ongoing trouble with peer relationships.

Unfortunately, I could offer Bobby's parents no hard-and-fast scientific guidelines about treating ADD—no proof that any form of treatment in childhood makes a difference in the long-term outcome. Studies that have followed children into adulthood indicate that *medication alone makes no difference*—and I try to convey this to all parents.[1] Taking Ritalin in childhood neither improved nor worsened outcomes in adolescence and adulthood, as measured by incidence of failure in school, dropout rates, teenage delinquency, substance abuse, and relative success in holding on to jobs and marriages.

For the past thirty-five years, the multimodal model has been recommended by the psychiatric establishment as the treatment of choice. A study completed in the 1980s by James Satterfield, a child psychiatrist at UC Irvine, and colleagues including Jim Swanson, is cited as the best proof for the value of this approach.[2] This study followed two groups totaling a hundred boys for nearly ten years, into late adolescence. Years earlier, both groups had received treatment with Ritalin, along with very brief counseling for one group, while the other group received more intensive individual and family counseling and special education services. When they were evaluated at the end of adolescence, the latter group was significantly less likely to be in trouble with the law.

The National Institute of Mental Health (NIMH) is currently sponsoring a major five-year study of 600 carefully screened children diagnosed with ADD, to determine which of several methods or combinations of treatment, including Ritalin, works best (if at all) in addressing their problems.[3] The active treatment phase of the study (referred to as the MTA study) ended in August 1997, with several years of follow-up to come. Everyone in the field looks forward to the results, although some veteran researchers question whether any study can come up with specific answers for individual children.[4]

Given the lack of definitive answers, what are parents to do when a child has been diagnosed with ADD and/or is experiencing symptoms that make life a struggle at home, with friends, or at school? I suggest learning about a variety of approaches to treatment—from professionals, books, support groups, and the electronic media, as well as relatives and friends. Not all need be given equal weight, but I think parents should get a wide range of views, then use their own judgment and make up their own minds. What are the likely benefits and costs of various interventions? (The cost side includes any discomfort, pain, or inconvenience the child or family may experience, as well as the investment of emotion, time, and money entailed.) Is a lot of travel necessary? Will it mean cutting the child off from established friendships? Is the level of effort required viable for a single parent? Are there potential undesirable effects to worry about? Taken all in all, does the intervention seem worth it?

Ideally, both parents should agree on any plan, or at least be willing to go along with it. Very rarely does an intervention succeed when one parent is dead set against it, and some effective methods are doomed to failure unless both are committed.

Once parents have chosen a form of treatment, they should try to stick with it for at least several weeks—longer may be needed, depending on the severity of the problems. Exceptions should be made if medication produces unacceptable side effects or if an intervention places someone in clear physical danger (for example, using physical restraint is usually okay for younger children but inadvisable with a teenager). However, it's also true that some of the most effective interventions may make things worse at first—for example, taking a firm stand on behavior often causes tantrums to escalate in intensity. Only with persistent effort does the situation improve. At such times, the support of other family members or a professional is very useful, both in encouraging parents to stick with it and in helping them judge when enough is enough. It's especially important in these cases that parents concur on their actions.

Support from outside the immediate family is also critical. It is less likely, for example, that the doctor or evaluator who performs a twenty-minute exam for ADD will be as able or willing to provide vital backup and follow-through for a particular strategy (including medication) as a physician who spends more time on the assessment. For some patients, medication alone works sufficiently well that minimal follow-up is needed. But even in those situations, teachers need to cooperate with evaluations performed by the school, and with subsequent recommendations for adjustments in the child's schoolwork and classroom situation.

THE CASE FOR MULTIMODAL TREATMENT

Current positions on ADD treatment tend toward one of two extremes. One (minority) view is that ADD represents a unique temperament and personality with both useful and less useful aspects, and that the child's environment ought to adapt to the child's needs and temperament. This position is reflected by such titles as *The Myth of the A.D.D. Child, Attention Deficit Disorder: A Different Perception*, and *No More Ritalin: Treating ADHD Without Drugs*.[5] Usually the use of medication is sanctioned only as a last resort or in a crisis situation, and in combination with multiple nondrug interventions.

The great weight of opinion, however, supports Ritalin as the primary or central treatment for this "brain-based" disorder. Hallowell and Ratey's *Driven to Distraction* is probably the best-known book taking this position, though it does cover strategies other than medication.[6] Recently a few experts have expressed the more daring opinion that for some children with ADD, Ritalin *alone* may appropriately be used as the first and only intervention—and even that the physician "need not feel guilty" if other services are not provided.[7] Although many researchers see inadequate evidence to support this claim,[8] it has already been widely aired and is likely to encourage more Ritalin-only treatment.

Based on two decades of clinical experience, I remain committed to a multicausal, nonpathological view of ADD in which both brain chemistry and environment contribute to children's problem behaviors. In this view, ADD symptoms express a "living imbalance" between the child's inherent capabilities and the demands of his or her environment. In this belief I feel a bond with those who want society to appreciate and adapt to the range of diversity in children's personalities. On the other hand, I recognize that the ADD child must learn to cope with socially approved expectations and responses, and that this may sometimes require the use of medication. It seems to me critical to raise questions about a society where several million children are taking Ritalin. In everyday terms, however, children and families must adapt to social norms, while we work on broader levels to make room for all kinds of people with all kinds of strengths and weaknesses.

Even in the absence of the "perfect" study supporting the role of psychosocial interventions in ADD treatment, there are compelling logical and practical reasons for using them. For one thing, the best drugs for treating ADD symptoms—Ritalin and other stimulants—cannot be used in the evening or near bedtime because they cause insomnia. This is the time of day when both parents can most often spend time with their children, yet these precious hours can be terribly vexing for families with an ADD-diagnosed child. Parent training, a central component of behavioral interventions, enables parents to cope more effectively when medication can't be used or is not elected. Even Russell Barkley, who doubts that family environment (unless it is truly horrendous) much affects long-range outcomes for ADD children, says that "undertaking specific changes in our family environments and our parenting . . . may produce immediate and short-term benefits, a reduction in stress for both parent and child, and a better quality of family life."[9]

Effective parenting and appropriate education can reduce a child's ADD symptoms and allow the frequency and dosage of Ritalin to be lowered. Conversely, medication alone will not teach the child or his or her caregivers appropriate coping skills for dealing with the ADD temperament, making it more likely that Ritalin will be needed over the long term.

The use of medication to treat ADD has clear advantages. For many children, medication works quickly to relieve symptoms. Ritalin and other drugs also can enhance the effectiveness of psychosocial or behavioral interventions, producing short-term improvements in attention and the ability to control impulsive and hyperactive behavior, so that the child can take in information more easily and respond more readily. Further, there are times when it's difficult or simply impractical to make an immediate response to problem behavior, so vital to the success of behavioral approaches—on the playground during recess, for example. Thus the use of medication as part of a multimodal program can allow the child a less restricted environment. These real benefits of medication, of course, have contributed to the Ritalin boom.

Whether it is ethical or "better" to use medication alone as a first response to ADD is discussed in the final chapter. I believe that *in most situations* psychosocial interventions should be tried first; if problems have not improved after several weeks, only then should medication be offered. This chapter outlines the strengths and weaknesses of various nonmedication approaches. None is a specific recipe, but I hope this survey will help equip readers to evaluate the advice they may encounter in books, doctor's offices, schools, and the company of friends and relations.

THERAPY FOR THE CHILD

"Talk therapies" have a place in treating some ADD-diagnosed children, as long as one doesn't expect too much of them. While the thrust of my interventions is usually with the parents and school, I do find it useful with unhappy or angry children to work with them alone. Depending upon the severity of the child's problems I might meet with the child as often as once a week, although such frequent visits are quite rare in my practice.

At a minimum, I believe it's respectful of the child and dignifying to the whole process to involve him directly. If he is old enough and can attend sufficiently to interact with me in this way, I try to lay out his situation and how I'm going to help him. I make an effort to focus on the specific behaviors that are causing the most grief, rather than just telling a child he "has" ADD and that's the reason for all his trouble. My aim is to form an alliance with the child, who is probably feeling like a rotten person the world has ganged up on, and who needs to feel that I'm on his side. Then he can be helped, in varying degrees, to understand what's going on and gradually enlisted in managing his behavior.

My office can be a safe place for a kid to ventilate and work through his feelings. However, the kind of talking I do with kids is quite different from traditional psychotherapy, in which a child would be encouraged to express himself without restraint. This is not a good idea with the kind of child who can so easily be carried off in a whirlwind of escalating emotions— usually fury or frustration—so that he loses any capacity to interact at all. Similarly, techniques that rely on a child making cognitive choices about his behavior are likely to fail; he may know the right thing to do in a given situation, but there's always the danger that his impulses will take over. In fact, ADD in many kids is a state of constant war between their cognitive, wanting-to-please side and their impulsive side.

The commonest treatment for children arising from the old Freudian model is play therapy, in which the child plays for, or with, the therapist; such opportunity for self-expression within a physically and emotionally safe, neutral environment is felt to be therapeutic in and of itself. The therapist also may offer insights into the meaning of the play. The child is supposed to resolve inner conflicts, and in the process gain better control over unconscious drives that manifest as problem behaviors. Play therapy sessions are conducted at least weekly. Parents are not included; rather, after an initial interview, the therapist may meet with the parents every three months or so to discuss the child's progress.

I often find playing with a child very useful in the initial evaluation. Experts overwhelmingly agree, however, that this kind of therapy offers scant value to the child struggling with ADD behavior.[10] There are exceptions, of course. A child who has experienced a trauma or chronic stress, such as child abuse or a major loss (the death of a parent or even divorce), may benefit. And for adolescents and adults, insight-oriented therapy may prove valuable in understanding the emotional baggage accumulated by living with ADD symptoms for a long time.

Cognitive behavioral therapy, or CBT, is a more directive approach. The therapist does more talking and determines the content of sessions much more vigorously than in play therapy. CBT may be summarized as teaching children rules about performance and behavior. Through a variety of methods—conversation, workbooks, role playing—the child and therapist review common problem situations: for example, waiting your turn; staying in your seat; accepting the decision of a parent, teacher, or peer. The child's feelings and current actions are highlighted ("You feel eager. You think you know the answer. You want to get up."). He is offered strategies, implemented in small steps, for becoming more aware of his emotions and responses, and is instructed in alternative ways of coping ("If I stand up, I'll feel bad later. I should raise my hand."). The child is praised and rewarded for appropriate answers and behavior during the session, and is supposed to practice these techniques with his parents and teacher, who have been briefed on them.

To the extent that CBT focuses on changing behavior, it can be of some value in working with ADD kids. Unfortunately, the very personality and problems of children with ADD or other "externalizing" disorders (Oppositional Defiant Disorder, Conduct Disorder) make CBT—and play therapy, for that matter—less likely to succeed, compared to the child who has "internalizing" problems.[11] Anxious children with strong and unusual fears (phobias), those with unusual compulsions and rituals (Obsessive-Compulsive Disorder) and those who don't like being "bossed around" by such feelings are the best candidates for CBT treatment.[12] They are more able to follow through on their genuine desire to beat the power of the anxiety and resume a more normal life.

The desire of the ADD or ODD child to "be good" may be no less genuine, but the temperamental and emotional qualities of their "disorders"—the inattention and impulsivity of ADD and the contrariness of ODD—tend to sabotage any therapy that requires cooperation and slowing down to think. A few studies of CBT for ADD children have demonstrated short-term improvement within restricted settings, but researchers note that these positive effects have not "generalized" to other settings.[13] I use elements of CBT in trying to give ADD patients a clear picture of their situation and ways of getting a grip on it. In general, though, I rely less on children's ability to modify their own behavior and more on the role of external controls—parents and teachers—in helping children make the right choices when their impulses threaten to take over.

I did a certain amount of talking with Bobby Hall soon after we met, about eight years ago. (At that time, insurance plans were more generous about covering such sessions.) With nearly all children (and many adults), I like to "personify" their problem. To Bobby I said, "Bobby, we've got to figure out a way to beat this anger stuff. It's ruining your life. You seem to be a pretty good kid when this feeling isn't in charge of you." (His guarded expression changed slightly at this.) "The first thing we have to do is give these angry feelings a name, so we can clearly identify them as the enemy. Some kids call their angry feelings 'Mr. Anger.' Can you think of a not-so-nice name for your angry feelings?"

Bobby got into the idea of fighting and beating "the enemy," and quickly came up with an idea for a name. "What about 'Red Hot Chili Peppers'"? he offered. "That's great!" I told him. "What if we just call them 'Red Hots' for short?" He agreed, and that became his and his parents' code word for his angry feelings. Parents also take to this personification, because it gives them a vivid way to warn their child when his behavior is getting out of hand: "Uh-oh—I see the Red Hots coming on." Naming a problem works for inattention and other symptoms, too: "Mr. Distraction" is one I've used a lot, or, for impulsivity, "Mr. I-just-want-to-have-fun-right now"—"Mr. I" for short. But kids often come up with more colorful names on their own; one child called his anger "the Bad King of the Mean Feelings."

Bobby and I then tried to identify those times when he was especially vulnerable to the "Red Hots": when he felt sad or tired, when his feelings were hurt by another child, when he'd had a bad day at school. I like to take the positive tack of finding out what a child may already be doing to try to control himself better, so I asked Bobby to think of times when he could have gotten really mad but stopped when he was only a little angry. Once, he said, a kid had claimed it wasn't Bobby's turn in a game. It made Bobby angry, but that time he walked away and started drawing by himself. Moving away and getting involved with another activity or person is a common technique. Kids know what works for them—but sometimes I can add to their repertoire.

Most often Bobby lost it when other kids teased him. He'd use foul language and strike out physically, which inevitably led to the principal's office. To ignore teasing is really hard, despite the advice and support of parents, teachers, and friends, and I thought Bobby could use another weapon. "Would you like to learn a really easy comeback for when kids tease you?" I asked. "Sure would," he replied in his oddly clipped tone. "It's simple—just three words," I said. "When a kid teases you, the three words to remember and say to him are, 'Say it again.' The kid will do it again, and you say the same thing: 'Say it again.' So as long as this kid keeps it up, you just keep saying, 'Say it again.' It'll drive him crazy—he won't want to tease you if he thinks it's what you want him to do. If he starts getting physical, run away and tell the teacher," I concluded. "What do you think?"

"I like it," Bobby said with some finality. We practiced the technique in a role play—first he was the teaser, then I was, using the taunts that Bobby heard ("You dork!—Say it again—You dork!—Say it again," and so on). By now Bobby was enjoying himself immensely and clearly appreciated the help. His parents were clued in to the Red Hots and Say It Again, so they could remind Bobby on a daily basis to use these and other techniques. This was the start of building a team that included Bobby, his parents, his teacher, and me, to fight the real enemy.

I also played games with Bobby quite often. I might occasionally use a psychological game such as the child therapy classic, The Talking-Feeling-Doing Game. But we were just as likely to play a board game like Sorry or Stratego. Such play was quite different from traditional play therapy, which is usually open-ended, with the child allowed to do whatever he wants. In play therapy, for example, he might get violent with a toy and then be encouraged to discuss what that's really about—the idea being that once he realizes why he's getting angry, this awareness will enable him to be more in control. Much more useful to an impulse-driven child are games that can model peer relationships. Board games, which involve taking turns as well as winning and losing, are metaphors for the luck and arbitrariness of life. In this case, I would take the role of Bobby's peer (but one who stayed in control). And as his peer, I would insist that he play by the rules.

I encouraged his parents to play these kinds of games at home, too. Their primary purpose was teaching Bobby to honor the rules of sportsmanship, rather than just to have fun (though that might happen). For example, if he spun the spinner or shouted an answer out of turn (an almost irresistible urge for an ADD-type kid), he'd get one warning. The second time, he might lose his turn or forfeit $100 in Monopoly money. If it happened a third time, he might have to sit out for five minutes and watch the game go on, while the adults (per instructions) acted like they were having an especially good time. If the penalty provoked a tantrum, a time-out resulted, with Bobby still in the room. This exquisite form of torture would make him so eager to rejoin the game that he would try extra hard to control himself.

GROUP EXPERIENCES FOR THE ADD CHILD

Other child-based treatment efforts include group therapy and structured group activities, also known as social skills training. These can offer distractible and/or impulsive children emotional support and guidance within a controlled arena, helping them develop restraint and sensitivity to others, so that they're not regularly alienating their peers. After Bobby's treatment had progressed for a few years, his parents tried sending him to summer camp and to some after-school art programs, and he did pretty well in both settings. He had been taking medication for some time by then, and his parents' skills at managing him had improved greatly.

The ADD summer program developed by William Pelham at the Western Psychiatric Institute and Clinic in Pittsburgh has become a model for this kind of "milieu" treatment for ADD.[14] Children spend three hours each day in a classroom format. The first hour resembles an academic special-education class; in the second, the children use computers; and the third hour is an art class. In all three settings, a behavioral system based on collecting or losing points operates. Points can be exchanged for privileges, social honors, or rewards at home. CBT is used both in the morning classes and in the afternoon, which is devoted to highly supervised sports and other recreation. Parents meet at least weekly with counselors to review their child's progress, and they receive training on how to implement reinforcement plans at home and at the child's regular school.

During the school year, the Pittsburgh program continues on Saturdays—a day when many parents would like to give their child some unstructured time, perhaps without the usual dose of Ritalin. Behavior flare-ups can torpedo such plans, and a well-run weekend program can help relieve the stresses. While such comprehensive group programs are not available in many communities, it's worth seeking out some kind of

structured, group-based experience. Unlike play therapy or CBT, these offer the ADD child real-time practice in learning to cope with the demands
of his world.

Beyond structured forms of therapy, what kind of life situations are
likely to be helpful to an ADD-diagnosed child? Parents should consciously seek opportunities for their child to feel successful outside the academic realm. Many children who have problems with attention and
behavior in school concentrate just fine on activities or subjects that interest them, or where they feel competent. Bobby, for example, could sit still
for many minutes drawing cartoon figures, so I encouraged Bill and June
Hall to find situations where he could be rewarded for this. Finding the
right arts or sports or drama program may represent yet another task for
parents, but the rewards, measured by a child's improved sense of self-
worth and social success, make the effort highly worthwhile. Parents
should try to ensure that the activity is supervised by adults who are clued
in to their child's personality and the best ways of keeping him or her focused and well behaved; for the impulsive youngster, a situation with lots
of children and no one clearly in charge is a prescription for disaster.

Recently parents have been asking me about two "alternative" treatments offered directly to the ADD child—biofeedback and meditation.
Non-Western, noninvasive interventions have become popular among
many people open to New Age ideas, yet both techniques would seem to
share the limitations noted for using CBT with impulsive or oppositional
children. Teaching a child who can't sit still to meditate sounds like a particularly thankless task. It might be more useful for teenagers or adults,
though I'm not aware of any demonstrated success. Biofeedback is used to
promote an awareness of when one is in a calm or agitated state through
signals such as colored lights or sounds that respond to changing brain
wave patterns. But in order to utilize this technique, someone must maintain enough cognitive presence to recognize the feelings that correspond to
those cues—again, very unlikely for the impulse-driven child. The few
studies on the use of biofeedback in ADD have been inconclusive.[15]

A final caveat for parents in search of treatment for any childhood disorder: *Never cede control of the child's therapy to the therapist.* While parents
needn't participate in or know the details of every meeting between a child
and his or her therapist, they should stay involved with the process by asking the therapist regularly how things are going and by letting the therapist know what's been happening, at home and at school. Too many
long-term courses of therapy for children have ended in parental disap-

pointment and anger over lack of results, when the treatment nearly always could have been shortened or modified had the parents been more vocal and informed. The principle of doctor-patient confidentiality is sacrificed in a good cause here. With teenagers, however, confidentiality becomes more of an issue; it's best if the teen willingly shares the information with his parents himself. How much the therapist divulges may depend on whether the therapy is meant more for the child or for the family.

PARENTAL GUIDANCE AND FAMILY THERAPY

I have always been slightly at a loss to know when simply talking to someone becomes therapy. "Parental guidance" sounds rather neutral and innocent—an experienced doctor giving a family advice on handling a difficult-temperament child—while "family therapy" may carry connotations of a more serious treatment or overtones of parent-blaming. But in my practice, the only real difference is one of degree. Most families with ADD-type problems can benefit from one or two visits wherein parents review their methods of handling their kids. Family therapy can be considered simply as an extension of that process, occurring if family and doctor agree that more visits could be useful.

Other issues in the family—adult depression, marital problems or divorce, job and economic stresses, alcohol or drug use, problems of the siblings—need be discussed only if they hinder coherent, effective parenting of the ADD-diagnosed child. It's important that such issues be brought up with the doctor, because if serious, such problems invariably harm the parents' ability to provide consistent affection and control. In practice, when a family is comfortable with the doctor, these issues do come up over time.

Children with ADD symptoms *can* learn ways to manage them—to keep a firmer handle on anger, persevere through distractions, take more responsibility for their actions, and get along better with other children. But they can't do it by themselves, or even with one-on-one help from a doctor or therapist. Parents play a definitive role by providing externally the control that the child is unable to supply from within. When this is available, the child becomes more able to make the "right" choices even when his impulses are pulling him in the wrong direction.

PARENTING FUNDAMENTALS FOR THE DIFFICULT CHILD

The essence of good parenting for ADD-type children is the same as for all children. It's simply harder to provide, yet even more necessary, because of the kind of children these are. Even as I offer opinions about what works best, I am humbled by the knowledge that my wife and I have raised our two "easy-temperament" sons only to ages eleven and nine. As a parent, I have a long way to go: adolescence looms! However, I have watched close to two thousand sets of parents try hard with difficult children, and they have my deepest respect. I have also had the pleasure of seeing many families and children improve—sometimes quickly—with the application of the principles that I'm about to share.

First, there is no prescription for loving your child. I believe that nearly all the parents I see love their children. Whether they are able to demonstrate it is another matter. Many are constrained by time pressures and other priorities. Spending time with your child, at play or in other contexts, is the surest way to let him know that you care about him and to validate his sense of self-worth. Even the most difficult child is more likely to act more cooperative when he feels loved and good about himself. However, a difficult child poses special challenges to any parent's expression of love, and ineffective parenting only makes that expression harder. Parents who do not set effective limits may see their attempts at loving devolve into mutual anger and a struggle of wills. Even a good time can be ruined when it's time to stop but Johnny doesn't want it to end.

Rather than fearing outside control, all children seek a steadiness of response from their parents. A child "in charge" of his parents is an insecure person, with an internal script that runs like this: "I'm too little to take care of myself, yet I regularly find myself more powerful than the adults I depend on for my care. I 'beat' them with my persistence and intensity. I will continue to challenge them until I get a degree of reliable intensity from them that allows me to feel they are stronger and more consistent than I am. Because my security needs are so great, I will challenge them even when I know that I'm doing something wrong." Admittedly, no child has ever expressed these exact sentiments to me directly, though more than a few adolescents have said as much—even a couple of children as young as eight. But their testing behaviors in defiance of caring and rational parents say it all.

Presuming that abundant love and affection are in place, probably the single most important component of any psychosocial approach to treating

ADD symptoms—the effort most likely to result in happier, more secure children with a decent self-image—is a form of parenting that emphasizes structure, consistency, and immediate, tangible, *action-oriented* responses to a child's behavior. Parents often ask me to suggest specific responses to their child's behavior; they want to know what works. In reply I first ask them, "What do you do when you are finally pushed to anger by your child?" Then I recommend they consider taking that action much sooner—long before they have become angry—and use that method on a consistent basis. And I emphasize that it should be an action rather than words.

When my own sons were about two and four, their noisy play sometimes got to me in the evening when I'd come home tired. When the play turned into fighting, I'd tell them to stop, but usually the noise level indicated they weren't listening. Though tired, I knew I should *do* something rather than continue to issue commands, so often I'd get up without knowing exactly what I was going to do. I might separate them from each other, remove a toy, turn off the TV, or give them a time-out. The boys, too, didn't know exactly what their dad was going to do, except that it was probably something unpleasant. It got so that, in time, I would simply get up from my chair and the misbehavior would cease. They had learned that if Dad had to get up, *something* was going to happen. This became a sufficient signal— and because of this, I think, they often responded just to my words.

Effective action is immediate action: missing dessert, losing a turn in a game, getting sent to bed early. Any response that is even moderately delayed (for younger children, by no more than a few minutes) becomes just words, mere threats or promises, and is a much less effective reinforcer. Many parents hope they can meet all their children's behavior challenges with rational explanations and positive reinforcers (rewards) alone. But realistically, in dealing with the temperament of ADD/ODD-type children— distractible but persistent, impulsive yet intense—cognitive or positive responses by themselves cannot resolve the child's emotional-security issue: who's stronger and steadier, the child or the parent. Another tactic of hopeful parents, ignoring a child's challenge, might be seen as not rewarding misbehavior, yet experience shows that if a parent doesn't actively intervene, the misbehavior usually escalates to a point where he or she must respond negatively. By then the behavior is probably bad enough that the parent's response must be far stronger than if it had occurred earlier.

Positive reinforcers are important, too: being allowed to play with a favorite toy, watch a favorite TV show, or have a story read at bedtime are privileges earned by good behavior. Making it clear that they *are* privileges helps a lot—nowhere is it written that watching *The Simpsons* is any child's inalienable right. However, it's impossible completely to avoid negative responses to a difficult-temperament child. Most parents I encounter know this intuitively, but many have been overwhelmed by their child's personality and handcuffed by the propaganda of politically correct parenting. This is demonstrated to me over and over when parents tell me that the technique of time-out doesn't work with their child. The time-out is a kind of paradigm of the action-oriented intervention, and it can occur in varying degrees of intensity, depending on the child's capabilities. Sometimes the action needs to be strong and/or physical. Over the past few decades, the condemnation of physical discipline in all forms has made many parents fearful of taking such action, putting those with really challenging kids in a terrible bind.

BEHAVIORAL TRAINING: AN INDISPENSABLE TOOL

The time-out is part of a repertoire of techniques for coping with child behavior that fall under the general category of behavior modification or behavior management training. To some parents and other observers, behavior modification—with its vocabulary of terms such as *reward, punishment, reinforcement,* and *extinction*—connotes negative ideas about heartless mind control and Pavlovian experiments. They sometimes ask: "Isn't it better if Susie works for herself rather than for gold stars or tokens? Aren't we bribing her?"

Despite its cold and clinical ring, however, behavior modification is simply a set of strategies that address the reality of how humans (and other creatures, for that matter) experience their world: what evokes a desirable response and what doesn't. All behavior is learned, though we come into life with inherent temperamental and developmental givens. Whatever we have integrated deeply into our psyches arrives first through experience—whether that experience begets affection, generosity, cooperation, or less positive attributes. Theorists such as B. F. Skinner and E. O. Wilson have shown that even altruism and love can be accounted for by behavioral principles.

Recent work with autistic children has demonstrated that very intensive forms of behavioral training (in children under age five) can produce remarkable improvements in a condition once thought to be "wired in" at birth and resistant to therapy. (See Chapter 5.) Reading about these discoveries and other evidence of great plasticity in the brains of young children has led me to speculate about the developmental aspects of ADD—how inherent temperament interacts with a child's early experience of life to influence whether ADD symptoms develop, or how severely. Based on my experience of a vast range of parental responses to ADD-type children, it seems likely that behavioral training in the early years might make a big difference. In other words, there may be many potential ADD children whose parents *did* meet their temperamental challenges with optimal responses, so that by age three or four, these active, spontaneous kids can pretty well control themselves, rather than look like ADD candidates. I'd like to see more research done along these lines.

Many of the books available on ADD provide detailed guidelines for using behavioral techniques and describe creative approaches to specific situations. One book I often recommend to parents is *Beyond Ritalin*, by Stephen Garber, Marianne Garber, and Robyn Spizman.[16] Most of the techniques described make significant demands on parents' time and energy at the start but should make their lives easier once the program is in place. Here in outline are a few of the most common strategies:

1. Structure tasks into smaller components. For example, instead of just telling a child, "Clean your room," break the job down into stages: "First pick up your clothes off the floor and put them in the hamper. Next pick up your toys and put them in the bins," and so on. A timer is often used to limit each subtask—for example, five minutes to get the clothes off the floor.

2. Reward the successful completion of tasks with a star, token, or check mark on a chart. Failure to complete the task in time may result in a loss of TV time or an earlier bedtime. Tokens may be turned in for special prizes or privileges, such as a small toy, increased TV time, or time with Dad.

3. Chart the child's behavior on a daily basis; post the chart somewhere in the house where parents and child can easily refer to it.

4. Target only one or two problem situations at a time. Once there is clear improvement (the child is doing a much better job cleaning his room, for instance) move on to the next priority.

5. Respond to failures by withdrawing privileges or giving time-outs.

A few comments are in order about *how* these techniques are put into practice. To parents who have done their reading or consulted experts, this deceptively simple advice—focus on discrete tasks, chart behaviors, bestow immediate rewards for good behavior—can begin to sound like a tedious litany. So often parents have told me, "We tried that, but . . ." I'm certain they believe they *have* tried it, yet by observing their child's unabating poor behavior I must conclude that they did not try with enough immediacy, intensity, or consistency for that child. These are by no means easy tasks for any parent, and in families with ADD children there's a good chance that one or both of the parents have problems themselves with organization and following through. In combination with their children's temperament, this makes successful parenting experiences extremely hard to come by.

Yet I have seen parents succeed when they really scrutinize their own behavior, calibrate their responses to the intensity of their child, communicate their power and consistency in a controlled way, and receive steadfast support and "permission" to take the actions necessary. Parents should realistically limit their goals to ones they are sure they can handle. When all this happens, things do get better.

Let's take as an example the time-out, the current societally approved "bottom line" for child discipline. In most time-outs, the child is restricted to a nonstimulating location—in most households a chair, bed, or quiet room—either for a defined period of time or until he or she calms down. Some expression of anger generally is permitted during time-out, but most parents draw the line at hitting, kicking, throwing things, or taking apart the room. Yet what is a parent to do when the child will not honor the rules of time-out? It's tricky, because solutions that occur to desperate parents can verge on the abusive, such as locking a child in a closet. Using a harness to keep a child of three or under on a bed has been recommended, but even this strikes me as too much. Nor I do much like the idea of closing a gate or locking the bedroom door. Rather than using any artificial restraint or barrier, which obscures the power issue, I believe that briefly but unpleasantly returning the child to the room or bed is more effective at delivering the message "I'm stronger and steadier than you."

Most books, if they discuss the dilemma at all, suggest lengthening the confinement time or imposing additional consequences such as losing privileges. However, all these consequences are of lesser intensity than the action of the time-out itself, or are sufficiently delayed as to render them ineffective with an out-of-control child. Telling a screaming, thrashing five-year-old who won't stay in the time-out area that he *has* to stay there ten minutes longer, or else he won't be allowed to watch his evening cartoons, will have little effect at that moment. One might as well be threatening that he won't have a birthday party next year. He wants to miss neither his cartoons nor his party, but he is simply unable to utilize that information while in the grip of his anger. Of course, when he eventually calms down, he'll feel really bad about missing his cartoons (if the parents have been practicing consistency, they will feel obliged to follow through), but that's too late for quelling the tantrum and his sense at that moment that he is stronger than his parents.

What's missing from the parent's repertoire and comfort level in such cases is a technique I have come to call the "emphatic no." This involves a combination of verbal sharpness, parental body language, and (if necessary) physical contact with the child, in an escalating pattern to break through an impulsive child's nonresponsiveness and allow him to access his cognitive knowledge of "right behavior." I believe this technique is among the most useful skills that parents of difficult-temperament children can learn.

The Emphatic No

Deke was two and a half when I first met him. His mother, Michelle, was frantic. She and her husband, Frank, had just been told that their son (their only child) was autistic, and they wanted another opinion. Since they wanted feedback quickly, I agreed to their bringing Deke along to the first visit.

I wanted to observe the family's interactions, so I set out some age-appropriate toys—cars, large Legos, and a dish set with plastic food—and asked Deke's parents to play with him. "He doesn't really talk," Michelle cautioned me, noting that he might say "ma" for Mom, "da" for dog, and "ba" for ball but not necessarily in the right context. Autistic children typically have language delay or do not use language in practical or useful ways.

Even as the parents and I talked briefly, I saw how Deke expressed his needs. When he tried to get onto the table with the toy bins, his parents asked which one he wanted and then proceeded to move all of them to the floor. As Deke tried to open each one, his parents would help him. Deke spent a maximum of fifteen or twenty seconds on any object, then threw it away and picked up another. As he ignored us and careened from one thing to the next, I could see how the previous evaluator might have judged that he was "unconnected" to people, the key diagnostic finding for autism.

But there were contradicting signs, too. When the parents made an effort to interact, they and Deke played nicely, albeit for periods of less than a minute. Deke seemed to enjoy and seek out being held by Michelle, whereas autistic children reject physical contact. He also played with toys appropriately. An autistic child will take a car and bang it on the floor rather than roll it and say, "Vroom!" After watching for about twenty minutes, I asked permission to join in the play. I was much more forceful and directive with Deke, pushing all the other toys aside and concentrating on the dishes with the fake food. I made plates of food for everyone and, while talking, gave each a dish filled with hot dogs, hamburgers, or pizza. Deke accepted his plate and tried to bite the hamburger. Then, handing him a cup, I poured pretend milk into my cup and his, drank out of mine, and said, "Yum." Deke responded by drinking out of his cup, and his parents laughed. He was able to stay with this play for almost five minutes. "That's the longest he's focused on anything besides TV or videos," Frank noted.

I never saw Michelle or Frank attempt to physically restrain or refocus Deke. Instead, they used words of encouragement or acted interested in the toy he had been playing with, but Deke seemed oblivious to their contributions. After a half hour I was convinced that Deke wasn't autistic. I did believe that he had significant language delay and probably manifested criteria for ADD in an incipient way. (Enough two-year-olds are very active to make determining what is "overactive" difficult.) Deke's problems were serious but lacked autism's devastating prognosis of inability to form emotional relationships. The parents were greatly relieved to hear my opinion and told me they planned to meet with a speech and language therapist for Deke's language problem. I also tried to tell them that their parenting style was less than ideal for coping with Deke's level of activity and impulsivity.

It was six months later when I heard from them again; Michelle wanted me to see the progress Deke had made in his language skills. Deke, now three, had twenty or more words, occasionally used two-word combinations, and babbled constantly. His focus was slightly improved: He could stay with one toy for a few minutes but still would abruptly end his play and impulsively roam around the room. But behavior-wise, things were going downhill. "Frank's in Asia on business for two months, and I'm feeling totally overwhelmed," Michelle confessed. "I can't remember a time when Deke's responded if I say no to him." Indeed, during that visit, he went to the door of my waiting room, turned the handle, and headed out, completely ignoring his mother's entreaties. Michelle agreed to another visit to help her get Deke to listen.

We decided to work on just one thing during the next session. Deke wasn't to touch the door handle to the waiting room; if he did, Michelle's response would be an emphatic no. The first time Deke touched the handle, Michelle was to say "No" loudly and physically remove him from the area if he didn't move away on his own. The second time, she would *shout* "No!" and remove him again. If he touched the handle again during the half-hour session, she would yell *"No!"* even more sharply and seat him on a designated time-out chair.

Michelle was dubious at first: "I've tried time-outs at home, but he'll never stay." I replied that she could either hold Deke in the chair so he couldn't get up, or if he did, she could grab him and place him down on the chair with some force while saying "No" in a loud voice. She should do this two or three times at most; if he still got up after that, she should ignore him for a minute or two. Deke weighed less than forty pounds and Michelle three times that—still, I wasn't sure Michelle could outlast her son in a test of wills. "I'll coach you the first few times if you feel like you need help," I promised. "Are you comfortable with this plan?"

One thing confused her: "If I let him go after the second or third time, won't he think he's won?" I explained that it wasn't critical that she "win" every time. More essential to the ultimate success of her efforts was their immediacy, her self-control, and the unpleasantness of the experience for Deke. Most important were consistency and her willingness to follow through the next time Deke challenged her. I suggested that Michelle limit herself to three physical responses per episode; more, and I worried that she might get too angry and lose control of herself. This would frighten both her and Deke and encourage the old pattern of avoiding conflict by giving in to his demands. "Just tell Deke after the third time, 'Okay, Deke, you won this time. But the next time you do that, I'm going to do the same thing.'" Deke would quickly get the idea, I assured her. If she felt too uncomfortable, or that she might be losing control of herself, she could stop at any time, I emphasized. (Only two or three times have a parent's actions while disciplining their child in my office worried me enough to call a halt.)

Deke had been wandering around but had not gone over to the door yet. Michelle called him over, sat him on her lap, and said, "See that door, sweetie? Don't touch the handle or you'll have to have a time-out. Understand?" She pointed to the chair. Deke squirmed and fussed while she spoke; it was hard to tell whether her words penetrated at all. Within a few minutes Deke facilitated the trial by going to the door. Michelle said "No" loudly, and Deke ignored her. She went to the door and moved him away, but he immediately went back. Then she yelled "No!" and pulled him away from the door. At that Deke moved to another part of the room; it wasn't clear whether he had responded to her or simply become distracted.

However, after a minute or two, he went back to the door. Michelle again yelled "No!" and then pulled him off the door handle and took him to the time-out chair. When she put him down, he immediately popped off the chair. She picked him up and gently put him back on the chair; Deke once again got off and tried to run away. "Do you think Deke thought that was very hard, Michelle?" I asked. Michelle knew it was a rhetorical question. She grabbed hold of Deke and put him on the chair a third time, and again he just jumped up and ran off. It was possible he thought that she was playing a game. Since that was the third effort, she let him go but ignored him for a few moments.

Within minutes Deke was back at the door, and we went through the procedure again. This time, after the first time-out attempt I told Michelle, "You'll know you've put Deke down forcefully enough if he hesitates for a moment before getting up, or starts to cry. Are you willing to use a bit more of your strength?" She was, she said. "Do you feel angry, or like you're close to losing control?" I continued. She didn't. So I encouraged her to try again, knowing she had a long way to go between her current ineffectiveness and getting through to Deke without seriously hurting him. He hadn't even cried yet or indicated any discomfort. Michelle picked Deke up and put him down on the chair with enough force that he looked surprised. He began crying right away and tried to get up, at which she picked him up again and put him down on the chair with slightly more force. By now Deke was crying loudly, but he sat on the chair for a couple of moments while Michelle and I moved back to the couch. Then he got up off the chair. I thought Michelle had made an impression, so I suggested she just ignore him for a while. Deke came over and tried to get Michelle to hug him, but she continued to talk to me. Then she and I started playing with toys; after less than a minute Deke happily joined us on the floor.

About five minutes later Deke got up and started wandering again. Michelle and I glanced at each other as he edged toward the door. When he put his hand on the door handle, Michelle let out a loud "No!"—and Deke dropped his hand and moved away from the door with apparent apprehension. Quietly Michelle said: "That's the first time he's ever listened to me." I offered her a high five in congratulations, and to our surprise,

Deke came over and wanted a high five as well. Delighted, I gave him some skin, and his mother gave him a big hug.

It took work, but she had gotten through. We agreed that she would focus on one activity at home during the next week, using the same technique. When Michelle and Deke returned, both seemed noticeably calmer. Michelle reported that she had used the emphatic no (for her that meant a forceful return to the time-out chair) a couple of times, but mostly Deke responded to her loud verbal "No!" They'd had their best week together in many months. Michelle admitted, "I was kind of concerned and scared the first time I put Deke down hard on the chair here—but since you didn't seem upset, I felt okay about going on." When she saw that it was working and Deke was doing better, she was pleased and excited. She'd talked about it by phone with Frank, who sounded surprised but interested.

I saw Michelle and Deke a few more times over the next two months and noted with satisfaction that Michelle definitely had Deke figured out. I saw her growing more comfortable and effective in her authority—much more active, ready to move physically if Deke didn't respond. She was needing to use physical means less and less often, however. For his part, Deke was less frantic and more able to stay focused in our play, though he still "wandered" more than the average three-year-old. When Frank rejoined the family, he too had a chance to use a time-out with Deke in the office, and I could see that Michelle would have to coach her husband. Theirs was not a typical male–female dichotomy over comfort with discipline; Frank was actually less comfortable with it than his wife. Nevertheless, this family had taken an important step toward addressing their son's temperamental and emotional needs.

Deke's impulsivity, one of the core features of the ADD temperament, in combination with his intense, defiant behavior, demanded an immediate and intense response from his parents to enable Deke to utilize his cognitive abilities—to access his knowledge that "I'm not supposed to touch the door handle." The child labeled as ADD does better faced with stark black-and-white choices and consequences. Adults with similar problems sometimes complain that they can function only when the sword of Damocles is about to fall on them. To the uninformed or faint of heart, successful parenting of the spontaneous, strong-willed child can appear harsh—and indeed, there's a fine line between skillful drill instructor and martinet. But a tougher, hands-on style is actually kinder and a better fit for this temperament profile than the more cognitive approaches in vogue.

To some parents, any use of physical force to direct or correct a child feels "wrong," and nothing can make them comfortable with it. Understandably, people who were abused as children often feel this way. For them, parenting a tough kid is truly a dilemma, for some way of setting limits still must be found. Yet the reluctance to use physical interventions with children is much more widespread than the actual experience of abuse can account for, approaching the level of a social pathology. "Aren't you teaching a child to use violence by physically restraining him or putting him down?" is the fear often expressed. To the contrary, there is no evidence that the controlled, appropriate use of physical discipline leads to children acting more violent later in life—indeed, as I noted in Chapter 8, the opposite has been shown. To universally proscribe the use of physical force, especially for children with difficult temperaments, is to unnecessarily tie parents' hands. Paradoxically, this often leads to prolonged and severe conflicts more likely to *provoke* abuse.

Appropriate physical interventions are not in themselves dangerous, but the context in which they are used is crucial. Is the intervention preplanned, methodical, and limited? Is the parent upset but not out of control? The answers determine whether the action frightens the child or reassures him that the parent is in charge of both herself and him. Above all, parents should remember that physical action is a choice, not a necessity—another tool in the parenting repertoire.

Some specific caveats should be mentioned. Most important, parents should *never* use physical discipline with a child when they feel out of control. A parent's first responsibility is to calm down before he or she says or does anything, however difficult that may be. Further, there are parents whose own personalities are so volatile that physical means as an option carry too much risk. I caution parents to walk away from situations when they are exhausted or upset about other things, or if they've had anything to drink. If I suspected drug or alcohol abuse, or if a parent seemed particularly volatile, I would try to convey that effective parenting is probably out of the question until they can sort out their own problem first. Finally, the child's age is a factor. Immediate physical interventions to back up one's words are most appropriate beginning in the second year of a child's life and become much more problematic after about age eight or nine. After that, many children are too large to restrain or forcefully put down with safety.

Physical force also can be used methodically outside of parenting to useful effect—for example, in sports, where in well-run programs children can learn the difference between force used in anger versus controlled strength to achieve a culturally approved goal. An especially good activity for many impulsive and hyperactive children is martial arts classes, which emphasize and teach self-control in the use of force while allowing the child to blow off steam through physical activity. Other good choices are swimming, gymnastics, and track, where the level of activity is relatively constant. I've known several boys who did well in Pop Warner football, where there's a lot of contact and the coaches tend to be strict, with immediate physical consequences—push-ups or laps—for misbehavior. On the other hand, Little League baseball is probably a sport to avoid. The kids are scattered around the field, and given baseball's leisurely, on-and-off rhythm, the outfielder is all too likely to be contemplating the grass when a fly ball comes his way.

INTERFACING WITH THE SCHOOL

In addition to effective parenting, therapy for the child, and in some cases medication, any multimodal approach to treating ADD symptoms must include efforts to obtain a school experience that's closely tailored to the child's needs. Not only does ADD behavior make it harder for a child to succeed in school, but learning disabilities frequently are part of the picture. This is a circular trap: the child's frustration, caused by learning deficits, exacerbates his ADD behavior, while inherent temperament problems make it harder for him to stick with academic challenges. For this reason, good ADD evaluations and interventions address both behavior and learning abilities.

Parents of a child with educational and behavioral weaknesses have two jobs. The first is to make sure, as best they can, that the school is addressing their kid's abilities appropriately, both in the general classroom and in any specialized learning environment. The second is to reinforce at home the kind of behavior that is expected in the school setting. This does not mean trying to *teach* the child at home, which is too emotionally laden for parents and children in general but is especially so when the child has a difficult personality and/or a learning problem. Except when the school asks parents to help, as in completing homework assignments, teaching the learning-disabled or ADD child should be left to teachers or tutors. Another exception, of course, is if parents and child have positive experiences over schoolwork; however, this is rare when the child is developmentally or temperamentally challenged.

How do parents determine whether their child's behavior and abilities make him or her a candidate for special educational help? They can seek an outside evaluation from a family doctor or behavioral specialist, which will help them understand the problems and support their attempts to obtain special help at school. However, federal law requires that the school make its own evaluation before offering special services, so many parents— often for financial reasons—elect to start there. An alert, caring teacher often brings behavior or performance problems to the family's attention, but parents should not count on this signal from busy teachers. They must be vigilant and knowledgeable about their child's life at school, and about the rights and responsibilities shared by families and schools in providing an appropriate education.

WHAT SCHOOLS CAN OFFER

Federal laws, specifically the IDEA and Section 504 (see Chapter 7), provide legal guidelines for evaluating and remediating educational disabilities. At any time a parent can request a screening evaluation of a child's performance. A teacher, psychologist, or doctor may also initiate such an evaluation, with the parents' approval. If the screening suggests a problem, a more detailed and formal evaluation must ensue, culminating in the development of an individualized educational plan (IEP).

Each state sets time limits for completing these procedures. In California, for example, the initial screening must be done within fourteen days of the request. An IEP can take more time to complete, sometimes up to three months. Of course, these evaluations and the recommendations for service that follow may be accomplished much more quickly given persistent pressure from parents, an outside health professional, or an attorney. I do not suggest that every evaluation is marked by foot-dragging and/or an adversarial relationship between school and family. Most are performed with honesty and diligence. However, there are real pressures on schools, and the squeaky wheel (the persistent parent) gets attention first.

Once it is determined that a child qualifies for special services, these may take various forms. It is beyond this book's scope to detail the approaches and techniques of special education for specific learning problems. In general, though, such methods try to teach the child alternative ways to learn required material. They exploit the child's relative developmental strengths while providing practice in areas where he is weak. For example, a child with a visual processing problem often reverses letters and has trouble paying attention to detail when reading and spelling; he may make frequent er-rors (such as reading ball for doll) or read very slowly. The special-ed teacher may ask him to pay attention to the shapes of the letters and give him cognitive reminders ("Remember, *b* bumps the next letter and *d* drags behind"). In addition, accommodations are made to give the learning-disabled child more time to learn the same material as his classmates, and grading may be adjusted to reflect not only his reduced accomplishments but his efforts to compensate.

This is how things are supposed to work. I must add that many parents find it hard to know if a school really is meeting the needs of their child, learning-disabled or not. Some parents, after encountering delays or what seem to them inadequate responses, become skeptical of school efforts at evaluation and remediation. Despite a genuine commitment to serve the special-needs child, many schools are strained to their limits of personnel and materials. This creates a clear conflict of interest—school officials may be loath to provide special services at increased cost if they feel this will lower the standard of education for the majority of pupils. Cost and staffing pressures also affect how school personnel view individual children and the source of their problems. For instance, the underperforming child who is not a behavior problem (in the pre-high-school grades, girls most often fit this profile) may be overlooked by the harried teacher or school psychologist preoccupied by acting-out boys. Even the behavior of "problem boys" can be seen as solely reflecting inherent emotional problems or troubled family dynamics—and therefore as the parents' responsibility rather than the school's.

Jenny Carter, the quiet fourth-grader introduced earlier, was just the sort of girl who doesn't immediately present as a problem, because she had good social skills and wasn't a troublemaker—but she was falling farther and farther behind in her schoolwork. Her parents, Susan and Peter, faced the potentially daunting challenge of making certain the school was doing its job with their daughter. The special-education teacher at Jenny's school, Mrs. Cronin, was sympathetic, but her own screening indicated that Jenny's reading difficulty was not sufficient to qualify her for special tutor-ing.

With my support, Susan and Peter pressed for a full IEP evaluation. Thus Jenny was scheduled for a series of tests with the school psychologist, a speech and language specialist, and Mrs. Cronin. Everyone agreed that Jenny's physical abilities were not in question, so the occupational/physical therapist assigned to the school was not involved. Taking the tests went relatively smoothly: Jenny would leave her regular classroom at various times during her day to meet with the evaluators. Two months after the initial request for an IEP, a meeting was held at the school, attended by all the evaluators as well as Jenny's parents, teacher, school principal, and myself.

THE IEP PROCESS: ONE FAMILY'S EXPERIENCE

Attending an IEP meeting for one's child shouldn't be an unpleasant experience, yet parents regularly report how difficult and scary it can be. As we waited outside the meeting room, Susan Carter remarked to me, "Why do I feel like I'm about to go into the dentist's office?" Her feelings were understandable, since she and Peter were about to publicly receive the opinions and judgments of several professionals about Jenny's problems. Me, they could hire and fire, but they were truly dependent upon their community's public education system. Sending Jenny to private school would have been next to impossible for them.

In the usual scenario, each evaluator reviews his or her findings, which by law they must—but not necessarily all in one hour-long meeting. Typically these specialists provide far too much technical data, such as detailed scores of subtests, quickly causing parents without a special-education background to become confused and overwhelmed. Far too much time tends to be devoted to data presentation, leaving too little time for interpreting what the data mean, or for the vital tasks of defining goals and interventions. I regularly request that the information be shortened and summarized, even if this necessitates another meeting with one or more of the evaluators later.

At Jenny's IEP meeting, I politely interrupted the psychologist's presentation to ask if the parents understood why the variations in Jenny's subtest scores on the WISC III intelligence test were significant. Susan's and Peter's response to my query indicated their confusion, and the psychologist appropriately slowed down and reexplained the data.

Susan and Peter were confident people with successful careers, yet they still felt lost in the meeting at times and later told me how much they appreciated my presence. Many parents have said that the single most useful hour of my time was the one spent at an IEP meeting. I strongly urge that both parents attend such meetings. If one parent is absolutely unable to do so, then the other should take a friend along, if only for a second set of eyes and ears to take in the information. If a qualified health professional can attend, so much the better—family doctors occasionally make time for this. Certain school districts provide their own ombudsperson, often a paraprofessional and parent who knows the IEP process and the laws.

Jenny's IEP evaluation found that she was behind in her reading and spelling and did have moderate visual processing problems. The IEP also turned up a mild weakness in her auditory sequential memory—her ability to remember a series of commands was somewhat below age level, another developmental disability that frequently accompanies or mimics ADD-type behavior. She had no problem concentrating on art projects but appeared to drift in class during silent reading and written assignments, often failing to complete her work in those areas. Her relative strengths were in math and in her basic demeanor, especially with her peers; her teacher and the psychologist judged that Jenny was among the most mature and well-liked children in her class.

Mrs. Cronin had been correct in guessing that Jenny's test scores were not low enough to qualify her for special services such as in-school tutoring. However, the teacher planned several changes for her within the classroom. She was to be moved to the front of the room and given shorter reading assignments in class and for homework. Her grades would reflect her performance with her adjusted workload, not necessarily how she fared compared to her peers. Mrs. Cronin would try to check more often to make sure Jenny was understanding written or verbal instructions. While she had to continue practicing her reading and writing, her parents would be allowed to read to her during homework aimed chiefly at obtaining information. Finally, Susan and Peter were referred to outside tutors who might be willing to reduce their fees slightly to help Jenny with her reading.

Along with these adjustments in her schoolwork, Jenny was to be held more accountable for completing work. Longer assignments would be broken up and she would be given a specified amount of time to complete them. If she finished in time, her teacher would give her a bronze, silver, or gold certificate redeemable for prizes at the end of the week. (This teacher used such rewards for a variety of behavioral and performance reinforcements.) Failure to complete the work could result in losing recess time. Susan and Peter would get a daily note informing them about Jenny's performance.

Susan and Peter were advised against punishing their daughter if she failed to complete classwork or homework. They could ask her about what she was finding hard at school, or if she did well, they could reward her with slightly more TV time or staying up an extra fifteen minutes. In general, parental efforts to improve a child's performance through punishments based on what happened at school—"You must go to bed early because you had a bad day at school"—are not especially fruitful. A more effective approach is to model expectations and responses at home along the lines of what the school would demand. Thus, for Jenny, Susan broke down home chores into smaller tasks. If told simply to clean her room, Jenny would take "forever." Instead, she first had to make her bed, then get her stuff off the floor, and lastly tidy up her desk, with five minutes for each task. As in school, redeemable rewards could be accumulated for successful efforts. Homework likewise was broken down into smaller increments, with rewards for completion.

The IEP team left it to me to decide whether or not Jenny met criteria for ADD—inattentive type. Strategically, I deferred a decision on the ADD diagnosis (her parents and I had discussed this previously) and on using Ritalin. I preferred to see what accommodations and services the school might offer Jenny, and how the parents and school could work together to support and structure her environment to improve her performance and attention. I could justify an ADD diagnosis later, if it was needed to obtain Section 504 services. A trial of Ritalin might be added if the renewed efforts of Jenny, her parents, and the school did not significantly improve things.

After an IEP meeting, the parents are asked to agree to the findings and recommendations, and to sign the IEP documentation. The Carters were leery at first, fearing that doing so might permanently bar Jenny from receiving any extra services. However, I advised them that the school's plan seemed reasonable, and that signing an IEP document is not an irrevocable sentence. The signatures indicate one's presence and agreement with the current goals and plans for the child. A family may at any time ask for another meeting or for a reassessment of the educational setting and plan.

After following the recommended program for six to eight weeks, the family and school would check in and confer with me. If Jenny had made little or no progress, a trial of Ritalin might be considered at that point. As it turned out, the results were not definitive; there was some progress, but later in the year Jenny did try Ritalin, which seemed to make completing her work a bit easier. For the fifth grade, however, she had a male teacher who gave her a lot of positive attention and was fairly strict; in his class, it seemed that things clicked for Jenny without medication. I lost touch with the Carters after that.

OTHER CHILDREN, OTHER EDUCATIONAL OPTIONS

When a child persistently struggles in the regular classroom, parents need to consider the advantages and disadvantages of the other available choices. Some choose to send their underperforming child to private school, where the student-teacher ratio is typically lower and the child can receive more individual attention. Jenny's family considered this option but couldn't afford it, which may have led to their eventual willingness to try Ritalin. Cost aside, the drawbacks of moving a child to a private school can include extra distance to travel, the loss of school friends, and the fact that new school pals aren't around to play with at home.

Transfer to a special class, or daily tutoring outside the regular classroom can help remediate learning problems. The trade-offs here are that special-ed children may be stigmatized by their peers or just feel "different," while the kid who regularly goes off for tutoring misses activities going on simultaneously in his or her regular classroom, as well as having to endure some stigma of difference.

Special day classes (SDCs) are for children with more serious learning and behavioral disorders. The typical SDC provides a full-time special-education teacher, usually assisted by an aide, for a class of not more than twelve students. A drawback is that the SDC population may include youngsters even considerably more troubled than the standard distractible/hyperactive child. Moreover, not every school has an SDC, so travel may be required.

To date, the most successful programs for children significantly impaired by distractibility, impulsivity, and hyperactivity have been those where children do spend time in a specialized, highly structured classroom. After they have experienced success there, children are returned to the regular classroom—but all too often, gains made in the special environment have not persisted. Unless ADD children and their teacher get support and assistance in the behavioral techniques used in the special class, the kids tend to fail once back in the normal classroom.[17]

An increasingly popular option is the use of full-time aides to monitor and support the special-needs child in the regular classroom.[18] This "shadow," as he or she is sometimes called, keeps the distractible child on task and in control, responding immediately when the child is struggling. The aide may work with other children but usually has one student as a primary responsibility. With such intensive help, many children are able to cope, and in the younger grades at least, little stigma attaches to such kids.

Even in middle school and high school, any social opprobrium must be weighed against the sense of failure the child might feel without such help, or against the label of attending a special class. Cost is a factor in making aides available, but schools may find it more economical than other means of achieving legal compliance. Parents also may be able to pay directly for an aide if the school's evaluation doesn't mandate one. In some places, young-adult volunteers serve as aides, at negligible cost to school and families, and to their own benefit.

A historical lack of success in returning special-education children to regular classrooms is among the arguments for a growing movement known as "full inclusion." This promotes efforts to meet the needs of *all* children within the regular classroom, by making adaptations for special-needs children with the support of teacher aides, parent volunteers, and paraprofessionals (or shadows). In these programs, the special-education teacher visits the regular classroom to assist the primary teacher both in direct teaching and in developing special plans for identified children. Full inclusion has some critics, including parents of learning-disabled children who feel it's a cosmetic solution and that only a special day class will work.

For the special-needs student, then, rarely does a perfect environment exist. Rather, the solution tends to be a series of compromises. Parents and teachers should monitor the child's progress regularly, with the overall aim of educating the child in the least restrictive environment.

Jenny Carter's case was a little different from that of many ADD-type children with difficulties in school, in that she didn't display the typically disruptive behavior of a hyperactive/impulsive child. Interfacing with the school poses somewhat different challenges for parents of a child such as Bobby Hall, who was constantly getting in trouble for clashing with other kids, both in class and in the schoolyard, and being rude or abrupt with his teacher. He would also tend to fixate on one activity that made him feel competent, such as drawing, when he was supposed to be doing other work. About five months after I first saw Bobby, in September of his third-grade year, he was finally scheduled for an IEP evaluation. By then he had been taking Ritalin for several months. I'd done some work with him and with his parents, and his overall attitude and performance were showing some improvement, mostly at home. His temper and foul language were still in evidence, though.

The school principal and psychologist took part in Bobby's IEP evaluation, along with his new teacher, his parents, and me. The school did have a system of consequences for misbehavior, though it didn't seem to work well for Bobby. A colored card for each child was displayed in the classroom to reflect his behavior. Normally it was green, but if a child misbehaved, he'd get a verbal warning and his card would be changed to blue. A second infraction resulted in a yellow card and loss of a recess period. The third time he acted up in any one day, he'd get a red card, and a note was sent home to the parents. I thought these responses might be too time-delayed to make an impact, given Bobby's personality: of course he wanted to have recess, but unless it was to come within moments of his misdeed, the prospect of losing this privilege probably wasn't enough reinforcement for him to keep control.

Based on my recommendations, some adjustments were made in the system for Bobby. He was moved to the front of his classroom, and if he misbehaved, his teacher was encouraged to act immediately, before events and emotions escalated. For his first rule violation he would put his head down on the desk for a minute or two. The next time he'd have to sit in the back of the room for five minutes. If a third incident occurred, he would immediately be taken to the principal's office to sit in a boring place for ten minutes. If he physically struggled with an adult at any time while being disciplined, his parents would be called and he'd be picked up from school. Notes were sent home daily reporting good and bad behavior. Staying in control could earn Bobby tokens, turned in for prizes from the teacher's "grab bag" at the end of the week.

Other techniques were used during recess. A stable and responsible kid might be assigned to hang out with Bobby, who was figuratively kept on a short leash—he wasn't allowed to range beyond ten yards of so of the yard duty (a teacher or other adult), who could thus immediately intervene if he started to go off. If he wandered farther, he'd be "benched." With practice and the help of medication, the distance would be increased. If he had a good day in the yard, he might be rewarded by leading the kids back inside or opening the door for everyone.

Bobby was briefed about the new procedures in advance and reminded on a regular basis. I had warned those taking part in his IEP evaluation that if he had to be sent home more than two or three times over a short period of time, the plan probably wasn't working and he might indeed have to be moved to a more specialized class environment. Fortunately, the teacher was able to adapt her style to his needs; his ongoing medication and work with the family also helped. Bobby had to be sent out of class only twice over the course of that school year, and the threat of a special class gradually receded.

PUTTING THE PIECES TOGETHER

For most families with an ADD-type child, finding the right combination of home environment, schooling, and other forms of treatment is an ongoing challenge. Bobby Hall provided an especially vivid illustration of this for me, as I've had the opportunity to watch over several years while his family worked to put all the pieces together.

Because of his anger and unhappiness, we initially considered long-term individual therapy for Bobby, but this was never pursued. The changes in Bobby's home and school environment, along with medication, proved sufficient to improve his mood and behavior. His daily experience began to include more success and less failure. His episodes of sadness and outbursts of temper decreased in frequency and intensity.

The Halls certainly had their share of work to do on parenting. When we first met, Bobby was going down the tubes emotionally, and his mother, June, was losing it herself on a regular basis. Bill, while more effective with Bobby, exercised lower standards than June and was not around a lot. I suppose our work together over several months could have been called family therapy. While most of the talk revolved around Bobby, the couple had disagreements to work out between themselves as well. How often would Bill work late? What were the behavior standards for Bobby to be? To their credit, they were quick learners, with the emotional flexibility and confidence to take certain risks with their son. Like Michelle, June faced a moment of crisis with Bobby and within herself when she attempted to hold firm and not back down. Bobby wasn't quite as persistent as Deke and didn't require a lot of physical intervention, but June recalled on many occasions "locking eyes" with Bobby, "ready to pounce on him if he moved away. He knew I wasn't kidding."

Bobby's unhappiness troubled Bill deeply, prompting him to become more consistent and to realize the need for him and June to agree on standards. If he let Bobby slide on things June felt were important, such as bedtime, it only made things harder for his wife and son. Basically Bill thought his wife's standards were fine, but he'd felt sorry for his son or was lazy about following through when he was in charge. Later in our acquaintance, Bill surprised me by remarking on how important those early meetings had been for him. I had genuinely forgotten how hard it had been to get Bill in the first time. Having fathers join the meetings is such a matter of routine that I don't always realize the profound effect an outside opinion can have on a family.

As Bobby progressed through the grades, his aggression decreased markedly, though he was still socially awkward and his behavior could be eccentric—at one time, his interest in a videogame character known as Sonic the Hedgehog bordered on the obsessive. He continued to challenge his teachers to find creative ways of integrating him into the standard class-room. Academically, he performed at an average level, with occasional bursts of achievement when something really engaged him. Once into mid-dle school, he began regularly to produce A's and B's on his report card.

The final ingredient in Bobby's treatment, as it is in many other multi-modal treatment programs, was Ritalin. He was started on the medication very soon after being evaluated, based on my judgment that it would sig-nificantly facilitate the psychosocial interventions we would try—and this proved to be the case. After several months of intensive involvement, I con-tinued to see him every six months. These visits also gave me an opportu-nity to check up on the overall scene for him and his parents.

At this writing, Bobby is thirteen and has taken medication for six years. Keeping him on medication was a team decision in which I concurred. Once or twice a year Bobby's parents would intentionally not give him Ri-talin for three to four days, while his teacher was alerted only that his med-ication was being "adjusted." Invariably both the teacher and Bobby would report more fidgeting and impulsive behavior, and a negative effect on his work completion. Bobby always agreed to resuming his medication. I'll be interested to see if Bobby continues to benefit as clearly from Ritalin as he moves into full adolescence.

When Bobby turned thirteen, I asked the Halls if they would consent to take part in a news program about ADD and Ritalin. I thought they repre-sented a good example of a family where Ritalin, *in combination with* par-enting/family therapy and monitoring the school situation, had helped a child. Bobby had matured nicely. He could sit quietly and carry on a re-laxed conversation with me; his speech had lost its mechanical, robotic quality. His range of interests had expanded—he was less likely to get lost in a single activity, such as Nintendo, as if it represented his salvation. He also acted more generous, had several friends, and seemed much happier in general. His activity level was normal and his parents no longer were con-stantly challenged—though even now, June said, there were moments when she needed to give Bobby "the look," upon which he would get it to-gether immediately.

In talking to the reporter, June made it clear that while she felt Ritalin had been helpful, she thought the change in their parenting was even more important. Bobby, articulate as always about his feelings, agreed that he was getting along better with his parents and in school. He also said he thought his medication had helped him, and that he wanted to continue taking it. (Not all preteens who have been treated with Ritalin feel this way, as we will see in the next chapter.) Hearing Bobby and his family discuss their experiences, I felt proud of them and certain that our efforts had made a critical difference in his prognosis. He'd been heading downhill and could have looked much worse in a few years; now it seemed like this interesting, difficult, yet winning kid had a future. As I like to tell kids like Bobby, "I knew you had it in you."

Chapter 11

←——————→

THE MEDICATION OPTION:
MAKING THE MOST OF A
DRUG INTERVENTION FOR ADD

Medicine is far more of a spectator than a participator sport. One needs to learn to respect the power of nature to heal and the relative impotence of medicine to influence this process except, often, adversely.

—John S. Werry, M.D.

When should a child take Ritalin? Despite decades of use and literally hundreds of scientific studies, there is no simple way to determine this for every child who seems like a candidate. Factors such as accompanying (comorbid) emotional problems, family circumstances, and evaluator biases complicate each decision. Most experts feel, as I do, that some reasonable effort should be made to address the child's problems by other means before resorting to Ritalin, but there is no consensus on what constitutes a reasonable effort. Furthermore, how families feel about using psychiatric medication for their children—whether they find it acceptable or prefer to try almost anything else—often represents a cultural bias rather than a "scientific" decision; this is discussed more fully in the final chapter.

Thus, the issue of if and when to use Ritalin remains a clinical judgment, undoubtedly leading to cases of both inadequate and excessive medication. Doctor, parents, and sometimes the child, depending on his or her age and maturity, decide together. Few parents are eager at first to place their child on any medication that affects the brain and personality. Nor do many children rush to take a pill. Still, the time often comes when all parties decide it makes sense to try Ritalin or another drug. For Bobby Hall's family, the decision to use medication was made early on—right after the evaluation. Jenny Carter's family allowed several months to elapse while exploring other methods before they consented to a trial of Ritalin. And Michael Sturdevant's parents elected to change schools rather than treat him with a drug that might have helped him cope sufficiently at his original school.

PRESCRIBING FOR ASHLEY

The decision to recommend Ritalin is easier when a child's symptoms are extremely pronounced. Ashley Barnes was one of the most hyperactive children I've met in twenty years of practice. She had just turned four when her parents, Steve and Sally, brought her in for the first meeting along with her sister, Kristy, and I truly wondered how they all had survived those four years. Ashley literally did not sit down for more than a few seconds; she was constantly on the go. It was hard to assess her development accurately because she spent so little time with any one item or activity. She also spoke quickly, in a high-pitched, squeaky voice. Her language abilities seemed okay (I could understand her well enough), but I was concerned about her overall development. According to her pediatrician, Ashley's head size was small for her age, and such decreased head circumference is sometimes associated with delays in neurological development.

Steve and Sandy were overwhelmed by their daughter's headlong activity and seemed paralyzed by uncertainty about what was wrong with Ashley. They wondered: Could she control herself? Should they discipline her more? Meanwhile, they did virtually nothing to influence her behavior and hardly spoke to each other at all. The parents' emotional reactions to this perpetual family crisis differed: Sandy seemed mainly sad to me, while Steve acted angry. I suspected that each experienced both feelings about their life with Ashley, but they didn't express them to each other. Two-year-old Kristy didn't seem much affected as yet, playing happily with blocks on my office floor. She'd duck her head when Ashley rushed by, or temporarily yield a suddenly desired toy to Ashley—I think Kristy already knew she'd get it back quickly when her sister moved on. Eventually, though, the amount of the family's energy Ashley consumed was bound to take its toll on Kristy.

Generally I'm fairly conservative about recommending Ritalin for children under age six if they are not in a formal educational setting—Ashley did not attend preschool. I feel there's a good chance that young children will respond to changes in their home environment even more than do their older counterparts. But I was dubious about this family's ability to effect changes significant enough to make this approach viable. I needed to learn much more about both Ashley and her parents; in particular, while I understood that Sandy and Steve were stunned by their daughter's personality, I thought there had to be other reasons for their astonishing passivity in the face of her incredibly overactive behavior. In the meantime I was worried about them all. The situation struck me as nightmarish—possibly even a setup ripe for child abuse in the continued absence of some effective intervention.

I thought that Ritalin could provide critical symptomatic relief to this family while we explored the reasons behind Ashley's problems. In the Barneses' case, I believed both child and parents would be helped equally by the medication. This isn't always so; sometimes I end up medicating children mainly because they cause problems for their parents or teachers, and the child benefits more indirectly. Because he is constantly failing and getting in trouble, the child feels bad, and if Ritalin helps him perform better, it follows that he feels better because the adults are pleased. With Ashley, however, I genuinely felt that medication could help her directly. Her hyperactivity was such that I doubted she could enjoy much of anything—obviously a value judgment on my part. Steve and Sandy were open to trying anything (including, as it turned out, medication for themselves). For a trial period of medication, I suggested they give Ashley one 5 mg tablet of Ritalin each morning, and increase the dose every three days by half a tablet (rather than the usual full tablet, because of her young age and small size).

The whole family returned the following week, and, with no exaggeration, they were a tabloid TV cliché come to life. The change was dramatic. On 7.5 mg of Ritalin, given two hours earlier, Ashley sat down on the floor in my office and played almost normally! She was still active, but she could now play "dishes and food" with her parents and me for a considerable time. Some of her improvement could have been due to greater familiarity and comfort with being in my office, but her parents had noticed equally impressive changes in her attention span and activity level at home.

All was not rosy for Ashley, however. Her increased ability to pay attention made some developmental deficits more noticeable. She acted and played like a child between the ages of three and three and a half, rather than one who had just turned four. Her language abilities also lagged a bit.

Because of her extreme hyperactivity, developmental delay, small head size (microcephaly), and somewhat unusual facial features, I referred Ashley to a pediatric geneticist for a chromosome study. If a genetic diagnosis could be made, it would not help Ashley directly but might comfort the family by identifying a major source of her problems, as well as telling her parents whether they or Ashley were at increased risk of having similar children in the future. The chromosomes showed no abnormality, however, nor did Ashley fit any recognizable hereditary condition.

During later sessions without the children, the parents and I discussed parenting this unusual child, and I learned more about Steve and Sandy's personal and marital issues. Sandy showed obvious signs of depression, including a marked lack of confidence and low self-esteem; she was considering trying an antidepressant. She complained that Steve was often physically and emotionally unavailable to her; at times she felt virtually abandoned with their troubled child. It wasn't hard to see why. Steve was a big wheel in his law firm, a very brainy and work-oriented guy who'd done well financially. He had to work long hours, no doubt, but the turmoil at home made him even more reluctant to leave the office, he admitted. Having a child like Ashley had come as a shock to this upwardly mobile couple, accustomed to expecting good things from life, and they were clearly struggling with a measure of grief and mourning.

Sandy and Steve ultimately showed that they were committed to their marriage and family, however. Over time they made some changes in how they dealt with their children and with each other. Sandy decided she didn't need medication herself. Each took a more active and direct role in discipline and in playing with the kids. (In the past they had let the children determine the play, so that things tended to go all over the place, literally and metaphorically.) A very positive step for Ashley occurred when she qualified for a special prekindergarten program for developmentally delayed children, where she did very well—with the help of her parents and medication.

Over the two years I worked with them, Ashley continued on twice-daily doses of 7.5 mg of Ritalin. Since Ashley was doing much better during the day, Sandy found that she could handle her daughter's activity in the late afternoon and evening without a third dose. Eventually Ashley's general pediatrician took over managing the medication.

I describe my involvement with Ashley in the hope that nearly everyone can agree that this child qualified for a trial of Ritalin. Very few children in my specialty practice are so handicapped by their personalities. The severity and pervasiveness of a child's symptoms are my chief guideline to whether medication should be tried, sooner or later. But even less severely affected children may receive medication immediately after a thorough evaluation—though always within the context of a multimodal treatment plan. There are various reasons for this. For example, the family may already have a history of counseling that did not make enough difference, or one or the other parent may be so stressed out by the situation that symptomatic relief must be offered before any further work is contemplated. In other cases, I'm likely to delay using Ritalin to see if alternative interventions make a sufficient difference for the child, family, or school.

THE WHAT, WHEN, AND HOW OF TAKING RITALIN

Brand-name Ritalin, manufactured by Novartis (formerly Ciba-Geigy), comes in the form of 5 mg, 10 mg, and 20 mg tablets, as does its generic counterpart, methylphenidate, produced by MD Pharmaceuticals. Despite claims from the ADD underground (encountered often on the Internet) of the brand-name drug's superiority, Ritalin and generic methylphenidate have been rated as bioequivalent in their actions by the Food and Drug Administration.[1] Unless a family insists on Ritalin, I prescribe generic methylphenidate because it is less costly. (An article in the *Journal of the American Academy of Child and Adolescent Psychiatry*, the leading child psychiatry journal, reported on two children who responded differently to the two different preparations, but the psychiatrists could not account for the differences.[2]) I have trouble accepting that the two versions of the drug really are different. If a child wasn't responding to methylphenidate, I would consider another medication entirely—say, Dexedrine—rather than switching to Ritalin.

Ritalin is a little pill, yellow or white. Even children describe the 5 mg tablet as small (it's about 6 mm across), and the larger-dose tablets are only slightly bigger. It has a somewhat bitter taste. No flavored liquid preparations of Ritalin, or any other stimulant for that matter, are available. On one hand, this is surprising, since the drug is prescribed for children as young as three; even Prozac now comes as a mint-flavored drinkable solution. However, the manufacturers of stimulants are probably concerned that a liquid form of the drug would be attractive to abusers, who might attempt to inject themselves. (Crushing the tablet and making a solution of the drug is a more labor-intensive effort.)

In any case, ingesting such a small pill isn't usually a problem for kids. One doctor's claim to fame was a method for teaching youngsters how to swallow Ritalin tablets by practicing with edible cake toppings. Some families crush the tablets and put them in yogurt or other soft foods; one mother put the tablet inside a small marshmallow. Children as young as five learn to swallow the tablet whole.

One of the chief attractions of Ritalin is the rapidity of its effects. Unlike some of the older antidepressants, for example, which could take up to two or three weeks to work, Ritalin begins working within twenty to thirty minutes after the child swallows it. So results are often observed immediately—but finding the ideal dosage amount and frequency may take from several days to a few weeks. It's pretty much a process of trial and error, because studies so far have failed to correlate body weight, dosage size, and blood levels of the drug to a reliable clinical response.[3] Researchers therefore recommend in most cases simply starting children on the smallest-dosage tablet. After monitoring the desired and undesired side effects for several days (I use three days), the dosage is increased by one 5 mg tablet.

Thus, when starting Ritalin, a typical dosing schedule would be to take one 5 mg tablet for the first three days, then take two together on days four through six. Every fourth day a pill is added, up to a total of 20 mg per dose—unless the patient experiences significant and persistent negative side effects, in which case no higher dose is attempted. Curiously, this 5 mg to 20 mg range applies to three-year-olds weighing only forty pounds as well as to full-grown men weighing six times that amount. I hypothesize (partly in jest) that the response to Ritalin has more to do with the number of brain cells one possesses, which doesn't change that much as young children become adults.

The purpose of this trial-and-error process, or titration, is twofold: to find the lowest dose at which the best response is achieved, and to minimize side effects. For most children, one 5 mg tablet is not enough to produce any observable change in behavior or performance. Incrementally increasing the dose allows the family to determine the dosage that produces the optimal response. If 10 mg of Ritalin works better than 5 mg and as well as 15 mg, then the child should take only 10 mg. In certain cases, however, even 5 mg may make a child jittery or bring on a headache (both rare at 5 mg but possible). If such complaints persist for more than a day or two, no further Ritalin is offered. As for the three-day time frame, this allows for surer determination of the medication's effects. The causes of behavior are complex, and it's difficult to attribute any one day's good or bad behavior to a drug. Three days of consistent results make it more likely that the medication is responsible.

If a patient, child or adult, is not responding to 20 mg, it is unlikely that raising the dosage will make a difference. One medical report cites the use of higher dosages—double the generally recommended limit—with much higher frequencies of side effects.[4] Despite the undesired effects, this practitioner claimed the method worked for him and his patients, though the journal later received critical letters about publishing the report. Experts are nearly unanimous in advising against single dosages of more than 20 mg.

The ideal frequency of dosing is also determined in the first several weeks. Ritalin's effects last about three to four hours. School lasts about six hours, and most children are awake for at least twelve. Yet many children do very well all day on just one dose of Ritalin, taken before they leave home in the morning. This cannot be explained solely by the drug's pharmacological action, since it is no longer detectable in the bloodstream after four hours. It's possible that the child who manages on a single daily dose of Ritalin has a milder temperament problem. In such a case, the medication helps him succeed in the morning, when the bulk of academic instruction takes place in elementary school. Afternoons are typically taken up with less challenging activities like projects, art, or physical education. Having had a good morning, the child feels better about himself, is able to delay his impulses toward immediate gratification, and can concentrate on the more enjoyable afternoon activities without need of more medication. Then, having experienced a happy and successful school day, he returns home in a sustained good mood, able to cooperate relatively well in the more flexible home environment.

However, many children (and nearly all teenagers and adults) benefit from more than one dose of Ritalin during the day. If deterioration in performance or behavior is noted after lunch (at school or at home), a second dose of Ritalin can be given around the lunch hour. The dosage amount is titrated, like the morning dose, in three-day increments. This need for a noontime dose accounts for the lines of children forming around the school secretary's office in many American schools. With a written note from the doctor, school staff must deliver medication to children. School nurses are the logical and best-qualified personnel for the task, but with nationwide cutbacks in public education, most elementary schools no longer have a nurse regularly on the premises. Other school personnel—secretaries, teachers, even janitors—have been delegated the job of doling out medication.[5]

Most school districts have a policy that prohibits children from taking their pills by themselves. Such rules are difficult to enforce and regularly ignored by both families and school officials. In particular, most teenagers I know who take a second dose of Ritalin at school do not bother going to the office. This laissez-faire attitude toward self-dosing is strongly challenged by law enforcement officials, who have found children giving or selling their Ritalin to friends who subsequently abuse the drug—primarily by snorting it. Indeed, in some areas Ritalin is said to be easier and cheaper to buy on the grounds of middle schools than on the adjacent neighborhood streets.[6]

A third dose of Ritalin can be given around four o'clock in the afternoon, again if observations of behavior seem to warrant it; this is happening with increasing frequency. Despite the findings of a recent study indicating that most children can handle a third dose without problems, that third dose does increase the possibility, for some children, of unacceptable side effects during the dinner hour and at bedtime.[7] I'm not aware of any children who receive more than three doses of Ritalin a day. For adolescents and adults, whose attention and performance requirements remain constant through most of their waking hours, two or three daily doses are the norm.

From a strictly physical standpoint, it appears Ritalin can be taken safely every day. On the other hand, one can cease taking it for a day, a month, or a year, and it should work pretty much the same as the last time it was taken. Some argue that Ritalin should be taken on a fixed dosage schedule, 7 days a week, 365 days a year—the frequently used analogy is to insulin for the diabetic.[8] While I object to the Ritalin/insulin analogy on several grounds, one need only note that even daily insulin dosages are adjusted according to how much the patient eats and how active he is. It doesn't make sense to take a drug every day if it isn't needed. For individuals more severely affected by attention or behavioral problems, taking multiple daily doses of Ritalin seems reasonable. But for many children, problems manifest only in the school setting; they do quite well without medication on weekends, holidays, and vacations. For such children at such times, Ritalin seems unnecessary.

I am often asked by the parents of a child who doesn't normally take Ritalin on weekends whether it's okay to give him the medication on a Sunday, for example, when they all plan to attend a family wedding or dinner party. Event-driven dosing makes sense in some ways. Why not give a child (and family) some chemical assistance in dealing with a potentially demanding event? From a physical standpoint, there's no harm at all. From a psychological perspective, the question becomes more complex: Can use of the drug "as needed" or on demand encourage a psychological dependency? The child, and even more so the parents, may come to believe that they can cope with such situations only with the drug's help. (The issue of unwanted psychological side effects of Ritalin is discussed at length in the final chapter.) In my practice, I suggest that each family decide whether it works best to go case by case—the child taking the extra dose or attending the event without medication—or to move to a regular, seven-days-a-week dosing schedule.

Based on my experience, I'm sure that a huge dip in Ritalin sales nationally occurs during the summer months, when schools are out. "Drug holidays"—regularly scheduled times on weekends or vacations when there are fewer demands on a child—were vigorously advocated at one time, when concern about Ritalin's effects on long-term growth was greater; it was felt that drug-free periods allowed for catch-up growth. More recent studies have diminished such concerns (see the next section) and thus the medical importance of a drug-free period. The issue now is: If a child functions well enough without medication, why give it?

How long a child should continue taking Ritalin is more controversial. More and more, experts are proposing lifelong stimulant treatment for those with ADD, but my clinical experience runs counter to this monolithic recommendation. While many children continue to benefit from Ritalin throughout childhood, and often stop the medication themselves when they reach adolescence, many borderline ADD kids experience significant variations in behavior and performance problems year to year. Educational settings and teaching styles can have a great impact. If a child has been off medication for the summer, parents often stick to the status quo when school starts, to see how things go.

As with Bobby Hall, if a child seems to be doing well on medication but the family is motivated to do without it, it's reasonable every six months or so to drop the pills for three or four days, or to use a reduced dose, and see what happens. Of course, some parents (and children) are convinced that medication is essential to a child's success and don't want to risk even short-term failure with a drug-free trial. How much that view represents the child's true physical need versus some degree of psychological dependency would be hard to sort out without a placebo-controlled trial. Practically speaking, it may not matter. In such cases it's likely the child will stay on medication until someone (usually the child-become-teenager) wants to try doing without it.

GAUGING THE EFFECTS

My main source of information about the effects of Ritalin on a child is the simple feedback forms I ask the parents and teacher to complete. Each form covers seven days, with sections for the morning and afternoon. While I do not use questionnaires for the purpose of diagnosis (see Chapter 9) and recognize that the same problem of observer bias operates in these feedback forms, I find them the best way to get specific details about a medication's effects on the child's behavior and how those effects vary at different dosages and different times of day. The form asks the parents and teacher to rate the child on three characteristics—attention, impulsivity, and task completion—and provides space for daily comments. These observations help me to determine what dosage and frequency are working best for the child.

Most of the time the teacher is not aware if the child has taken Ritalin on any particular day or how much is being taken. (He or she does know that the purpose of the report is to determine the correct dosage.) This is an advantage in that the teacher is less likely to be influenced by the placebo effect (any desired and undesired effects that derive from the act of treatment itself—pill taking, injection, and so on—rather than from the active ingredient in the pill or shot). All treatments have some placebo effect, and that of Ritalin has been rated quite high; in one study, up to 30 percent of its effects were attributed to this phenomenon. (Other studies show lower but still significant placebo effects with Ritalin.)[9] Concern has been expressed about a placebo response this high. Why expose a child and his community to a potentially dangerous drug, some ask, if improvements could come from taking a sugar pill? Such rhetoric should be viewed in its proper context, as it usually comes from those who wish to criticize Ritalin in any way possible. The very real improvements of performance it can bring about well outweigh any placebo effect.

Interestingly, unwanted Ritalin-like side effects also occur with placebos. In studies, nearly one in five children on the placebo were rated as irritable, and one in ten were anxious. In one study, more children reported headaches or stomachaches on placebo than they had from taking low-dose Ritalin! Only loss of appetite and insomnia are reported statistically more often from the drug itself.[10] How a doctor presents or "sells" a drug may also contribute to placebo effects; I've wondered, in fact, whether some of my patients find Ritalin less effective because I don't tell them it will work miracles.

In fact, given the titration procedure I've described, a stimulant "works" 60 to 90 percent of the time, according to studies.[11] (My own experience using either Ritalin or Dexedrine is closer to 90 percent.) In the relatively few cases where it doesn't help, factors other than simple ADD—such as anger, depression, or anxiety—are probably operating.

As mentioned, Ritalin's effects on hyperactive, impulsive behavior can be observed within minutes, when the proper dose is given. Thus, for children who exhibit these kinds of behaviors, change can be noticed and recorded over a matter of days. But in the child who gets the medication primarily for inattentiveness, the effects can be far more subtle. Improvements in work completion, for example, may be not as quickly evident as changes in activity and impulsivity. Since most teenagers and adults given Ritalin are not hyperactive, it can take several weeks to fully determine the medication's dosing levels, frequency, and overall value.

HOW CHILDREN FEEL ABOUT TAKING RITALIN

Naturally, I also solicit the child's opinions about the medication's effects. For younger children, I might frame the question as "What's good and bad about taking this medicine for you?" Interestingly, few elementary-school-age children report any major differences, good or bad, during the initial weeks of taking Ritalin. Generally, the self-observations of teenagers and adults are more helpful in reaching decisions about the benefits of the drug and its dosage and frequency. Even so, I rely on the teenager's parents or the adult's spouse to provide another slant on the Ritalin user's behavior and performance; it can be quite different.

Finding out how children really feel about taking Ritalin isn't easy—how hard it is depends on their age, development, and relative dependency on their parents. A 1982 study of fifty-four hyperactive children, titled "How Do Hyperactive Children Feel About Taking Stimulants and Will They Tell the Doctor?" found that "a large fraction of the children dislike the medication and often tried to avoid taking it."[12] About 42 percent disliked or hated taking the medication, while 30 percent said they liked taking it, and the same percentage felt indifferent (this group included some who said they looked forward to stopping medication). In an interesting sidelight, many of the children told the doctor they had no problem taking the medication, while their parents reported having to chase them around the room to get them to take it. These results led the researchers to advise doctors against relying solely on the child's report to determine the medication's acceptability.

In a later study, more of the children who complained took regular Ritalin versus Ritalin SR, the sustained-release form, making the researchers wonder whether the hassle or stigma associated with multiple doses of Ritalin (especially at school) led to greater unhappiness about taking it.[13]

Finding a discrepancy between how a child reports his or her behavior relating to medication and what others say actually happens is not unusual in pediatrics, but may be more common among children labeled with ADD. Some studies have found that ADD children hold themselves less accountable and blame others for their problems and failures, compared to children who do not meet ADD criteria.[14] This is understandable for a child who often finds himself in trouble and needing to explain why ("Tommy made me do it").

A more important fact is that children who take Ritalin tend to attribute their improved performance to their own efforts, not to the drug's effects, while blaming failures on the fact that they hadn't taken their pill.[15] This is in contrast to parents and teachers, who clearly attribute improvements in behavior and performance to the drug. Studies based on children's own statements have not found that children become psychologically dependent on Ritalin. Ironically, the adults close to them may be more psychologically dependent on it than is the child himself ("Oh my God, we forgot to give him his Ritalin this morning"). Despite such findings, however, it's hard to imagine that a child who has misbehaved doesn't make the connection between this and hearing the refrain: "Did you take your pill this morning?" On some level, he must feel that the pill makes a difference in his behavior—or at least he knows that's what the grown-ups think.

To what extent a child should be involved in decisions about his taking medication depends on his age and maturity. I believe children should be truthfully informed about the drug, as their understanding permits. The potential exists to hurt a child by misinformation or indifference, even while the drug improves his performance. If Ritalin is being considered, I'll always ask the child, with the parents' permission, how he feels about taking it. If he is younger than eleven, I usually start by telling him that the decision to try Ritalin is not his alone; his parents and I will decide after hearing from him. This is not to oppress or put down the child; rather, the responsibility entailed is too great a burden for most children. If a child feels pressure to decide alone, he is more likely to avoid making the choice, saying something vague like "I don't care" or "It's okay." Instead, I tell him his opinions are important to his parents and me and will help us decide.

I especially want to hear specifics from the child if he doesn't want to take the medication: What are his reasons, and can they be addressed? The most frequent concern from younger children is about the pills themselves. Do they taste bad? How large are they? Are they hard to swallow? Some might ask a more sophisticated question: Do they have any bad effects? I try to answer all the questions—better still, I ask the parents to talk to their child in my presence, which helps me learn what the parents know about the drug. To kids, I describe Ritalin's effects as "helping you do what you want to do." Most of them will acknowledge that it's hard for them to complete their work, that they talk to their friends too much, or that they get into trouble. I tell them the Ritalin can help them pay better attention in class or at home. Sometimes it's useful to say, "It may get you to think before you do something stupid," or "It may make it easier to get your schoolwork done" (which often convinces them).

I am very clear about telling children that Ritalin is not a pill that will automatically make them "good." I explain that it cannot make them perform or behave unless they want to. "These pills will not make you do your homework if you don't want to," I say. "If you don't want to do what your teacher or mother says, the pill won't make you do it." It's very important that the child retain a sense that his performance is self-determined. This approach also reflects the fact that virtually all children *want* to be good and to please their parents and teachers.

When a child returns for follow-up, I avoid asking, "How are the pills?" Like asking, "How was school today?", such general questions tend to elicit minimal and vague responses like "Fine" and "Okay." Instead, I typically ask, "Tell me one good thing and one bad thing about taking these pills." As mentioned, a younger child often doesn't report behavioral and performance improvements, but his parents and teacher do—and the child usually seems pleased to hear that. With an older kid, I often hear, "I'm doing better in school. I haven't gotten into any trouble in a week." Asked how he feels about that, almost *every* kid says he feels good. I may then congratulate him: "I knew you had it in you."

Negative comments range from "The pills are hard to swallow" to "I don't like going to the secretary's office and missing class." Addressing such concerns occasionally can mean stopping the medication; this is much more likely for older children and adolescents. The hardest responses to deal with are the nonspecific ones, such as "I don't like it." If asked why not, a child may simply repeat, "I don't know. I just don't like it." Sometimes running through a list of side effects, both physical and psychological, determines the source of unhappiness, but here one risks putting words in the child's mouth. At the least, negative comments may indicate that a child feels bad about himself because he has to take pills. The feeling may arise from having overheard a parent speak defensively about putting a child on medication. If he is feeling bad, or at best ambivalent, it's important to review the reasons why he's taking medication.

Both at the start and at every six-month follow-up visit, I make a point of asking the child, "And what is Ritalin supposed to do?" If he answers, "Make me act good," I ask the parents to correct him: "It helps you concentrate and think more before you act." I'm not sure if this really changes the child's point of view—especially if he hears something else outside my office—but I feel it's important to keep repeating the message, in the hope that the child retains his sense of free will and choice about his behavior.

SIDE EFFECTS AND OTHER CONSIDERATIONS

Research studies have determined a few unwanted effects of Ritalin, both immediate and long-term. Ritalin in low doses lowers the heart rate and raises blood pressure. These changes have not been found to be significant, either in the short or long term. Ritalin can be taken with or without food. Complaints of abdominal distress are commonly associated with taking any medication in pill form, and Ritalin is no exception. These complaints pass with continued use, however, and are rarely a reason for discontinuing the drug.

Decreased appetite is common while Ritalin is working, but as soon as the drug's effects have worn off (typically less than four hours), hunger returns, often with greater intensity. Therefore, in a typical dosing pattern—two or three doses a day, beginning right after breakfast—the medication likely will decrease a child's desire for lunch, but as its effects wear off, his appetite for an afternoon snack and larger-than-usual helpings at dinner may increase. (Dinner may need to be a bit later than normal for children taking three doses daily.) Many parents worry that Ritalin use will cause persistent weight loss or failure to gain weight—important in growing children—but this has been much studied and occurs only rarely. Similar concerns that Ritalin use in childhood could decrease eventual adult height were raised in studies during the 1970s. Attempts to replicate these findings were inconsistent, however, and very recent analyses of long-term growth patterns reveal no such effects.[16]

Children may have trouble falling asleep if Ritalin is taken too late in the day; thus, it is common practice to give the last dose not later than 4:00 P.M.—both to prevent insomnia and to allow the appetite to return in time for dinner at a reasonable hour. A certain number of children cannot take a late-afternoon dose because of these side effects. However, many children and most adults can tolerate an afternoon dose without problems.

Rebound is a term used to describe the worsening of symptomatic behavior after a drug has worn off. Rebound from Ritalin is not uncommon; some parents feel that their child becomes even more "hyper" in the late afternoon or evening, as the drug wears off. In studies of the phenomenon using Ritalin and Dexedrine, some but not all of the children showed some aspects of rebound, but none were so severely affected that stopping their medication was indicated.[17] Dexedrine (see below) or longer-acting preparations of Ritalin are often recommended in situations where rebound persists. Some physicians prescribe a second drug such as clonidine to treat the rebound. I try to identify behavioral ways of dealing with late-day problems.

Another possible effect of Ritalin, though scientifically equivocal and relatively rare, is that the medication can unmask the existence of involuntary tics or the more serious condition, Tourette's syndrome. (Unmasking means that symptoms manifest sooner than they normally would.) This link was identified by researchers in the 1980s, but today there is growing consensus that the link between tics and Ritalin is inconsistent. It's now thought that the medication can be used for children with Tourette's (or a family history of the disorder) if the child's behavior warrants treatment and responds to Ritalin.[18]

Higher doses of Ritalin (more than 20 mg) usually lead to children's complaining of nervousness, palpitations (feeling one's heart beating), tremor (shakiness), and/or headaches. Teenagers and adults may experience similar discomfort but also report mild euphoria when Ritalin is taken orally in higher doses. Such doses given to children generally do not result in euphoria, but there are exceptions. A recent report noted that an eleven-

year-old boy was stealing his own medication from his grandmother because the tablets made him feel "nice" and "very happy."[19] And a twelve-
year-old patient of mine was caught by his father taking an extra 10 mg
tablet of Ritalin before playing in a Pop Warner football game. He said it
made him feel "sharper," though his father felt he was "acting strange." In
a culture where professional athletes still attempt to use performance-
enhancing drugs despite stiff penalties, such occurrences should not be
surprising. However, most of the time, the younger child on a higher-than-
normal dose doesn't care for the experience and will say something like, "I
feel weird."

Experiencing euphoria is, of course, one of the features of a drug that
makes it a candidate for abuse. The most serious drugs of abuse are those
that readily cause users to develop tolerance (the need for a higher and
higher dose to obtain the same effect) or addiction (a physical and emotional craving for the drug). In the typical dose range of 5 mg to 20 mg, up
to perhaps 60 mg total per day, Ritalin does not produce either tolerance
or addiction. Ritalin does not accumulate in the bloodstream or elsewhere
in the body, and no withdrawal symptoms occur when someone abruptly
stops taking the drug, even after years of use. However, with teenagers and
adults who abuse Ritalin—by taking high doses, sometimes via snorting or
shooting the drug—the phenomena of tolerance, addiction, and withdrawal can occur.

No serious diseases have been linked with Ritalin use. The only slim evidence of such a possible link is a 1996 study by the FDA of rats given large
daily doses of Ritalin over their whole life, which resulted in an increased
rate of liver cancer in these animals.[20] In releasing the study, however, the
FDA assured doctors and patients that it was highly unlikely that Ritalin
was carcinogenic in humans. Liver cancer is common in rats and uncommon in people. FDA checks found no correlation between records of liver
cancer victims and the use of Ritalin, nor have there been reports of increased liver cancer in children or adults who've taken Ritalin.

I mention this study only to highlight the possibility, however unlikely,
that despite sixty years of stimulant use with children demonstrating remarkable physical safety, some as-yet-undiscovered negative effect of Ritalin still could be found. Each parent must weigh the use of Ritalin for a
child on the evidence of clear short-term improvements in behavior and
performance with the absence of long-term negative or positive consequences directly attributable to the drug. However, the long-term negative
consequences of continuing failure and declining self-worth are well

known. The possibility that Ritalin can assist in breaking that pattern must be weighed against any downside to the drug.

RITALIN VERSUS DEXEDRINE

Among medications other than Ritalin used for problems of attention, behavior, and performance, by far the most common first-line treatment is dextroamphetamine, or Dexedrine. Virtually everything that has been said about Ritalin applies to Dexedrine. Structurally and pharmacologically the two are very similar, and studies of groups of children have shown the benefits and disadvantages of Dexedrine to be the same as for Ritalin. Nevertheless, for reasons that are unclear but may have to do with subtle differences in chemical structure, some people who do not respond well to Ritalin or who experience significant unwanted effects from it can take Dexedrine successfully, and vice versa. Some doctors prefer one over the other based simply on their experience; some are influenced by unsubstantiated claims such as that Ritalin causes fewer side effects than Dexedrine or that Dexedrine doesn't cause tics as Ritalin can.

Unlike Ritalin, ordinary Dexedrine comes only in 5 mg tablets (Ritalin comes in 5 mg, 10 mg, or 20 mg doses), but it requires the same kind of dosing trial to titrate the optimal dosage and frequency. Some experts believe that less Dexedrine per dose—some say half as much—works as well as a larger dose of Ritalin, but the dosage is always determined by the clinical response. In sum, there is no absolute advantage to taking one over the other. Typically, Ritalin is tried first, and only if it is not successful is Dexedrine then prescribed.

Both Ritalin and Dexedrine come in preparations that stay active in the body longer than the standard tablet: Ritalin SR (for sustained-release) and Dexedrine Spansule. Ritalin SR comes only as a 20 mg tablet and cannot be divided; cracking the pill's surface destroys the slow-release mechanism. Dexedrine Spansule comes in 5 mg, 10 mg, and 15 mg dosages.

Other long-acting preparations are appearing as the ADD market continues to grow. A medication called Obetral, originally developed for weight control, had been off the market for years when Richwood Pharmaceutical bought the company that made it and simply renamed the drug, calling it Adderall. Currently Richwood is widely promoting Adderall as a long-acting stimulant that combines the two slightly different structural forms of amphetamine. The *Medical Letter*, a highly respected journal that reviews drugs and therapeutics, judged that Adderall did not constitute a significant addition to the medication previously available for ADD, and that it had not been studied as thoroughly as Ritalin or Dexedrine.[21] As yet I have not had a reason to try Adderall with any children I've treated, though I'm sure to encounter some who have received it. And a whole new generation of stimulants and drug delivery systems is in the pipeline for production and distribution, as the pharmaceutical industry gears up to meet the increased demand for ADD treatments.[22] A slow-release skin patch has already been tested in children.

A longer-lasting stimulant has obvious value, and not just to the manufacturer. (Until quite recently Ritalin SR had no generic competitor. Novartis could charge more for it than for regular Ritalin, which is available in generic form. Now MD Pharmaceutical is making a generic methylphenidate sustained-release pill.) Taking pills less frequently is easier, especially for young patients, and increases what doctors call "compliance" (the patient following doctor's orders). A child or teenager taking a longer-lasting preparation can avoid the hassle and possible stigma of taking a midday dose of medication at school. In addition, some physicians feel that the long-acting versions "smooth out the ride" of stimulants, mitigating their up-and-down effect or the rebound phenomenon. There is no documented evidence of this, however.

The drug industry offers studies demonstrating that, in these preparations, the active ingredient indeed remains in the bloodstream longer. However, a more recent study, comparing one dose of Ritalin SR with two separate 10 mg doses of generic methylphenidate, found that the two-dose approach produced better ratings of behavior and performance over eight hours than the single dose of Ritalin SR.[23] Further, long-acting amphetamines have a greater likelihood of causing sleep problems, even when taken only in the morning. In my experience, long-acting preparations can be helpful in precluding the need for a noon dose in cases where a drug effect for eight-plus hours is needed. It is less clear that they make any difference in reducing rebound. I have found (without any systematic investigation) that Dexedrine Spansule seems to work better than Ritalin SR and rarely causes sleep problems when taken only in the morning. That it comes in three different dosages is an added advantage.

ALTERNATIVES TO RITALIN:
WEIGHING THE BENEFITS AND RISKS

Ritalin and Dexedrine remain the mainstays of medication for children and adults with attentional or behavior problems. During the 1990s, however, the rising rate of ADD diagnosis in concert with belief in ADD's biological origins has led to great interest and activity in exploring a range of other drugs for ADD treatment. Some, such as pemoline (Cylert) and the tricyclic antidepressant imipramine (Tofranil), were employed for ADD before this decade but have been prescribed much more often in the last several years. Other tricyclics or clonidine (Catapres) have very little history of use with ADD-related behavior problems. They are mostly tried with children who show co-morbid problems such as depression or oppositional behavior, or whose ADD symptoms are very severe.

All these drugs have their partisans, but all have their problems as well. They have produced documented side effects ranging from dry mouth to sudden death. And compared to Ritalin and Dexedrine, their use in children has been studied only minimally. Once we move beyond Ritalin and Dexedrine, the number of published studies on the effects of other drugs for ADD drops precipitously.[24]

Research on the use of most drugs with children is inhibited by several factors. For one thing, there are ethical and legal hurdles to clear when performing research on children; what constitutes a child's "informed consent" continues to be a source of controversy.[25] But probably the chief barrier to more research involving children is the lack of a perceived market (and thus a financial return) for the pharmaceutical industry, which prefers to invest in drug investigations more certain to generate increased profits. So funding for research focused on children comes primarily from the federal government and some private foundations.

This situation may be changing, however, at least for certain kinds of medication. A 1997 headline in the *Wall Street Journal* announced "Antidepressant Makers Study Kids' Market"; other major media have since reported on this.[26] The articles describe how, after several years of rapid growth, a plateau in antidepressant use among adults has prompted pharmaceutical companies to explore more vigorously the potential use of psychotropic medications in children. Both to secure formal FDA approval and to convince physicians that these medications are useful to children, more industry-supported studies are planned to test drugs in the pediatric age group. Such studies are required in order to advertise the benefits of such drugs to physicians and patients. That's the good news.

This trend also has worrisome aspects, however. While it's important to learn whether these medications actually are beneficial to children, it's unfortunate that the scope of such research probably will be limited to the medication alone. The constituency for psychosocial approaches simply is not as powerful or well organized as the drug industry, and the profit incentive is lacking. A second caveat stems from the pressure on researchers funded by commercial interests to report only positive findings.[27] One researcher, under threat of a lawsuit, delayed for more than two years her report that a brand-name drug offered no advantages over a generic.[28] With pharmaceutical companies funding research, some bias seems inevitable; whatever the result, it gets a positive spin.

Apart from Ritalin, amphetamine, and pemoline, every other drug used to treat ADD must be prescribed by physicians for off-label use. This means that the federal government has not approved the drug specifically for the condition the doctor wishes to treat, though he/she still may prescribe it for that purpose. (To win FDA permission to manufacture and distribute a medication in this country, pharmaceutical companies must do extensive testing that demonstrates a drug's efficacy for a particular condition or set of conditions. Once a drug is approved by the FDA, however, a doctor may prescribe it for any reason he sees fit. Sometimes, if there is sufficient promise of profit, a company will organize new or existing studies of a drug and petition the FDA to add a condition to the official list of diseases the drug treats.)

No drugs besides Ritalin, amphetamine, and pemoline have been added to the FDA's list of drugs recommended for ADD treatment. This, however, has not stemmed the enthusiasm for trying alternative compounds. In practice, doctors prescribe many medications off-label for a wide range of problems in psychiatry and general medicine. They are supposed to disclose to patients when they are prescribing a drug for off-label purposes, but many fail to do so—whether due to absent-mindedness, haste, or concern that the information will unnecessarily worry the patient and make compliance less likely. The Clinton administration, recognizing the prevalence of off-label prescribing, called in 1997 for increased spending and regulatory changes to monitor drug effects and safety in connection with treating children. The industry met these proposals with resistance, citing cost and safety issues; to date, no action has been taken.[29]

CYLERT

Pemoline, known by the brand name Cylert, is FDA-approved for ADD but is used far less frequently than either Ritalin or Dexedrine. Despite being touted as a once-a-day drug and heavily marketed to physicians by its manufacturer, Abbott Laboratories, Cylert is taken by only 2 percent of all children taking medication for ADD, according to a 1996 survey.[30] Like its more popular competitors, Cylert belongs to the stimulant class of drugs, but its structure is quite different from that of methylphenidate, amphetamine, or cocaine. As with other stimulants, its mechanism of action on ADD is unknown. Curiously, Cylert does not appear to be abusable (surely it has been tried).

Cylert can cause a transient inflammation of the liver (chemical hepatitis), and a blood test every six months to assess liver function is recommended. This may partly account for the drug's relative unpopularity. Perhaps more significant, Cylert may take up to three weeks to work, in contrast to the immediate effects of Ritalin or Dexedrine. A recent study suggested that such delayed effects are caused by starting the titration of Cylert at the manufacturer's recommended dosage level, which the researchers deemed too low.[31] In their hands, apparently, Cylert worked as quickly as Ritalin. It remains to be seen whether Cylert increases in popularity, but there's good reason why it should not.

Until recently, Cylert was being considered by some as potentially a first-line drug for ADD. As I was writing this chapter, however, I received a mailing labeled in bold red type on the envelope: *Important—Drug Warning!* Inside was a letter from Abbott Laboratories alerting doctors to an important change in their package insert and labeling for Cylert.[32] The insert would now inform readers of thirteen cases of acute liver failure in children who had been taking Cylert; eleven of the cases had resulted in either death or the need for a liver transplant. All the children had been taking Cylert for at least six months. The onset of liver failure was rapid, usually within four weeks of the first signs of trouble—most often jaundice, or yellowing of the skin and eyeballs. Normal periodic testing of liver function did not pick up these impending medical disasters. "Because of its association with life-threatening hepatic failure," Abbott stated in the letter, "Cylert should not ordinarily be considered as a first-line drug therapy for ADHD."

THE TRICYCLICS: FINDING NEW USES FOR OLD DRUGS

All the drugs discussed below are considered second-line, meaning that their use should be reserved for children who have not improved with Ritalin or Dexedrine, or who have experienced unacceptable side effects on those drugs. Problems of behavior and/or performance must be unusually severe or persistent to justify the use of these off-label medications. Typically, children considered as candidates for such drugs have co-morbid diagnoses with ADD—that is, serious problems in addition to inattention or hyperactivity. Child psychiatrists are far more likely than general pediatricians to use these second-line drugs, in part reflecting the more complex and difficult problems the specialists see. Some should be prescribed only by a child psychiatrist or pediatric behavior specialist, and used only under close supervision and management. Seeking a second opinion is reasonable if one of these medications has been recommended for your child.

The tricyclic class of drugs for ADD includes chiefly imipramine (Tofranil), desipramine (Norpramin), and nortriptyline (Pamelor). Venlafaxine (Effexor), while technically not a tricyclic, is often considered in this class because of its similar actions and side effects. These and other tricyclics formerly were classified as antidepressants and, indeed, since their discovery in the 1950s were the most widely prescribed drugs for depression—until Prozac. Recently the tricyclics have been tried and used for various conditions besides depression, from panic disorder to headaches.

The tricyclics have the advantage of being morning and bedtime medications. Their use has not been associated with the tics of Tourette's syndrome. And they do not have abuse potential, an important factor to consider in prescribing to people who potentially self-administer: adolescents and adults. (A recent article reported an intriguing side effect—apparently several teenage boys found that taking tricyclics made their use of marijuana unpleasant.[33]) Because a frequent side effect is sedation, the dose is divided and tricyclics most often are taken twice a day. The other typical complaints are dry mouth, constipation, and blurred vision. These unpleasant effects are similar to those of antihistamines, which are closely related to the tricyclics. The effects tend to be more severe with the tricyclics and occur more frequently as the dosage gets higher.

The use of tricyclics with children for ADD has been long championed by the influential Harvard Pediatric Psychopharmacology Clinic.[34] They recommend daily dosages they describe as high—3 mg to 5 mg per kilogram of body weight, which, for an eleven-year-old, might be as much as

250 mg per day—to achieve maximum effectiveness. (The upper limit of 5 mg per kilo is twice as high as most adult dosages for depression.) They acknowledge, however, that the specific effects of tricyclics on ADD symptoms may not be as "robust" (a popular term among psychopharmacologists to characterize a high frequency and degree of improvement) as those obtained from using Ritalin.[35]

Until recently, imipramine and desipramine were believed quite safe. They were regularly used by child psychiatrists to treat childhood depression, and pediatricians for years had used low doses of imipramine to relieve nighttime bed-wetting. So practitioners were shocked and dismayed when, in the late 1980s, reports in the medical literature implicated the use of desipramine in the sudden deaths of five young children.[36]

Three of the children had died during or after exercise, and while the exact cause of their deaths is uncertain, fatal cardiac arrhythmia (a major disturbance in the electrical pacing of the heart's contractions) was suspected. All the children had been properly managed: that is, they were being treated for ADD or depression, and their drug dosages and blood levels were within normal limits before their deaths. One child had had a previous episode of arrhythmia that was considered relatively benign and had resolved. While desipramine was the drug used by all five children, all the tricyclics have come under increased scrutiny, because after ingestion, imipramine is converted into the same active metabolite as desipramine.

In 1995 the furor over tricyclics culminated in a debate in the pages of the leading child and adolescent psychiatry journal on the acceptability of desipramine for treating children. John S. Werry, an internationally respected child psychiatrist, took the position that it was unacceptable. Since no study had documented the efficacy of any pharmacological treatment for childhood depression, he argued, any significant risk (not the highly unlikely possibility of death, but rather any profound unwanted effect) of a particular drug made its use for this purpose unacceptable. Furthermore, he said, its use should be discouraged in the treatment of other conditions such as ADD, where alternatives are available.[37]

A team led by Joseph Biederman of the Harvard group took the position that its use was acceptable, arguing that for conditions such as ADD, the tricyclics were of proven value and the increased risk of death was extremely small. Even for childhood depression, where the drugs' value was unproven, they claimed that children should not be denied the possible benefits of treatment with a tricyclic, because great suffering and even death (by suicide) can ensue from unsuccessfully treated psychiatric disorders.[38] At other times, Dr. Biederman's group has suggested that up to 10 percent of American children may suffer from psychiatric disorders amenable to treatment with tricyclics.[39]

Biederman and others point out that more children die each year from extreme allergic reactions to penicillin than from the effects of tricyclics, yet no one is suggesting a ban on the use of penicillin or other common antibiotics for children. However, one can test for penicillin allergy and thus avoid using the drug with those who are sensitive. Also, unlike tricyclics for childhood depression, penicillin has been proven effective in the treatment of infection. Finally, there are no psychosocial treatments for an acute ear infection, whereas for childhood depression they do exist.

A year after the journal debate, in 1996, the American Academy of Child and Adolescent Psychiatry, the primary organization of child psychiatrists, reported on a task force that evaluated the relative risk of desipramine use in childhood. That Joseph Biederman was the lead author of the task force's report reflects his expertise, experience, and leadership within the academic psychiatric community.[40] However, since Biederman and his group have strongly promoted the tricyclics, putting him in charge of the investigation was like assigning the fox to guard the henhouse. Based on several assumptions and a vast amount of statistical analysis, the task force concluded, not surprisingly, that the link between desipramine and sudden death in children was "weak." The normal rate of sudden death in children, 2.5 per million, increased to perhaps 4.2 per million with desipramine use. Statistically this is insignificant, but it's almost impossible to judge the accuracy of these figures. And if you are the parent of one of the two or so children who need not have died, the risk appears in a different light.

Further extensive electrocardiographic (EKG) studies of children on tricyclics have tried to tease out a possible heart abnormality that might instigate the fatal reaction, and might also serve as a marker or danger sign to predict it.[41] It's recommended that child psychiatrists and pediatricians obtain an EKG both before and after a child begins treatment with a tricyclic. Nevertheless, some experts feel that no test can effectively screen out this very low yet devastating risk.[42] Since the original reports, two more children have died suddenly on tricyclics, one of whom was taking imipramine.[43]

CLONIDINE

Another drug that has seen increased interest and use for ADD is clonidine (trade name Catapres). Clonidine is used mainly to treat hypertension; like some other drugs for high blood pressure, it works on the central nervous system. In the late 1980s and early 1990s, based on just four studies involving a total of 122 children, clonidine was deemed useful for treating ADD in children.[44] It quickly developed a reputation among child behavior specialists as good for ADD children who were also oppositional, aggressive, or had trouble falling asleep at night. (Its most frequently reported side effect is sedation.) Like Ritalin, clonidine remains in the bloodstream for only three or four hours, but unlike Ritalin, it is often used only at night, or once or twice during the daytime. One possible advantage to this drug is that it comes in a skin patch that can deliver a steady dose of the drug throughout the day.

Guanfacine (Tenex), another antihypertensive very similar to clonidine, but purportedly providing day-long action with a single dose, also has been reported as beneficial in treating childhood ADD. (The study was done by the same principal investigator who reported on clonidine's benefits.)[45] Both drugs may cause postural hypotension (dizziness when standing up), and neither should be stopped abruptly because of the small possibility of a withdrawal hypertensive reaction (headache and malaise are common, and stroke an extremely rare possibility).

Clonidine is used both alone and in combination with Ritalin for ADD. It was estimated that more than a hundred thousand children were taking the combination in 1995, but lately the bloom on clonidine's use for ADD seems to be fading.[46] Articles questioning its efficacy and safety have appeared, and it was recently been reported that, tragically, three children taking Ritalin and clonidine in combination suddenly died.[47] Once again, cardiac arrhythmia is suspected, and EKGs are being recommended when this drug is used in children.

LESS-USED DRUGS AND COMBINED PHARMACOTHERAPY

Still other drugs have been used and studied in children with ADD-type behavior, though with much less frequency than those discussed above. The major tranquilizers—chlorpromazine (best known by its trade name, Thorazine), thioridazine (Mellaril), and haloperidol (Haldol)—were more extensively used for this purpose in the 1960s and 1970s. Because they act nonspecifically and pose the risk of serious and permanent muscle-movement disorders (tardive dyskinesias), their use today is reserved for children whose ADD is accompanied by other very significant problems. These heavy-duty drugs are approved for use only in treating seriously disturbed or psychotic children and adolescents, but they are far more often prescribed to control extremely disruptive and aggressive behavior.

Not surprisingly, the serotonin-specific drugs—Prozac (fluoxetine), Zoloft (sertraline), and Paxil (paroxetine) among them—have been tried for ADD. Researchers have had little success, however, and these drugs have been relegated to secondary status in ADD treatment. On the other hand, a structurally unique antidepressant called bupropion (Wellbutrin), has demonstrated some benefit for ADD.[48] Like the tricyclics, Wellbutrin is usually reserved for those who are not considered good candidates for a stimulant; alternatively, it is used in combination with Ritalin. In general, this is a well-tolerated drug, but a small increase in the incidence of grand mal seizures has been reported. And it's not as effective as Ritalin in addressing core ADD symptoms.

Mood-stabilizing drugs, such as lithium carbonate (Eskalith or Lithobid) and valproic acid (Depakote), have been studied and recommended for use when ADD is complicated by bipolar disorder (manic-depressive illness). Again, the child's behaviors must be extreme for him or her to be considered a candidate—but in some circles, such extreme cases seem to be common. At the Harvard Pediatric Psychopharmacology Clinic, bipolar disorder was found in an estimated 23 percent of children with ADD, according to a 1996 report.[49] Such a high percentage of bipolar illness in ADD children—or, for that matter, in any child psychiatry setting—elicited astonished responses in letters to the journal that published the study.[50] Academic quibbling aside, a consequence of asserting such a high rate of combined bipolar-ADD diagnoses is to increase and justify the use of drugs with more serious and/or frequent side effects. Thanks in part to publicity about such findings, parents are starting to describe their children to me as "bipolar," even over the telephone, with disconcerting frequency. That their kids are severely troubled doesn't necessarily indicate a troubled environment, in the current way of thinking, but a more severe diagnosis that warrants a more risky drug. This is a disturbing new trend in treatment.

What remains is a kind of pharmacological grab bag. Dilantin and carbamazepine (Tegretol), two commonly used anticonvulsants (that is, they're used for seizures), have also been tried for ADD. And a group of drugs called monoamine oxidase inhibitors (MAOIs), used primarily in resistant depressions, have been found useful for ADD but are rarely employed because of the need to maintain a diet strictly devoid of the amino acid tyramine. (For example, eating cheddar cheese along with these drugs can cause blood pressure to skyrocket.) Since restraint is not among the hallmarks of the ADD personality, this risk associated with MAOIs is unacceptable to most physicians and families.

No discussion of medication for ADD can be complete without mentioning the latest trend in child psychopharmacology: using multiple psychotropic agents in combination. Once disparagingly called "polypharmacy" and now referred to as "combined pharmacotherapy," the use of two or more drugs for children has gained respect and is even being promoted by leading researchers.[51] This reflects a major attitudinal change in psychiatry. Until twenty years ago, doctors were reluctant to put a child on any psychotropic medication. If it was deemed truly necessary or useful, drugs were used parsimoniously. It was believed that using more than one drug complicates the picture tremendously—for example, it's harder to determine each drug's effects if two or more are acting concurrently. Most also felt that the risk of side effects was greater when using drugs in combination. And compliance was an issue: Medical students are taught that the use of more than one drug dramatically reduces the likelihood that patients will remember to take the right pill at the right time.

All that has changed as child psychiatry, along with its adult counterpart, has followed the lead of general medicine, where multiple medications are often prescribed—for example, for hypertension. The hope and assumption of biological psychiatry have been that categorizing behavior into discrete diagnostic entities would allow physicians to target diseases with specific treatments. Clinical reality belies that fantasy, so if there occurs a "less than satisfactory response to single agents," the clinician is encouraged to address individual problem symptoms with different drugs.[52] The managed-care industry also has had a hand in promoting the use of drugs in combination, and psychotropic drugs in general, as lower-cost alternatives to counseling and other forms of treatment for psychiatric problems.

The most popular medication "cocktails" for ADD mate Ritalin with a tricyclic such as desipramine or with clonidine. Conversely, Ritalin is often added to another drug for the treatment of aggression or conduct disorder, depression, mania, tic disorders, and obsessive-compulsive disorder. The frequent occurrence of such co-morbid symptoms and their clinical persistence ostensibly justify the use of multiple agents. In yet another study coming out of the Harvard clinic, 47 percent of the children being treated there were receiving more than one psychotropic agent.[53]

FIRST, DO NO HARM

Much of what is "news" in the field of ADD and in research on the whole range of behavioral problems is made by doctors working in academic settings. It's inevitable that these doctors see a somewhat different population of ADD cases than do most clinical practitioners. In the latter category are family-care doctors and pediatricians, who handle the majority of "plain vanilla" ADD cases and kids with minor problems of attention and impulsiveness, as well as behavioral specialists like myself, who do see more difficult cases. In contrast, child psychiatrists, especially those in university centers, tend to treat children who manifest very severe and resistant behavior problems, and they encounter higher rates of co-morbid disorders.[54] These doctors therefore are far more likely to use combined pharmacotherapy than are general pediatricians.

Academic researchers set the trends in medicine, however, and many on the front lines of clinical practice try to emulate them. Since the focus in research is so overwhelmingly on medication (and recently, on drugs in combination), following this fashion often leads clinical practitioners to ignore potentially useful psychosocial interventions. Again, managed care colludes in this trend. Furthermore, the evaluations and medication therapies offered by some front-line doctors too often do not display the level of training, expertise, and rigor reflected in the published work of university teaching and research centers. This can create a real risk of practicing bad medicine—for example, prescribing drugs inappropriately and/or without the close management that is essential. In such a situation, the healer can violate medicine's fundamental dictum: *Primum non nocere* (First, do no harm).

Even within psychiatry, the current enthusiasm for intervening with a menu of psychotropic drugs has its critics. Often these are older, respected researchers—leaders of an earlier generation of psychiatrists who feel distanced from their contemporary counterparts.[55] Among them is John Werry, the New Zealand child psychiatrist and author of psychopharmacology textbooks. Werry represents a link between American psychiatry and the international psychiatric community, and is one of the few experts willing to speak frankly in peer review journals. He talks about what he calls the "next generation of psychopharmacologists" in this way:

> I stand in awe of their swashbuckling style, the sophistication of their theories and the elegance of their high-tech methods, compared with the "by gosh and by god" art that those of us of the older generation . . . used. However, 40 years has slowly and painfully taught me that medicine is far more of a spectator than a participator sport. One needs to learn to respect the power of nature to heal and the relative impotence of medicine to influence this process except, often, adversely.[56]

I appreciate John Werry's accumulated wisdom and share his sentiments. I prescribe a good deal of Ritalin and believe the drug is relatively safe when used as recommended. I recognize the risks entailed in not treating or undertreating a serious behavioral problem with medication, and I do occasionally use nonstimulant drugs, though never for uncomplicated ADD symptoms. Even less frequently do I prescribe two agents for combined use. I'm reluctant to expose children to even a small risk of serious side effects from a drug whose efficacy has not been proven to me, and I want parents to know these risks and their options in weighing their decisions. Often a child is referred to me after having been treated elsewhere with two or three drugs, and I try to work with the parents and teachers to modify the child's environment so as to reduce the number of medications needed.

I do not question the sincere desire to heal on the part of today's innovators in American psychiatry. But the enthusiasm for treating children's emotional and behavior problems with powerful drugs, relatively untested on children, ought to be tempered with hard-earned wisdom about the limitations of such medicines. I do not believe that the problems of simple ADD merit even a small risk of dying from its treatment.

Chapter 12

<———>

RITALIN BEYOND CHILDHOOD:
TEENAGERS, ADULTS, AND ADD

Does the combination of repeated failures in my earlier years without any continued period of success, missed opportunities to learn, and the battering taken by my sense of self-worth as I endeavored to keep up with my peers account for much of my situation today, or is it entirely constitutional? It is most likely a tangled mixture of many forces, both internal and external.
—An adult ADD patient, quoted by Gabrielle Weiss, M.D., and
Lily T. Hechtman, M.D., *Hyperactive Children Grown Up*

Before 1980, when ADD was largely defined by excessive motor activity and impulsivity, it was believed to be a condition that ended when the child reached adolescence. It's true that extreme hyperactivity tends to diminish and eventually disappear by adulthood. But with the appearance of DSM-III, ADD was reconceptualized as a problem chiefly of inattention, and a person no longer had to demonstrate hyperactivity in order to meet the diagnostic criteria. This meant that the diagnosis could embrace many more teenagers and adults.

More important, follow-up studies of hyperactive children as they passed through adolescence and into adulthood indicated that many continued to have behavior and performance problems. These long-term studies of ADD children, which started to appear in the 1980s, have shown that, as a group, they are less likely to complete high school, and more likely as teens to experience academic problems, juvenile delinquency, substance abuse, and car accidents than children without ADD signs.[1] The teen years seem to be the most difficult, though many of the people studied continued to have problems in adulthood. They tended to be under-achievers in their careers and to have trouble working without supervision. Sometimes they persisted in antisocial behavior.[2]

These findings have been well publicized and, in combination with the widespread and intense public attention paid to ADD in the last decade or so, have led to an enormous rise in the number of teenagers and adults receiving the ADD diagnosis. Not surprisingly, we're also seeing a phenomenon of teens and adults attributing all kinds of life adjustment problems to the possibility that they "have" ADD. While the number of people over eighteen who take Ritalin is still dwarfed by the number of children age five to eighteen, the adult group has been the fastest-rising segment of Ritalin users over the past five years.

WHAT'S DIFFERENT ABOUT ADD POST-CHILDHOOD?

Teenagers and adults with ADD symptoms face quite different issues than do the children (or parents of children) diagnosed with ADD.[3] By the time such children hit puberty, even as hyperactivity and impulsivity slack off to some extent, other factors are conspiring to make life more challenging: coping with the larger world of middle school, an increased academic workload, and the whole juggernaut of emotional change that accompanies early adolescence, from asserting one's identity independent of parents to issues of peer acceptance to the emerging awareness of sexuality. And year after year, more emotional burdens heap up around the person's unsatisfactory behavior and performance: conflict-laden relationships, poor self-esteem, and a growing stock of negative feelings.

In broadest terms, moving from childhood to later life for those with ADD involves a shift from problems with *behavior* to problems with *performance*. The simple fact of hyperactivity or impulsivity is not the chief concern for teens and adults; rather, it's their disorganization, irresponsibility, procrastination, and inability to complete tasks that most often lead them or others to believe they have ADD. Another crucial difference is that older adolescents and adults are far more self-critical about their failures to perform than are younger children, who generally prefer to forget (that is, deny) their problems. With children, the decision to pursue evaluation for possible ADD is always made by parents, perhaps under the urging of a teacher who perceives a serious problem. While teens and adults also are influenced by parents, teachers and peers (and/or significant others), people increasingly set their own standards for performance as they mature. Their decision to seek out (and participate in) evaluation and treatment for ADD-type problems is far more self-determined.

Another profound difference: many teenagers and all adults have control over their own medication. By high school, the lines outside the school nurse's office have disappeared. Legally, teenagers are usually not permitted to self-medicate—especially with a controlled substance—on school grounds. Realistically, nearly all of them do.

The power to choose whether and when to take medication is a symbol of adult responsibility, but it poses certain risks for individuals who use Ritalin. Parents rarely, if ever, overmedicate their children; nor do children enjoy the experience of higher-than-recommended doses of Ritalin. But for adults taking prescribed Ritalin, or for some teenagers whose parents may not carefully supervise their dosage, the potential for overuse or abuse does exist. Just how many or what proportion of self-administrators overuse the drug, or use it erratically, is simply not known.

Many teens and adults who are truly handicapped by their ADD symptoms rely on Ritalin to help them function in certain basic ways that are expected of every mature or maturing person: to get by in school, to hold down a decent job, to manage life's endless organizational challenges, to moderate a difficult personality so that relationships can thrive better. But there's an ill-defined difference between these goals and the aim of achieving "optimal" performance with help from pharmacology. Where the line should be drawn between real need and cosmetic life enhancement is currently being hotly debated. Offering Ritalin to teenagers and adults for ADD opens a Pandora's box of questions about normal and supranormal achievement.

To what degree does ADD persist beyond childhood? The percentage of children diagnosed with ADD who continue to have problems as teenagers and adults has been variously estimated to be from 30 to 80 percent. Nearly two thirds of those followed from childhood into later life complain about persistent problems of inattention, impulsivity, or hyperactivity. Adolescence is a particularly difficult time, but by the time they reach young adulthood, many people with a childhood diagnosis of ADD have learned to cope with their personality. About half of all hyperactive kids do as well as their normal peers by the time they reach their twenties, a statistic not often stressed. In fact, one study indicates that the rate of ADD problems in any given age group seems to decline by about half every five years.[4] And another study found that people in their twenties who were hyperactive as children were employed at rates *equal* to those of a "normal" control group.[5] A key difference was that those in the once-hyperactive group were more likely to find jobs in the trades (carpenters, electricians, builders) than in the professions or service industries.

Virtually all the follow-up studies on ADD persisting into adolescence and adulthood have focused on children who were hyperactive, rather than those with the milder inattentive form. As noted previously, children diagnosed with hyperactivity twenty to twenty-five years ago very probably had more severe behavior and performance problems than many of those being diagnosed in the current ADD epidemic. A 1996 editorial in the *American Journal of Psychiatry* notes that long-term outcomes for ADD are worse for those children who were more severely affected, as logic would suggest.[6] So today's parents who hear about poor outcomes for ADD children in later life may be somewhat reassured by the knowledge that no one yet has followed, for more than three or four years, the "new" ADD child or adolescent—especially those who show only problems of inattention. I am convinced the outcomes for this large subgroup of recently diagnosed children will be much better than for their hyperactive and impulsive counterparts.

ADOLESCENT ADD: BLACK AND WHITE AND ALL OVER THE PLACE

The predictable adolescent crisis of identity is tough under any circumstances and is usually intensified by ADD symptoms. Teenagers must cope with strong and volatile feelings while dealing with a list of psychic chores: trying to decide what they want, learning to set their own limits and meet responsibilities, coming to terms with mature sexuality and relationships. Everyone has distinct personality strengths and weaknesses, but these variations are especially threatening to the self-image during the early teenage years, when insecurity about one's identity and the need for peer acceptance are high. For children with extremes of personality, this time of life carries even greater burdens and risks but also presents new opportunities for their diverse talents to be appreciated.

Teenagers, bless their hearts, tend to view things as black and white, wonderful or awful, and to feel passionate about virtually everything. This, along with their normal need to assert independence and autonomy, often makes it hard for them to accept a first-time diagnosis of ADD or the need to take Ritalin. And many teenagers who obediently took Ritalin as chil-

dren refuse the drug as young adolescents (between, say, thirteen and sixteen). At this moment in their lives, the idea that they are different is unacceptable. I've noticed an informal correlation between the age when kids
no longer want to dress up for Halloween and young patients refusing to
take Ritalin; it happens around age twelve or thirteen in both cases. Both
actions intolerably threaten a shaky identity.

Children who feel this way tell their parents and me that they "can handle things without Ritalin." I've noticed that kids who have had more severe problems as younger children more often tend to want "to do it on
their own," compared to the milder cases of ADD—for me a telltale sign
that the more severely affected kids have a lower self-image that's more
threatened by the medication. Interestingly, when they reach their later
teens or early twenties, many young patients decide on their own to resume
taking Ritalin.

I followed one young patient named Kevin O'Rourke for nine years, beginning in 1989, when he was seven. He was one of those kids for whom
Ritalin made a huge difference; I don't know if it saved his life, but when I
first saw him, he was about to get expelled from school for the second time.
His single mother, Janice, had been reported to the local child abuse
agency for allegedly hitting him. She also had a younger son and daughter,
and little control over any of the three; their family life was chaotic. But
Kevin was her major headache.

Kevin was exquisitely sensitive to Ritalin, meaning that with adequate
doses (ranging over the years from 10 to 20 mg twice or three times daily),
he could perform at a very high level in school—though always within a
special day class environment. He was very bright, but without medication
he was one of the most hyperactive and impulsive children I'd ever met.
His thought patterns and conversation were extremely tangential, jumping
from one subject to the next with the barest of connections. With Ritalin,
though, he and his mother could manage without either of them losing
control. And as we worked together in the first few years, Janice's parenting skills improved.

Kevin's was not a simple case of ADD. An anxious child, he worried that
his performance was inadequate, yet he rarely admitted this openly. In fact,
he almost always denied having any problems—a clear sign that he was too
scared to acknowledge them. It's not unusual for children to engage in denial as a form of coping, and very common in children with ADD problems. A common sign of this is "forgetting" to take medication, and when
Kevin "forgot" to take his pill, his behavior deteriorated markedly, in-

evitably prompting a call from the school. Every so often his mother would intentionally withhold the pills on weekends "just to see if they still helped." But she too would always notice right away the return of his "hyperness and jumping around," as she called it.

Kevin himself must have been well aware of Ritalin's effect on his ability to cope with life's demands, but he rarely acknowledged the drug's benefits or deficits, even when I asked him directly. Over the years I did so often, but he'd just say, "It's okay," and wouldn't elaborate, even when pressed. But neither did he rebel against taking the medication, which involved going to the school office—until he was twelve and had been taking Ritalin for five years. At first he would just "forget" to go to the office and have to be reminded. Soon his mother was reporting that she had to hunt for him in the morning when it was time to take his pill. Later he started verbally protesting against taking it, but Janice always prevailed.

When I learned what was going on, I again tried to get Kevin to express his feelings about taking Ritalin, specifically if he wanted to continue it. "I don't want to take it anymore" was his unequivocal reply. Janice, who was at the meeting, became quite upset: "Kevin, you know how different you act when you don't take the pills." He calmly held his ground: "I just want to try it on my own without the pills for a while." His mother's voice took on a pleading note. "But we've already done that, and you know how bad you always act." Clearly Janice felt very threatened by the idea that she'd have to cope with Kevin without Ritalin. In fairness to her, I knew she cared about her son and that it *would* be much harder for both of them. Yet I felt I had to respect Kevin's feelings; he couldn't explain why he wanted to try it on his own, but he was very firm about it. So despite Janice's and my own misgivings, we agreed that he would go without medication for a week's trial. His teacher would be told only that his dose was being "adjusted." Predictably, he and those around him had a difficult week, and he was referred to the principal's office for the first time in more than a year.

Kevin resumed taking Ritalin, though the issue was never formally settled. I continued to see him and Janice about every six months—about as often as a crisis seemed to occur in some aspect of his condition. Unlike many children who grow out of their hyperactivity entirely, he remained somewhat fidgety and impulsive. Meanwhile, though, he matured into a tall, strong young man who performed very well in school. He could read twelfth-grade-level material on entering high school, and was a whiz in science. He still attended special-ed classes, and once admitted to me that he was frightened of giving up that support. While Kevin continued to reiterate that he didn't want to take Ritalin (and I emphasized it was up to him), the prescriptions would invariably be filled. I haven't heard from him recently, but I suspect that he did eventually stop taking medication. Perhaps he'll get back in touch when he's in his twenties and reconsidering its benefits. Or he may have found a calling in which he can perform without its assistance. I'd like to know in either case.

WHEN TEENS ARE DIAGNOSED FOR THE FIRST TIME

It's a somewhat different situation when an underperforming or acting-out child is first considered in adolescence as an ADD candidate. There are varying reasons for a delayed diagnosis. Sometimes problem behavior can be ignored in younger children, predictably leading to much less tolerable trouble when the child reaches the teen years. An evaluating physician usually seeks some evidence that the problem began earlier in childhood, but no history may exist because the child coped well enough until middle school or high school. Realistically, many teens and adults seeking evaluation don't recall their early childhood well. And pragmatically, Ritalin will usually help, whether or not symptoms appeared before age seven.

Sometimes the kid just isn't performing up to his potential, and parents want to leave no stone unturned in discovering why. Social and media sources have spread the word about possible undiagnosed ADD, and it seems a promising avenue to explore. This was the case with Gavin Donaldson, the easygoing fifteen-year-old mentioned in Chapter 1, whose high-achieving parents thought his "concentration problems" were standing in the way of his getting top grades. In laying out to Gavin and his parents the pros and cons of using Ritalin, I emphasized that in his case it was truly elective, and I spent some time discussing values and goals: what it meant to be successful in school and in life. Gavin did wind up trying Ritalin. He said it made him work harder and more efficiently—he could concentrate better—but he didn't like its effect on his spontaneity and the way he related to his friends. He stopped taking the drug after several weeks, and his parents accepted his decision. I was glad when he stopped.

In fact, Gavin's openness to trying the drug is uncommon among younger teens. Many teenagers simply don't buy the concept of ADD. They're more comfortable attributing performance problems to laziness or lack of motivation than accepting the idea that something is wrong with their brains. And many are confused by the therapeutic use of Ritalin, a potential drug of abuse, having been endlessly told how terrible drugs are. Within the black-and-white, all-or-nothing worldview of adolescents, their cynicism about those same adults offering them Ritalin is understandable.

More rarely with younger teens, but more commonly with those over sixteen, an individual's own perception of his performance deficits may lead him to seek evaluation for ADD and treatment with medication. Sometimes just a one-year age difference can produce a major shift in the locus of concern and responsibility. Whether it's the child or the parents who contact me, I prefer in the evaluation stage that the teenager attend the first meeting, in contrast to my procedure with younger children. If the parents have reported over the telephone that their child is very angry and unwilling to cooperate, they may come alone the first time—but that circumstance in itself gives me some useful insight about problems within the family.

By the time a child reaches adolescence, the persistent negative experiences of coping with a difficult personality invariably cause ADD symptoms to be entwined with emotional problems: anxiety, depression, anger ("an attitude"), or a volatile mix of all three. The presence of such comorbid conditions makes evaluating and treating adolescents a special challenge. What may look at first glance like a simple case of teenage ADD often becomes complicated as I get to know the child and family, with reports of suicide attempts, running away, protracted battling between parents and child, or trouble with the law.

Adolescence is also a time when more serious psychiatric disorders begin to show up. While moodiness is as common as acne among teenagers, I do occasionally meet a profoundly depressed and isolated young person, unable to attend to the daily tasks of living, never mind going to school or maintaining friendships. A child whose behavior is perceived as "different" in elementary school may seem bizarre in high school. It's not always easy to distinguish the pathological from extreme forms of rebellion, but certain signs should be taken seriously. Not only is hearing voices (unconnected with hallucinogen use) an upsetting experience for a teenager, but to a physician it may be an early signal of a thought disorder or schizophrenia. I'm glad to say that such tragic developments are relatively rare in my practice.

I try hard to make a connection with the teenager and speak directly about his or her problems and choices. If there's a lot of conflict between the kid and his parents, I walk a fine line between empathizing with the child while maintaining an alliance with the parents. Parents seldom find the panacea they are hoping for by consulting a doctor. Desperate parents with an unhappy, angry, acting-out adolescent want help; they've heard that ADD might be the problem, and many believe that Ritalin could be their salvation. In most such situations, however, the use of medication is academic. If the teen were willing to consider Ritalin, he'd already be over his major problem, which is opposition to everything his parents and other adults want. Neither an ADD diagnosis nor a drug will resolve this struggle; feelings and interactions must be addressed first. While problems of attention and impulsivity may exist, they are secondary to emotional and family issues. Usually some child and family therapy are needed before anything else can happen.

ADD and Conduct Disorder in Teenagers

With depressing regularity these days, unwilling teens are hauled into my office by parents who have heard from a school or drug counselor that their child's high-school failures or substance abuse problem may be due to un-diagnosed ADD. Tom Francis, age fifteen, was one of them. I first met his mother, Bunny, who breathlessly recounted her adopted son's difficulties, along with some background on the family. They were quite wealthy: Tom's father, Harrison, was CEO of a medium-sized computer hardware producer and was too busy to come to the meeting—in a pattern that proved consistent, he'd leave family matters to his wife until they reached a crisis. Of Tom, she said, "He's always been an underachiever at school." She rattled off a list of prior learning evaluations that had cleared her son of any serious learning disability, though (like most people) he had relative strengths and weaknesses in various subjects. He wasn't great at math, and he found it easier to learn by listening than by seeing new material. If he didn't really apply himself, his performance would decline sharply.

As Bunny talked (and talked), it became clear that his parents had done everything for Tom except set limits for him as he was growing up. Bunny was quite ready to admit her impotence: "I've never been able to get Tom to mind. But he was such an easy boy until he reached puberty." Tom hadn't displayed significant behavior problems until his sophomore year in high school, according to Bunny; in fact, before then, the family had been in counseling because of his shyness and social withdrawal.

During later sessions, it also became apparent that Bunny and Harrison had serious marital problems, usually swept under the rug. When they dis-agreed, Harrison pretty much ignored Bunny's wishes and requests—a fact not lost on Tom, who observed that his mother usually lost any power struggles. This surely contributed to his own failure to heed her. Bunny's hectic, scatterbrained, motor-mouth style probably encouraged her family's tendency to tune her out. That her comfortable lifestyle was due solely to her husband's earnings didn't make it easier for her to assert herself effectively. While Bunny and Harrison seemed to accept their status quo, it (along with Harrison's frequent absences) increasingly posed problems in dealing with Tom. The earlier family therapy hadn't helped.

Now Tom was acting out in ways that caused concern. Ironically, he was no longer a social wallflower, but his society was questionable. He'd begun hanging out with an older crowd, including some kids in their late teens who were into virtual-reality games, music, and drugs (not necessarily in that order). Tom would ask for a ride downtown on school nights and not come home until nearly midnight; Bunny went along with it. "What else could I do?" she asked plaintively. She realized that her reluctance to say no to Tom caused problems, but she feared he'd get angry with her and couldn't bear disappointing him.

Meanwhile, he was getting straight F's at his private school, where he was on probation and under threat of dismissal before the next school year. This alarmed even Harrison. The school thought his dreaminess and passivity in class might be related to ADD (or maybe his late nights were depriving him of sleep). The diagnosis had been considered in earlier learning evaluations, but "Harrison was against using drugs," Bunny explained. A couple of things had since changed, prompting their call to me: Harrison had reconsidered the acceptability of Ritalin, and a few days earlier Tom had set fire to his school books on his desk after Bunny (for once) had refused to drive him downtown.

When I hear a story like Tom's, I know immediately that this isn't a simple case of ADD and that there's much more going on with this child and his family. Certainly ADD symptoms may have been part of the picture for Tom—and indeed, Bunny's own behavior led me to speculate that she might be a candidate for evaluation. (It would be interesting to document ADD rates in adoptive parents and their children, to compare them with the already established genetic connection in families.) But compared to this family's problems in dealing with behavior and emotions, I felt that Tom's degree of inattention and impulsivity were well down the list of importance.

My next meeting was with Tom himself, who turned out to be a pleasant, even-tempered fellow, talking easily and frankly with me. "I don't really feel like going to school," he said flatly. "I know I'm supposed to, but I don't care enough to do the work." The fact that he was on the brink of expulsion didn't seem to bother him greatly; he thought he could go to public high school, where most of his friends were, anyway. Tom displayed the denial and sense of invulnerability common to adolescents, but to an extreme degree. In considering an ADD diagnosis, I wondered how much of Tom's indifference to school might be a case of "can't" versus "won't," and whether he might be an example of the ADD child's "insensitivity to delayed consequences," about which Russell Barkley speaks. Tom didn't think much about his future, but he had some ideas about music that were rather thoughtful and intelligent. He was clearer on his feelings about his family. He despised his mother ("She's a flea") and felt fear and anger toward his father, who, he said, "never did anything with me when I was growing up." Though he recognized that Harrison held the power in the family, Tom believed that "he'd never do anything" in the way of real discipline. From his point of view, his father tolerated more misbehavior than Bunny did.

Because of Tom's daydreaming, disorganization, and procrastination in school, I felt he might adequately meet the criteria for the inattentive type of ADD. Tom knew about Ritalin—some of his friends took it—but he didn't think he needed it. Some of those friends had been prescribed the drug, and a few others had tried it on their own in middle school, though Tom denied he'd done this himself. He also denied having used other drugs, while freely acknowledging that some of his friends smoked marijuana and took hallucinogens. Usually I interpret such remarks as highly suspect; a teenager who talks like this probably is somewhat familiar with drug use himself.

The first visit with the whole family present brought a lot into the open. Harrison sounded simultaneously patient and exasperated with both his son and his wife. About Tom, he told me, "He's basically a good boy," and in the next breath turned to his son, asking, "Don't you care if you're kicked out of school?" He went on to say, "This has been mainly Bunny's responsibility," but admitted that his wife was pretty ineffectual with Tom. When I asked if he'd ever tried to take over the parenting, he said, "Oh, yes, I've tried to"—at which Bunny shot back angrily, "For about two weeks! That's how much time you give your son." Then she addressed me: "He'll give him a car in six months; he'll give him a new electric guitar." Then back to her husband: "You know, Harrison, you just don't say no to Tom."

As the couple settled in to fight, I glanced over at Tom, who was sitting on a separate couch with his head back and eyes closed. I figured he'd seen them bicker like this thousands of times and was checking out; I didn't find it hard to extend the metaphor of checking out to his current attitude about school and life in general. Of course, there was more to his situation, but the family dynamic certainly played into his overall cynicism. Later I learned from his parents that Tom was more depressed than he'd let on with me. He had threatened to run away and even hinted at ending his life if his parents carried out a plan to send him away to boarding school, saying things like, "What's the point of living?" (I never view such statements merely as attempts to manipulate, even if they sometimes have that intention or effect; teens can be tragically prone to act on impulse.) Over the next few months, he also complained of trouble sleeping. That he was anxious didn't surprise me, and with his parents' permission, I offered him some low-dose imipramine (an antidepressant), which might help him sleep better and also improve his mood and attention.

However, I didn't think that treating him with medication would make much difference. Tom's underperformance at school may have been traceable in part to an inherent biological problem manifesting as ADD symptoms, but it was also connected with his feelings of anger, sadness, and alienation; his low self-image; and the troubled family relationships. Tom needed both a crash course in limits and a lot of understanding—maybe a safe place to talk after he reached some sort of crisis or hit emotional bottom—and I didn't believe his parents could provide the appropriate environment, structure, and monitoring needed. Few parents, in fact, can make the quick and profound change in long-established patterns that's called for in such cases.

Bunny and Harrison must have sensed this on their own, because without my prompting they had already surveyed some special boarding schools for problem teens. Tom's father was dismayed by the prospect of his son's attending the local high school, where he believed students were more tempted to use drugs and alcohol, and finally agreed with Bunny that Tom needed to be in a different environment. The first step was to send him to a summer boarding school program for struggling teens in the East. Tom again threatened to run away, but faced with the choice of going along or being hospitalized, he wound up getting on the plane for New Hampshire quietly. He did reasonably well without medication there—the last I knew, it remained to be seen how he would do after returning home.

DEALING WITH ACTING-OUT ADOLESCENTS

Tom's family had the luxury of considering this expensive option. Most parents struggling with an out-of-control teen do not, and others are unwilling to send a child away. The hard choices they are left with include local drug treatment programs (some offer short-term boarding), calling in the police, or kicking the child out of the house. In truth, it's very hard, if not impossible, to control an acting-out teenager who is determined to go his way. And most parents are understandably reluctant to make the really tough choices that might make a difference at this stage; instead they attempt milder measures, such as grounding for a weekend, that are likely to have little effect. This is not meant critically, only to report what happens in real life. I hope never to face such choices as a parent—they mostly all stink, and the risks and costs are high.

To parents in such a dilemma, the appeal of medication is great. If the teenager is willing and the side effects not too serious, the typical reaction is, "Why not try it?" Because of their abuse potential for teens, stimulants are often passed up in favor of broader-acting drugs such as the antidepressants imipramine or desipramine, which can affect mood as well as attention deficits. (The sudden-death risk associated with the tricyclics has been reported only in prepubertal children.) Prozac or another SSRI might be considered because of their minimal side effects, but these typically have little effect on ADD symptoms. If the family continues to work with a psychiatrist, ultimately a mood stabilizer such as lithium may be tried, often in combination with another drug. There is no evidence that any of these drug interventions are widely effective with kids who meet criteria for conduct disorder, but any one of them might make a difference in a particular case. When multiple drugs are used, it becomes harder to sort out which may be helping or hurting. Given the number of psychotropic medications available, the continuing ambiguities of psychiatric diagnosis, and the desperation of families seeking help, the search may go on for months for a drug or combination of drugs that will "cure" a teen's "chemical imbalance."

Trying to offer advice to any parent of a badly struggling teenager is a test of any professional's self-confidence. Often it seems there's little you can do except ride out the storm until the kid makes it to the magic age of maturity (seventeen or eighteen, with luck; at the latest, one hopes, the early twenties). Nonetheless, when parents ask for advice, I tell them it makes sense to me to maintain some broad limits such as a curfew and the need to make passing grades. Other principles include trying to spend time with the teen (even if he protests), getting to know his friends, and taking a consistent position with the other parent.

It's a truism that the most influential part of parenting takes place fairly early in a child's life; by the time he reaches adolescence, his sense of what's acceptable and expected in his family is pretty well set. This holds in spades for families with an ADD-personality kid; even parents who have provided clear and firm limits will find them tested during these years. If they have let behavior problems slide, they're in for a much harder time. I wish that parents who are afraid of hurting a younger child's feelings with an emphatic no could foresee how much greater the stakes and risks will be with that same child as a teenager. The amount of testing and risk taking teens engage in is inversely related to how much love and respect has been built between them and their parents since childhood. Those who consciously restrain themselves do so on the basis of not wanting to hurt or disappoint their parents. With ADD kids, the question is often raised about how much self-restraint they are capable of—the "won't" versus "can't" equation. The teen with ADD-type problems may have more difficulty restraining himself, but all except the most emotionally disturbed adolescents retain some volition and the ability to judge what's right and wrong.

In responding to unacceptable behavior, short-term consequences such as withholding phone privileges or restricting activities may or may not have any effect. Parents must be willing to establish and convey that there's a bottom line, usually that the child cannot continue to live in their house. I recognize how traumatic this choice would be for any parent and never propose they exercise it without offering some alternative living situation—preferably the home of a relative or friends, otherwise a group home arrangement. Circumstances that generally call for a teenager to be placed in a different environment or even psychiatric hospitalization, at least temporarily, include the threat of suicide; running away or threatening to do so with the means at hand (for example, a credit card); substance abuse in conjunction with school failure, defiance, or keeping bad company (usually this means marijuana or alcohol use on weekdays, or any use of harder drugs); physical threats or acts toward family members; known lawbreaking; and persistent promiscuity. An essential element is to at least ensure the teen's physical safety; no major psychotherapeutic or drug intervention can take place unless he or she feels safe and secure. This means the teen must be clean of alcohol and street drugs and protected from physical and emotional violence.

At the worst, if things have progressed too far or resources are too limited to create such a safe environment, the teen may be forced to learn life's rules in the school of hard knocks: incarceration, pregnancy, or worse. Even when parents can't control their children, they face choices about how much to protect or rescue them. Again, as the children get older, the ante is raised: conferencing with the third-grade teacher is one thing, and talking to an arresting officer or judge is quite another. At some point during adolescence, parents no longer can protect a child from the most serious consequences of his actions, even if they still wish to.

I don't want to paint too black a picture. Kids with ADD complicated by severe conduct disorder are a relative minority (though they get a lot of attention). As I've said, of hyperactive children followed into their teenage years in studies, about half were judged to be reasonably well adjusted, and the numbers improved as teens passed into adulthood. All teenagers who engage in a certain amount of acting out through ADD-like behavior should be receiving multimodal treatment that includes some individual and family counseling. Group counseling or therapy can be especially helpful for teens (and adults). While it may carry some stigma or the risk of exposure to more seriously troubled kids in the group, it has advantages in that teens tend to listen to and respect their peers' viewpoints. Hearing the experience of others their age often can draw them out more than going one-on-one with a therapist. But an adult therapist is on hand to guide the group process, which can become a comfortable, safe place for young people to at least talk about their problems.

The teenager's school continues to have a role in any such effort. Evaluation for learning problems should take place, if it hasn't in the past, and accommodations in teaching can be made. High schools increasingly offer some nontraditional settings that may work better for an ADD adolescent. Some operate on shortened days; others send work home to be completed throughout the week, and the student reports in only once weekly for teaching and coordinating the following week's assignments. Through such alternative arrangements, kids can obtain a high-school education outside the fairly inflexible standard classroom environment, and some work at jobs in addition to their schoolwork. There remains some stigma about attending such programs, though that's changing—partly due to the example of young role models such as tennis stars or actors who get their education this way.

A few more thoughts on medication. While I caution teens (as with younger children) that taking a drug won't miraculously clear up all their problems, talking about medication in a metaphorical way can sometimes help them articulate their goals. Lately I've been asking teenagers who are considering taking medication this question: If you could take a magic pill that had no bad effects and could help you in the exact ways you wanted, what effects would you like that pill to have? (I used to ask a similar question about a magic wand, but a magic pill seems more up-to-date.) Responses have included: have stronger motivation, more willpower, more energy; be smarter; pay attention better; feel happier; be less sensitive (to emotional pain); get things done; be less shy and more outgoing; talk to my parents more; lose weight. A number say they wish such a pill could last longer than four hours. This wish list then becomes a reference point not only in determining medication but in setting goals for counseling and family therapy.

Teenagers have had interesting thoughts on the difference between taking drugs that I prescribe and taking drugs on their own; I've talked about this with some teens who have abused drugs, including speed (methamphetamine). A case has been made by several researchers, including Joseph Biederman and his colleagues, that teenage and adult substance abuse represents an individual's attempts to self-medicate their biological disorders. There's undoubtedly some merit to the idea that people use alcohol and drugs to cope with their emotions and problems, biologically based or not. Some see their doctor; others see their dealer. Since I prescribe Ritalin, an abusable substance, the parallels can get uncomfortable.

The possibility always exists of using Ritalin deliberately to get high. Children don't like the effects of high-dose Ritalin, so they are at virtually zero risk. However, teenagers and adults who take Ritalin can use the medication in this way, and a rare few develop an addiction to the drug. My own experience (and that of most other doctors) in treating teenagers with Ritalin reveals very little obvious or chronic abuse. I've suspected it among only two or three teens, out of scores for whom I've prescribed the medication, and in two of those situations I believed the teens may have been giving or selling Ritalin to their friends rather than abusing it themselves. Another possibility is that the parents of children or teenagers being treated with Ritalin may begin using the drug themselves, but again my experience leads me to believe that this is relatively rare.

OLDER TEENS: CONTEMPLATING THE FUTURE

The later teenage years typically mark a transition in which adolescents begin to worry about their own performance and future, and make decisions for themselves. In this the teen has the tacit support of society, which encourages increased self-responsibility with increasing age. A few enterprising seventeen- and eighteen-year-olds have contacted me directly to request an appointment for ADD screening; I'm happy to go along, but still insist that their parents come to the first meeting.

If the oppositional, acting-out teen represents one end of the adolescent ADD spectrum, the young person who is personally motivated to improve her performance but feels held back by her personality occupies the other. She usually wants to meet the expectations and hopes of her parents, but her standards are more internalized and self-directed. In contrast to younger adolescents, she is generally willing, if not eager, to try medication. A tendency to hope for too much from drug interventions can be one problem in working with these young people; another is that their dreams and ambitions may not be a good fit with their personality and capabilities. Where kids with conduct-type problems expect too little of themselves, these kids sometimes expect too much.

Susie Cohn, a seventeen-year-old high-school junior, was one of those who insisted that her parents arrange an evaluation for ADD; indeed, Susie called me herself the first time. She lived mostly with her mother, Sharon, but spent time with her father, Hank, as well—her parents had been divorced for about three years. She had two older brothers away at college. At my request, both parents accompanied her to the first visit. A cute, perky young woman, Susie had a flair for drama, according to her parents, and that flair was apparent as she launched into her explanation of why she thought she had ADD.

"Well, for one thing, I've *never* been on time in my *whole life*," she confessed with a disarming grin. "I've *never* finished a book [it turned out she *had* finished that teen manifesto, Salinger's *A Catcher in the Rye*] and I'm *always* behind in my schoolwork, even with tutoring help." Susie had been assessed for learning problems in elementary school, though none were found. She had heard about ADD from her psychotherapist: "I think it really fits me, except that I'm not hyper." Sharon wasn't as ready to accept this self-diagnosis, expressing concern that ADD could become a stigmatizing label for Susie or that she would use it as an excuse for poor performance. It quickly became clear that Susie and her mom regularly locked horns over many issues, though their relationship seemed basically loving and close. Hank spoke up for Susie's motivation: "She tries really hard. I think the schools aren't doing their job. The public school system in this state is going to hell." I sensed that Sharon had always been the more demanding parent and Hank the more laid-back one, and that Susie occasionally took advantage of their failure to agree on standards. However, both seemed eager to do what was best for their daughter and cooperate in the effort.

When I met with Susie alone, she made it clear that she wanted to go to college, and she even knew where. She aimed to attend Georgetown University and major in political science or international relations. She had visited Washington, D.C., had made some friends there, and was stimulated by its aura of power. In general, Susie's attitude seemed positive: She had a social life and didn't seem especially bothered by her parents' divorce, saying, "I think they've actually been happier since they separated." She did acknowledge that she and her mom fought quite often, one reason she looked forward to living away at college. Academically, she was on shakier ground. When I asked her to read aloud some tenth- and eleventh-grade material and answer some comprehension questions, I became alarmed by her obvious struggle to decode some of the harder words and to extract meaning from the text. Her spoken-language abilities clearly were adequate, but she was also pretty weak in math skills. Throughout the academic screening, she showed a tendency to rush ahead and answer impulsively.

I got another view from Susie's therapist, who said that her upbeat demeanor belied a more troubled youngster. In previous years major battles had taken place between the parents and between the girl and her mother, and Susie had gone through an acting-out phase, hanging out with "stoners" and failing to come home on a few nights. There had been threats of running away and suicide. More recently things had cooled down a lot; now, instead of challenging her parents, Susie seemed to be applying her persistence and intensity toward the goal of college. The therapist shared my concern about Susie's academic skills. Although no specific learning disability had been diagnosed, she was receiving weekly tutoring and had had some accommodations made in her school program.

The therapist, whom I respected, thought that ADD might be contributing to Susie's difficulties, or at least wanted to look into the possibility by referring her to me. She felt that Susie was at low risk for abusing Ritalin and could handle the responsibility of taking it, and in this I tended

to agree. Some aspects of Susie's profile met criteria for ADD; more pragmatically, the diagnosis might get her extra help in school, and medication
might help her cope better with its demands. But something else was troubling me about Susie's situation. In thinking about her goals and aspira-
tions, I wondered how well they fit her developmental and temperamental
strengths.

With teenagers of this kind—who are motivated yet feel they may
"have" ADD—I try to ask three questions: What do they *want* to do in the
future (their personal dream)? What do they think they *should* do (that is,
what is expected of them)? What are they good at? For the teenager (or
adult) hounded by problems of distractibility and impulsivity, the answers
to each can be quite different. Susie *wanted* to go to Georgetown; this was
clearly her dream. She thought she *should* go to college, in part because
both her brothers did (though according to the parents, both boys had
found academics easier than Susie did). She wasn't sure what she was good
at—she enjoyed theater and acting but felt it lacked substance and security.
Here was an odd reversal of typical parent/child ideas about college and careers; neither Sharon nor Hank felt Susie had to go to Georgetown, or any
college, for that matter. They felt their daughter's strengths lay in drama,
and were prepared to send her to an arts program either at the college level
or as an apprentice in a theater company. They agreed that a career in the
arts promised less financial security than one in government but argued
strongly that it was just as valid a choice, and, moreover, one in which they
would support her.

Susie was not to be easily talked out of her goal—and who was I to end
her dream of a life in international relations or government? However, I
had trouble envisioning her getting through a highly competitive college
and then going on to law school without taking Ritalin. Even with medication it promised to be a struggle, given her academic weakness. Looking
ahead, it was possible that Susie would need to continue taking Ritalin to
accomplish the reading and writing required throughout such a career—
and even then, I felt the odds were high that she could fall short. Nearly all
the adults I've met who complain that attention problems seriously impair
their work are pursuing careers for which they are ill-suited by their skills
or personality.

Susie's response to Ritalin was at best equivocal, at least in terms of her
grades. She reported that it helped her concentrate but sometimes left her
irritable and cut down on her sociability—which she saw as a negative. After a while she said she thought Ritalin's effects were wearing off too

quickly. I briefly considered trying Dexedrine Spansule but decided against it when she began missing appointments. I hadn't seen Susie for three months when she called to say she was out of pills and the SAT was that weekend. This increased my concern about her reliability. I didn't think she was abusing Ritalin to get high, but rather suspected she was slipping into a pattern of using the drug intermittently on an "as needed" basis, to study or take exams. I worry that this kind of use permits or even promotes an "ADD lifestyle" marked by denial and procrastination, alternating with frantic catching up.

Every grown-up gets to determine how she wants to live, yet this pattern of dealing with responsibilities is the very reason many adults seek treatment in the first place—indeed, it is often labeled as typical adult ADD behavior. I'm not sure if I'm helping or hurting by prescribing Ritalin, as I did for Susie on this occasion, if it becomes incorporated into such a lifestyle. Susie may have reached a similar conclusion—she eventually stopped calling for prescription refills. I'm not aware of her current career path.

RITALIN: "GLASSES" FOR THE UNDERPERFORMING TEENAGER?

Whether Ritalin should be used to achieve optimal performance is, for me, one of the thorniest issues in treating teenagers and adults with medication. An incident in my professional career several years ago brought it into sharp focus. While attending a week-long review course in psychopharmacology offered by Harvard Medical School and Massachusetts General Hospital, I had the opportunity to hear Joseph Biederman, perhaps the most published researcher in the field, speak on ADD. The talk was stimulating and clearly new to many in the audience, and the question period afterward went on for a long time. When it was over, Dr. Biederman offered to continue the discussion outside the conference hall. I eagerly left my seat to join those interested, for I had a question of my own.

I'd been thinking of one kid in particular. Jim Hassler was sixteen when I first met him, and he had already been taking Ritalin for several years. His parents were strong believers in the chemical-imbalance theory of behavior. What made Jim's case unusual (at that time) was that he wasn't underperforming at all. He was clearly both bright and hardworking; he was getting straight A's in high school. Even off medication, which had been tried now and then, Jim earned excellent grades, though an occasional B-plus or A-minus might slip into his record. But he was very clear about how much harder it was for him to concentrate and stay at the top of his class without the Ritalin.

I thought Jim had anxious and obsessional qualities in addition to any possible attention deficits; his parents, both postdoctoral graduates, seemed equally driven. They were open to talking about the meaning and costs of success, and they approved of Jim's continuing to meet with me to discuss his anxieties. They were even willing to take him off Ritalin—but when the medication was discontinued, Jim reported that he was having much more trouble keeping up his performance level. Though his parents did not notice any difference in Jim's performance on or off the drug, they supported and respected his wish to resume taking it.

I was uncomfortable in my role, however. If I stretched his symptoms, Jim might vaguely have met DSM criteria for ADD. He didn't seem to experience any ill effects from taking Ritalin (only later, when in his early twenties, did he tell me that it sometimes left him feeling cranky and irritable). Yet I never felt that I was treating an illness. Was I acting ethically—both in my care of Jim and in relation to his peers—by boosting his performance with medication? Jim was in the running for valedictorian, the top performer of his high-school class; was it fair to other high achievers that Jim was taking Ritalin?

I didn't raise this question with his family, but I did with Joe Biederman. Patiently fielding a swarm of questions in the conference corridor, he struck me as intense, forthright, and knowledgeable; he projected a sense that he knew everything there was to know about ADD. When I spotted an opening, I quickly jumped in, sketching out my two-year experience with Jim and the essence of my dilemma. Was I treating illness or just enhancing performance? Dr. Biederman seemed unfazed, as if he had addressed the question many times before.

"It's like wearing glasses to achieve twenty-twenty vision," he explained. "If inattention or distractibility is preventing optimum performance, why not give Ritalin?" The alternative, he said, expanding on the analogy, would compel the child to squint to self-correct a fundamental defect in his vision. A doctor could allow a child to struggle along on his own, Biederman surmised, but he felt that Ritalin was the better choice for the patient. He paused to see if I had understood, and as it seemed to make sense, I nodded agreement and he moved on to the next question. Yet something about his response left me unsatisfied. I continued to ponder it, along with a colleague, Dr. Tom Boyce, then director of the UCSF Division of Behavioral and Developmental Pediatrics, who was also at the meeting. As we talked I began to discern the flaws in Dr. Biederman's glasses metaphor.

For one thing, the standards for good vision are much more precise and objective than those for good behavior or performance. The measures for 20/20 vision are well defined. Some doctors and patients find 20/30 vision acceptable, but nonetheless there's a clear difference; it's a less subjective matter than accepting B's instead of A's on a report card. With ADD, however, the lack of a biological marker or standardized test, like the Snellen chart for visual acuity, hampers any accurate measurement of behavior. The standards of what's acceptable exist very much in the eye of the beholder. As I've pointed out, special-education teachers generally see less ADD-type behavior in a given child, compared to regular classroom teachers. Fathers generally handle ADD-type children more effectively than mothers. Various ethnic groups feel differently about the need for kids to sit quietly and concentrate. ADD questionnaires are by nature imprecise because they raise questions like how many fidgets is a lot—and so on.

As it turned out, Jim Hassler himself became dissatisfied with Ritalin, saying it made him less sociable. More to the point, it didn't address what he and I came to call his "existential angst"—never feeling quite happy or contented with himself. So Jim and I embarked on a grand tour of the psychotropic drugs used to treat ADD, depression, and anxiety disorders: we went through several SSRIs (the Prozac family), desipramine, Welbutrin, and BuSpar, among others. Typically, Jim would report that the newest drug was finally "the one," but a few months later he would complain again that he wasn't feeling right. When he reached college, Jim did his share of self-medicating with alcohol, marijuana, cocaine, and an occasional hallucinogen. He had some difficult times, and at his low point as a freshman, he even contemplated suicide. With some help, he pulled himself out of it and graduated with a 4.0 average.

Jim's quest for the perfect medication eventually led him to the Hallowell Clinic in Concord, Massachusetts, a mecca for ADD sufferers. He returned with a drug new to him: nortriptyline (Pamelor), a tricyclic known among psychiatric cognoscenti as good for generalized angst like Jim's. As usual, he hailed the new medication as a breakthrough, and while cautiously supportive, I reminded him that we'd been down this road before. I'm still in touch with Jim, who is twenty-four at this writing. He's feeling stuck at the moment, is seeing a therapist, but hasn't found the right job for himself. Recently he asked (at his parents' urging) to try Ritalin again; I wasn't against it but asked for specific goals and measures so that we could determine if it was making a difference. Jim's is a good demonstration of a life that defies a simple drug solution.

As for me, I still haven't completely sorted out where I stand on the issue of optimizing performance with Ritalin and other medications. It's sometimes useful to think in terms of whether a person's ADD symptoms can be said to constitute an impairment, legally or otherwise. Jim, surely, was not impaired in relation to his peers. Explaining this idea can help clarify the issue for families, and some accept my opinion as to when medication doesn't seem called for. Others go in search of a more cooperative doctor.

ADULTS WITH ADD: MY DAY ON A STIMULANT

When it comes to evaluating and treating adults for ADD, I sometimes feel I'm at a curious disadvantage. Neither I nor anyone in my family "has" ADD or takes Ritalin, in contrast to many leaders of the ADD-Ritalin movement. There's no question that sharing a common experience with patients has advantages for the professional helper: promoting understanding and deeper empathy about the trials of the condition and what it takes to cope. But there's also a danger that viewing life through the lens of ADD may limit one's vision.

Because I don't suffer the effects of an ADD personality, perhaps I have to listen harder and pay closer attention to what I hear from patients, just as I must try harder to understand the experience of a mother (I'm not a woman), a parent raising teenagers (my kids are still in grade school), or someone living in the country (my experience has been urban and suburban). My task, then, is to try to imagine what it's like for that person or family, while bringing a different perspective to their problem and possible solutions. Perhaps, in not "being" ADD myself, it's easier for me to look at the bigger picture of ADD and Ritalin and to raise concerns.

One observation about myself gives me a clue, I think, about coping with a nervous system that makes concentrating difficult. I think I concentrate well unless I am in a room where a TV is on. Even with the sound turned down or off, if the screen is within my visual field, I get distracted by the video image and have trouble communicating. I can read a book with no problem around TV, but carrying on a conversation takes real effort. I try to sit with my back to the TV or ask if it can be turned off. I've been told by many ADD sufferers that this is what it's like for them virtually all the time.

Unlike many of my generation, I never had the experience of using amphetamine, or "speed," either recreationally or to cram for exams. I was really a virgin when it came to familiarity with the effects of the medication I prescribed so often. One day I remarked as much to the mother of an eleven-year-old I'd been treating. Joan said she'd been curious, too, and had tried one of her son's Dexedrine Spansule pills. (I suspect that many parents try their children's medication, and not just Ritalin; even when prescriptions are tracked through triplicate records, it's hard to notice if an occasional pill is diverted to someone other than the patient.) Anyway, Joan said the drug hadn't done much for her, but she had a bunch left—we had discontinued it because her son wasn't responding. She offered to give me some. This transaction was mildly unethical and probably illegal; I would never, for example, write a Ritalin prescription for one of my friends or family. But I trusted Joan and, after weighing the pros and cons, decided to try a 10 mg Dexedrine Spansule. (I did advise her to throw out the rest so that no one else had access to it.)

It wasn't until several months later that I found an occasion to conduct my experiment. Because I couldn't predict its effects on me, I didn't want to take the Dexedrine on a day I was seeing patients, nor did it make sense to take it during a time when I wanted to kick back, such as on a weekend. I waited, in fact, until Christmas Eve day; I take that day off and there's always much to do. I didn't tell my wife, Denise, when I took it because I wanted to get her "blind" reaction to me on the drug. I took the pill after breakfast, around 9 A.M. About an hour later I went out to do some gardening; it had been raining and I hadn't weeded in nearly a month. For the next ninety minutes I power-weeded with great energy and drive. It felt good to work, and I knocked off the whole front yard.

Heading back inside, I noticed my younger son's GI Joe lying on the living room floor. He and his brother have many spaces in which to create their elaborate setups of toy soldiers—even the living room is okay, but we tell them they must pick up there. "Louie!" I shouted into their bedroom, "I've warned you many times about GI Joes in the living room. I know I'm being short with you, but this one is mine for the rest of the day." "Okay, Dad," was Louie's no-big-deal response.

At lunchtime, I warmed up two slices of leftover artichoke pizza that I liked, but ate only one. Around one in the afternoon I went downstairs to the study to work on a rewrite of an article for a professional journal; it was a major job of thinking and reorganization, and I felt up for it. In fact, as I worked over the several hours, I thought I was really "killing" it. I came up for air as it was getting dark, feeling I had put in a very productive day.

When I told Denise I had taken the pill, she seemed mildly annoyed. "So now I know why you had only one piece of pizza. And you know you were short with Louie." I protested that I'd acknowledged being impatient, but he'd left his GI Joe in there one too many times. "But there was an edge to your voice," she insisted. "It wasn't necessary." At dinner shortly thereafter, I ate what I suspect was a normal amount: the drug should have worn off by then. Later in the evening I reviewed the work I'd done on the paper. It was okay but not as good as I'd thought while under the Dexedrine's influence. After the kids went to bed, Denise and I wrapped gifts and retired early in anticipation of being awakened at dawn. I had no problem falling asleep.

Clearly, this very limited experience cannot represent the entire range of adult responses to Ritalin and its fellow stimulants. However, what I felt and how I acted is pretty consistent with the reported experience of these drugs—for those with problems of concentration and performance *and* for those who don't have such problems. More than a few adults who consult me about a possible ADD diagnosis have not been aware of Ritalin's across-the-board effects; they've had occasion to try it and made the error of assuming that because it affected them, they had ADD.

Matilda, age fifty-five, was such a patient. One day when she called to refill a Ritalin prescription for her eighteen-year-old daughter, Musette, she asked if she could make an appointment for herself. Matilda confessed she had taken one of the 20 mg Ritalin pills before a class—she'd recently gone back to school part time—and felt that her concentration was remarkably improved. Moreover, she said, she had always struggled to pay attention, just like her daughter: "Maybe I have ADD, too?"

I asked Matilda to come in with her husband, whom I already knew from my evaluation of Musette. Matilda's husband confirmed her reported symptoms and supported her in her desire to try Ritalin. Acceptance of medication for performance and emotional problems seemed pretty high in this family; he himself had been taking Prozac for a while, and Musette eventually switched to Prozac as well. Whether Matilda really met criteria for ADD was a borderline call, but Ritalin did seem to help her. She currently uses it three or four times a week when she attends school or works at her part-time clerical job. Her husband agrees that she's more satisfied with her performance and hasn't noticed any downside effects. This is a fairly typical case today for a physician treating child and adult ADD—the gray area is vast.

COMPLICATING FACTORS IN ADULT ADD: THE RISK OF ABUSE

Given the publicity surrounding ADD and the complex demands of contemporary life, the upsurge in adult ADD diagnoses is not surprising. Many adults feel overwhelmed by their situations, and many no doubt have experienced problems with focus and attention since childhood. In the past, however, if they were not clearly hyperactive, such problems were most often attributed to laziness, bad parenting, or just a general deficiency of character. No wonder, then, that adults with such a history experience tremendous relief to find they are not alone in this situation, or feel unburdened to discover that their problem can be diagnosed as a chemical imbalance rather than some kind of moral or emotional failure. And some adults seem to prefer a diagnosis of ADD to other possible psychiatric explanations for their problems, because it's perceived as a medical rather than mental disorder.[7]

But if ADD in teenagers is rarely uncomplicated by emotional baggage, this is even more true of adults. Inherent strengths and weaknesses of personality are by this time of life overlaid with decades of responses from parents, siblings, teachers, peers, lovers, bosses, and coworkers. For some people, a dominant emotion such as anger, sadness, or anxiety adds an extra burden to functioning normally, and many adults have already been treated for such emotional problems by the time they "discover" they have ADD. Others have chosen to treat their own woes with the aid of substances legal and illegal: alcohol, marijuana, prescription drugs, and so on. For someone who is generally successful and believes he or she has good self-control, slipping into substance abuse can be an almost unnoticed process.

A patient named Paul Ford provides a good picture of the tangled web of adult ADD. The Fords first came to see me about Cameron, their hyperactive seven-year-old; they also had a daughter, Shannon, who was about to enter adolescence and was a good student. I worked with Paul and his wife, Jeri, to help them provide more immediate and consistent responses to Cameron, who also was started on Ritalin. At a follow-up meeting both parents reported that things with Cameron were much better, and then Jeri said, "Now that you fixed Cameron, maybe you can deal with the real problem." She gestured toward her husband, who looked sheepish.

Jeri went on to elaborate on Paul's history of irresponsible behavior and intermittent alcohol use, which had driven their marriage to the brink several times. Paul had been sober for the past six months, but certain patterns had persisted—procrastination at work, unfinished projects around the house—that Jeri thought might be caused by ADD. Despite his history of alcohol abuse, which might indicate more severe psychiatric problems, I felt I knew Paul and his family well enough by then to take him on.

Paul, when we met again, told of a life of highs and lows. An entrepreneur who had succeeded and failed in a number of businesses, currently he was making good money but was dissatisfied with his business partners and looking to start his own company. He complained of distractibility: he would begin one project and then abandon it for another. His home was a jumble of uncompleted stretches of Sheetrock and exposed plumbing. He would put off doing things he found boring until his wife or business partners literally had to scream at him. Paul had abused both amphetamines and alcohol, though he was currently attending AA because Jeri had threatened to leave him. He didn't know how to relax, except by drinking or taking a rare fishing vacation with a buddy; his last vacation had been three years earlier.

This wasn't the first time Paul had sought professional help—he'd had several courses of individual psychotherapy over the years, mostly exploring his feelings that he could never please his father. A previous doctor had prescribed the antidepressant imipramine, which he took for almost a year without being sure if it had helped him. His history did seem consistent with a personality marked by distraction and impulsiveness, and just as I was mulling over other possible causes for his problems, he suddenly interrupted me, blurting, "Doctor—do you know one of your socks is inside out?" I looked down at my dark-colored socks to see that, indeed, the ribs on the left one were facing out and those on the right were facing in. This may in part have prompted me to offer Paul a Ritalin trial, together with developing a coherent plan for responsible action worked out with him and Jeri. Both were agreeable to this.

Paul quickly found that 20 mg of Ritalin three times a day did a lot to keep him focused, and his wife agreed. He was no longer wasting half his day on useless distractions, he talked to his family more in the evenings, and he even completed some home projects. Jeri thought he seemed less depressed. For a while I continued to meet with Paul and/or Jeri every other week to talk over issues in their relationship and Paul's business, but as things seem to improve, we met less frequently. Though I still filled his prescription once a month, it wasn't necessary for me to see him each time.

About four months had gone by without a meeting when Paul called to say he needed to see me. Several things were happening at once. Paul had launched his own business and was on call "all the time." Jeri's job situation had suddenly become tenuous and she was in danger of being laid off. Cameron was doing well but Shannon had begun acting strangely; her parents thought she was doing drugs (marijuana, not Ritalin). Paul, when I saw him, looked terrible, bloated and exhausted. When he asked for another prescription of Ritalin, I said I'd have to talk to Jeri first. On the phone, she said that Paul had begun drinking again, and she thought he was using Ritalin erratically—sometimes he would stay up most of the night. "At first I thought the Ritalin was a big help, but now I'm not so sure," she said. "I do know I can't stay in this marriage if he keeps drinking."

Both came to the next visit, at which Paul looked and sounded depressed, like a little boy caught with stolen candy. It took a few minutes for him to admit he'd been using Ritalin to try to stay awake and get more work done. It worked, but in the mornings he would feel absolutely depleted. The business was demanding, he wasn't making as much money as he'd hoped by this time, and he was worried about that, as well as about Shannon's behavior. In reaction to all this, he had stopped going to AA and started drinking again. As he seemed so depressed, I asked if he'd had any suicidal thoughts; it had crossed his mind, he said, but he wouldn't do that to his family.

Paul wasn't in bad enough shape to warrant psychiatric hospitalization, but his current emotional state and alcohol use precluded his continuing to take Ritalin. He had slipped into a chronic abuse pattern with the drug: trying to do more and more, then needing it to keep going or to avoid the inevitable crash. His drinking contributed to the damage. I referred Paul to a psychiatrist colleague who agreed that he seemed depressed and started him on Zoloft, a Prozac relative. For several months Paul did all right but then began drinking again. This time Jeri moved out for three weeks, and at his internist's suggestion, Paul began taking Antabuse, a drug that if combined with alcohol produces nausea. Paul's business partner, who valued his contribution to the company and didn't want to lose him, helped out by making sure Paul took his Antabuse on most days. Jeri liked that a lot because it kept her from being the policeman, and Paul went back to AA.

About a year after Paul's relapse, he wanted to resume taking Ritalin, in a smaller dose and only twice a day. Since he'd been away from alcohol for months, was taking the Antabuse, and seemed calmer overall, his wife, the psychiatrist, and I agreed to it. Jeri would monitor the Ritalin and notify me immediately if she thought Paul was drinking again or was taking Ritalin inappropriately. Paul did resume taking Ritalin, 15 mg twice a day, and checks in with me about every three months. At this writing, he and Jeri have done reasonably well for about three years. Their kids have been up and down. Cameron hung on with decent grades until he reached high school, where he's been suspended once or twice—marijuana use was suspected. He still takes Ritalin and wants to continue doing so. Shannon turned into a major problem, sneaking out at night, doing alcohol and drugs, having sex indiscriminately. She was put into therapy and later sent off to a special school for eighteen months. Since then she's been better, apparently; she earned a GED diploma and has a steady (though much older) boyfriend.

Paul's story is more dramatic than that of many other adults I've treated, though not so untypical of the kinds of problems that adults diagnosed with ADD may have. Anyone who self-administers Ritalin runs the risk of overdoing it—trying to extend the wake–sleep cycle to accomplish more and slowly slipping into an abuse pattern where one stays up too long and then needs the drug to get going again in the morning, or whenever it wears off. Running his own business, Paul was especially vulnerable, but in this time of downsizing and heightened job insecurity, the temptation exists for many.

Other pitfalls include hoarding the drug and using it for its euphoric effects. One parent, a former amphetamine abuser, told me how easy it was for him to get Ritalin prescriptions from the doctor they formerly had seen for their son. He complained of ADD symptoms (which he genuinely believed he had), was started on Ritalin, and then was able to obtain prescriptions on a monthly basis by sending in a self-addressed stamped envelope. He received Ritalin this way for over a year without a follow-up meeting, and after several months began saving up the drug and using it for weekend binges. Only when he felt he was losing control of his use did he stop sending in the envelopes; he thought it was too dangerous for him to have the drug around. Stories like this spur me to pay especially close attention to the rate and regularity of prescription refills among my teenage and adult patients. Ironically, failure to refill a prescription may also be a danger sign; the patient may be taking the medication erratically rather than according to plan.

SOME APPROACHES TO HELPING ADULTS

The appeal of Ritalin to a busy, harassed adult whose life is further complicated by ADD symptoms is obvious: Take a pill and the fuzzy picture will magically sharpen; those annoying distractions will subside. As with other age groups, it seems that a medication intervention too often is the only one pursued by adults with ADD. But even if it seems like an investment of time that can't be spared, counseling or other psychosocial treatment is vital for people who think they suffer from ADD, to address the impact of their special temperament and accompanying emotional issues. A few basic principles should guide such efforts.

For one thing, anytime an adult consults a mental health professional about concentration and organization problems, it's important if possible to involve a significant other or family member, to get a balanced perspective. A patient named Pete, for example, had tried Ritalin to improve his concentration, but his wife was more concerned about his outbursts of temper. So in addition to some marital and individual counseling, we tried Prozac, which seemed to help him stay on an even keel. His wife remarked, "Before Ritalin, Pete and [their son] Jay used to forget Jay's baseball glove before a game, and Pete would blow his stack. With Ritalin, he'd remember the glove but get mad over other things Jay did. Now that he's taking Prozac, he forgets the glove now and then—but he doesn't get mad. It's much better."

In addition to professional counseling, it can be useful for adults who suspect ADD to obtain psychoeducational testing to check for any learning weakness—especially if their work involves much reading and writing. Such testing is quite reliable in identifying specific weaknesses in information processing, which can be reassuring to someone who's frustrated and confused by his or her inability to work efficiently. More practically, such specialists can suggest compensatory techniques that make it easier to live with learning problems.

Traditional, insight-oriented psychotherapy is not effective for many ADD-type adults. They often bounce from topic to topic, have trouble locating and staying with their feelings, and free-associate very fast and without much real connection to their emotions. More useful to most is a directive approach aimed at changing behavior rather than just understanding it. Here the patient is helped to set goals, develop strategies, and analyze ongoing successes and failures. The work typically includes teaching organizational skills and the use of tools such as lists and calendars; it also involves exploring how "significant others"—not just intimate partners but friends and mentors—can help keep an ADD adult on track. The patient is taught ways to manage mood instability and reduce self-defeating behaviors—procrastination, task avoidance, and avoiding intimacy—and encouraged to develop more productive ways of coping.

Working with a professional is ideal, at least to get started, but one can take a self-help approach by consulting some of the books aimed at adult ADDers. Hallowell and Ratey in *Driven to Distraction* recommend "50 Things You Can Do if You Have ADD"—some self-evident, others that may strike readers as useful.[8] The authors' suggestion to enlist a "coach" seems to me a good idea. A coach is someone to whom the ADD adult reports on a regular basis to develop plans, strategies, and goals. He or she needn't be a therapist, but should not be a spouse or boss. In a sense, the coach represents an external, supportive, friendly superego who can police the tendency to deny, avoid, and procrastinate so common among those who have coped with distractibility and impulsivity all their lives. A coach may break down and structure complex tasks into manageable components for an ADD adult. Say a business presentation is due in several weeks: the coach will help divide the project into discrete jobs, each with its own deadline. Many coaches call their clients to make sure they are working on an assigned task within the appropriate time frame. A coach can be the even-tempered, responsible, consistent, mentoring "parent" such adults still need. Coaching, by the way, has become something of a growth industry, to judge from ads in *Attention!* magazine and on the Internet—some of which claim it can be conducted over the phone.

FINDING THE WAY THAT FITS

Most studies on adult ADD have looked at what's gone wrong in the subjects' lives. In contrast, a small but provocative study of thirty-two ADD adults attempted to identify characteristics and coping strategies of those who were successful (based on their own report and on measures of occupational status and educational achievement).[9] The study found that women and those who went on to higher education generally were more successful, though IQ was not necessarily a prime factor. The strategies most often cited included setting up rituals and routines, making and using lists, using one's social network for support, and choosing a job with variety and activity.

These ADD survivors repeatedly emphasized how important finding the right job was, and I've had occasion to think about this a lot. Interestingly, my wife's career has suggested to me the kind of job profile that seems to fit well with the ADD temperament. Denise works in film production, and I've met many of her colleagues on various crews. Talking with them about their jobs and histories, I've been struck by how many of them—men in particular—describe behavior that could be diagnosed as ADD. Many struggled in school and had a fairly troubled adolescence. Some went to film school; others began as production assistants, the gofers of the industry. Over time they picked up other skills, some rising to positions of authority and creativity.

Film production is a demanding business with potentially long days. When you're working, you're *on*, and the intensity and pressure at those times are terrific. On the other hand, when you're off, responsibilities drop away and there's plenty of opportunity to kick back and space out. This kind of working rhythm seems to suit the ADD personality, which typically can focus intensely for brief periods, appreciates variety, and shows quick adaptability to new challenges. The entertainment business has been a growth industry for years; the pay can be excellent, and such work generally doesn't require a four-year college degree.

These reflections are certainly not meant to direct everyone with distractibility and other ADD signs to Hollywood. But I hope they illustrate the need to pose certain key questions to teenagers and adults contemplating their education and future.[10] To reiterate: *What do you want to do, what do you think you should do, and what are you good at?* In the last thirty years, young people have been encouraged to attend a four-year college as the surest preparation for career success: more recently, we've realized that this isn't the best route for everyone. More attention should be paid to jobs that do not require a four-year degree, and more role models identified in such employment areas.[11] As noted earlier, a study found that among a group of adults who'd been hyperactive as children, more were successfully employed in trade jobs than in professional or service-industry careers.[12] Based on this study and my own experience, people with ADD-type personalities also are drawn to entrepreneurial endeavors and to the arts.

Another patient of mine offers an interesting example of midlife career change based, in part, on coming to terms with his ADD symptoms. Harvey, introduced in Chapter 6 as he was helping me research the Internet, was an insurance broker when we first met. He was also a confused bundle of symptoms who had survived any number of psychiatric diagnoses. He'd enjoyed relative economic success, but money was constantly a problem. He and his wife, Julie, also had long-standing marital problems. Harvey spoke of a punitive, erratic, alcoholic father, who he felt had contributed to his lifelong pattern of challenging authority. But he was much more inclined to attribute his problems to undiagnosed ADD. While I thought Harvey had several different problems (in the jargon, he could have been co-morbid with anxiety, depression, or bipolar disorder), I felt he had enough signs of adult ADD to warrant Ritalin, and enough responsibility to use it safely.

Harvey reported that he worked more efficiently on the drug, but he still hated his job. He performed well enough as long as selling a policy went smoothly, but if he had to make more than one or two phone calls to pursue a client, he'd put it aside. Another problem was that, in the nature of the work, he'd go for weeks without income and then connect on a few big deals—but he didn't manage money well. Meanwhile, Harvey had developed an interest in computers, devising systems for himself and coworkers and spending hours on the Internet when it was still in its infancy. Julie fretted about their bills, resented the amount of time he spent online, and generally felt angry with her husband over what she saw as his irresponsible behavior. To her, ADD was just an excuse for his unwillingness to pursue clients, his avoidance of tasks around the house, and his evasiveness in discussing their marital issues. Julie herself had a problem with alcohol, and it was only after she entered a program, joined AA, and stopped drinking that she came to a meeting with her husband and me—nearly a year after I first met Harvey.

During that meeting, the talk turned to Harvey's problems at work and his failure to follow up with potential clients, with all of us trying to figure out what made it so hard for him. "I don't mind the easy policies," he said, "but if they don't call back, I hate calling them. I just don't want to have to beg or hear that no." Julie appeared stunned; she'd never heard him talk about this so forthrightly. "But Harvey," she asked with mixture of sympathy and incredulity, "how can you be at a job where rejection is a daily possibility and you can't stand hearing no?" Looking embarrassed and depressed, Harvey extended his arms, palms up, in an unmistakable gesture: "I don't know."

Six months later, when I heard from Harvey again, he told me that he'd left the insurance company and was now a full-time computer consultant, earning a more regular income from the services he provided. With this new work, he felt he could concentrate well enough without Ritalin, and had stopped taking it—that's why he hadn't called earlier. Our relationship after that was limited to my providing some counseling in exchange for his giving me information about ADD and the Internet. The signs looked hopeful for continuing success in his new career and, according to Harvey, he and Julie were still struggling but doing better.

The researchers who studied successful ADD adults proposed that the next step should be to learn if and how strategies for surviving ADD can be taught.[13] They speculated that adaptability, as a childhood trait, may be a factor in adult success, and that the ADD-type person requires a higher level of intensity to respond to teaching. This potentially valuable research remains to be done.

For now, a great many adults and teenagers are taking Ritalin in the absence of any studies evaluating the long-term experience of these age groups on the drug. This kind of data is also needed. Long-term use of Ritalin from childhood through adulthood may be the answer for some people. But taking this stimulant is not without risks. We now know that the supposed "paradox" of stimulants is a myth—that they have the same effect (in low doses) on all adults as on children. Given the uncertain outcomes and higher risks of abuse and addiction after childhood, the real paradox about Ritalin may be that it's actually safer for children than for teenagers and adults.

Chapter 13

PERFORMANCE IN A PILL:
WHAT RITALIN SAYS ABOUT US

No scientific undertakings or hypotheses are completely divorced from the social values of their time and place.

—Russell A. Barkley, Ph.D.

In late twentieth-century America, when it is difficult or inconvenient to change the environment, we don't think twice about changing the brain of the person who has to live in it.

—Ken Livingston, *The Public Interest*

On the campus of a small private college in the wooded hills of New York's affluent Westchester County, an unremarkable shingled building houses the nation's most prestigious think tank for bioethics. For more than thirty years the Hastings Center at Pace College in Briarcliff Manor has been at the forefront of analyzing and addressing the increasingly complex and thorny ethical questions that have accompanied the breakthroughs and failures of modern medicine. Its monthly publication, *The Hastings Center Report*, is read not just by those in the medical field, but by judges, lawyers, legislators, sociologists, philosophers, and journalists.

I came to the Hastings Center in the late spring of 1996 to join thirty other experts in exploring the frontiers of human performance and medicine. The conference was one of four in a project entitled, "Technologies Aimed at the Enhancement of Human Capacities."[1] Its twin focus: psychoactive drugs and cosmetic surgery.

Peter Kramer had come to speak on Prozac, of course, but also about the range and potential—positive and negative—of other new psychotropic agents. Peter Whitehouse, a leading neuropsychologist, was there to discuss how new drugs for Alzheimer's disease might also enhance memory and intelligence in normal people.[2] Needless to say, I was there to talk about Ritalin.

A theme that emerged early and persistently in our discussions was the difficulty of differentiating between *enhancement* of the normal or well and *treatment* of the sick or disabled.[3] Different approaches were invoked to tease out the differences—from statistical analysis to attempts to construct universal standards of disability (for example, a statement such as "Everyone would agree it is better to be able to see than be blind.") However, in a roomful of ethicists, there always occurred at least one and usually several challenges to such "obvious and true" conclusions.

The statistical approaches were open to the same criticisms I've leveled at ADD questionnaires: how is it decided how many fidgets are too many?[4] For many of the conditions discussed, the problem came down to the arbitrariness of the judgment—at what point does difference become disease, and by whom and for whom is disease being determined? Supposedly neutral observation turned out to be deeply subjective: What to one group appeared to be a clearly disabling or disadvantageous condition—blindness, deafness, big nose, dark skin color—to another group could represent opportunity for growth and understanding, and/or cultural and developmental pride. I was powerfully struck by how these same problems apply to the diagnosis of ADD. When does spontaneity become impulsivity; sensitivity to stimuli, distractibility? At what point does ADD temperament become ADD disease? Who defines it and for whom?

As I listened to Kramer talk about Prozac and Peter Whitehouse about Cognex (the first of a new generation of drugs for Alzheimer's), it occurred to me that "my" drug was different in at least one signficant way. Ritalin and other stimulants have been in use for a hundred years. While other participants spoke of the exciting possibilities and grave concerns that lay ahead, I felt that I had seen the future, and that it was happening right now, across the country, with Ritalin.

SUMMARIZING THE RESEARCH: WHAT EXPERTS BELIEVE

We know a great deal about Ritalin, yet serious questions about its ultimate value persist. In 1993 Jim Swanson and colleagues published a "review of reviews" that summarized the literature on Ritalin use in children.[5] Its conclusions provide a succinct portrait of our present knowledge about Ritalin's use in treating ADD.

• Ritalin does, *in the short term*, improve concentration and effort, and decrease motor activity and impulsivity. It tends, in the short term, to increase compliance, decrease defiance and aggression, and improve family and peer interaction.

• It does not have a "paradoxical" effect on children or those with ADD; everyone basically responds in the same way to Ritalin, in varying degrees.

• There exist no neurological, physiological, or biochemical means to predict or determine response to Ritalin.

• Ritalin does not improve complex skills such as reading, athletic ability, and social behavior. Grades may improve, but Ritalin cannot correct a learning disability. Ritalin produces short-term improvement in tests of physical strength, endurance, and speed, but only while someone is under the direct influence of the drug. Ritalin does not improve significant emotional problems.

• There is no evidence of long-term improvement in children taking Ritalin. No improvement in academic outcome can be attributed solely to its effects, no decrease in antisocial behavior or arrest rates, and only small effects on learning and achievement.

• The unwanted effects of Ritalin are (commonly) problems with eating and sleeping, possible negative effects on cognition (diminished creativity) and self-image, and rare or disputable increases in motor or verbal tics.

Swanson and his colleagues note candidly that the authors they reviewed displayed a remarkable range of viewpoints.[6] For some, Ritalin is the greatest thing since sliced bread; for others, it is a dangerous, addicting substance used to control the minds of children. Ritalin as manna or Ritalin as poison: among so many studies one can find evidence to support virtually any position. Of course, both Swanson and I have our own viewpoints. Mine undoubtedly emerges between the lines of my foregoing summary.

Since so many reports about Ritalin and ADD claim to be "scientific and neutral," let the reader beware.

Jim Swanson himself is an interesting figure. He took a leading role in the professional organizations that, together with CHADD, were instrumental in getting ADD included as a disability under the Individuals with Disabilities Education Act (IDEA) in 1991. Swanson acknowledges that this was the single biggest factor in the explosion of ADD diagnoses and Ritalin use in this country. However, he now states publicly that ADD is being overdiagnosed and Ritalin overused. Whereas some leaders on the academic front of ADD, including Harvard's Joseph Biederman, believe that ADD may affect up to 10 percent of America's children, Swanson (along with many other experts) feels that its prevalence is between 3 and 5 percent.

Swanson's position on treatment also departs significantly from others in the academic mainstream. He has no doubt that psychosocial efforts alone—especially changes in a child's school environment—can effectively address ADD symptoms. He has the data to back such beliefs, gleaned from years of study at the clinic-cum-school he directs in Irvine, California. However, he questions whether Americans have the moral will and financial resolve to mount a major effort to counter ADD with psychosocial methods, rather than continue to rely on Ritalin.[7]

A CULTURE INCLINED TOWARD RITALIN

Why does the United States produce and use 90 percent of the world's Ritalin? Among other countries, only Canada and Australia have reported recent increases. In Canada, which absorbs many cultural trends from across the border, Ritalin use has quadrupled since 1990, but the per capita rate there is still only half of ours. Australia uses a tenth as much Ritalin on a per capita basis. Neither Western Europe nor the developed nations of Asia have seen any significant rise in Ritalin use during the 1990s. Some neurogeneticists have proposed that Americans typically are descended from an especially adventurous, rootless, "hungry" cohort of Europeans: in other words, those who emigrated here. However, most sociobiologists doubt such explanations, questioning how just three hundred to four hundred years of separation—a short time by evolutionary standards—could produce such distinct differences.

In truth, the differences are far more likely to be cultural than biological. Cultures differ, for example, in the degree to which their members accept emotional distress or tolerate underperformance.[8] They also vary in how people feel about seeking professional assistance for emotional problems and in their acceptance or disapproval of drugs to relieve distress or improve performance.

America is the only nation to include, in its declaration of existence, the right to the "pursuit of happiness"; outsized expectations are part of our birthright. In countries such as Great Britain and Japan, the reality of class and station is acknowledged, while Americans cling to our deeply embedded ideals of equality and unlimited opportunity. A new generation of Horatio Algers—say, Steve Jobs or Bill Gates—perpetuates the dream of upward mobility, even as the gap between the richest and the rest of us widens. Such culturally contrasting attitudes are especially visible in what young people are led to expect of themselves and life. In Japan, national exams taken at middle-school age direct children permanently toward vocational or college-educational tracks. In America, on the other hand, nearly every child is considered a candidate for college education and the success that is supposed to follow. We're great believers in the perfectability of humankind.

But the pursuit of happiness can become a tyranny. If society says you should be successful and happy and you're not, there must be something wrong with you. In such a society, persistent difficulty, disappointment, and sadness are not acceptable aspects of the human condition; rather, they are subversive enemies we must somehow defeat. During National Mental Health Week a few years ago, an official billboard urged: "Let's Wipe Out Depression in America!" To struggle with weaknesses or sadness becomes, in itself, a problem—a disorder to be diagnosed and treated. No other culture seems to have such intolerance for the negatives of the human condition.

With regard to ADD, America's cultural rejection of underperformance translates into less restrictive criteria for diagnosis than elsewhere. In Europe, a child must still demonstrate hyperactivity to receive the diagnosis, and symptoms must pervade all life situations.[9] In general, doctors there are much more ready to acknowledge the role of psychosocial factors in illness, and there is greater skepticism about treatment with medication.[10] In Great Britain especially, child psychiatrists are less likely than their American counterparts to use psychotropic medication.[11] It's not that English children don't have problems paying attention, completing tasks, or controlling their impulses. But their difficulties tend to be viewed less as disease symptoms and more as individual or social problems, rooted in willful misbehavior or in poverty or oppression.

In earlier chapters, I've discussed factors in American society that I believe are contributing to the rising rates of ADD diagnosis—the changing structure and function of the family, an overtaxed educational system, an emerging culture of disability, and the exigencies of managed care. Others have theorized that diet and environmental toxins are possible contributing factors, though as I've noted, most studies do not support this. Yet another intriguing if unproved idea is that the "cultural tempo" of society has speeded up, giving us an overstimulating environment to which some children are particularly sensitive.

The main problem with the cultural tempo theory (aside from the difficulty of studying it scientifically) is that similar overstimulating conditions exist in other industrial societies that show very low ADD rates—Japan, for instance. Another hypothesis about culture and ADD makes more sense to me: In 1982 Dorothea and Sheila Ross proposed a link between hyperactivity and the relative consistency of the cultural and institutional messages children receive.[12] Consistent cultures—such as Japan and China—emphasize group cohesiveness, and reward conformity rather than individual achievement.

In contrast, "inconsistent" cultures "maximize individual differences, emphasize individual achievement, and segregate individuals on the basis of achievement, socioeconomic status, [and] religion." America is the prime example, of course. Ross's conclusion is that more consistent cultures represent good-fit situations for hyperactive-type children, whereas inconsistent ones become "provocative ecologies": they cause latent ADD tendencies to manifest. In current American society, moreover, a kind of Catch-22 is operating. Individual achievement is prized, but conformity is still expected—the least good fit imaginable for an ADD personality.

Of course, even within America there's considerable cultural variation in attitudes toward ADD. As I've noted, the ADD diagnosis and Ritalin use remain overwhelmingly a phenomenon of white, suburban, middle- and upper-middle-class children. It's in this slice of society, of course, that expectations run highest and anxieties about performance shortfalls lately have become acute. It's this group of parents who worry that their children's future may be jeopardized by not getting into the right preschool. Little wonder they so often see the wisdom in Ritalin.

Ritalin use is rising most rapidly among adults, teenagers, females, and preschoolers, in that order, but as of 1997 these groups still accounted for small percentages, compared to boys ages six through twelve. It's been doc-umented that in some communities up to 17 percent of boys at certain grade levels were receiving the drug. This equals one in six boys taking Ri-talin. That figures strikes many people, myself included, as unacceptably high, but others, like Joseph Biederman, believe that Ritalin use is simply catching up to the need. If indeed 10 percent of children are affected by ADD (an estimate he calls conservative), then a 17 percent treatment rate among boys is just what the doctor ordered, given that boys manifest symp-toms by a ratio of four or five to one over girls.

Even within the United States, however, Ritalin usage varies fivefold among states and twentyfold by communities within states. The recent trend, of course, has been to stretch the boundaries of the ADD diagnosis: Hyperactivity is no longer required; children need not have shown symp-toms before age seven; adults are suffering an ADD epidemic. And more and more subtle and recondite variations of ADD are being diagnosed as experts struggle to pin down the core problem. There is one constant, however: Ritalin.

RITALIN—UNIVERSAL PERFORMANCE ENHANCER OR PATENT MEDICINE REDUX?

There's an inescapable sense that American medicine is "rediscovering the wheel" with regard to the performance-enhancing properties of stimulants. That stimulants improve short-term concentration and performance has been known for a *century*. American medical practice seems to have a re-curring love affair with stimulants, beginning in the late nineteenth century with cocaine, reviving from about 1930 to 1980 with amphetamine, and, since 1990, with Ritalin as the drug of choice. All have been legitimately prescribed for a variety of ills from rheumatism to obesity. But if we've learned anything from this long history of medical stimulant use, it's that problems of abuse eventually surpass the unfulfilled promises of long-term improvement.

With children, the safety record of sixty years of stimulant use is quite good overall. However, Ritalin's growing use by teens and adults carries more risks, and the erratic pattern of Ritalin prescribing has alarmed the federal Drug Enforcement Administration. In some areas just one or two doctors prescribe nearly all of the Ritalin used. DEA officials find it virtually impossible to determine if these patterns represent legitimate specialty practices or Ritalin mills, because standards of diagnosis have become so broad and vague.[13]

The pervasive confusion among doctors as to what constitutes Attention Deficit Disorder parallels our Hastings Center debate about the distinctions between treatment and enhancement. Where should we draw the line on Ritalin use? Because Ritalin to some extent sharpens focus and diminishes impulsivity in anyone, I must view it as performance enhancer for everyone. Some people—often those we diagnose with ADD—need improvement more than others. But virtually all situations viewed as problems of inattention, impulse control, or hyperactivity will clinically improve with Ritalin use, unless the picture also includes a lot of anxiety, anger, or depression. Therefore, the task of diagnosing becomes strictly a matter of degree. The question I find myself asking most often is not who should get Ritalin, but who shouldn't.

The Hastings Center discussion, being philosophical in nature, went in search of some bottom-line propositions that all could agree on. Dan Brock, a professor of philosophy and bioethics at Brown University, spoke persuasively about the "absolute" disadvantage of some conditions.[14] Some, like blindness and loss of mobility, he felt were "objectively and uncontroversially bad for a person." On the other side of the coin, what kind of performance-enhancing treatment might be an absolute good? Brock believed that "enhancements to all-purpose means, such as memory or *the capacity to focus one's attention* [my italics] . . . would be beneficial in virtually any life plan."[15] Logically, then, if a drug or therapy existed that could improve attention without any significant cost or risk to the user or society, this would be a good thing. Does this apply to Ritalin?

Who Decides for Whom?
Issues of Choice and Consent

In considering treatment for any condition, Dr. Brock made it clear that a higher standard for good must be met when "the authority, moral or legal, of one individual, group, or institution act[s] in a way that affects the life and capacities of another." In other words, the benefits must clearly outweigh the costs. For example, the use of fluoride in drinking water and vaccines to prevent serious illness in children appear to have passed this test of values. Is this also the case, when parents, in concert with doctors and teachers, decide to give Ritalin to a child?

Informed consent has become the legal and moral standard of decision making in medical practice, but when it concerns making choices on behalf of a child, the issues can get complex and controversial. All the more so when the condition being considered for treatment is as amorphous as ADD.

These days, it's often argued that even young children should be allowed to participate in treatment decisions—for example, in the continuation of chemotherapy for cancer when the prognosis is uncertain.[16] For most children younger than eleven or twelve, there's really no such thing as informed consent or choice—at best they can give their parents and doctor "informed permission" to treat them. If a child says he doesn't want the shot or the medicine, his parents can overrule him, but the possible need for coercion, subtle or forceful, raises the ante. Considering the child's wishes is a delicate matter: One must guard against burdening the child with too much responsibility, yet allowing him or her to participate is a step in the right moral direction. Too often in the past, children have been barely informed, or not at all, about medications and procedures prescribed for them.

This was certainly true of Ritalin in times past. In a study that followed hyperactive children into adulthood, Gabrielle Weiss and Lily Hechtman asked adults who had been treated with Ritalin as children how they had felt about taking the medication then, and how they felt about it in retrospect.[17] Their subjects uniformly expressed sadness and anger; they didn't understand, as children, why they were taking the medication and had felt bad about it. These memories, of course, were from a time (around 1970) when the whole climate surrounding psychotropic medications was very different than it is today. Nearly universally, these patients wished that someone had explained the medication to them more fully.

Far more serious accusations have been leveled by some who believe that taking Ritalin in childhood heightens the risk of stimulant abuse later in life. For example, the story has circulated of a gifted professional athlete who was repeatedly bounced from his sport for cocaine use.[18] He had taken Ritalin as a child and said that, when he first used cocaine, "I thought it was okay because it reminded me of Ritalin." However, any such connection remains entirely unproven. My opinion is that no parents should feel guilty on this score about offering their child Ritalin.

Individual choice is of course limited by Ritalin's status as a prescription-only, federally controlled substance. At this time you cannot simply walk up to a pharmacy window in the United States and ask for a hundred 20 mg Ritalin tablets. (You can, however, do just that at the Mexican *farmacias* that proliferate legally in border towns near San Diego and Laredo, Texas). In America, you must receive a doctor's permission to use the drug; the doctor in turn is monitored by the government. Should we, in fact, have more freedom to use a substance that may enhance performance for everyone?

In other circumstances—and these are occurring more often lately—an individual's choice to *refuse* Ritalin becomes problematic. Already, at certain schools, some parents are receiving unmistakable messages that their child should be on Ritalin in order to continue in his special-education or regular class. I encountered this personally with Michael Sturdevant's family. Anecdotally, I've been told of a school district where children weren't allowed to return to classes after a suspension unless they were taking the medication.[19] And a private school in my own area has a well-known reputation for referring children to one specialist, who invariably prescribes Ritalin.

Even without direct pressure, a person may be subtly persuaded to choose Ritalin by realizing that more and more of his peers are using it to obtain a competitive edge. Whether this occurs in a daily classroom setting, in preparing for exams or the SAT, or in a fast-track workplace, the increasing acceptance of Ritalin may prompt people who feel they are barely coping to ask for the drug. In all these examples of "free choice under pressure," no one is specifically ordering the parent or individual to use the drug, but they are strongly influenced by their situation to try it.

In raising these kinds of concerns about Ritalin use, I and others have been accused of creating unnecessary anxiety in parents who are considering medication for their children's problems.[20] I don't buy it, in part because there are plenty of voices raised in Ritalin's praise. And I believe that by posing questions about the drug, on both individual and societal levels, I am helping to equip parents (and children) to make informed decisions about treatment. For a parent to feel ambivalent or worried about a treatment is not necessarily bad. Many of those I counsel eventually do consent to a trial of Ritalin for their child, and most seem to appreciate being informed about all sides of the issue.

Does Ritalin Treat "Motivation Deficit"?

As I've pointed out, a lot of the confusion about ADD boils down to the "can't" versus "won't" conundrum. Joseph Biederman says that if a person's IQ is higher than his or her academic performance indicates, then Ritalin can be appropriately used for improvement. But aren't other factors involved when someone isn't performing up to potential? Of course, Dr. Biederman would consider the usual "co-morbid" suspects of opposition, depression, and anxiety. But what about motivation? Don't people who care more try harder, and conversely, do less if they care less? You can have a spectacular IQ, but if you don't apply yourself, no one except the psychologist and your mother will know.

Back in the early 1980s, Russell Barkley proposed that "deficits in rules-governed behavior" or "insensitivity to consequences" best account for the behavioral and performance problems of ADD.[21] These concepts clearly involve motivation: If a child is insensitive to the consequences of his actions—if he cannot connect failure to finish his homework with the likelihood of getting a poor grade—it will look to most people as if he does not care.

In his most recent writings, Barkley refines and expands these ideas into a model of ADD as a disorder of self-regulation.[22] He now sees *timing* as the critical element. In other words, compared with normal children and adults, someone with ADD is less able to take account of consequences *if those consequences are less immediate and more distant in time*. He finds this diminished capacity to be a largely inheritable trait.

If a person's ability to behave "correctly" is not under his control—is, in fact, neurologically determined—the moral and social implications are vast. Barkley himself declares that he "would go so far as to say that *ADHD impairs the human will and one's volition.* [His italics] He goes on to acknowledge, "I fully appreciate the conundrum that such conclusions about ADHD pose for the notion of personal accountability and responsibility within society."[23]

This strikes to the heart of our decision-making as parents and teachers. We want to know whether a child is really trying, whether his efforts are really hindered by brain chemistry, and for what he or his family should be held accountable. We make allowances and exceptions for people with inherent physical or mental disabilities. When the issue is blindness or deafness, such judgments are comparatively easy. When it's proposed that neurologically based lack of motivation or self-control is a disability, we get very uneasy.

Barkley is right about the challenge for society. ADD becomes a paradigm for our confrontation with the idea of problem behavior as a disease. Responsibility and free will are the cornerstones of Western society, reinforced by much of Western religion and ethics. Lack of motivation was once viewed as laziness or sloth, one of the seven deadly sins. Will this fundamental "vice" of our culture come to be viewed as genetic and biologic, inherent and unchangeable?

COSMETIC RITALIN: HONING THE COMPETITIVE EDGE

To give medication for a condition whose chief trait is the failure to perform up to one's potential—or to manage one's life efficiently—crosses the line, in my view, between treating a disorder and enhancing a particular aspect of personality. In essence, it is "cosmetic psychopharmacology."[24] There's nothing inherently wrong about enhancing human potential; it's condoned, even supported, by society on many levels. We insist on compulsory education to equip people to perform as citizens. Special tutoring is fine, even for extra credit. Children get music, ballet, and skating lessons; SAT preparatory classes are in demand. So why not Ritalin? Proponents say that Ritalin only serves to level the playing field for individuals with attention deficit. But since the drug exerts similar effects on everyone, why should only those operating below the norm have access to its performance-enhancing qualities?

Most people can muster arguments against the idea of Ritalin on demand. It's easier to accept that children or adults who are disabled by ADD symptoms deserve whatever extra help they can get. But what in fact constitutes a disability? From CHADD's national magazine, *Attention!*:

> Consider a college student who achieves at an above-average level overall. Specifically, suppose that, due to dyslexia and ADD, his reading speed is 50% of the average student's reading speed. Suppose further that he spends twice as much time as his classmates on reading assignments. Does his extraordinary effort, resulting in overall above-average performance, mean that he should not be permitted accommodations (e.g., books on tape) for his reading difficulty? And Ritalin for his ADD?[25]

Some might say that the student CHADD is defending qualifies as disabled. Yet in condoning Ritalin for such students, we venture onto a slippery slope where our foothold on what constitutes real effort and achievement is increasingly unsure.

In competitive sports we appreciate not only the speed, strength, endurance, courage, or grace of the athlete but also the effort and time entailed in reaching a high level of performance. We know intuitively that taking a pill to finish faster or leap higher cheapens the achievement. Furthermore, if drugs such as stimulants or anabolic steroids were permitted, athletes not using them would exercise this "free choice" under the severest kind of pressure: Their refusal to take the drug could greatly affect their ability to stay competitive.

Recently it has been argued that since ADD is a "medical" condition, an exception to the stimulant ban should be made for athletes with ADD.[26] As of 1993, the National Collegiate Athletic Association acceded to this thinking; all it takes is a letter from the team physician to waive the ban for that athlete. An NCAA official cites legal jeopardy as one reason the organization changed its policy.[27] The U.S. Olympic Committee still hews to international rules, under which an athlete who tested positive for stimulants would be disqualified.[28] But how long will they hold this line? During the 1996 Olympic Games in Atlanta, it seemed like every other competitor had asthma; you could watch them on TV taking their "hit" of bronchodilating inhalant before their event. If Ritalin becomes more widely acceptable in sports, might we expect a similar epidemic of ADD among Olympic athletes?

Of course, it can be argued that competition is not the point of education, that the real purpose is to learn the knowledge and skills necessary to succeed in life. But competing for grades is how children get assigned to academic tracks, get into the better colleges and universities and go on to the better jobs. And Ritalin can improve academic performance as measured by grades. True, in the early grades academic success may not be a prime concern; some parents decide on Ritalin in the hope that its effects on behavior will help their child's self-image and peer relations. But later on, performance becomes critical.

Here is where serious questions about fairness arise. Take two students with borderline attention problems: Does the child who tries hard without the aid of Ritalin simply live with lesser grades, while his fellow student taking Ritalin gets A's? As more students turn to Ritalin for help in completing assignments and taking examinations, will this influence others to try it? Will they, like athletes, have to exercise "free choice under pressure" to win their academic race? And should colleges, grad schools, and corporations be informed that applicants use Ritalin when scores are evaluated?

Many Americans still strongly believe that taking a pharmaceutical shortcut somehow undercuts achievement—that it's "cheating." We retain a cultural belief that it's better to cope by developing one's inner resources and social bonds than by resorting to psychotropic agents. This attitude, for which psychiatrist Gerald Klerman coined the phrase "pharmacological Calvinism,"[29] has been undermined by the siren song of biological psychiatry and the increasingly acceptable use of Prozac and related drugs to smooth out life's bumps.

We still do not know, however, how using Ritalin affects people's self-image in the long term. Do they feel fundamentally more in control of their lives, or do they lose confidence in their ability to cope without medication? We do know that children—especially teenagers, whose identities are notably vulnerable—are susceptible to feelings of inadequacy when taking Ritalin, even as they perform better; and we have heard from adults who feel emotionally harmed by having taken Ritalin as children. But the rising acceptance of cosmetic drug use may eradicate such negative feelings or stigmas as time goes on. If this process eventually overwhelms our belief in the power of the unmedicated self, is this a good thing?

BIOLOGICAL PSYCHIATRY AND THE NEW DETERMINISM

Biological psychiatry has convinced Americans that emotional, behavior, and performance problems arise from some malfunctioning of the brain. It has been embraced for reasons ranging from the emotional (parents are relieved of blame for their child's problems) to the economic (if ADD is a biological disorder, it should be treated with medication, which is much less expensive than other forms of treatment).

There's no doubt that heredity and inherent neurochemistry are important factors in behavioral traits expressed from birth onward. There *are* "difficult" children by nature. It probably *is* harder for certain adults to concentrate or follow through on tasks because of their inherent temperaments. And the metaphors of biological psychiatry—including chemical imbalance and the concept of brain disorders—can be very useful in clinical practice, as long as they are part of a broader view of how a person's biology interacts with his environment.

But there are also significant drawbacks to a purely biological explanation of ADD. Ritalin enthusiasts like to draw analogies to medical conditions that are clearly physiological, as in comparing Ritalin for ADD to glasses for vision correction. I explained in Chapter 12 why this medical analogy just doesn't sit right with me. In another frequently used comparison, Ritalin is said to correct a chemical imbalance just as insulin replacement corrects the insulin deficiency in diabetes. There are several flaws to this logic. First, it doesn't explain why Ritalin affects people with apparently normal brain chemistry. Second, ADD is not caused by a "Ritalin deficiency," whereas insulin deficiency causes diabetes. (As I noted earlier, no one speaks of an "aspirin deficiency" causing headaches.) Further, the insulin analogy suggests that, like the diabetic, the "ADDer" is wise to accept the chronic, physical nature of his condition and resign himself to the use of a chemical replacement, probably for the rest of his life. To believe otherwise would be engaging in denial.

There's something still more troubling about the insulin metaphor. However serious a problem diabetes may be, a person with this condition does not define himself in terms of a malfunctioning pancreas. In fact, he or she may resent such a limited view. But we do define ourselves by our brains and our personalities. Tinkering with character and behavior raises complex questions about who we are and how much control we have (or should have) over something as fundamental as personality—our own and our children's. A colleague once lamented to a group of behavioral pediatricians: "You know, we regularly overtreat ear infections with amoxicillin, even though bacterial resistance to antibiotics has become a serious problem. So why isn't there the same kind of hue and cry over this as we're seeing with Ritalin? How come amoxicillin isn't on the front page?" We all knew the answer: Society is not ready to accept the notion that chemical interventions for behavior and personality are equivalent to those for ear infections.

In general, biological psychiatry overstates both its theoretical case and its successes. It's one thing to believe that biology contributes to behavior. But if we ignore or minimize environmental expectations and responses—that all-important fit described by temperament experts—we fall into the trap of bioreductionism, the idea that every human trait can be traced to a specific gene. For the last half century, the elegant models of genes and DNA have enthralled scientists and the public alike, and psychiatry has been quick to climb aboard the bandwagon. But, notes a recent *New York Times* article, paraphrasing theoretical biologist Richard Goodwin, "this 'genocentric' view of biology is both misleading and dangerous . . . because it engenders simplistic thinking, which prompts social acceptance of genetic determinism and turns personal responsibility into genetic destiny."[30]

Is it really a good idea to categorize people by saying that their inherent ADD-type personality is a disease? It may be useful in our present social context, by making them eligible for disability services and the like, but what if the culture changes and becomes less sympathetic toward those with the trait—even discriminatory? Yes, the characteristics of ADD may be inheritable, but the problems that lead it to be called a disorder are socially defined.

Furthermore the specter of stereotyping and stigmatization haunts any model that categorizes humanity in this way. Around the turn of the century, such thinking was invoked to justify the eugenics movement, in which the physically and mentally "enfeebled" (often poor, immigrant, or black citizens) were sterilized to prevent erosion of the American gene pool. Sterilization for the same purpose was practiced as recently as the 1970s in Sweden and Finland.[31]

It took the genocidal horrors of the Nazi Holocaust to totally discredit—at least for the time being—the notion of a "superior race."[32] However, current genetic theory is generating a new wave of social and political controversy in this country, in particular over alleged racial connections with intelligence. Already concerns have been expressed about insurance companies and employers who deny coverage or jobs based on an applicant's genetic profile (if, for example, they are seen as high-risk for breast or colon cancer), even if the individual is asymptomatic.[33] The consequences of neurogenetic determinism are not necessarily benign or forgiving to those with "disorders."

ADD as Disability: "Field Trials" in the Courtroom, Classroom, and Workplace

In early 1997 I spoke to Patricia Latham, a Washington-based attorney for the National Center for Law and Learning Disabilities, which specializes in disability strategies. I was curious whether she knew of any criminal cases in which ADD had been used as a defense in court. She wasn't aware of any, but literature from her center did state that "ADD and learning disabilities could be a factor in decreasing the severity of an offense."[34] For example, a crime requiring proof of intent might be reduced to one involving merely "reckless behavior." Later I learned of three cases in Ventura County, California, where defendants had tried to absolve themselves of culpability based on having ADD. While none of these resulted in a not-guilty verdict, neither the trial nor the appeals courts opposed the principle of using ADD as a defense.[35]

One morning in July 1997, I opened my *San Francisco Chronicle* to the following headline: "Kingpin in Boy's Torture Under Medical Watch."[36] The story, datelined San Jose, continued as follows:

> The 14-year-old ringleader in the gang torture of a Mountain View youth was ordered yesterday into the care of California Youth Authority doctors to determine if he has a disorder that might have influenced his behavior. [A judge took this action] after hearing testimony that brain photography had revealed an apparent abnormality. The teen has admitted his role in the torture and beating last November of a middle school student by five teenagers, but his attorneys contend he is a victim of attention deficit disorder that might have led to his violent behavior.

I doubt that brain scan evidence will survive in court, but a case like this throws the ambiguity of the ADD diagnosis into clear relief. Most experts would agree that pathological violence on this level is not typical of uncomplicated ADD. Rather, such a severely acting-out kid—if one wants to give him the benefit of a psychiatric diagnosis—surely is displaying behavior linked with anger, opposition, and Conduct Disorder symptoms.

I found myself meditating on the broader questions raised by the case: If a troubled person feels better and more powerful when he engages in sadistic behavior, is this an expression of inherent personality? In part, it may be. Is a person affected by ADD aware of right and wrong? Yes. Is he capable of enough self-control to choose not to act this way? Perhaps, though it's true that a person's ability to restrain himself may be compromised by impulsivity. Should an ADD diagnosis mitigate assignment of responsibility for criminal behavior? It may or may not. The current legal standard for "diminished capacity" defenses is that a person is not criminally responsible only if, at the time of the crime, he or she did not know the nature of the act or that it was wrong.[37]

It's only a matter of time until such questions are played out in public. I predict that clinicians and researchers will not have the last word on what constitutes ADD, how it is diagnosed, and its effects on performance and responsibility. Rather—as with cases involving multiple personality disorder,[38] sexual abuse, and recovered memory[39]—the civil and criminal courts sooner or later will define the standards for and legal implications of ADD, both explicitly and by the impact of their decisions on the professional and lay communities.

Economic imperatives of the workplace will also be a factor, I think, in limiting the concessions offered to people with ADD-related deficits. When corporate America feels sufficiently threatened by the costs of disability regulations covering ADD, it will seek support from the media and government to change them.

Already a backlash to the victims' rights movement is in full swing. Sympathy for what began as a courageous fight for the rights of black Americans, women, and the severely disabled has devolved into suspicion of disability rights and identity politics. Russell Barkley worries about what this means for ADD: "Overly loose standards for legal or clinical determinations . . . only serve to trivialize the disorder. Those who truly suffer from this condition stand to lose tremendously if the public comes to see ADHD as nothing more than an label applied to an individual who experiences frustration with himself or herself or with his or her children. . . ."[40]

As I noted in Chapter 7, it makes sense that parents of children struggling in overcrowded classrooms seek aid for their children through an ADD diagnosis. However, the diversion of funds and other resources to special services for ADD and learning-disabled children makes the general classroom that much less tolerable for the others. Naturally, government and political leaders are attending to protests from both sides, eager to discern where the majority opinion lies. It is in this cultural maelstrom that the confusions of ADD diagnosis and treatment will be thrashed out.

THE ETHICS OF COMPLICITY

The 700 percent jump in Ritalin production in the 1990s does reflect an imbalance, but I characterize it as a "living imbalance" rather than a neurochemical one. Parents and teachers alike are trapped in a web of fear and anxiety about their own and America's future. This translates into demands for higher performance in school (and at an earlier age), even as class size has climbed, and funding for public education has stagnated or shrunk. It makes "average" grades and vocational or artistic tracks unacceptable to middle-class families. The same anxiety paradoxically makes parents less available to their children, as they work longer and harder to achieve economic security.

In such times, Ritalin seems to many like the right prescription: It works fast, it's relatively cheap, and it usually improves behavior and performance in the short term. It permits children and adults who are "square pegs" to fit into the "round holes" provided by the culture.

My awareness of the pressures on parents and children is always with me as I evaluate for ADD, a "disorder" that makes the child's brain fully responsible for any imbalance between performance and expectations. There's little I can do to change the big picture: I can't reduce class sizes, nor increase funding for public education, nor alter America's changing role in the global economy. I can, however, address as many remediable factors as possible in my evaluation. And, in the end, I can help this child or that grown-up cope a bit better by offering him Ritalin.

Still, this doesn't seem like enough. As far back as 1980, in *Hyperactive Children: The Social Ecology of Identification and Treatment*, Carol Whalen and Barbara Hencker discussed the "social trap" doctors face when they prescribe Ritalin for a child.[41] While the physician may be "doing good" on an individual basis, they note, by enhancing the child's performance with medication, he or she may unwittingly be contributing to a "social bad." It's a well-known conundrum of child psychiatry that even an effective psychopharmacological intervention may permit a poor environment to continue or worsen. When American doctors distribute fifteen tons of Ritalin to children in just one year, are they accepting and abetting the fact of overcrowded classrooms, overwhelmed parents and teachers, and unreasonable standards?

My use of the term *complicity* to describe this dilemma is borrowed from an intriguing presentation made at the Hastings Center by Margaret Olivia Little, a philosopher from the Kennedy Institute of Ethics at Georgetown University, who spoke on cosmetic surgery.[42] Essentially, she challenged the typical defense of the practice—that it makes women "feel better about themselves"—by proposing that it reinforces oppressive social values: chiefly, the idea that women's self-worth rests on appearance. Little drew some interesting parallels to point up the moral dimensions of the issue: Should a child teased unmercifully by his peers on account of his protuberant ears be offered cosmetic surgery? This probably would raise few moral qualms. But, what if there was a treatment that could make dark-pigmented skin lighter, that is, make a black person "white"? The argument could be made that white skin offers social and economic advantages; however, such a treatment would only reinforce the morally bankrupt position that skin color is a measure of a person's worth.

Little remains sympathetic to women who want to improve their appearance in response to social norms and, by extension, to those who seek self-enhancement for any perceived deficiency. Nor does she unduly censure the cosmetic surgeons. Her solution to the ethical dilemma is that, even as the treatment is pursued, both doctor and patient should acknowledge the social forces that led to their decision. She believes that doctors have an extra moral obligation to publicly challenge such values, because they profit from them. To do less is to be complicitous in perpetuating them.

Reviewing a paper in which I voiced similar ethical concerns about ADD, a colleague asked: "Would Dr. Diller not treat a child's diarrhea until he was absolutely sure of its etiology [medical cause]?" My answer: Yes, I would treat the child's diarrhea. However, if I suspected it was caused by drinking river water that contained untreated sewage or chemicals from a factory upstream, it would be unconscionable merely to treat the symptom. I'd feel compelled to alert others to the possible cause and try to stop the pollution.

I'm not "against" Ritalin, nor do I like to answer the frequent question of whether it is overprescribed. I don't think that's the right question to ask. No doubt it is both over- and underprescribed, depending on which community you assess. However, I am against employing Ritalin as the first and only treatment for a host of behavioral and performance problems in children. I'm concerned that we might be *too* successful in medicating the sharp edge off our obsession with performance. If this is true, we might further delay addressing some of the larger issues, such as public school funding and support for parents who stay home. What most worries me is the sense that we are postponing some later reckoning with the "living imbalance" our children are experiencing today.

I think the Ritalin explosion should be regarded rather like the proverbial canary in a coal mine: When the bird is overcome by low levels of gas in the shaft, the miners know to get out, for a literal explosion may follow. The surge in ADD diagnosis and Ritalin treatment is a warning to society that we are not meeting the needs of our children and that adults are struggling, as well. It should serve as a flashing red light for the white middle class—analogous to the deaths of inner-city children from violence and illicit drugs—alerting us to the need to allocate greater resources to children and their families. Experience tells us that a society using drugs to cope does so at its own risk.

IF NOT RITALIN . . .

As I move toward my conclusion, I anticipate the question "So what are his solutions to the ADD/Ritalin dilemma?" with much ambivalence and humility. I am daunted by the immensity of the social, economic, and cultural factors at work, and aware that my own social and cultural hypotheses on the ADD phenomenon are difficult to assess scientifically.

I am sure of one thing: that the united efforts of all concerned parties will be needed. Beyond the most directly affected groups—parents of ADD-diagnosed children, adolescents and adults with ADD, and professionals involved in research and clinical practice—I would urge anyone concerned about our children and Ritalin use to take action. This can begin simply by talking to others: friends, parents, educators, colleagues, doctors. Sharing information and resources is useful in itself, and by opening lines of communication, people can realize that they are not alone in their concerns—and that they have a surprising amount in common with others on various sides of the issue. In any such discussions, assigning fault will be counterproductive. Children, parents, teachers, and doctors have all received more than enough blame, and blaming children's brains doesn't help either if it leads to passivity.

I've had the opportunity—in my office practice, in school meetings to develop a child's educational plan, at professional gatherings, at conferences sponsored by CHADD, the DEA, or other groups—to speak to most of the constituencies who have an interest in ADD diagnosis and treatment, and in Ritalin use. I'll try to summarize some things I've said, and things I haven't yet had a chance to say, to those most affected by ADD, personally or professionally.

To the parents of children diagnosed with ADD, or those who suspect their child has ADD, and to ADD adolescents and adults:

• Insist on an adequate evaluation of your child (or yourself)—one that takes account of all the circumstances of the person's life and world. Bear in mind that bias operates in any evaluation; find out all you can about your doctor's approach to evaluating for and treating ADD.

• Do not accept the problems and behaviors associated with ADD solely as manifestations of a brain-based abnormality. Rather than a "chemical imbalance," it's more useful to think of an imbalance between the brain's inborn tendencies and the demands of a person's environment.

• Resist the use of diagnostic labels like "he's ADD" to describe your child. He or she will be better served if you and your doctor describe and address specific strengths and weaknesses. Words like "personality" or "temperament" can substitute for "disorder" in the interest of relieving guilt or blame.

• Do not feel guilty about giving your child Ritalin if you feel confident in the medical evaluation and advice you've received. The medication can be used safely and thoughtfully by children and adults.

• At the same time, consider and pursue other avenues of intervention. Ritalin can often substitute for behavioral or educational approaches to treatment, but it may not be "morally equivalent" to them.

• Think long and hard about the choice between working more to achieve a better lifestyle or spending more time with your children. Parents are caught between a rock and a hard place: the desire for a high standard of living versus the benefits to a child with more parental supervision. A child with a challenging temperament lends the decision greater urgency: choosing work may also mean choosing Ritalin so the child can cope successfully. If this must be your choice, you should not be faulted for it; your dilemma is rooted in our social and economic reality.

• Don't be intimidated by political correctness from disciplining a difficult child in a firm and consistent fashion.

• Know your rights under educational disability laws. If your child qualifies for special help at school because of behavior problems, insist that teachers, doctors, and administrators develop a suitable educational plan.

• Try to distinguish between meeting the basic criteria for ADD and being impaired by such symptoms. If you function as well as most people despite your ADD, you surely have a right to seek treatment to improve your performance further, but don't be suprised if not everyone supports you in this. The same goes for parents wanting extra help for children who are performing at least as well as their peers, even if they may have "higher potential."

To teachers, school administrators, and other educational professionals and policy makers:

• Whenever possible, special-needs children will do better within the regular classroom.

• Support efforts to add paraprofessional assistants to the regular classroom. Putting more adults in the classroom is good for all kids, but especially for those who need more immediate feedback and attention. More highly trained ADD specialists could float between classes to provide specialized help and to train teachers and aides.

• Put more men in the classrooms. Teacher's aides typically are female, but the positive way in which ADD children respond to their fathers suggests that male paraprofessionals might have more impact. College undergraduates—especially those majoring in education or psychology—represent an untapped, relatively low-cost source of such support. Programs could be developed for college credit.

• Restore the traditional physical classroom structure in some classes—teacher in front and children's desk in rows—for the benefit of those children who work better without a friend within reach.

• Destigmatize the use of a quiet place in the classroom where a child can go to escape distraction. A child shouldn't have to get into trouble to use such a space, or feel bad about it.

• Children should be held to rigorous standards of performance, but those standards should be tailored to a child's capabilities. Provide a wider choice of electives, approaches (such as computer-based learning) and alternative schools, even on the elementary grade level, for youngsters with different abilities and interests.

• Make it possible for some students to continue in a one-on-one relationship with a teacher past the sixth grade—in other words, delay until high school the transition to a multi-teacher environment that now takes place in middle school. This option should be available to any child whom it suits better, not just those with ADD or learning disabilities.

• Bring back the option of a vocational or artistic track in high school. Teenagers in effect make that choice themselves when they drop out or concentrate on after-school activities rather than their studies; when this happens, it looks like failure to most parents. More children could stay in school and off Ritalin if schools restored and destigmatized alternative educational tracks, and if parents were reeducated as to their value.

To my fellow doctors in private practice and medical research, to professional medical organizations, and to health care and insurance administrators:

• Recognize the persistantly subjective nature of the ADD diagnosis and its frequent overlap with other problems, despite efforts to standardize criteria and draw hard distinctions.

• Support pragmatic approaches to diagnosis and treatment, and reserve DSM primarily for research purposes, as was originally intended. Either a dimensional or needs-based system would more accurately reflect the reality of ADD symptoms and be more useful to patients and doctors. The categorial "disease" model forces doctors to make all-or-nothing decisions on ADD diagnoses—and since insurance claims and disability services ride on a diagnosis, doctors are motivated to fudge for their patients' benefit. The recently published *Diagnostic and Statistical Manual—Primary Care* (pediatrics' version of the DSM) does offer a dimensional model, and needs-based systems have been developed for mental retardation and learning disorders.[43]

• Establish a bare minimum standard for a physician-conducted ADD evaluation of not less than 30 minutes. The process should include talking to the child and obtaining information about the child from at least one other source besides the mother or primary caregiver.

• Bring the power of managed health care to bear on mandating physician practices for quality care. One HMO, northern California's Kaiser Permanente, has taken the lead in developing a cost-conscious, multimodal ADD evaluation.[44]

• Promote multimodal interventions for the treatment of ADD. Parents, doctors, and patients will see better long-term outcomes when medication is used in combination with behavioral training and educational modifications that involve an individual's entire support system. Treatment approaches that demand more time from professionals are bucking the cost-cutting trend in medicine—but if doctors won't work to change the system for their patient's benefit, who will?

• Acknowledge the effects of ADD on families, and the effects of family dynamics on ADD. Ideally, the treating physician should meet with the patient's whole family at least once. If this is impossible in primary care, where time and space are especially costly, find ways to work closely with a specialist or mental health professional who can take on the task of a full-family assessment.

• Support access to a full range of counseling services, which may include parent effectiveness training (PET), group parenting classes for ADD or difficult children, and behavior management training. An ADD diagnosis should not be required in order for families to get financial support for such counseling.

Finally, I hope that all of the concerned parties will translate their concern into public advocacy:

• Get some other parents and professionals together to have a discussion about schools, families, ADD, and Ritalin in your community. Such meetings can be informal or sponsored by professional or parent groups.

• Identify acceptable local standards for ADD diagnosis and Ritalin use. Identify schools and medical practices where standards seem particularly loose or vague, and where many children receive medication. Conversely, identify schools and practitioners where the ADD diagnosis is not accepted at all, even when it might be reasonable to offer a trial of medication.

• Use local community forums (PTA meetings, churches, civic functions) to raise the issues of ADD and Ritalin use to larger groups.

• Urge government support of quality day care, and options that allow parents to spend more time at home, such as flex time and telecommuting.

• Support efforts that will reduce class size for *all* children, especially in the early grades.

• Employers should shoulder some of the financial burden of managing ADD as a public health issue—one that by its nature is difficult to categorize strictly as medical, emotional, or educational.

• If you are active in CHADD or other ADD self-help groups, you are in a unique position to promote positive change. Urge your group toward a more balanced position on ADD as a biological disease. Ask that CHADD give at least equal support to the multimodal treatment model. And look beyond the sometimes restricted view of "special interests": advocacy for a worthy personal cause does not cancel out our responsibility as citizens to the larger social good.

If you are accustomed to hearing advocates argue about ADD and Ritalin from a particular side, my "solutions" may seem inconsistent with any one position. In my role as a doctor, my mandate and instinct are to help individual patients and their families as best as I can. In my practice, that very often means perscribing Ritalin and/or saying yes to a marginal ADD diagnosis so that a family can receive benefits. Multiply my practice by thousands of doctors doing likewise, and we start to see medicine contributing to a social problem. My growing awareness of this, and my sense that in succeeding as a doctor I may be failing as a citizen has led, ultimately, to this book.

A DIFFERENT PRESCRIPTION FOR A RITALIN NATION

A thoughtful English psychiatrist once asked me if I believed Ritalin would go the way of Valium, America's prescription drug of choice from the 1950s through 1970s, which later fell out of favor. Or would Ritalin be a permanent feature on our psychic landscape? As Peter Kramer has noted, Valium was popular during a time when aggressive, dominant women were not appreciated at home or in the workplace; it was the perfect drug to help relieve their anxieties and frustrations.[45] By the 1980s, however, more women were working outside the home, and assertiveness had become an asset. Besides its dangers of addiction, Valium's effects were not as useful to women in the marketplace. Prozac, on the other hand, with its mild stimulatory quality and uncanny ability to make people less sensitive to emotional stress and pain, is the perfect drug to salve the bumps and bruises of the business world.

A similar point can be made about Ritalin's appeal in the 1990s. In the broadest sense, I believe that Ritalin encapsulates our attempt to keep pace as life gets more complex and demanding and as our anxiety level about performance increases. Given Ritalin's universal enhancing properties I realize with some irony that a book meant to question Ritalin may actually popularize and increase its use.

Societal expectations about behavior and performance can change very quickly, perhaps over as little as a decade or two. In contrast, temperament and development evolve very slowly, over hundreds of thousands of years, with changes governed largely by the available gene pool. Hence a personality that was valued in the 1960s could be problematic only thirty years later—and it's the out-of-step individual who suffers.

Today, in middle-class America, it's expected that one will work hard in school, attend college and maybe graduate school, and focus on securing gainful, meaningful employment, with a few stops along the way to find a suitable mate and probably produce a child or two. Even just a few decades ago, college was not a given for middle-class kids; between now and then the perceived need for higher education has climbed from "it would be nice" to "it's important" to "it's urgent." And the kind of performance required to attain these life goals has changed. We push our children harder and earlier to succeed—and we demand that schools and other institutions give them every advantage needed to compete. Performance as reflected by grades has become a near-obsession—but to what end?

Since the 1980s we've seen an unprecedented emphasis on material success, and with the gap between richest and poorest widening, the middle class is scrambling to reach the first category and stay out of the second. We are bombarded every waking moment by messages that we can find emotional contentment by buying things; our state religion is consumer-based capitalism.[46] If success continues to mean merely getting the sort of education needed for U.S. consumer citizenship, then performance enhancers such as Ritalin—which allow those on the verge of success to compete effectively—will remain popular.

But inevitably there are some who aren't cut out to compete on this level, or who just don't want to. Should we then, even with the best intentions, force them into academic and career paths not well suited to their personalities and abilities, and then medicate them to raise their motivation? I think this is what's happening to a great extent with ADD-type children.

Much of what is treated in psychiatry today can be viewed as unappreciated diversity within the human personality. Thomas Bouchard has had a principal role in the research on identical twins that demonstrated how much of behavior is genetically guided. Nevertheless, in concluding his landmark article in *Science*, Bouchard expresses strong feelings about the creative interplay of culture and genes:

> A human species whose members did not vary genetically with respect to significant cognitive and motivational attributes . . . would have created a very different society than the one we know. Modern society not only augments the influence of genotype on behavioral variability . . . but permits this variability to reciprocally contribute to the rapid pace of cultural change.[47]

Valium, Prozac, Ritalin: all these are drugs that smooth the edges off human diversity, making our culture less rich and interesting and perhaps affecting, in ways we cannot predict, the time-honored "co-evolution" of personality and society.

On a more individual level, I worry about the possibility that people with "ADD personalities" and their families—overwhelmed by the weight of genetic evidence that seems to predestine behavior, psychiatry's commitment to biochemical explanations, outsize performance demands, and Ritalin's quick results—may give up trying to improve their lives by means other than drugs. All these factors, and more that this book has detailed, are conspiring, I think, to make people see the challenge of a difficult personality as a glass half-empty rather than half-full. As another writer on twins, Lawrence Wright, reminds us: "Genetic traits are best understood as inclinations, not as mandates. . . . We can change our behavior and the course of our lives, even though it may entail a struggle against our natural tendencies. . . ."[48] In this very struggle lies the essence of our humanity and our individuality.

Hopeful signs can be found that the compass needle of America's values is being pulled in new directions. Clearly there's a deep yearning for greater meaning and satisfaction than can be gained through acquisition. Both spiritual and secular trends reflect the growing discontent with consumer culture.

It is all too easy to cope with an anxiety-inducing world by adopting an every-man-for-himself stance. Some, conscious of deeper needs, seek solidarity and meaning within an identified group. Visionary social theorists direct us toward a "communitarian" path, one that looks to redress an imbalance between the rights of individuals and special interests and responsibility to the community.[49] Some see service to others as an antidote to America's current cynical materialism.[50]

It takes a conscious effort, real work, to resist the pressures of a culture of performance. I need only look at my own children, at their more-or-less normal struggles and gifts, to realize how much I worry about them and their future. Both my wife and I try to find a balance between asking for their best and accepting who they are, and we know we don't always succeed. So I can only try to imagine what coping in this culture is like for families with greater extremes of temperamental diversity than ours. The struggles surely are greater, but perhaps so might the rewards be.

Sometimes I don't have to imagine: people tell me. A mother active in CHADD recently and eloquently described her evolving feelings about her son, Jeffrey, diagnosed with ADD at age six and now thirteen. "Jeff's been in and out of special schools and has taken three medications to help him fit in with his friends and at school," she said. "It's been really hard for him and for us. Especially for me, because I kept wanting him to change in some fundamental way that wasn't going to happen." Her tone became more optimistic. "Lately, in spite of everything, I've come around to just accepting Jeff for who he is—and the funny thing is, it's actually been a lot better between him and me. I know it still won't be easy," she went on. "We'll keep trying to help him and get him to help himself, but *I* feel different. Instead of just seeing him as someone who's ADD and has a disease, now he's . . . just Jeffrey. He's himself." All of us might envy this mother her hard-earned wisdom.

For the present, the anxious compulsion to fit in and to get our share first remains very much with us. Until we can discover other culturally approved paths to contentment, the model of achievement at any cost—which demands an unforgiving level of performance, at school, at home, and at work—will predominate. Only when America somehow regains its balance between material gain and emotional and spiritual satisfaction will conditions that have fueled the ADD epidemic and the Ritalin boom change. Only then will diversity of personality be valued for what it has offered our species since civilization began.

Notes

Chapter 1: Ritalin Ascendant

1. Based upon data from the Drug Enforcement Administration (DEA), U.S. Department of Justice. Ritalin production and use are presented in great detail in the following chapter.

2. The Mental Research Institute (MRI) is considered by many the "birthplace" of family therapy and family systems theory. Gregory Bateson, the noted anthropologist and cybernetician, founded MRI in the late 1950s. Many of the early pioneers and subsequent luminaries of the family therapy movement—Virginia Satir and Jay Haley, to mention just two—worked and taught at MRI. In the 1970s MRI was one of the few training centers that welcomed and trained nonpsychiatrist physicians, like myself, in family therapy.

3. Peter D. Kramer, *Listening to Prozac* (New York: Viking Penguin, 1993).

4. Edward M. Hallowell and John J. Ratey, *Driven to Distraction: Recognizing and Coping with Attention Deficit Disorder from Childhood Through Adulthood* (New York: Pantheon Books, 1994); *Answers to Distraction* (New York: Pantheon Books, 1994).

5. Joseph Biederman, "Are Stimulants Overprescribed for Children with Behavioral Problems?" *Pediatric News*, August 1996, p. 26.

6. Monika Guttman, "The Ritalin Generation," *USA Weekend*, October 27–29, 1995, pp. 4–6.

7. Based upon about a 4:1 or 5:1 ratio of boys to girls currently diagnosed with ADD.

8. Lawrence H. Diller, "The Run on Ritalin: Attention Deficit Disorder and Stimulant Medication Treatment in the 1990s," *The Hastings Center Report*, vol. 26 (1996), pp. 12–18.

9. Gina Kolata, "Boom in Ritalin Sales Raises Ethical Issues," *New York Times*, May 15, 1996, p. C8.

10. Based upon statements from Gene R. Haislip, deputy assistant administrator, Drug Enforcement Administration, Office of Diversion Control. The pharmaceutical industry is discussed in more detail in the next chapter.

Chapter 2: Stimulant of Choice

1. Alice's story about Joe was told at a conference at which I spoke in 1997. Alice prefers to remain anonymous but gave me permission to adapt her story for this book.

2. Arthur L. Hughes, "Epidemiology of Amphetamine Use in the United States," in

Amphetamine and Its Analogs: Psychopharmacology, Toxicology, and Abuse, A. K. Cho, D. S. Segal, eds. (San Diego: Academic Press, 1994), pp. 439–57.

3. Laurence L. Greenhill, "Pharmacologic Treatment of Attention Deficit Hyperactivity Disorder," *Psychiatric Clinics of North America*, vol. 15 (1992), pp. 1–27.

4. *Goodman and Gilman's The Pharmacological Basis of Therapeutics, ninth edition*, Joel G. Hardman, Lee L. Limbird, et al., eds. (New York: McGraw-Hill, 1996), p. 221.

5. Bernard Weiss and Victor G. Laties, "The Enhancement of Human Performance by Caffeine and the Amphetamines," *Pharmacological Review*, vol. 14 (1962), pp. 1-36.

6. Victor G. Laties and Bernard Weiss, "The Amphetamine Margin in Sports," Federation Proceedings, vol. 40 (1981), pp. 2689-92.

7. *Goodman and Gilman's The Pharmacological Basis of Therapeutics, ninth edition*, p. 571 (see note 4).

8. The history of methylphenidate and Ritalin is drawn from several main sources: Greenhill, "Pharmacologic Treatment" (see note 3); Gabrielle Weiss and Lily Trokenberg Hechtman, *Hyperactive Children Grown Up: ADHD in Children, Adolescents and Adults*, second edition (New York: Guilford Press, 1993); Russell Barkley, *Attention-Deficit Hyperactivity Disorder: A Handbook for Diagnosis and Treatment* (New York: Guilford Press, 1990); Timothy E. Wilens and Joseph Biederman, "The Stimulants," *Psychiatric Clinics of North America*, vol. 15 (1992), pp. 191–222; James M. Swanson, Keith McBurnett, et al., "Stimulant Medications and the Treatment of Children with ADHD," *Advances in Clinical Child Psychology*, vol. 17 (1995), pp. 265–322.

9. Charles Bradley, "The Behavior of Children Receiving Benzedrine," *American Journal of Psychiatry*, vol. 94 (1937), pp. 577-85.

10. Mortimer D. Gross, "Origin of Stimulant Use for Treatment of Attention Deficit Disorder" [letter], *American Journal of Psychiatry*, vol. 152 (1995), pp. 298–99.

11. Bradley, "Behavior of Children" (see note 9).

12. Charles Bradley, "Benzedrine and Dexedrine in the Treatment of Children's Behavior Disorders," *Pediatrics*, vol. 5 (1950), pp. 24–37.

13. Melvin Grumbach, chairman emeritus of the Pediatric Department at the University of California, San Francisco, told me about this use of amphetamine in children at Columbia during the 1940s and 1950s.

14. Todd Forte, public relations officer, Novartis, personal communication, 1996.

15. Laurence L. Greenhill, "Methylphenidate in the Clinical Office Practice of Child Psychiatry," in *Ritalin: Theory and Patient Management*, Laurence L. Greenhill and Betty B. Osman, eds. (New York: Mary Ann Liebert, Inc., 1991), p. 98.

16. See sources cited in note 8 for more extensive reviews of studies on the short- and long-term effects of Ritalin.

17. Lori Jeanne Peloquin and Rafael Klorman, "Effects of Methylphenidate on Normal Children's Mood, Event-Related Potentials, and Performance in Memory Scanning and Vigilance," *Journal of Abnormal Psychology*, vol. 95 (1986), pp. 88–98; H. S. Koelega, "Stimulant Drugs and Vigilance Performance: A Review," *Psychopharmacology*, vol. 111 (1993), pp. 1–16.

18. Steven R. Pliszka, James T. McCracken, and James W. Mass, "Catecholamines in Attention-Deficit Hyperactivity Disorder: Current Perspectives," *Journal of the American Academy of Child and Adolescent Psychiatry*, vol. 35 (1996), pp. 264–72.

19. Thomas J. Spencer, Joseph Biederman, et al., "Growth Deficits in ADHD Children Revisited: Evidence for Disorder-Associated Growth Delays?" *Journal of the American Academy of Child and Adolescent Psychiatry*, vol. 35 (1996), pp. 1460–69.

20. Kenneth D. Gadow, Edith Nolan, et al., "School Observation of Children with Attention-Deficit Hyperactivity Disorder and Comorbid Tic Disorder: Effects of Methylphenidate Treatment," *Journal of Developmental and Behavioral Pediatrics*, vol. 16 (1995), pp. 167–76.

21. N. L. Feidler and D. G. Ullman, "The Effects of Stimulant Drugs on Curiosity Behaviors of Hyperactive Boys," *Journal of Abnormal Child Psychology*, vol. 11 (1983), pp. 193–206.

22. Jeanne B. Funk, John B. Chessare, et al., "Attention Deficit Hyperactivity Disorder, Creativity, and the Effects of Methylphenidate," *Pediatrics*, vol. 91 (1993), pp. 816–19.

23. Kenneth D. Gadow, "Prevalence of Drug Treatment for Hyperactivity and Other Childhood Behavior Disorders," in *Psychosocial Aspects of Drug Treatment for Hyperactivity*, Kenneth D. Gadow and John Loney, eds. (Boulder: Westview Press, 1981).

24. ". . . And Pep in America" [editorial], *New England Journal of Medicine*, vol. 283 (1970), pp. 761–62.

25. Einar S. Perman, "Speed in Sweden" [editorial], *New England Journal of Medicine*, vol. 283 (1970), pp. 760–61.

26. "Methylphenidate (A Background Paper)," Drug and Chemical Evaluation Section, Office of Diversion Control, Drug Enforcement Administration, Department of Justice, Washington, DC, October 1995.

27. Gretchen Feussner, Drug Enforcement Administration, Office of Diversion Control, April 1997, personal communication. While Michigan continues to employ triplicate prescriptions they are no longer required for Ritalin. It cost too much money to maintain and monitor the data for the large number of Ritalin prescriptions being written.

28. Robert Maynard, "Omaha Pupils Given 'Behavior Drugs,'" *Washington Post*, June 29, 1970, p. 1.

29. E. T. Ladd, "Pills for Classroom Peace?" *Saturday Review*, November 21, 1970, pp. 66–68, 81–83; Nat Hentoff, "The Drugged Classroom," *Evergreen Review*, Decem-

ber 1970, pp. 31–33; J. M. Rogers, "Drug Abuse—Just What the Doctor Ordered," *Psychology Today*, September 1971, pp. 16–24.

30. A. S. Neill, *Summerhill: A Radical Approach to Education* (New York: Hart Publishing Co., 1964).

31. Peter Schrag and Diane Divoky, *The Myth of the Hyperactive Child, and Other Means of Child Control* (New York: Pantheon Books, 1975).

32. Joel Sapell and Robert W. Welkos, "Suits, Protests Fuel a Campaign Against Psychiatry," *Los Angeles Times*, June 29, 1990, p. A48; "Review and Outlook: The Prozac Posse," *Wall Street Journal*, September 27, 1991, p. A10.

33. Both the persistence and insidious quality of Scientology's attack lead me to often introduce myself when I speak at public forums with the qualifications, "I am not against Ritalin nor am I a member of the Church of Scientology."

34. Judith L. Rapoport, Monte S. Buchsbaum, et al., "Dextroamphetamine: Cognitive and Behavioral Effects in Normal Prepubertal Boys," *Science*, vol. 199 (1978), pp. 560–63.

35. Judith L. Rapoport, Monte S. Buchsbaum, et al., "Dextroamphetamine: Its Cognitive and Behavioral Effects in Normal and Hyperactive Boys and Normal Men," *Archives of General Psychiatry*, vol. 37 (1980), pp. 933–43.

36. Gadow, "Prevalence" (see note 23).

37. Daniel J. Safer and John M. Krager, "A Survey of Medication Treatment for Hyperactive/Inattentive Students," *Journal of the American Medical Association*, vol. 260 (1988), pp. 2256–58.

38. "Methylphenidate Yearly Production Quota (1975–1996)," Office of Public Affairs, Drug Enforcement Administration, Department of Justice, Washington, DC, 1996.

39. Rachel G. Klein and Paul Wender, "The Role of Methylphenidate in Psychiatry" [commentary], *Archives of General Psychiatry*, vol. 52 (1995), pp. 429–33.

40. Claudia Wallis, "Life in Overdrive," *Time*, July 18, 1994, pp. 42–50.

41. Edward M. Hallowell and John J. Ratey, *Driven to Distraction: Recognizing and Coping with Attention Deficit Disorder from Childhood Through Adulthood* (New York: Pantheon Books, 1994).

42. "CH.A.D.D. Facts 8," Children and Adults with Attention Deficit Disorder, Plantation, Florida, 1993.

43. Warren E. Leary, "Blunder Limits Supply of Crucial Drug," *New York Times*, November 14, 1993, p. 20.

44. "Methylphenidate (A Background Paper)," pp. 12–13 (see note 26).

45. *Federal Register*, December 17, 1996; 61FR66311.

46. Daniel J. Safer, Julie M. Zito, and Eric M. Fine, "Increased Methylphenidate Usage for Attention Deficit Disorder in the 1990s," *Pediatrics*, vol. 98 (1996), pp. 1084–88.

47. Lawrence Diller and Robert Morrow, "The Case of the Missing Methylphenidate" [letter], *Pediatrics*, vol. 100 (1997), pp. 730–31.

48. "Background Information on Methylphenidate (Ritalin)," Office of Public Affairs, Drug Enforcement Administration, Department of Justice, Washington, DC, 1993.

49. Barbara Crossette, "Agency Sees Risk in Drug to Temper Child Behavior," *New York Times*, February 29, 1996, p. A7.

50. James M. Swanson, Marc Lerner, and Lillie Williams, "More Frequent Diagnosis of Attention Deficit-Hyperactivity Disorder" [letter], *New England Journal of Medicine*, vol. 333 (1996), p. 994.

51. While dextroamphetamine production has risen at a rate similar to that of methylphenidate, it is more difficult to extrapolate usage levels for ADD because the drug is used in some other combinations.

52. Lillie Williams, Marc Lerner, and James Swanson, "Prevalence of Office Visits for ADD," unpublished.

53. Paul Wilson, "Trends in the Diagnosis and Treatment of ADHD," *Conference Report: Stimulant Use in the Treatment of ADHD*, Drug Enforcement Administration, Department of Justice, Washington, DC, December 1996.

54. Beth Spanos, "Quotas, ARCOS, UN Report and Statistics," *Conference Report: Stimulant Use in the Treatment of ADHD*, Drug Enforcement Administration, Department of Justice, Washington, DC, December 1996.

55. Paul Wilson, vice president, statistical services, IMS America, personal communication, 1996.

56. Katherine Maurer, "African-American Children Less Likely to Get Ritalin," *Clinical Psychiatry News*, vol. 24 (1996), pp. 1–2.

57. Luke Chang, Richard F. Morrisey, and Harold S. Koplewicz, "Prevalence of Psychiatric Symptoms and Their Relation to Adjustment Among Chinese-American Youth," *Journal of the Academy of Child and Adolescent Psychiatry*, vol. 34 (1995), pp. 91–99.

58. Robert C. Morrow, "Methylphenidate/ADHD: A Virginia Study," *Conference Report: Stimulant Use in the Treatment of ADHD*, Drug Enforcement Administration, Department of Justice, Washington, DC, December 1996.

59. Robert Files, a narcotics detective from Alexandria, Virginia, said school nurses in his district claimed 38 percent of the children had taken Ritalin, but he could not provide confirming data. Presented at "Stimulant Use in the Treatment of ADHD," Drug Enforcement Administration Conference, San Antonio, TX, December 1996.

60. UN International Narcotics Control Board, *Report of the UN International Narcotics Control Board, 1994* (New York: UN Publications, 1995).

61. Data from Jean-Marie Ruel, M.D., Special Medical Advisor to the Bureau of Drug Surveillance of Health Canada, Ottawa, 1998.

62. Phillip L. Hasell, Michael J. McDowell, and Jane M. Walton, "Management of Children Prescribed Psychostimulant Medication for Attention Deficit Hyperactivity Disorder in the Hunter Region of NSW," *Medical Journal of Australia*, vol. 165 (1996), pp. 477–80; Allan Carmichael, "Improving Diagnosis and Management of Attention Deficit Hyperactivity Disorder in Australia" [editorial], *Medical Journal of Australia*, vol. 165 (1996), pp. 464–65.

63. Crossette, "Agency Sees Risk" (see note 49); Spanos, "Quotas" (see note 54).

64. Gene Haislip, "Readin, Ritin, and Ritalin," presented at "Stimulant Use in the Treatment of ADHD," Drug Enforcement Administration Conference, San Antonio, TX, December 1996.

65. Spanos, "Quotas" (see note 54).

66. Marsha D. Rappley, Joseph C. Gardiner, et al., "The Use of Methylphenidate in Michigan," *Archives of Pediatric and Adolescent Medicine*, vol. 149 (1995), pp. 675–79.

67. Charlotte Mapes, assistant U. S. attorney, Appellate Division, Denver, CO, presented at "Stimulant Use in the Treatment of ADHD," Drug Enforcement Administration Conference, San Antonio, TX, December 1996.

68. "Petition for Rulemaking to Reclassify Methylphenidate from Schedule II to Schedule III," Methylphenidate Review Document, Drug and Chemical Evaluation Section, Drug Enforcement Administration, Washington, DC, 1996.

69. Martin Stein, M.D., chairman of the American Academy of Pediatrics, Committee on Psychosocial Issues and the Family, 1995–1996, personal communication, 1995.

70. Harold I. Schwartz, "An Empirical Review of the Impact of Triplicate Prescription of Benzodiazepines," *Hospital and Community Psychiatry*, vol. 43 (1992), pp. 382–85.

71. Lawrence H. Diller, "Decreasing the Controls on Stimulants: A Reconsideration," *California Pediatrician*, Fall 1995, pp. 21–22.

72. John Merrow, "Reading, Writing and Ritalin," *New York Times*, October 21, 1995, p. 15.

73. "Methylphenidate (A Background Paper)," pp. 14–15 (see note 26).

74. "Ritalin Maker Opens Drive to End Abuse," *New York Times*, March 26, 1996, p. A13.

75. Hughes, "Epidemiology," p. 440 (see note 2).

76. Weiss and Laties, "Enhancement" (see note 5).

77. Hughes, "Epidemiology," pp. 441–43 (see note 2).

78. T. Silvertone, "The Place of Appetite-Suppressant Drugs in the Treatment of Obesity," in *Obesity: Theory and Therapy*, second edition, Albert J. Stunkard and T. A. Wadden, eds. (New York: Raven Press, 1993).

79. Perman, "Speed in Sweden" (see note 25).

80. Darryl Inaba, head pharmacist of the Haight-Ashbury Free Clinic for the past thirty years, personal communication, 1995.

81. "Methylphenidate (A Background Paper)" (see note 26).

82. Reported on CNN in 1996: A seventeen-year-old Roanoke, Virginia, male snorted Ritalin obtained from a friend's prescription medicine at a party. The autopsy revealed no other drugs and a lymphatic myocarditis (inflamed heart muscle), the same pathology found in acute cocaine overdoses. Details of this case were provided to me by Robert Morrow, Department of Pediatrics, Eastern Virginia Medical School, 1997.

83. Gretchen Feussner, "Actual Abuse Issues," *Conference Report: Stimulant Use in the Treatment of ADHD*, Drug Enforcement Administration, Department of Justice, Washington, DC, December 1996.

84. Ibid., p. 38.

85. Janice Gabe, addiction counselor, New Perspectives of Indiana, Inc., Indianapolis, IN; Johnny Hatcher, assistant commander of narcotics, Texas Department of Public Safety Narcotic Service, Austin, TX; Ronald Files, detective, Arlington County Police Department, Community Resources Section, Arlington, VA. All publicly talked about Ritalin's easy availability at the DEA conference "Stimulant Use in the Treatment of ADHD," San Antonio, TX, December 1996.

86. I feel it is necessary to clarify my relationship with the Drug Enforcement Administration. I do share with the DEA many of the same concerns about the *potential* abuse of prescribed stimulants in the United Sates. In 1994, when I learned of the efforts to decontrol Ritalin, I was one of the few physicians concerned who spoke and wrote publicly about it. Too many physicians and psychologists had become cavalier about Ritalin's abuse potential. To that end, at the conclusion of the DEA's conference "Stimulant Use in the Treatment of ADHD," held in December 1996, Jim Swanson, representing most of the major researchers present at the conference, acknowledged to the conference and the press that leaders in the field of ADHD had been lax about conveying the abuse potential of the drug. They agreed to make efforts to publicize this aspect of the treatment and did so at the next national CHADD meeting, held in October 1997. I do disagree with some of the DEA's positions on Ritalin. Most important, I think they may at times overstate the risks and the evidence for Ritalin's abuse and addictive potential. For example, at the DEA conference it seemed premature, based on the evidence, to link to humans the rat

studies of preexposure to methylphenidate that led to faster addiction in rats. Those efforts undercut their otherwise reasonable concerns.

87. James M. Swanson, Keith McBurnett, et al., "Effect of Stimulant Medication on Children with Attention Deficit Disorder: A 'Review of Reviews,'" *Exceptional Children*, vol. 60 (1993), pp.154–61.

88. Lily Hechtman, "Attention-Deficit Hyperactivity Disorder," in *Do They Grow Out of It? Long-Term Outcomes of Childhood Disorders*, Lily Hechtman, ed. (Washington, DC: American Psychiatric Press, 1996), pp. 17–38.

89. Susan Schenk, "Is the Treatment with Psychostimulants a Risk Factor for Substance Abuse?" *Conference Report: Stimulant Use in the Treatment of ADHD*, Drug Enforcement Administration, Department of Justice, Washington, DC, 1996.

90. Timothy E. Wilens, Joseph Biederman, and Thomas J. Spencer, "Attention-Deficit Hyperactivity Disorder and the Psychoactive Substance Use Disorders," *Child and Adolescent Psychiatric Clinics of North America*, vol. 5 (1996), pp. 73–91.

91. *A Comprehensive Guide to Attention Deficit Disorder in Adults: Research, Diagnosis and Treatment*, Kathleen G. Nadeau, ed. (New York: Brunner-Mazel, 1995).

92. Russell Barkley, "Special Report: Attention Deficit Hyperactivity Disorder," *Psychiatric Times*, vol. 13 (July 1996), pp. 38–41.

93. Lawrence H. Diller, "Muffling the Chant?" [letter], *Psychiatric Times*, vol. 13 (October 1996), pp. 6–7.

94. Joseph Biederman, "ADHD Through the Life Cycle," presented at Psychopharmacology Review, Massachusetts General Hospital and the Harvard Medical School, October 1994. Also Paul Wender and Edward Hallowell, among others.

Chapter 3: Attention Deficit Disorder

1. Edward M. Hallowell and John J. Ratey, *Driven to Distraction: Recognizing and Coping with Attention Deficit Disorder from Childhood Through Adulthood* (New York: Pantheon Books, 1994), pp. 209–14.

2. Claudia Wallis, "Life in Overdrive," *Time*, July 18, 1994, pp. 42–50.

3. William Carey at the Society for Developmental and Behavioral Pediatrics Annual Meeting, September 1996, San Francisco.

4. Russell Barkley, *Attention-Deficit Hyperactivity Disorder: A Handbook for Diagnosis and Treatment* (New York: Guilford Press, 1990), p. 40.

5. Thom Hartmann, *Attention Deficit Disorder: A Different Perspective* (Grass Valley, CA: Underwood Books, 1993).

6. Much of the following history comes from Barkley, *Attention-Deficit Hyperactivity Disorder* (see note 4).

7. Virginia I. Douglas, "Stop, Look and Listen," *Canadian Journal of Behavioral Science*, vol. 4 (1972), pp. 259–82.

8. *Diagnostic and Statistical Manual of Mental Disorders, Third Edition* (Washington, DC: American Psychiatric Association, 1980).

9. Stuart A. Kirk and Herb Kutchins, *The Selling of DSM: The Rhetoric of Science in Psychiatry* (New York: Aldine De Gruyter, 1992).

10. *Diagnostic and Statistical Manual of Mental Disorders, Third Edition, Revised* (Washington, DC: American Psychiatric Association, 1987); *Diagnostic and Statistical Manual of Mental Disorders, Fourth Edition* (Washington, DC: American Psychiatric Association, 1994).

11. Gerald L. Klerman, "The Advantages of DSM-III," *American Journal of Psychiatry*, vol. 141 (1984), pp. 539–42.

12. Mary Sykes Wylie, "Diagnosing for Dollars," *Family Therapy Networker*, May/June 1995, pp. 23–33.

13. *DSM-IV*, pp. 83–85 (see note 10).

14. Ibid., p. xxiii.

15. Keith McBurnett, Benjamin B. Lahey, and Linda J. Pfiffner, "Diagnosis of Attention Deficit Disorders in DSM-IV: Scientific Basis and Implications for Education," *Exceptional Children*, vol. 60 (1993), pp. 108–17.

16. Herman M. van Praag, *"Make-Believes" in Psychiatry, or the Perils of Progress* (New York: Brunner-Mazel, 1993), p. 31.

17. *The Classification of Child and Adolescent Mental Diagnoses in Primary Care: Diagnostic and Statistical Manual for Primary Care (DSM-PC), Child and Adolescent Version*, Mark L. Wolraich, ed. (Elk Grove Village, IL: American Academy of Pediatrics, 1996).

18. Stan F. Shaw, Joseph P. Cullen, et al., "Operationalizing a Definition of Learning Disabilities," *Journal of Learning Disabilities*, vol. 28 (1995), pp. 586–97; *Mental Retardation: Definition, Classification and Systems of Supports*, ninth edition (Washington, DC: American Association on Mental Retardation, 1992).

19. Michael Rutter, "Behavioral Studies: Questions and Findings on the Concept of a Distinctive Syndrome," in *Developmental Neuropsychiatry*, Michael Rutter, ed. (New York: Guilford Press, 1983), pp. 273–74.

20. Michael Rutter, personal communication, 1996.

21. Saro Palmeri, "Attention-Deficit Hyperactivity Disorder: Sometimes a Disorder, Often a Clinical Tautology," *Journal of Development and Behavioral Pediatrics*, vol. 17 (1996), pp. 253–54.

22. DSM-III-R does provide additional descriptors called "axes" or "domains of information" that could be used to enhance a description of the ADD diagnosis. Axis 4 is intended to account for environmental stressors on the individual, while Axis 5 is supposed to reflect the patient's current level of overall functioning. The stress factors in Axis 4 are not well specified, and Axis 5 does not rate the seriousness of the specific disorder. In either case, these descriptors are often ignored or left out when communicating a diagnosis of ADD.

23. Daniel L. Zeidner, "Teacher Deficit Disorder" [letter], *Pediatrics*, vol. 96 (1995), p. 378.

24. Russell A. Barkley and Joseph Biederman, "Toward a Broader Definition of the Age-of-Onset Criterion for Attention-Deficit Hyperactivity Disorder," *Journal of the American Academy of Child and Adolescent Psychiatry*, vol. 36 (1997), pp. 1204–10.

25. Peter S. Jensen, David Martin, and Dennis P. Cantwell, "Comorbidity in ADHD: Implication for Research, Practice and DSM-V," *Journal of the American Academy of Child and Adolescent Psychiatry*, vol. 36 (1997), pp. 1065–79.

26. Jessie C. Anderson, Sheila Williams, et al., "DSM-III Disorders in Preadolescent Children: Prevalence in a Large Sample from the General Population," *Archives of General Psychiatry*, vol. 44 (1987), pp. 69–76. This 1987 study used a group of nearly eight hundred children from a single town in New Zealand, and its results can be questioned on several counts. For one thing, because Ritalin use in the United States is so much greater than anywhere else in the world, how does one accurately project from a study of children from New Zealand to children in this country? Furthermore, the researchers qualified their ADD findings: Of the fifty-three children who met ADD criteria, only thirty-five demonstrated the symptoms strongly and in all situations. If one limits the positive finding to the "most impaired" children, this distinction lowers the overall prevalence of ADD by nearly a third, to 4.4 percent.

27. David Shaffer, Prudence Fisher, et al., "The NIMH Diagnostic Interview Schedule for Children Version 2.3 (DISC-2.3): Description, Acceptability, Prevalence Rates, and Performance in the MECA Study," *Journal of the Academy of Child and Adolescent Psychiatry*, vol. 35 (1996), pp. 865–88.

28. Anna Baumgaertel, Mark L. Wolraich, and Mary Dietrich, "Comparison of Diagnostic Criteria for Attention Deficit Disorders in a German Elementary School Sample," *Journal of the Academy of Child and Adolescent Psychiatry*, vol. 34 (1995), pp. 629–38; Mark L. Wolraich, Jane N. Hannah, et al., "Comparison of Diagnostic Criteria for Attention-Deficit Hyperactivity Disorder in a County-Wide Sample," *Journal of the American Academy of Child and Adolescent Psychiatry*, vol. 35 (1996), pp. 319–24.

29. Joseph Biederman, "Are Stimulants Overprescribed for Children with Behavioral Problems?" *Pediatrics News*, August 1996, p. 26.

30. James M. Swanson, "Discussion," in *Learning Disabilities: Proceedings of the National Conference*, James F. Kavanagh and Tom J. Truss, eds. (Parkton, MD: York Press, 1988), p. 524.

31. Janet Wozniak, Joseph Biederman, et al., "Mania-like Symptoms Suggestive of Childhood-Onset Bipolar Disorder in Clinically Referred Children," *Journal of the Academy of Child and Adolescent Psychiatry*, vol. 34 (1995), pp. 867–76.

32. Mark L. Wolraich, Scott Lindgren, et al., "Stimulant Medication Use by Primary Care Physicians in the Treatment of Attention Deficit Hyperactivity Disorder," *Pediatrics*, vol. 86 (1990), pp. 95–101.

33. Peter D. Kramer, *Listening to Prozac* (New York: Viking Penguin, 1993), pp. 32–33.

34. Russell A. Barkley, *ADHD and the Nature of Self-Control* (New York: Guilford Press, 1997).

Chapter 4: Coping with a "Living Imbalance"

1. *Project Head Start: A Legacy of the War on Poverty*, Edward Zigler and Jeanette Valentine, eds. (New York: Free Press, 1979).

2. James Atlas, "Making the Grade," *New Yorker*, April 14, 1997, pp. 34–39.

3. No. 626: Employment Status of Women, by Marital Status and Presence and Age of Children: 1960 to 1995," in *Statistical Abstract of the United States: 1996* (Washington, DC: Department of Commerce, 1996).

4. NICHD Early Child Care Research Group, "Mother-Child Interaction and Cognitive Outcomes Associated with Early Child Care: Results of the NICHD Study," presented at the Biennial Meeting of the Society for Research in Child Development, Washington, DC, April 1997.

5. Frederick Mosteller, "The Tennessee Study of Class Size," *The Future of Children*, vol. 5 (1995), pp. 113–27; Helen P. Bain and C. M. Achilles, "Interesting Developments on Class Size," *Phi Delta Kappan*, May 1986, pp. 662–65.

6. Robert B. Gunnison, "Class Sizes in California Shrink Fast," *San Francisco Chronicle*, December 3, 1996, p. 1.

7. Mary B. W. Tabor, "Homework Is Keeping Grade-Schoolers Busy," *New York Times*, April 6, 1996, p. 6.

8. Stan F. Shaw, Joseph P. Cullen, et al., "Operationalizing a Definition of Learning Disabilities," *Journal of Learning Disabilities*, vol. 28 (1995), pp. 586–97.

9. Sally Shaywitz, "Dyslexia," *Scientific American*, November 1996, pp. 98-104.

10. Under the Individuals with Disabilities Educational Act (IDEA) and Section 504 of the Vocational Rehabilitation Act of 1972; see Chapter 7 for details.

11. Jacquelynne S. Eccles, Constance Flanagan, et al., "Schools, Families and Early Adolescents: What Are We Doing Wrong and What Can We Do Instead?" *Journal of Developmental and Behavioral Pediatrics*, vol. 17 (1996), pp. 267–76.

12. Amanda Bennett, "Facts and Figures Add Up to Big Money for SAT Tutor," *Wall Street Journal*, January 28, 1994, p. B1; Lisa Leff, "Students Get Leg Up on SATs," *Washington Post*, November 2, 1991, p. A1.

13. Arlie Hochschild, *The Time Bind: When Work Becomes Home and Home Becomes Work* (New York: Henry Holt and Co., 1997).

14. Matt Murray, "Thanks, Goodbye: Amid Record Profits Companies Continue to Lay Off Employees," *Wall Street Journal*, May 4, 1995, p. 1; A New York Times Special Report, *The Downsizing of America* (New York: Times Books, 1996).

15. Joseph Biederman, Sharon Milberger, et al., "Family-Environment Risk Factors for Attention-Deficit Hyperactivity Disorder," *Archives of General Psychiatry*, vol. 52 (1995), pp. 464-70; Joseph Biederman, Sharon Milberger, et al., "Impact of Adversity on Function and Comorbidity in Children with Attention-Deficit Hyperactivity Disorder," *Journal of the American Academy of Child and Adolescent Psychiatry*, vol. 34 (1995), pp. 1495–503. The researchers acknowledged that by excluding the lowest socioeconomic group they may have underestimated the impact of poverty. By the nature of their investigations, the doctors could only make an association between these social factors and ADD; they could not determine causality. For example, did family conflict or the mother's mental health cause the child's ADD, or did the child's ADD behavior contribute to family conflict or the mother's problems? Most likely there is a bidirectional effect operating.

16. "One in Four: America's Youngest Poor," National Center for Children in Poverty, Columbia School of Public Health at Columbia University, New York, December 1996.

17. Gerald H. Block, "Hyperactivity: A Cultural Perspective," *Journal of Learning Disabilities*, vol. 10 (1977), pp. 236–40.

18. Victor C. Strasburger, "Electronic Media," in *Developmental-Behavioral Pediatrics*, second edition, Melvin Levine, William Carey, and Allen Crocker, eds. (Philadelphia: W. B. Saunders and Co., 1992), pp. 171-77.

19. Robert Sege and William Dietz, "Television Viewing and Violence in Children: The Pediatrician as Agent for Change," *Pediatrics*, vol. 94, suppl. 4 (1994), pp. 600–7.

20. S. Landau, E. P. Lorch, and R. Milich, "Visual Attention to and Comprehension of Television in Attention-Deficit Hyperactivity Disordered and Normal Boys," *Child Development*, vol. 63 (1992), pp. 928–37.

Chapter 5: Blaming Johnny's Brain

1. Harold S. Koplewicz, *It's Nobody's Fault: New Hope and Help for Difficult Children and Their Parents* (New York: Times Books, 1996).

2. Alvin Pam, "Introduction," in *Pseudoscience in Biological Psychiatry: Blaming the Body*, Colin A. Ross and Alvin Pam, eds. (New York: John Wiley, 1995), p. 1.

3. Here I'm referring to the discovery of the association of long-term treatment with phenothiazines leading to the development of a permanent involuntary movement disorder called tardive dyskinesia and the failure of the phenothiazines to have much effect on the apathy and depression of psychosis known as the negative signs of schizophrenia. Regarding the overall impact of tricyclic antidepressants on the suicide rate, see N. Retterstol, "Death Due to Overdose of Antidepressants: Experiences from Norway," *Acta Psychiatrica Scandinavia*, suppl. 371 (1993), pp. 28–32.

4. The professional and lay public were unaware that a statement proposing a biological basis for the psychiatric disorders was initially included by Spitzer and his colleagues for DSM-III but then was deleted before the final version was published. From Stuart A. Kirk and Herb Kutchins, *The Selling of DSM: Rhetoric of Science in Psychiatry* (New York: Aldine De Gruyter, 1992).

5. Bernie Zilbergeld, *The Shrinking of America: Myths of Psychological Change* (Boston: Little, Brown and Co., 1983), p. 89.

6. Steven R. Pliszka, James T. McCracken, and James W. Maas, "Catecholamines in Attention-Deficit Hyperactivity Disorder: Current Perspectives," *Journal of the American Academy of Child and Adolescent Psychiatry*, vol. 35 (1996), pp. 264–72.

7. Russell A. Barkley, *ADHD and the Nature of Self-Control* (New York: Guilford Press, 1997), pp. 31–37.

8. Alvin Pam, "Biological Psychiatry: Science or Pseudoscience?" in *Pseudoscience in Biological Psychiatry*, Colin A. Ross and Alvin Pam, eds. (New York: John Wiley, 1995), pp. 7–35.

9. Lars F. Gram, "Fluoxetine," *New England Journal of Medicine*, vol. 331 (1994), pp. 1354–61.

10. "Operating Income Leaps 20% on Potent Sales of Prozac," *Wall Street Journal*, January 28, 1997, p. B4.

11. Peter D. Kramer, *Listening to Prozac* (New York: Viking Penguin, 1993).

12. Barkley, *ADHD*, p. 39 (see note 7).

13. Robert Plomin, personal communication, 1998.

14. Thomas H. Maugh, "Scientists Find Abnormal Gene Associated with Hyperactivity," *San Francisco Chronicle*, May 1, 1996, p. A4.

15. Nathan D. Childs, "Recent Study Fails to Find 'Daredevil' Gene," *Clinical Psychiatry News*, December 1996, p. 6.

16. Susan L. Smalley, "Behavioral Genetics '97—Genetic Influences in Childhood-

Onset Psychiatric Disorders: Autism and Attention-Deficit/Hyperactivity Disorders," *American Journal of Human Genetics*, vol. 60 (1997), pp. 1276–82.

17. Lawrence H. Diller, J. Lane Tanner, and Jon Weil, "Etiology of ADHD: Nature or Nurture?" [letter], *American Journal of Psychiatry*, vol. 153 (1996), p. 451.

18. Alison Pike and Robert Plomin, "Importance of Nonshared Environmental Factors for Childhood and Adolescent Psychopathology," *Journal of the American Academy of Child and Adolescent Psychiatry*, vol. 35 (1996), pp. 560-70.

19. Alan J. Zametkin, Thomas E. Nordahl, et al., "Cerebral Glucose Metabolism in Adults with Hyperactivity of Childhood Onset," *New England Journal of Medicine*, vol. 323 (1990), pp. 1361–66.

20. Alan J. Zametkin, Laura L. Liebenauer, et al., "Brain Metabolism in Teenagers with Attention-Deficit Hyperactivity Disorder," *Archives of General Psychiatry*, vol. 50 (1993), pp. 333–40; Monique Ernst, Laura L. Liebenauer, et al., "Reduced Brain Metabolism in Hyperactive Girls," *Journal of the American Academy of Child and Adolescent Psychiatry*, vol. 33 (1994), pp. 858–68; Monique Ernst, Robert M. Cohen, et al., "Cerebral Glucose Metabolism in Adolescent Girls with Attention-Deficit/Hyperactivity Disorder," *Journal of the Academy of Child and Adolescent Psychiatry*, vol. 36 (1997), pp. 1399–1406.

21. J. A. Matochik, Thomas E. Nordahl, et al., "Effects of Acute Stimulant Medication on Cerebral Metabolism in Adults with Hyperactivity," *Neuropsychopharmacology*, vol. 8 (1993), pp. 377–86; J. A. Matochik, Laura L. Liebenauer, et al., "Cerebral Glucose Metabolism in Adults with Attention Deficit Hyperactivity Disorder After Chronic Stimulant Treatment," *American Journal of Psychiatry*, vol. 151 (1994), pp. 658–64.

22. Daniel G. Amen and Blake D. Carmichael, "High-Resolution Brain SPECT Imaging in ADHD," *Annals of Clinical Psychiatry*, vol. 9 (1997), pp. 81–86.

23. Alan J. Zametkin, personal communication, 1997. Zametkin criticizes the study for its lack of reproducibility. The subjects were not well described and the scans themselves are not subject to quantitative analysis, but rather subjectively interpreted by the radiologist.

24. "Mental Health: Does Therapy Help?" *Consumer Reports*, November 1995, pp. 734–39.

25. Martin E. Seligman, "The Effectiveness of Psychotherapy: The *Consumer Reports* Study," *American Psychologist*, vol. 50 (1995), pp. 965–74.

26. Retterstol, "Death Due to Overdose" (see note 3).

27. Sharon Milberger, Joseph Biederman, et al., "Is Maternal Smoking During Pregnancy a Risk Factor for ADHD in Children?" *American Journal of Psychiatry*, vol. 153 (1996), pp. 1138–42; Eric Mick, Joseph Biederman, and Stephen Faraone, "Is

Season of Birth a Risk Factor for Attention-Deficit Hyperactivity Disorder?" *Journal of the American Academy of Child and Adolescent Psychiatry*, vol. 35 (1996), pp. 1470–76.

28. J. M. Schwartz, P. W. Stoessel, et al., "Systematic Changes in Cerebral Glucose Metabolic Rate After Successful Behavior Modification Treatment of Obsessive-Compulsive Disorder," *Archives of General Psychiatry*, vol. 54 (1996), pp. 109–113.

29. Susan B. Campbell, Elizabeth W. Pierce, Cynthia L. March, et al., "Hard-to-Manage Preschool Boys: Symptomatic Behavior Across Contexts and Time," *Child Development*, vol. 65 (1994), pp. 836–51.

30. Elizabeth A. Carlson, Deborah Jacobvitz, and L. Alan Sroufe, "A Developmental Investigation of Inattentiveness and Hyperactivity," *Child Development*, vol. 66 (1995), pp. 37–54.

31. Bryna Segal, "Decision Tree for Recommending Intensive Behavioral Interventions for Children with Autism and PDD (Revised 10/96)," presented at "Update in Behavioral and Developmental Pediatrics," University of California, San Francisco, February 1997.

32. Richard Perry, Ira Cohen, and Regina DeCarlo, "Case Study: Deterioration, Autism and Recovery in Two Siblings," *Journal of the Academy of Child and Adolescent Psychiatry*, vol. 34 (1995), pp. 232–37.

33. George L. Engel, "The Need for a New Medical Model: A Challenge for Biomedicine," *Science*, vol. 196 (1977), pp. 129–35.

34. Paul Genova, "The Shifting Metaphors of Biological Psychiatry," *Psychiatric Times*, vol. 13, September 1996, p. 24.

35. Alexander Thomas and Stella Chess, *Temperament and Behavior Disorders in Children* (New York: New York University Press, 1968).

36. Stella Chess and Alexander Thomas, *Temperament in Clinical Practice* (New York: Guilford Press, 1986).

37. Michael Rutter, "Temperament: Changing Concepts and Implications," in *Prevention and Early Intervention: Individual Differences as Risk Factors for the Mental Health of Children—A Festschrift for Stella Chess and Alexander Thomas*, William B. Carey and Sean C. McDevitt, eds. (New York: Brunner-Mazel, 1994), pp. 23–34.

38. Charles M. Siper and Sara Harkness, "Temperament and the Developmental Niche," in *Prevention and Early Intervention: Individual Differences as Risk Factors for the Mental Health of Children—A Festschrift for Stella Chess and Alexander Thomas*, William B. Carey and Sean C. McDevitt, eds. (New York: Brunner-Mazel, 1994), p. 116.

39. Michel Maziade, Chantal Caron, et al., "Psychiatric States of Adolescents Who Had Extreme Temperaments at Age 7," *American Journal of Psychiatry*, vol. 147 (1990), pp. 1531–36.

40. Sandra Scarr, "Genetics and Individual Differences: How Chess and Thomas Shaped Developmental Thought," in *Prevention and Early Intervention: Individual Differences as Risk Factors for the Mental Health of Children—A Festschrift for Stella Chess and Alexander Thomas*, William B. Carey and Sean C. McDevitt, eds. (New York: Brunner-Mazel, 1994), p. 172.

Chapter 6: Welcome to Ritalin Nation

1. Edward M. Hallowell, "What I've Learned from ADD," *Psychology Today*, May/June 1997, pp. 40–44.

2. Ibid.

3. Thom Hartmann, *Attention Deficit Disorder: A Different Perception* (Grass Valley, CA: Underwood Books, 1993).

4. John Ratey and Catherine Johnson, "Out of the Shadows," *Psychology Today*, May/June 1997, pp. 47–50.

5. Ibid.

6. Hallowell, "What I've Learned" (see note 1).

7. "CHADD Fact 1: The Disability of ADD—An Overview of Attention Deficit Disorders," CHADD, Plantation, FL, 1993.

8. Letter from Peter S. Jensen to Michael F. Parry, December 20, 1996.

9. "ADD and the Media: An Ongoing Battle for Responsible Coverage," *Chadder Box*, July/August 1997, p. 4.

10. *ADD: A Dubious Diagnosis* [videotape documentary], aired October 20, 1995, The Merrow Report, New York, NY.

11. "Phonies, Slackers, Frauds . . . ," CHADD fund-raising letter, September 2, 1997.

12. Hartmann, *Attention Deficit Disorder*, p. 124 (see note 3).

13. George Johnson, "Image Problem—Old View of the Internet: Nerds. New View: Nuts," *New York Times*, "Week in Review," March 30, 1997, p. 1.

14. Risa Beth Burns, " Medicine and the Media," *Hospital Practice*, vol. 29 (1994), pp. 91–92.

15. Alan Zametkin, personal communication, December 1996.

16. Daniel J. Safer and John M. Krager, "Effect of a Media Blitz and a Threatened

Lawsuit on Stimulant Treatment," *Journal of the American Medical Association*, vol. 268 (1992), pp. 1004–7.

17. Susan Schenk, "Is the Treatment with Psychostimulants a Risk Factor for Substance Abuse?" *Conference Report: Stimulant Use in the Treatment of ADHD*, Drug Enforcement Administration, Department of Justice, Washington, DC, 1996.

18. "Vital Signs: Spending on Consumer Advertising of R$_x$ Products" [graphic], *Clinical Psychiatry News*, May 1997, p. 1.

19. For this section on alternative causes of and treatments for ADD, I used the excellent review by Barbara D. Ingersoll and Sam Goldstein, *Attention Deficit Disorder and Learning Disabilities: Realities, Myths and Controversies* (New York: Doubleday, 1993).

20. Benjamin Feingold, *Why Your Child Is Hyperactive* (New York: Random House, 1975).

21. Esther H. Wender, "The Food Additive–Free Diet in the Treatment of Behavior Disorders: A Review," *Journal of Developmental and Behavioral Pediatrics*, vol. 7 (1986), pp. 35–42.

22. Mark L. Wolraich, Scott D. Lindgren, et al., "Effects of Diets High in Sucrose or Aspartame on the Behavior and Cognitive Performance of Children," *New England Journal of Medicine*, vol. 330 (1994), pp. 301–7.

23. Laurence Jerome, Michael Gordon, and Paul Hustler, "A Comparison of American and Canadian Teachers' Knowledge and Attitudes Towards Attention Deficit Hyperactivity Disorder (ADHD)," *Canadian Journal of Psychiatry*, vol. 39 (1994), pp. 563–67.

24. James M. Swanson and Marcel Kinsbourne, "Food Dyes Impair Performance of Hyperactive Children in a Laboratory Test," *Science*, vol. 207 (1980), pp. 1485–86.

25. James M. Swanson at "Changing Who We Are: Ritalin and the American Family," a panel discussion for the Stanford Health Library, March 1997, Palo Alto, CA.

26. Katherine S. Rowe and Kenneth J. Rowe, "Synthetic Food Coloring and Behavior: A Dose Response Effect in a Double-Blind, Placebo Controlled, Repeated-Measures Study," *Journal of Pediatrics*, vol. 125 (1994), pp. 691–98.

27. National Institutes of Health, "Defined Diets and Childhood Hyperactivity: Consensus Conference," *Journal of the American Medical Association*, vol. 248 (1982), pp. 290–92.

28. Daniel W. Hoover and Richard Milich, "Effects of Sugar Ingestion Expectancies on Mother-Child Interactions," *Journal of Abnormal Child Psychology*, vol. 22 (1994), pp. 510–15.

29. "CHADD Facts 6: Controversial Treatments for Children with ADD," CHADD, Plantation, FL, 1995.

Chapter 7: Making Accommodations

1. James M. Swanson, Marc Lerner, and Lillie Williams, "More Frequent Diagnosis of Attention Deficit Hyperactivity Disorder" [letter], *New England Journal of Medicine*, vol. 333 (1996), p. 994. Dr. Swanson subsequently confirmed this opinion directly to me.

2. Charles J. Sykes, *A Nation of Victims: The Decay of the American Character* (New York: St. Martin's Press, 1992), p. 12.

3. Ibid., p. 1.

4. Robert Reid and Antonis Katsiyannis, "Attention-Deficit/Hyperactivity Disorder and Section 504," *Remedial and Special Education*, vol. 16 (1995), pp. 44–52.

5. "CHADD Facts 4: Education Rights for Children with ADD," CHADD, Plantation, FL, 1993.

6. Matthew D. Cohen, "Section 504 and IDEA—What's the Difference: Limited vs. Substantial Protections for Children with ADD and Other Disabilities," *Attention!* Summer 1997, pp. 23–27.

7. James M. Swanson, Keith McBurnett, et al., "Stimulant Medications and the Treatment of Children with ADHD," *Advances in Clinical Child Psychology*, vol. 17 (1995), pp. 265–322.

8. Nick Penning, "Definitions of Handicapping Conditions Expands . . . Almost!" *School Administrator*, vol. 47 (1990), pp. 31–32.

9. For example, the use of the Weschler Intelligence Scale for Children—III is not permitted in California for assessment of African-American children following a successful suit in the early 1990s. See Robert Reid, "Assessment of ADHD with Culturally Different Groups: The Use of Behavioral Rating Scales," *School Psychology Review*, vol. 24 (1995), pp. 537–60.

10. Telephone interview with Phyllis McClure, March 1997.

11. Swanson, McBurnett, et al., "Stimulant Medications" (see note 7).

12. Memorandum, "Section C: Clarification of Policy to Address the Needs of Children with Attention Deficit Disorders Within General and/or Special Education," Office of Special Education and Rehabilitative Services, Department of Education, Washington, DC, September 1991.

13. "CHADD Facts 4" (see note 5).

14. Peter Applebome, "Push for School Safety Led to Proposed Rules on Discipline for Disabled Students," *New York Times*, May 14, 1997, p. A17.

15. "CHADD Facts 4" (see note 5).

16. Reid and Katsiyannis, "Attention-Deficit" (see note 4).

17. Robert Hanley, "A Test Case for Special Education Rights: Parent of Boy with Learning Disability Is Suing School for Damages," *New York Times*, February 18, 1996, p. 18; Davan Maharaj, "Ruling Renews Debate About Special Education," *Los Angeles Times*, July 23, 1995, p. B1.

18. "CHADD Facts 4" (see note 5).

19. Adam Clymer, "Senate Passes Bill on Teaching the Disabled," *New York Times*, May 15, 1997, p. A16.

20. Carol Brydoff, "Getting Their Attention," *California Schools*, Winter 1996, pp. 24–29.

21. Sam Dillon, "Special Education Absorbs School Resources," *New York Times*, April 7, 1994, p. 1; Jacques Steinberg, "School Budget Study Shows 43% Is Spent in Classrooms," *New York Times*, November 21, 1996, p. B8.

22. Sam Dillon, "Badillo Contends that the Cost of Special Education Is Inflated," *New York Times*, August 14, 1994, p. 1.

23. "Shift in Schools' Spending," *New York Times*, December 12, 1997, p. A15.

24. Sam Dillon, "Comptroller Report Faults Special Education Policy: No Way to Measure Gains for Its Students," *New York Times*, June 27, 1994, p. B3.

25. Michael Winerip, "A Disabilities Program that 'Got Out of Hand,'" *New York Times*, April 8, 1994, p. 1.

26. Helen Beck, learning disabilities specialist, Disabled Students Program, University of California, Berkeley, personal communication, 1994.

27. Tamar Lewin, "College Toughens Its Stance on Learning-Disabilities Aid," *New York Times*, February 13, 1996, p. 1.

28. Ruth Shalit, "Defining Disability Down," *New Republic*, August 25, 1997, pp. 16–22; Mary McDonald Richard, "Students with LD/ADD Win Landmark Court Decision over Boston University," *Attention!* Fall 1997, pp. 36–37.

29. Michael Gordon, Russell A. Barkley, and Kevin K. Murphy, "ADHD on Trial," *ADHD Report*, vol. 5 (August 1997), pp. 1–4; Patricia H. Latham, "ADD and Test Accommodations Under the ADA: Several Court Cases Shed Light on Who Qualifies," *Attention!* Fall 1997, pp. 41–44.

30. Marybeth Kravets, "Key Steps to Selecting a College," *Attention!* Fall 1996, pp. 8–12; Lei Ann Marshall-Cohen, "ADD and the Law: Legal Rights and Accommodations for College Students with ADD," *Attention!* Fall 1996, pp. 42–45.

31. Dyan Machen, "An Agreeable Affliction," *Forbes*, August 12, 1996, pp. 148–51.

32. Ibid.

33. Sykes, *Nation of Victims*, p. 133 (see note 2).

34. Robert Pear, "Employers Told to Accommodate the Mentally Ill," *New York Times*, April 30, 1997, p. 1.

35. Michael J. Grinfeld, "Needs of Mentally Disabled Topic of ADA 'Guidance': Employers Rankled; Fear False Claims and Added Expense," *Psychiatric Times*, June 1997, p. 1; Peter D. Kramer, "The Mentally Ill Deserve Job Protection," *New York Times*, May 6, 1997, p. A19.

36. Todd Zwilich, "Disability Guidelines Worry Some Psychiatrists," *Psychiatric News*, October 1997, p. 5.

37. Gary Eisler, "Attention Deficit Disorder Can't Be Ignored," *Wall Street Journal*, June 27, 1994, p. A12.

38. Mary Sykes-Wylie, "Diagnosing for Dollars," *Family Therapy Networker,* May/June 1995, pp. 23–33.

39. Barbara Strauch, "Use of Anti-Depression Medicine for Young Patients Has Soared," *New York Times*, August 10, 1997, p. 1.

40. Elizabeth Shogren, "Insurance Bill Seeks Parity Coverage for Mentally Ill," *Los Angeles Times*, September 18, 1996, p. A1.

41. Todd Zwilich, "Small Business Exemptions Limit Parity Laws' Scope," *Clinical Psychiatry News*, November 1996, p. 1.

42. Michael Quint, "New Ailments: Bane of Insurers," *New York Times*, November 28, 1994, p. C1.

43. Jeffrey S. Schwann and Michael J. Maloney, "Developing a Psychiatry Study Group for Community Pediatricians," *Journal of the American Academy of Child and Adolescent Psychiatry*, vol. 36 (1997), pp. 706–8.

44. Mark Olfson, Steve C. Marcus, et al., "Antidepressant Prescribing Practices of Outpatient Psychiatrists," *Archives of General Psychiatry*, vol. 55 (1998), pp. 310–16.

45. Jerome P. Kassirer, "Managed Care and the Morality of the Marketplace," *New England Journal of Medicine*, vol. 333 (1995), pp. 50–52.

Chapter 8: The Politically Correct Parenting Trap

1. Julie V. Iovine, "When Parents Decide to Take Charge Again," *New York Times*, November 7, 1996, pp. A17–18.

2. Steve Farkas and Jean Johnson, *Kids These Days: What Americans Really Think About the Next Generation* (New York: Public Agenda, 1997), p. 14.

3. Ibid., p. 15.

4. Anna Freud, *Normality and Pathology in Childhood* (New York: International Universities Press, 1965).

5. Robert Coles, *The Mind's Fate: A Psychiatrist Looks at His Profession—Thirty Years of Writings* (Boston: Little, Brown and Co., 1995), pp. 99–100.

6. Ibid.

7. Ann Hulbert, "Dr. Spock's Baby (How Benjamin Spock's Book 'Baby and Child Care' Has Changed)," *New Yorker,* May 20, 1996, pp. 82–90.

8. Benjamin Spock, *Baby and Child Care: New and Revised Edition* (New York: Hawthorne Books, 1968), p. 328.

9. Spock, *Baby and Child Care,* second edition (New York: Pocket Books, 1957), p. 2.

10. Spock, *Baby and Child Care,* p. 329 (see note 8).

11. Selma Fraiberg, *The Magic Years* (New York: Charles Scribner's Sons, 1959), p. ix.

12. Diana Baumrind, "Effects of Authoritative Parental Control on Child Behavior," *Child Development,* vol. 37 (1966), pp. 887–907.

13. Ibid.

14. Ruth S. Kempe and C. Henry Kempe, *Child Abuse* (Cambridge, MA: Harvard University Press, 1978).

15. Alice Miller, *The Drama of the Gifted Child: The Search for the True Self,* revised edition (New York: Basic Books, 1994).

16. Ibid., pp. 87–89.

17. For years, the only mental health expert advocating spanking was James Dobson, an avowedly Christian child psychologist. His books, beginning with *Dare to Discipline,* have sold millions of copies. James C. Dobson, *Dare to Discipline* (Wheaton, IL: Tyndale House Publishers, 1970).

18. The most recent spate of media interest was generated with a publication by a longtime anti-corporal-punishment advocate, Murray Straus of the University of New Hampshire: Murray A. Straus, David B. Sugarman, and Jean Giles-Sims, "Spanking by Parents and Subsequent Antisocial Behavior of Children," *Archives of Pediatrics and Adolescent Medicine,* vol. 151 (1997), pp. 761–67. By the variety and intensity of the reactions elicited, the article did little to settle the argument.

19. Stanley Turecki, *The Difficult Child,* revised edition (New York: Bantam Books, 1989).

20. Diana Baumrind, "The Discipline Controversy Revisited," *Family Relations,* vol. 45 (1996), pp. 405-14.

21. Benjamin Spock, *Baby and Child Care,* p. 336 (see note 8).

22. Ibid., p. 338.

23. Fraiberg, *Magic Years,* p. 20 (see note 11).

24. Ibid., p. 251.

25. "Short- and Long-Term Consequences of Corporal Punishment," Stanford B. Friedman and S. Kenneth Schonberg, eds., *Pediatrics*, vol. 98, suppl. (1996), pp. 801–60.

26. Robert Larzelere, "A Review of the Outcomes of Parental Use of Nonabusive or Customary Physical Punishment," *Pediatrics*, vol. 98, suppl. (1996), pp. 824–28.

27. Stanford B. Friedman and S. Kenneth Schonberg, "Personal Statements," *Pediatrics*, vol. 98, suppl. (1996), pp. 857–58.

28. In 1998, the AAP, which sponsored the 1996 meeting on corporal punishment, seemingly ignored the conference's findings. Its "Guidelines for Effective Discipline" (*Pediatrics*, vol. 101, pp. 723–28) come across squarely against the use of corporal punishment in children. The controversy continues.

29. Jeffrey G. Parker and Steven R. Asher, "Peer Relations and Later Personal Adjustment: Are Low-Accepted Children at Risk?" *Psychological Bulletin*, vol. 102 (1987), pp. 357–89.

30. Stephen P. Hinshaw and Sharon M. Melnick, "Peer Relationships in Boys with Attention-Deficit Hyperactivity Disorder with and Without Co-Morbid Aggression," *Development and Psychopathology*, vol. 7 (1995), pp. 627–47.

31. Stephen P. Hinshaw, Brian A. Zupan, et al., "Peer Status in Boys with and Without Attention-Deficit Hyperactivity Disorder: Predictions from Overt and Covert Antisocial Behavior, Social Isolation, and Authoritative Parenting Beliefs," *Child Development* (in press).

32. Jonathan F. Mattanah and Stephen P. Hinshaw, "Parental Predictors of Overt and Covert Anti-Social Behavior in ADHD and Comparison Boys," manuscript submitted for publication.

33. Russell A. Barkley, "Parents as Shepherds, Not Engineers," *ADHD Report*, December 1997, pp. 1–4.

Chapter 9: Evaluating for ADD

1. Robert Reid, "The Three Faces of Attention-Deficit Hyperactivity Disorder," *Journal of Child and Family Studies*, vol. 5 (1996), pp. 249–65.

2. American Academy of Child and Adolescent Psychiatry, "Practice Parameters for the Assessment and Treatment of Children, Adolescents, and Adults with Attention-Deficit/Hyperactivity Disorder," *Journal of the American Academy of Child and Adolescent Psychiatry*, vol. 36, suppl. (1997), pp. 85S–121S. For the purposes of research and of managed care, great effort has been made to validate the basing of a diagnosis on a single questionnaire or interview. The savings of time, energy, and money would be great if such a shorthand method could be proved valid. The usual proof hinges on an exercise involving a statistically significant number of children,

wherein the results of a very brief parent interview are compared with a so-called gold standard—the results of a full evaluation of the same group of children, requiring interviews with parents and child and the concurrence of two child psychiatrists. Statistically, the shorter method proved in this way is supposed to be valid, but the more frequently such shortcuts are used beyond the initial study group, the weaker becomes the statistical link with the gold standard. And that standard itself is not objective; it's established by the opinions of psychiatrists.

3. C. Keith Conners, *Conners Parents Rating Scale—Revised* and *Conners Teachers Rating Scale—Revised* (North Towanda, NY: Multi-Health Systems, Inc., 1989); Thomas M. Aschenbach and Craig S. Edelbrock, *Child Behavior Check List* (Burlington, VT: University Associates in Psychiatry, 1983).

4. Robert Reid and John W. Maag, "How Many Fidgets in a Pretty Much: A Critique of Behavior Rating Scales for Identifying Students with ADHD," *Journal of School Psychology*, vol. 32 (1994), pp. 339–54; Thomas Armstrong, "ADD: Does It Really Exist?" *Phi Delta Kappan*, February 1996, pp. 424–28; Regina Bussing, Elena Schuhmann, et al., "Diagnostic Utility of Two Commonly Used ADHD Screening Measures Among Special Education Students," *Journal of the American Academy of Child and Adolescent Psychiatry*, vol. 37 (1998), pp. 74–82.

5. Robert Reid, Stanley F. Vasa, et al., "An Analysis of Teachers' Perceptions of Attention-Deficit Hyperactivity Disorder," *Journal of Research and Development in Education*, vol. 27 (1994), pp. 195–202.

6. Dianne K. Sherman, William G. Iacono, and Matthew K. McGue, "Attention-Deficit Hyperactivity Disorder Dimensions: A Twin Study of Inattention and Impulse-Hyperactivity," *Journal of the American Academy of Child and Adolescent Psychiatry*, vol. 36 (1997), pp. 745–53.

7. Howard D. Chilcoat and Naomi Breslau, "Does Psychiatric History Bias Mothers' Reports? An Application of a New Analytic Method," *Journal of the American Academy of Child and Adolescent Psychiatry*, vol. 36 (1997), pp. 971–79.

8. Joseph Biederman, Sharon Milberger, et al., "Impact of Adversity on Functioning and Comorbidity in Children with Attention-Deficit Hyperactivity Disorder," *Journal of the American Academy of Child and Adolescent Psychiatry*, vol. 34 (1995), pp. 1495–1503.

9. Mark L. Wolraich, Jane N. Hannah, et al., "Comparison of Diagnostic Criteria for Attention-Deficit Hyperactivity Disorder in a County-Wide Sample," *Journal of the American Academy of Child and Adolescent Psychiatry*, vol. 35 (1996), pp. 319–24.

10. Robert Reid, "Assessment of ADHD with Culturally Different Groups: The Use of Behavior Rating Scales," *School Psychology Review*, vol. 24 (1995), pp. 537–60.

11. Robert Reid, George J. DuPaul, et al., "Assessing Culturally Different Students for Attention-Deficit Hyperactivity Disorder Using Behavior Rating Scales" (in press).

12. Joseph Biederman, Stephen V. Faraone, et al., "High Risk for Attention-Deficit Hyperactivity Disorder Among Children of Parents with Childhood Onset of the Disorder: A Pilot Study," *American Journal of Psychiatry*, vol. 152 (1995), pp. 431–35.

13. *Wechsler Intelligence Scale for Children*, third edition, Bruce A. Bracken, ed. (Cordova, TN: Psychoeducational Corp., 1993).

14. Melvin D. Levine, *Pediatric Examination of Educational Readiness at Middle Childhood* (Cambridge, MA: Educators Publishing Service, 1985).

15. Russell A. Barkley, *Attention-Deficit Hyperactivity Disorder: A Handbook for Diagnosis and Treatment* (New York: Guilford Press, 1990), pp. 328–29.

16. Janet A. Camp, Irv Bialer, et al., "Clinical Usefulness of the NIMH Physical and Neurological Examination for Soft Signs," *American Journal of Psychiatry*, vol. 135 (1978), pp. 362–63.

17. Michael I. Reiff, Martin T. Stein, and Mark L. Wolraich, "Working Forum on ADHD," presented at the Society for Developmental and Behavioral Pediatrics Annual Meeting, September 1996, San Francisco.

Chapter 10: Addressing the Imbalance

1. Lily Hechtman, "Attention-Deficit/Hyperactivity Disorder," in *Do They Grow Out of It? Long-Term Outcomes of Childhood Disorders*, Lily Hechtman, ed. (Washington, DC: American Psychiatric Press, 1996), pp. 17–38.

2. James H. Satterfield, Breena T. Satterfield, and Anne M. Schell, "Therapeutic Interventions to Prevent Delinquency in Hyperactive Boys," *Journal of the American Academy of Child and Adolescent Psychiatry*, vol. 26 (1987), pp. 56–64.

3. John E. Richters, L. Eugene Arnold, et al., "NIMH Collaborative Multisite Multimodal Treatment Study of Children with ADHD: I, Background and Rationale," *Journal of the American Academy of Child and Adolescent Psychiatry*, vol. 34 (1995), pp. 987–1000.

4. Carol K. Whalen and Barbara Hencker, "Therapies for Hyperactive Children: Comparisons, Combinations, and Compromises," *Journal of Consulting and Clinical Psychology*, vol. 59 (1991), pp. 126–37.

5. Thomas Armstrong, *The Myth of the A.D.D. Child: 50 Ways to Improve Your Child's Behavior and Attention Span Without Drugs, Labels, or Coercion* (New York: Dutton, 1995); Mary Ann Block, *No More Ritalin: Treating ADHD Without Drugs* (Clifton, NJ: Kensington Publishing Co., 1996).

6. Edward M. Hallowell and John J. Ratey, *Driven to Distraction: Recognizing and Coping with Attention Deficit Disorder from Childhood Through Adulthood* (New York: Pantheon Books, 1994).

7. Russell A. Barkley, "Special Report: Attention-Deficit Hyperactivity Disorder," *Psychiatric Times*, vol. 13 (July 1996), pp. 38–41.

8. Personal communications in 1996 from Jim Swanson and Steve Hinshaw, both principal investigators in the NIMH MTA Study.

9. Russell A. Barkley, "Parents as Shepherds, Not Engineers," *ADHD Report*, vol. 5 (December 1997), pp. 1–4.

10. Russell A. Barkley, *Attention-Deficit Hyperactivity Disorder: A Handbook for Diagnosis and Treatment* (New York: Guilford Press, 1990).

11. Russell A. Barkley, *ADHD and the Nature of Self-Control* (New York: Guilford Press), p. 337.

12. John S. March, Karen Mulle, and Byron Herbell, "Behavioral Psychotherapy for Children and Adolescents with Obsessive-Compulsive Disorder: An Open Trial of a New Protocol-Driven Treatment Package," *Journal of the American Academy of Child and Adolescent Psychiatry*, vol. 33 (1994), pp. 333-41.

13. Stephen P. Hinshaw, Barbara Hencker, and Carol K. Whalen, "Self-Control in Hyperactive Boys in Anger-Inducing Situations: Effects of Cognitive-Behavioral Training and of Methylphenidate," *Journal of Abnormal Child Psychology*, vol. 12 (1984), pp. 55-77; Philip C. Kendall, "Cognitive-Behavioral Therapies with Youth: Guiding Theory, Current Status and Emerging Developments," *Journal of Consulting and Clinical Psychology*, vol. 61 (1993), pp. 235–47.

14. William E. Pelham, E. Gnagy, et al., "A Summer Treatment Program for Children with ADHD," in *Model Programs in Child and Family Mental Health*, M. Roberts, ed., (Mahwah, NJ: Lawrence Erlbaum, 1996). (This summer program has been adopted as the child-based treatment component for the MTA multisite study of ADD.)

15. Barbara D. Ingersoll and Sam Goldstein, *Attention Deficit Disorder and Learning Disabilities: Realities, Myths and Controversial Treatments* (New York: Doubleday, 1993), pp. 176–79.

16. Stephen W. Garber, Marianne Daniels Garber, and Robyn Freedman Spizman, *Beyond Ritalin* (New York: Villard Books, 1996).

17. Ronald A. Kotkin, "The Irvine Paraprofessional Program: Using Paraprofessionals in Serving Students with ADHD," *Interventions in School and Clinic*, vol. 30 (1995), pp. 235–40.

18. Ibid.

Chapter 11: The Medication Option

1. James M. Swanson, Keith McBurnett, et al., "Stimulant Medications and the Treatment of Children with ADHD," *Advances in Clinical Child Psychology*, vol. 17 (1995), p. 271.

2. H. A. Weinberg, "Generic Bioequivalence" [letter], *Journal of the American Academy of Child and Adolescent Psychiatry*, vol. 34 (1995), pp. 834–35.

3. Mark D. Rapport and Colin Denney, "Titrating Methylphenidate in Children with Attention-Deficit/Hyperactivity Disorder: Is Body Mass Predictive of Clinical Response?" *Journal of the American Academy of Child and Adolescent Psychiatry*, vol. 36 (1997), pp. 523–30.

4. Sheldon Kesler, "Drug Therapy in Attention-Deficit Hyperactivity Disorder," *Southern Medical Journal*, vol. 89 (1996), pp. 33–38.

5. Ronald Files, narcotics detective , Alexandria, VA, at "Stimulant Use in the Treatment of ADHD," Drug Enforcement Administration Conference, San Antonio, TX, December 1996.

6. Reports from several narcotics officers; see note 5.

7. Martin A. Stein, T. A. Blondis, et al., "Methylphenidate Dosing: Twice Daily versus Three Times Daily," *Pediatrics*, vol. 98 (1996), pp. 748–56.

8. James M. Swanson, at "Changing Who We Are: Prozac, Ritalin and the American Family," a panel discussion at the Stanford Health Library, Stanford University, March 1997, Palo Alto, CA.

9. Swanson, McBurnett, et al., "Stimulant Medications" (see note 1).

10. Stuart Fine and Charlotte Johnston, "Drug and Placebo Side Effects in Methylphenidate-Placebo Trials for Attention-Deficit Hyperactivity Disorder," *Child Psychiatry and Human Development*, vol. 2 (1993), pp. 25–30.

11. Swanson, McBurnett, et al., "Stimulant Medications" (see note 1).

12. Ester K. Sleator, Rina K. Ullmann, and Alice von Neumann, "How Do Hyperactive Children Feel About Taking Stimulants and Will They Tell the Doctor?" *Clinical Pediatrics*, vol. 21 (1982), pp. 474-79.

13. Jennifer Bowen, Terence Fenton, and Leonard Rappaport, "Stimulant Medication and Attention-Deficit Hyperactivity Disorder: The Child's Perspective," *American Journal of Diseases in Children*, vol. 145 (1991), pp. 291–95.

14. B. Hoza, William Pelham, et al., "The Self-Perceptions and Attributions of Attention Deficit Hyperactivity Disorder and Non-Referred Boys," *Journal of Abnormal Child Psychology*, vol. 21 (1993), pp. 271–86; William Pelham, D. A. Murphy, et al., "Methylphenidate and Attribution in Boys with Attention-Deficit Hyperactivity Disorder," *Journal of Consulting and Clinical Psychology*, vol. 60 (1992), pp. 282–92.

15. Richard Milich, Barbara Licht, et al., "Attention-Deficit Hyperactivity Disordered Boys' Evaluations of and Attributions for Task Performance on Medication versus Placebo," *Journal of Abnormal Psychology*, vol. 98 (1989), pp. 280–84; Carol Whalen, Barbara Hencker, et al., "Messages of Medication: Effects of Actual versus Informed Medication Status on Hyperactive Boys' Expectations and Self-Evaluations," *Journal of Consulting and Clinical Psychology*, vol. 59 (1991), pp. 602–6.

16. Thomas J. Spencer, Joseph Biederman, et al., "Growth Deficits in ADHD Children Revisited: Evidence for Disorder-Associated Growth Delays?" *Journal of the American Academy of Child and Adolescent Psychiatry*, vol. 35 (1996), pp. 1460–69.

17. Charlotte Johnston, William Pelham, et al., "Psychostimulant Rebound in Attention Deficit Disordered Boys," *Journal of the American Academy of Child and Adolescent Psychiatry*, vol. 27 (1998), pp. 806–10.

18. Kenneth D. Gadow and Jeffrey Sverd, "Stimulants for ADHD in Child Patients with Tourette's Syndrome: The Issue of Relative Risk," *Journal of Developmental and Behavioral Pediatrics*, vol. 11 (1990), pp. 269–71; Kenneth D. Gadow, Edith Nolan, et al., "School Observations of Children with Attention-Deficit Hyperactivity Disorder and Comorbid Tic Disorder: Effects of Methylphenidate Treatment," *Journal of Developmental and Behavioral Pediatrics*, vol. 16 (1995), pp. 167–76.

19. Richard Corrigall and Tamsin Ford, "Methylphenidate Euphoria," *Journal of the American Academy of Child and Adolescent Psychiatry*, vol. 35 (1996), p. 1421.

20. "Study of Ritalin's Cancer Causing Potential," *FDA Consumer*, vol. 30 (1996), p. 3. Experts have reassured me that the kind of rat study used in this case reflects an older screening protocol for possible links between a drug and cancer, a protocol that is now being phased out.

21. "Adderall and Other Drugs for Attention Deficit Hyperactivity Disorder," *Medical Letter*, vol. 36 (1994), pp. 109–10.

22. Gene Haislip, deputy assistant administrator, DEA, Office of Diversion Control, "Readin, Ritin, and Ritalin," presented at "Stimulant Use in the Treatment of ADHD," Drug Enforcement Administration Conference, San Antonio, TX, December 1996.

23. Swanson, McBurnett, et al., "Stimulant Medications" (see note 1).

24. Thomas Spencer, Joseph Biederman, et al., "Pharmacotherapy of Attention-Deficit Hyperactivity Disorder Across the Life Cycle," *Journal of the American of Child and Adolescent Psychiatry*, vol. 35 (1996), pp. 409–32.

25. Leonard H. Glantz, "Conducting Research with Children: Legal and Ethical Issues," *Journal of the American Academy of Child and Adolescent Psychiatry*, vol. 34 (1996), pp. 1283–91.

26. Elyse Tanouye, "Antidepressant Makers Study Kids' Market," *Wall Street Journal*, April 4, 1997, p. B1.

27. Richard A. Devo, Bruce M. Psaty, et al., "The Messenger Under Attack—Intimidation of Researchers by Special Interest Groups," *New England Journal of Medicine*, vol. 336 (1997), pp. 1176–80.

28. Lawrence K. Altman, "Drug Firm, Relenting, Allows Unflattering Study to Appear," *New York Times*, April 16, 1997, p. 1.

29. Robert Pear, "Proposal to Test Drugs in Children Meets Resistance," *New York Times*, December 2, 1997, p. A14.

30. William E. Pelham, James M. Swanson, et al., "Pemoline Effects on Children with ADHD: A Time-Response by Dose-Response Analysis on Classroom Measures," *Journal of the American Academy of Child and Adolescent Psychiatry*, vol. 34 (1996), pp. 1504–13.

31. Ibid.

32. David Pizzuti, divisional vice president, Medical Affairs and Pharmaceutical Ventures, Abbott Laboratories, December 1996.

33. Timothy E. Wilens, Joseph Biederman, and Thomas J. Spencer, "Case Study: Adverse Effects of Smoking Marijuana While Receiving Tricyclic Antidepressants," *Journal of the American Academy of Child and Adolescent Psychiatry*, vol. 36 (1997), pp. 45–48.

34. Joseph Biederman, D. R. Gastfriend, and Michael S. Jellinek, "Desipramine in the Treatment of Children with Attention Deficit Disorder," *Journal of Clinical Psychopharmacology*, vol. 6 (1986), pp. 359–63.

35. Timothy Wilens, personal communication, December 1996.

36. Mark A. Riddle, Barbara Geller, and Neal Ryan, "Another Sudden Death in a Child Treated with Desipramine," *Journal of the American Academy of Child and Adolescent Psychiatry*, vol. 32 (1993), pp. 792–97.

37. "Resolved: Cardiac Arrhythmias Make Desipramine an Unacceptable Choice in Children," Affirmative: John S. Werry; Negative: Joseph Biederman, Ronald Thisted, et al., *Journal of the American Academy of Child and Adolescent Psychiatry*, vol. 34 (1995), pp. 1239–48.

38. Ibid.

39. Timothy Wilens, Joseph Biederman, et al., "Cardiovascular Effects of Therapeutic Doses of Tricyclic Antidepressants in Children and Adolescents," *Journal of the Academy of Child and Adolescent Psychiatry*, vol. 35 (1996), pp. 1491–1502.

40. Joseph Biederman, Ronald Thisted, et al., "Estimation of the Association Between Desipramine and the Risk for Sudden Death in 5- to 14-Year-Old Children," *Journal of Clinical Psychiatry*, vol. 56 (1995), pp. 87–93.

41. Wilens, Biederman, et al., "Cardiovascular Effects" (see note 39).

42. Barbara Geller, "Clinical Comment: Commentary on Unexplained Deaths of Children on Norpramin," *Journal of the American Academy of Child and Adolescent Psychiatry*, vol. 30 (1991), pp. 682–83.

43. Christopher K. Varley and Jon McClellan, "Case Study: Two Additional Sudden Deaths with Tricyclic Antidepressants," *Journal of the American Academy of Child and Adolescent Psychiatry*, vol. 36 (1997), pp. 390–94.

44. Spencer, Biederman, et al., "Pharmacotherapy" (see note 24).

45. R. D. Hunt, A. F. Arnsten, and M. D. Asbell, "An Open Trial of Guanfacine in the Treatment of Attention-Deficit Hyperactivity Disorder," *Journal of the Academy of Child and Adolescent Psychiatry*, vol. 34 (1995), pp. 50–54.

46. Dennis P. Cantwell, James Swanson, and Daniel F. Connor, "Case Study: Adverse Response to Clonidine," *Journal of the American Academy of Child and Adolescent Psychiatry*, vol. 36 (1997), pp. 539–44; "Clonidine for Treatment of Attention-Deficit/Hyperactivity Disorder," *Medical Letter*, vol. 38 (1996), pp. 109–10.

47. Michael J. Maloney and Jeffrey S. Schwam, "Clonidine and Sudden Death" [letter], *Pediatrics*, vol. 96 (1995), pp. 1176–77.

48. C. Keith Conners, Charles D. Casat, et al., "Bupropion Hydrochloride in Attention Deficit Disorder with Hyperactivity," *Journal of the American Academy of Child and Adolescent Psychiatry*, vol. 34 (1996), pp. 1314–21.

49. Joseph Biederman, Stephen Faraone, et al., "Attention-Deficit Hyperactivity Disorder and Juvenile Mania: An Overlooked Comorbidity," *Journal of the Academy of Child and Adolescent Psychiatry*, vol. 35 (1996), pp. 997–1008.

50. Gilles Pelletier, Guy Geoffrey, and Philippe Robaey, "Mania in Children" [letter], *Journal of the American Academy of Child and Adolescent Psychiatry*, vol. 35 (1996), pp. 1257-58; Sheryl M. Schneider, Donald Atkinson, and Rif El-Mallakh, "CD and ADHD in Bipolar Disorder" [letter], *Journal of the American Academy of Child and Adolescent Psychiatry*, vol. 35 (1996), pp. 1422–23.

51. Timothy E. Wilens, Thomas Spencer, et al., "Combined Pharmacotherapy: An Emerging Trend in Pediatric Psychopharmacology," *Journal of the American Academy of Child and Adolescent Psychiatry*, vol. 34 (1995), pp. 110–12.

52. Ibid.

53. Timothy Wilens, Joseph Biederman, et al., "Nortriptyline in the Treatment of ADHD: A Chart Review of 58 Cases," *Journal of the American Academy of Child and Adolescent Psychiatry*, vol. 32 (1993), pp. 343–49.

54. James M. Swanson, "Discussion," in *Learning Disabilities: Proceedings of the National Conference*, James F. Kavanagh and Tom J. Truss, eds. (Parkton, MD: York Press, 1988), p. 524.

55. Herman M. van Praag, Dean X. Parmalee, Barbara Geller, and Robert Coles, among others.

56. Werry, "Resolved" (see note 37).

Chapter 12: Ritalin Beyond Childhood

1. Lily Hechtman, "Attention-Deficit/Hyperactivity Disorder," in *Do They Grow Out of It? Long-Term Outcomes of Childhood Disorders*, Lily Hechtman, ed. (Washington, DC: American Psychiatric Press, 1996), pp. 17–38.

2. Ibid.

3. Esther W. Wender, "Attention-Deficit Hyperactivity Disorders in Adolescence," *Journal of Developmental and Behavioral Pediatrics*, vol. 16 (1995), pp. 192–95; *A Comprehensive Guide to Attention Deficit Disorder in Adults: Research, Diagnosis and Treatment*, Kathleen G. Nadeau, ed. (New York: Brunner-Mazel, 1995).

4. John C. Hill and Eugene P. Schoener, "Age-Dependent Decline of Attention Deficit Hyperactivity Disorder," *American Journal of Psychiatry*, vol. 153 (1996), pp. 1143–46.

5. Salvatore Mannuzza, Rachel G. Klein, et al., "Educational and Occupational Outcome of Hyperactive Boys Grown Up," *Journal of the American Academy of Child and Adolescent Psychiatry*, vol. 36 (1997), pp. 1222–27.

6. Gabrielle A. Carlson, "Compared to Attention Deficit Disorder . . . ," *American Journal of Psychiatry*, vol. 153 (1996), pp. 1128–30.

7. Kevin Murphy and Russell A. Barkley, "Attention Deficit Hyperactivity Disorder Adults; Comorbidities and Adaptive Impairments," *Comprehensive Psychiatry*, vol. 37 (1996), pp. 393–401; Peggy Peck, "Some Adults Seem to Prefer an ADHD Diagnosis," *Clinical Psychiatry News*, October 1997, p. 16.

8. Edward M. Hallowell and John J. Ratey, *Driven to Distraction: Recognizing and Coping with Attention Deficit Disorder from Childhood Through Adulthood* (New York: Pantheon Books, 1994), pp. 245–54.

9. Robert D. Wells, David M. Snyder, and Barbara Dahl, "Compensatory Techniques Used by Successful and Unsuccessful Adults with Attention Deficit Disorder," presented at the Society for Developmental and Behavioral Pediatrics Annual Meeting, September 1996, San Francisco, California.

10. Kathleen G. Nadeau, *ADD in the Workplace: Choices, Changes and Challenges* (Bristol, PA: Brunner-Mazel, 1997).

11. Ilana DeBare, "Good Pay Without a B.A.," *San Francisco Chronicle*, March 3, 1997, p. D1.

12. Mannuzza, Klein, et al., "Educational and Occupational Outcome" (see note 5).

13. Wells, Snyder, and Dahl, "Compensatory Techniques" (see note 9).

Chapter 13: Performance in a Pill

1. *Enhancing Human Traits: Conceptual Complexities and Ethical Implications*, Erik Parens, ed. (Washington, DC: Georgetown University, in press).

2. Peter Whitehouse, Eric Juengst, et al., "Enhancing Cognition in the Intellectually Intact," *The Hastings Center Report*, vol. 27 (May/June 1997), pp. 14–22.

3. Eric Juengst, "The Meanings of 'Enhancement' for Biomedicine," *Enhancing Human Traits* (see note 1).

4. Robert Reid and John W. Maag, "How Many Fidgets in a Pretty Much: A Critique of Behavior Rating Scales for Identifying Students with ADHD," *Journal of School Psychology*, vol. 32 (1994), pp. 339–54.

5. James M. Swanson, Keith McBurnett, et al., "Effect of Stimulant Medication on Children with Attention Deficit Disorder: A 'Review of Reviews,'" *Exceptional Children*, vol. 60 (1993), pp. 154–61.

6. James M. Swanson, Keith McBurnett, et al., "Stimulant Medications and the Treatment of Children with ADHD," *Advances in Clinical Child Psychology*, vol. 17 (1995), pp. 265–322.

7. James M. Swanson at "Changing Who We Are: Prozac, Ritalin and the American Family," a panel discussion for the Health Science Library, Stanford University, March 13, 1997.

8. Lee M. Pachter and Robin L. Harwood. "Culture and Child Behavior and Psychosocial Development," *Journal of Developmental and Behavioral Pediatrics*, vol. 17 (1996), pp. 191–98.

9. Dorothy Bonn, "Methylphenidate: U.S. and European Views Converging?" *Lancet*, vol. 348 (1996), p. 255.

10. Sir Michael Rutter [letter], where December 31, 1996.

11. David J. Bramble, "Antidepressant Prescription by British Child Psychiatrists: Practice and Safety Issues," *Journal of the American Academy of Child and Adolescent Psychiatry*, vol. 34 (1995), pp. 327–31.

12. Dorothea M. Ross and Sheila A. Ross, *Hyperactivity: Current Issues, Research and Theory*, second edition (New York: John Wiley and Sons, 1982).

13. Gene Haislip, deputy assistant administrator, Drug Enforcement Administration, Office of Diversion Control, personal communication, 1996.

14. Dan Brock, "Enhancements of Human Function: Some Distinctions for Policy Makers" in *Enhancing Human Traits* (see note 1).

15. The rejoinder to the concept of a universal "good" asks why should one capacity or feeling be exalted over another. Increased focus may sound good but

what if it comes at the expense of leisure time or relaxation, loving someone or feeling sensitive? Will enhanced focusing ability be "good" in all situations for everyone?

16. David Beyda, "Informed Pediatric Consent," presented at Stimulant Use in the Treatment of ADHD, Drug Enforcement Administration Conference, San Antonio, TX, December 1996.

17. Gabrielle Weiss and Lily Trokenberg Hechtman, *Hyperactive Children Grown Up*, second edition (New York: Guilford Press, 1993), pp. 293–300.

18. Fred Gardner, personal communication, 1997.

19. Detective Ronald Files of the Arlington County Police Department in Virginia at the DEA-sponsored conference "Stimulant Use in the Treatment of ADHD," December 1996, was quite emphatic that he had received reliable information that at some of the elementary schools in his district such a policy was in place in certain classrooms.

20. Joseph Biederman on the *NBC Nightly News*, May 1996.

21. Russell Barkley, *Attention-Deficit Hyperactivity Disorder: A Handbook for Diagnosis and Treatment* (New York: Guilford Press, 1990), p. 45.

22. Russell A Barkley, *ADHD and the Nature of Self-Control* (New York: Guilford Press, 1997).

23. Ibid., pp. 315–16.

24. Peter Kramer, *Listening to Prozac* (New York: Viking, 1993), p. xvi.

25. Peter S. Latham and Patricia H. Latham, "For Adults with ADD: Documenting ADD for College Accommodations," *Attention!* Fall 1996, pp. 48–52.

26. Paul G. Dyment, "Hyperactivity, Stimulants and Sports," *Physician and Sportsmedicine*, vol. 18 (1990), p. 22.

27. Frank Uryasz, director of sports science, National Collegiate Athletic Association, personal communication, 1997.

28. Billie Marseilles, pharmacist, United States Olympic Committee, personal communication, 1997.

29. Gerald L. Klerman, "Psychotropic Hedonism versus Pharmacological Calvinism," *The Hastings Center Report*, vol. 2 (1972), pp. 1–3.

30. Sandra Blakeslee, "Some Biologists Ask: Are Genes Everything?" *New York Times*, September 2, 1997, p. B7.

31. "Swedish Scandal: Revelations that Sweden Coerced Welfare Recipients into Racially-Motivated Sterilizations from 1935 to 1976," editorial, *New York Times*, August 30, 1997, p. A18.

32. Charles C. Mann. "Behavioral Genetics in Transition," *Science*, vol. 264 (1994), pp. 1686–89.

33. Ruth Hubbard and R.C. Lewontin, "Sounding Board: Pitfalls of Genetic Testing," *New England Journal of Medicine*, vol. 334 (1996), pp. 1192–93.

34. Patricia Latham, Goldstein, et al., "The Criminal Justice System and Individuals with Attention Deficit Disorder and Learning Disabilities," *National Center for Law and Learning Disabilities Publication* (Cabin John, MD, 1995).

35. Heather A. Foley, Christopher O. Carlton, and Robert J. Howell, "The Relationship of Attention Deficit Hyperactivity Disorder and Conduct Disorder to Juvenile Delinquency: Legal Implications," *Bulletin of the American Academy of Psychiatry and the Law*, vol. 24 (1996), pp. 333–45.

36. "Kingpin in Boy's Torture Under Medical Watch," *San Francisco Chronicle*, July 23, 1997, p. A20.

37. Henry J. Steadman, Margaret A. McGreery, et al., *Before and After Hinckley: Evaluating Insanity Defense Reform* (New York: Guilford Press, 1993).

38. A. Seltzer, "Multiple Personality: A Psychiatric Misadventure," *Canadian Journal of Psychiatry*, vol. 39 (1994), pp. 442–45.

39. Elaine Showalter, *Hystories: Hysterical Epidemics and Modern Media* (New York: Columbia University Press, 1997); Moira Johnston, *Spectral Evidence: The Ramona Case: Incest, Memory and Truth on Trial in Napa Valley* (Boston: Houghton-Mifflin Co., 1997).

40. Michael Gordon, Russell A. Barkley, and Kevin Murphy, "ADHD on Trial," *ADHD Report*, vol. 5 (August 1997), pp. 1–4.

41. Carol K. Whalen and Barbara Hencker, "The Social Ecology of Psychostimulant Treatment: A Model for Conceptual and Empirical Analysis," in *Hyperactive Children: The Social Ecology of Identification and Treatment*, Carol K. Whalen and Barbara Hencker eds. (New York: Academic Press, 1980).

42. Margaret O. Little, "Cosmetic Surgery, Suspect Norms, and the Ethics of Complicity," in *Enhancing Human Traits* (see note 1).

43. *The Classification of Child and Adolescent Mental Diagnoses in Primary Care: Diagnostic and Statistical Manual for Primary Care (DSM-PC): Child and Adolescent Version*, American Academy of Pediatrics.

44. Peter Levine, M.D., Permanente Medical Group, Walnut Creek, CA, personal communication, 1997.

45. Peter Kramer, *Listening to Prozac* (see note 24), p. 39.

46. George Soros, "The Capitalist Threat," *Atlantic Monthly*, February 1997, pp. 45–58.

47. Thomas J. Bouchard, David T. Lykken, et al., "Sources of Human Psychological

Differences: The Minnesota Study of Twins Reared Apart," *Science*, vol. 250 (1990), pp. 223-50.

48. Lawrence Wright, *Twins: And What They Tell Us About Who We Are* (New York: John Wiley and Sons, 1997), p. 155.

49. Amitai Etzioni, *The Spirit of Community: Rights, Responsibilities and the Communitarian Agenda* (New York: Crown Publishers, 1996).

50. Michael Lerner, *The Politics of Meaning: Restoring Hope and Possibility in an Age of Cynicism* (Reading, MA: Addison-Wesley Publishing, 1996).

INDEX

AAP (American Academy of Pediatrics), 188

activity, excessive, *see* hyperactivity

ADA (Americans with Disabilities Act), 162, 164, 165, 166

ADD, *see* attention deficit disorder

ADDA (Attention Deficit Disorder Association), 34, 129, 133, 149

ADD culture, 124–44
    alternative treatments and, 134, 139–44
    CHADD and, *see* CHADD
    drug advertising and, 134, 139
    media and, 135–38
    online, 127, 132–35

Adderall, 21, 21*n*, 37, 265–66

addiction, 23, 264, 293

ADD-ogenic culture, 75, 97–100, 315–18
    see also environment

ADHD, *see* attention deficit disorder

adolescents with attention deficit disorder, *see* teenagers with attention deficit disorder

adults with attention deficit disorder, 2, 34, 35, 64, 65, 278–81, 300–311
    abuse potential and, 305–7
    approaches to helping, 307–8
    and author's experience with stimulant, 300–302
    coaching and, 308
    complicating factors in, 303–7
    evaluation and, 199–200
    job choice and, 309–11
    Ritalin used by, 35, 255
    self-help approaches for, 308
    and using Ritalin for optimal performance, 297–300, 302–3
    work and, 96–97

advertising, drug, 134, 139

African-Americans, 36, 149–50, 196

alternative treatments, 134, 139–44

Amen, Daniel, 111–12, 127

American Academy of Child and Adolescent Psychiatry, 214, 253

American Academy of Pediatrics (AAP), 188

American Journal of Psychiatry, 281

American Psychiatric Association (APA), 53, 60

Americans with Disabilities Act (ADA), 162, 164, 165, 166

America Online, 133

amino acids, 141

amphetamines, 2, 20, 21, 40, 41, 268, 318
    abuse of, 27, 41
    Adderall, 21, 21*n*, 37, 265–66
    belief in calming effect of, in children, 24
    Dexedrine, *see* Dexedrine
    Dextrostat, 21, 21*n*
    epidemics of, 40–41
    long-acting, 266
    positives and negatives of, 22–23
    Ritalin vs., 25

Anafranil, 67, 69

Answers to Distraction (Hallowell and Ratey), 12

antidepressants, 267, 290
    Prozac, 11, 69, 106, 108–9, 253, 270, 274, 290, 338, 339
    tricyclic, 108, 116, 267, 270–72, 275, 290

antifungal medications, 140–41

anti-motion-sickness medication, 140

APA (American Psychiatric Association), 53, 60

appetite, 26, 262–63, 314

Asher, Steven R., 190

Asian-Americans, 36

Asperger's syndrome, 68

athletes, 14, 324

Atlas, James, 80

Attention!, 129, 308, 323

attention deficit disorder (ADD; attention deficit/hyperactivity disorder; ADHD), 1–2, 32–34, 332–34
    in adults, *see* adults with attention deficit disorder
    attention problems in, *see* attention problems, in ADD
    behavioral inhibition and, 73
    as biologically based, *see* brain-based theory of ADD
    bipolar disorder and, 274
    brain and, *see* brain; brain-based theory of ADD